TOP WALKS
in AUSTRALIA

Melanie Ball

EXPLORE
AUSTRALIA

CONTENTS

Introduction	vi
What to take	viii
Bushwalkers' code	x
How to use this book	xii
Map	xiv

WALKS

no.	walk	km	hours	grade	page
NEW SOUTH WALES & ACT					
1	Big Hole & Marble Arch	11.7*	4	easy/moderate	2
2	The Coast Track	28.7	2 days	moderate	8
3	Finch's Line & Devine's Hill Loop	11	3	moderate	20
4	Grand High Tops	12* or 14.5	4–6	moderate/hard	26
5	Mount Kosciuszko via Main Range Loop	22.5	7–8	moderate	33
6	Murrumbidgee River Corridor (ACT)	12.9	3–4	easy/moderate	41
7	National Pass Loop	9.5	4–5	moderate/hard	47
8	Nightcap Bluff	16.7*	5–7	moderate	55
9	Pigeon House Mountain (Didthul)	6*	3	moderate/hard	62
10	Spit Bridge to Manly	11	4	easy/moderate	67
VICTORIA					
1	Aire River to Johanna Beach	14	6	moderate	78
2	Cathedral Range South Loop	12	5–7	hard	84
3	Hollow Mountain	3.4*	2	moderate	91
4	Lake Mournpall Loop	9.6	2–3	easy	96
5	Mount Eccles Loop	8.6	3	easy/moderate	102
6	Mount Hotham to Falls Creek	23.5	1 day	hard	108
7	Ritchie's Hut Loop	12	1 day	easy/moderate	116
8	Walhalla Train, Tram, Trail Loop	16	4–5	moderate	122
9	Wilsons Promontory Lighthouse Loop	44.4	2–3 days	hard	130
10	Yarra Bend Loop	11.2	3–4	easy/moderate	139

* denotes return trip

no.	walk	km	hours	grade	page
SOUTH AUSTRALIA					
1	Adelaide 'Summit to Sea'	35	2 days	moderate	148
2	Alligator Gorge Loop	9.3	3–4	moderate	160
3	Bunyeroo Gorge	8.2*	2–3	easy/moderate	166
4	Dutchmans Stern Loop	10.8	3–4	moderate	171
5	Mount Ohlssen-Bagge	7.6*	3	hard	177
6	Rocky River to Sea	16.5	5–6	moderate	183
7	Waitpinga Cliffs	12.6	4	moderate	189
WESTERN AUSTRALIA					
1	Bluff Knoll	6.3*	3–4	moderate/hard	198
2	Cape to Cape Day Out	25	8–10	moderate/hard	204
3	Cathedral Gorge Loop	8	3	easy/moderate	212
4	Coalmine Beach to Treetops	27.8	2 days	moderate	217
5	Hellfire Bay to Lucky Bay	7.7	3	moderate	226
6	The Loop	9.4	3–4	moderate	234
7	Sullivan Rock to Monadnocks Campsite Loop	14.6	4–5	moderate	240
8	Wadjemup Walk Trail Loop	16	5	easy/moderate	246
9	Warren River Loop	11.3	3–4	moderate	257
10	Weano & Hancock Gorges	5	3–4	moderate	262
11	Weir & Wildflowers	9.6	3	easy/moderate	269
NORTHERN TERRITORY					
1	Alice Springs Telegraph Station	5.5 or 9*	2	easy	278
2	Jarnem Loop	7.7	3	easy/moderate	284
3	Jatbula Trail	63	6 days	moderate	290
4	Kings Canyon Loop	6.7	3–4	moderate	304
5	Mount Sonder	15.6*	6–7	moderate/hard	311
6	Mpulungkinya Walk [Palm Valley] Loop	5	2	easy/moderate	316
7	Ormiston Pound Loop	9.3	3–4	moderate	321
8	Uluṟu Base Walk	11.6	3–4	easy	327

WALKS CONT.

no.	walk	km	hours	grade	page
QUEENSLAND					
1	Carnarvon Gorge	25*	9	moderate	338
2	Kondalilla Falls Circuit	6.9	2-3	moderate	344
3	Lake Barrine Circuit	5.3	2	easy	349
4	Lake McKenzie-Central Station Loop	19	6-7	moderate	353
5	Mount Cordeaux	7.5*	2-3	moderate	360
6	The Pyramids Loop	5.7	3	moderate	366
7	Ravenswood Historic Town Loop	5	2	easy	372
8	Thorsborne Trail	32.7	4 days	moderate	379
9	Toolona Creek Circuit	18.5	6	hard	392
TASMANIA					
1	Bay of Fires	8.5-22*	3 hrs-1 day	easy	402
2	Cape Hauy	10.3*	3-4	moderate	407
3	Cape Queen Elizabeth	13*	4	easy/moderate	412
4	Coal Mines Historic Site Loop	4.7	2	easy	418
5	Growling Swallet & Junee Cave	3.6	2	easy	424
6	Historic Richmond Town Loop	5.2	2	easy	430
7	Lake Dobson & Tarn Shelf Loop	5.2	2	moderate	436
8	Maria Island Loop	18	2 days	moderate/hard	441
9	kunanyi/Mount Wellington Summit Loop	13.8	5-7	hard	449
10	Overland Track	65	6 days	moderate	456
11	Wineglass Bay & Hazards Beach Loop	12	4	moderate	471

* denotes return trip

Index	476
Acknowledgements	480

Sculpted boulders on The Coast Track, Royal National Park, NSW

Crossing the Rocky River on the Snake Lagoon Hike, Kangaroo Island, SA

TOP WALKS IN AUSTRALIA

The smallest, lowest, flattest and second driest continent on Earth (only Antarctica gets less rainfall), Australia is a patchwork of ancient geologies and rich human histories fashioned on a breathtaking scale.

Almost a fifth of Australia's nearly 8 million square kilometre landmass is classed as desert. Unsurprisingly, more than 80 per cent of its population lives within 100km of the 36,000km coastline. Separating the country's necklace of gorgeous beaches from its arid inland, collectively and affectionately called the outback, are diverse environments ranging from steamy tropical rainforest to glaciated alpine moors. Created by geological upheaval and patient weathering, these subtly and dramatically different habitats are home to a staggering assortment of flora and fauna. And there is no better way to experience these wonders than on foot.

Only while walking do you have the time to grasp the drama of volcanic sculpture, or the genealogy of a gnarled Antarctic beech tree whose ancestors spread their branches before the supercontinent Gondwana split up. Only at pedestrian pace will you spot that weird mushroom thrusting through leaf litter or that banded black cockatoo feather dropped by a squawking passer-by.

Bushwalking is also one of the most inexpensive ways to get and stay fit; an activity for all ages that liberates us from air-conditioned gyms, recorded music and reveal-all lycra.

Tasmania, Victoria and New South Wales are Australia's most recognised and celebrated bushwalking states, but there are fabulous hikes all across the country. Some are a few easy kilometres to a lookout or waterfall. Others stretch for hundreds and thousands of kilometres and can be walked in one-day clips, overnight hikes or epic end-to-end journeys. Whether named after a famous landscape artist (South Australia's Heysen Trail), the first Australians (Western Australia's Bibbulmun Track) or the country traversed (Australian Alps Walking Track, through the mountains of Victoria, New South Wales and Australian Capital Territory), these spectacular long-distance routes combined with shorter routes offer adventure for hikers of all levels of experience.

Ask bushwalkers to nominate their favourite Australian hike and each will say something different. Some won't say anything at all, preferring to stay mum about a recently discovered – or rediscovered – spot. Selecting walks for this book was always going to be challenging, and inevitably someone will ask, 'Why didn't you include …?'

I chose these walks because they showcase each state and territory's unique mix of environments, culture, history, flora and fauna; and because they are interesting and enjoyable and will, I hope, inspire you to bushwalk more. While some might test even a keen hiker's fortitude and taste for hills, there are no bush-bashes, and most are suitable for groups of mixed ages and abilities.

You can leave footprints on Victorian beaches buffeted by shipwrecking winds; follow in the footsteps of 19th-century convict chain gangs on the Hawkesbury River in New South Wales; explore Uluru's cultural significance to the Anangu people in the Northern Territory; peer over precipitous sea cliffs in Tasmania; have close encounters with some of the world's tallest trees in Western Australia; swim in perched lakes and plummeting waterfalls in Queensland; and tread old sea beds remote from any ocean in inland South Australia.

Whether you want to escape civilisation for a few days with all you need on your back, or string urban parks together; whether you want to test your physical limits or introduce your children to the delights of the great outdoors on a leafy stroll; whether you want to gaze upon landscapes whose splendour leaves you open-mouthed or narrow your focus to a wildflower found nowhere else in the world, Australia has a walk that nails the brief.

Slow down, walk with respect, and have fun.

Melanie Ball

This book is dedicated to all the people who have left only footprints across Australia: the first Australians who have done so for millennia, and the men and women who followed them, captivated by the country's natural and mythological history.

A huge thank you to the friends who have walked with me, and posed for more 'look natural' photographs than was reasonable, and to my husband Simon in particular. I look forward to clocking up more kilometres with you on new tracks and old favourites.

WHAT TO TAKE

To enjoy bushwalking you need to be comfortable. That doesn't mean you should never push yourself – it's just that blistered feet, bruised shoulders and chafing clothing can turn a great walk into a trial, and getting wet and cold or sunburnt and dehydrated can be life-threatening.

There have been great innovations in outdoor clothing and equipment since Livingstone went troppo in the African jungle and Robert Falcon Scott forced his hands into frozen fur gloves in Antarctica – but don't race off and buy a credit-card load of the latest gear from an adventure store! You essentially just need walking clothes that protect you from the weather and give you freedom to move.

There are some traditionalists who hate walking poles and converts who rave about them. Poles can help with balance when crossing creeks and ease the pressure on knees on descents. You could just use a stick, but the use of poles, plural, can lessen or prevent the fat fingers that some walkers suffer as a consequence of arms dangling from pack-strapped shoulders; and countless internet sites claim that walking with poles burns almost half as many calories again as walking without. Poles or not? One or two? It's up to you.

As is water. Water is essential on walks longer than an hour, in hot weather and in hilly country – but on a short wildflower ramble? Leave your water in the car and discover the joys of going bush empty handed. In other situations, consider your drinking habits; if you don't drink much and have to be reminded/encouraged, a water bladder with tube might be a good option, because it enables you to drink small amounts on the move rather than having to stop and pull out a bottle.

Footwear

The last thing you want on a walk is sore feet. Footwear should be appropriate for the conditions and comfortable for long periods of time. Closed shoes or boots give some protection from sticks and stones and a twisted ankle, but walking sandals may be more comfortable in open country or with creek crossings, because the water drains out. Some people still reminisce about hiking in Dunlop Volleys, while others pull on 'barefoot shoes' with individual toe pockets. Whatever you choose, it should fit properly, not move around on your feet, and be worn in. The road to bushwalking hell is littered with people wearing brand new boots on long hikes.

The ideal on any walk is to carry as little as is safe. Here are my suggestions:

Short, easy walk of an hour or so
Nothing

Moderate walk of a few hours
Daypack with 1l of water
Whistle (for attracting attention)
High-energy snack such as a muesli bar, nuts or chocolate
Rain- and wind-proof jacket/and or second layer
Camera

Half day tougher walk
Daypack with 1.5l of water
Whistle (for attracting attention)
Lunch
High-energy snack such as a muesli bar, nuts or chocolate
Rain- and wind-proof jacket/and or second layer
Basic medical kit – bandages, blister treatments, perhaps some antihistamine
Compass, map and/or GPS
Camera

Full day more remote walk
Daypack with 2l of water
Whistle (for attracting attention)
Lunch
High-energy snacks
Rain- and wind-proof jacket, and second layer; spare thermals, beanie, gloves and neck warmer if walking in cold weather
Torch
Waterproof matches
Full medical kit including a foil heat blanket
Compass, map and/or GPS
Camera
Leave plans of your walk with someone who will alert authorities if you do not return as planned

Very remote long walk
All the above
Consider taking a personal emergency beacon (these can be hired online)

BUSHWALKERS' CODE

The philosophy of 'take only photos, leave only footprints' is an oldie but a goodie, and worth revisiting here because it is surprising – and appalling – how many bushwalkers leave a mark on the beautiful environments their activity would otherwise suggest they love. It may be as minor as a dropped toffee wrapper or as extreme as toileting beside a waterhole and leaving the loo paper behind declaring 'I was here!'

The bushwalkers' code is a common-sense approach to limiting impact on the country we tread. This includes keeping your group small and not making or using shortcuts, because they cause erosion and increase the risk of walkers losing their way; camping on existing tent sites, lighting camp fires in existing fireplaces and not cutting down wood to burn; carrying out what you take in (everything weighs less empty); and washing and toileting well away from water. A personal bugbear is walkers who detour around bogs, exacerbating the damage, rather than risking wet and/or muddy feet walking through.

Minimal impact bushwalking is described in more detail at depi. vic.gov.au (search for 'bushwalking code'). A good source for tips on reducing your impact on the planet in general is Leave No Trace Australia: lnt.org.au.

Looking after your group is also important. Ensure everyone's safety and enjoyment by doing the following things: letting someone know where you're going, when you expect to be back and who to contact should you fail to show by a designated time; choosing a walk that fits the experience and fitness of your group (it's okay for groups to split, but no-one should be dropped off the back alone); being prepared to cancel a walk, even last minute, if weather conditions deteriorate significantly; and knowing what to do if someone is injured. Issues of timing, walk choice, weather and injuries are even more important when walking solo, which can be an exhilarating experience.

For 'how to' bushwalking hints, suggested walks by region, walking clubs around Australia and more, go to:
Bushwalking Australia: bushwalkingaustralia.org.au
Bushwalk Australia forum: bushwalk.com
Bushwalking New South Wales: bushwalkingnsw.org.au
Bushwalking Queensland: bushwalkingqueensland.org.au
Walking SA (South Australia): walkingsa.org.au
Bushwalk Tasmania: bushwalktasmania.com
Bushwalking Victoria: bushwalkingvictoria.org.au
Bushwalking Western Australia: bushwalkingwa.org.au

HOW TO USE THIS BOOK

Designed to inspire you to explore Australia on foot and assist you when you do, this book includes simple maps, and descriptions of routes, wildlife and plants. In some cases, such as overnight and more remote walks, you'll need to take a contour map and compass and/or a GPS, all of which you should know how to use; additional maps are suggested for these walks. In most cases, however, you should be able to safely navigate the walks using this book.

DISTANCE

The majority of walks in this book demand some effort. Included are loop walks (returning to the start point a different way), return walks or out-and-back and one-way walks. Some of the walks described follow formed trails, with a crushed rock or sandy surface, however, most bushwalking tracks are unsurfaced; the narrowest of these, often just a trail worn by feet, are commonly called foot pads, a term used in this book.

TIME REQUIRED

The most challenging aspect of writing a bushwalking guide is estimating how long a route will take, because people walk at different speeds in flat terrain and even more so in hilly country; some power along from A to B, others stop frequently for photographs. Food breaks, track finding, weather conditions, group size – large groups move more slowly than small groups – and opportunities for a swim all affect completion times.

Times in this book are estimated for fit, enthusiastic, middle-aged walkers who enjoy taking photographs, but who don't linger over lunch and snack breaks. Some people will take longer than the estimated time, some will finish earlier. Hopefully fit walkers will find these estimates fairly accurate.

BEST TIME

Most of these walks are suitable for walking year-round. Where there is a particular peak time (e.g. wildflower season) or a particularly poor time (e.g. the route is snowbound), this is noted.

GRADE

Reasonably flat walking on well-formed tracks usually gets an 'easy' tag, although longer distances might nudge that to 'moderate'; stairs, hills, rough tracks and some scrambling earn a 'moderate' tag; difficult terrain, steep or long hills, remoteness and distance all contribute to a 'hard' tag. The detail in the walk description should help you decide whether a walk is right for you.

GUIDED WALKS

Walking companies offer a great alternative to independent hiking; they organise the route, transport, accommodation and food, leaving you free to just enjoy the hike. Options include guided walks with hard-top lodging, and glamping trips in remote country. Some companies also offer self-guided itineraries, providing comprehensive walking notes and transferring your luggage to the next hotel or B&B while you walk on with only a day pack.

Recommended companies include:
Australian Walking Holidays:
australianwalkingholidays.com.au
Auswalk: auswalk.com.au
Life's An Adventure: lifesanadventure.com.au
Park Trek: parktrek.com.au
Willis's Walkabouts: bushwalkingholidays.com.au
World Expeditions: worldexpeditions.com/au

REFERENCES AND FURTHER READING

Cronin's Key Guide to Australian Wildflowers (2008), Leonard Cronin, Allen & Unwin
Cronin's Key Guide to Australian Trees (2007), Leonard Cronin, Allen & Unwin
The Slater Field Guide to Australian Birds (2009), Peter, Pat & Raoul Slater, New Holland Publishers

Map symbols

850	Contour with height
--→--◆--	Walking route with direction, steep track
---------	Walking track
=========	Freeway/highway
=========	Major road
·········	Other road
●	Point of interest
⋀	Cave
▲	Hill/mountain
●	Landform
◎	Vegetation
◎	Water feature
~	Waterfall
▬	Weir
⊗	Trail junction
⚒	Mine/diggings
⊺	Lighthouse
ER	Emergency radio
H	Heliport
⚓	Ferry terminal
🚉	Train station

LOCALITY

WORLD HERITAGE AREA

NATIONAL PARK

★	Attraction
🍖	Barbecue
⛱	Beach
🪑	Bench
🍴	Cafe/restaurant
⛺	Campsite
✋	Indigenous culture
i	Information
📷	Lookout
P	Parking
🎋	Picnic area
🎠	Playground
🪜	Stairs
🚻	Toilet
🔭	View
🦎	Wildlife
🚶	Walk start
🚶	Walk finish

Jarnem Loop

Cathedral Gorge Loop

Weano & Hancock Gorges

WESTERN AUSTRALIA

PAGE 196

The Loop

Weir & Wildflowers

Perth

Wadjemup Walk Trail Loop

Sullivan Rock to Monadnocks Campsite Loop

Cape to Cape Day Out

Bluff Knoll

Hellfire Bay to Lucky Bay

Warren River Loop

Coalmine Beach to Treetops

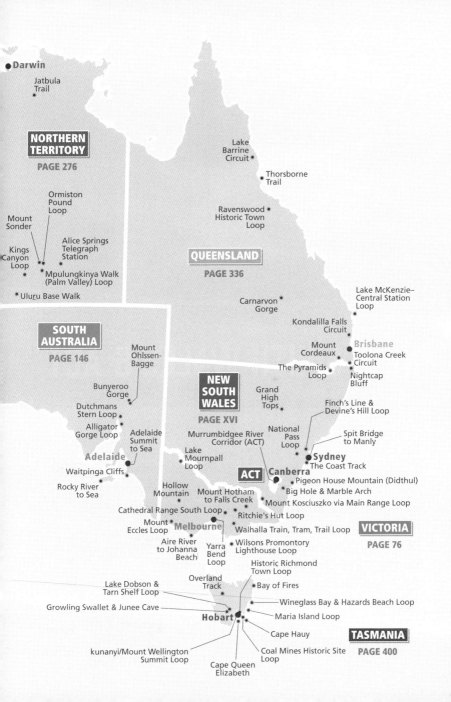

● Darwin

Jatbula
Trail

**NORTHERN
TERRITORY**
PAGE 276

Ormiston
Pound
Loop

Mount
Sonder

Alice Springs
Telegraph
Station

Kings
Canyon
Loop

Mpulungkinya Walk
(Palm Valley) Loop

● Uluru Base Walk

Lake
Barrine
Circuit ●

Thorsborne
Trail

Ravenswood ●
Historic Town
Loop

QUEENSLAND
PAGE 336

Carnarvon ●
Gorge

Lake McKenzie–
Central Station
Loop

Kondalilla Falls
Circuit

Mount
Cordeaux

Brisbane
Toolona Creek
Circuit

The Pyramids
Loop

Nightcap
Bluff

**SOUTH
AUSTRALIA**
PAGE 146

Mount
Ohlssen-
Bagge

Grand
High
Tops

Finch's Line &
Devine's Hill Loop

Bunyeroo
Gorge

**NEW
SOUTH
WALES**
PAGE XVI

Dutchmans
Stern Loop

Alligator
Gorge Loop

Adelaide
Summit
to Sea

Murrumbidgee River
Corridor (ACT)

National
Pass
Loop

Spit Bridge
to Manly

Lake
Mournpall
Loop

Adelaide

Waitpinga Cliffs

● Sydney
The Coast Track

ACT   **Canberra**

Rocky River
to Sea

Hollow
Mountain

Mount Hotham
to Falls Creek

Big Hole & Marble Arch

Pigeon House Mountain (Didthul)

Mount Kosciuszko via Main Range Loop

Cathedral Range South Loop

Ritchie's Hut Loop

Mount
Eccles Loop

Melbourne

Walhalla Train, Tram, Trail Loop

VICTORIA
PAGE 76

Aire River
to Johanna
Beach

Yarra
Bend
Loop

Wilsons Promontory
Lighthouse Loop

Historic Richmond
Town Loop

Lake Dobson &
Tarn Shelf Loop

Overland
Track

● Bay of Fires

Growling Swallet & Junee Cave

Wineglass Bay & Hazards Beach Loop

Maria Island Loop

Hobart

Cape Hauy

kunanyi/Mount Wellington
Summit Loop

Coal Mines Historic Site
Loop

TASMANIA
PAGE 400

Cape Queen
Elizabeth

Golden beaches and greened headlands run south from a lookout on the Coast Track

NEW SOUTH WALES & ACT

The term 'bushwalking' originated in New South Wales in the early 20th century, and hiking here will continue to expand your vocabulary as you reach for superlatives to describe the wonders revealed by hiking. Climb extraordinary volcanic plugs in the north and Australia's tallest mountain in the south; take in grandstand views of one of the world's most beautiful harbours from a city park, and a dissected sandstone plateau from a cliff track cut by men suspended in bosun's chairs. Get out there!

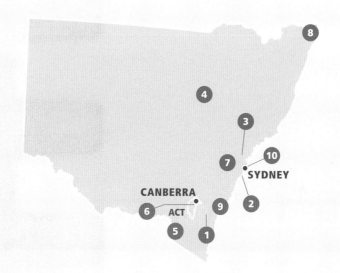

1	Big Hole & Marble Arch	2
2	The Coast Track	8
3	Finch's Line & Devine's Hill Loop	20
4	Grand High Tops	26
5	Mount Kosciuszko via Main Range Loop	33
6	Murrumbidgee River Corridor (ACT)	41
7	National Pass Loop	47
8	Nightcap Bluff	55
9	Pigeon House Mountain (Didthul)	62
10	Spit Bridge to Manly	67

1 BIG HOLE & MARBLE ARCH

Walk:	11.7km return
Time required:	4 hours
Best time:	Any dry day (river level permitting)
Grade:	Easy to moderate with one steep hill
Environment:	Eucalypt scrub, canyon, cave, some views
Best map:	This one
Toilets:	Pit toilet in Berlang camping and picnic area
Food:	None
Tips:	Before setting out, check the Shoalhaven River depth at bom.gov.au – click on 'New South Wales', then 'Rainfall & River Conditions'. Take water sandals for the river crossing and a head torch for navigating through and exploring Marble Arch.
	For a scenic drive from Canberra, travel to Deua National Park via Braidwood and back via the historic village of Captain's Flat.

The views are mere distractions on this walk to a huge hole in the ground and a canyon sliced through striped marble. It's a fun outing for adventurers of all ages.

Nature does some weird and wonderful things, such as punching a huge hole in Earth's crust. This walk in Deua National Park takes in the

A hill-and-valley view unfolds ahead of walkers returning from the Big Hole

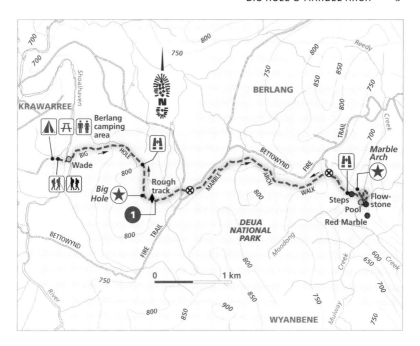

unimaginatively named Big Hole, sandwiched between a river crossing and a labyrinthine cave, for a fun few hours on foot in south-east New South Wales.

The departure point is Berlang picnic and camping area, about 45km south of Braidwood, off Cooma Rd, which is confusingly called Krawarree Rd on many maps. The turn-off to the park is signed, just south of some corrugated iron holiday cottages.

Walk through the picnic area towards a cream-on-green wooden sign giving distances to the Big Hole and Marble Arch, and on through open trees to the upper reaches of the Shoalhaven River. Early in its 300km-plus journey from the Southern Highlands to a south coast estuary, the Shoalhaven is usually fordable here, but it can deepen and speed up after heavy rain, making the crossing more difficult and occasionally dangerous.

You'll probably get wet feet whatever the river height, so take water sandals and a small towel so you can boot up on the other side.

On a warm day you might like to have a dip in the Shoalhaven after the walk, though the water is usually cold enough to make your feet ache.

Follow the track away from the river, through open forest of banksias, manna gums (also called ribbon gums), coarser, more fibrous-barked broad-leafed peppermints and scribbly gums, their smooth trunks graffitied with the curlicue trails of scribbly moth larvae. The furry grey-green plants are woolly grevillea, which produce pretty pink and cream flowers in winter and spring.

This rocky country is lumpy with termite mounds and sometimes embroidered with white orchids. Bald Hill, just to the right, is waist-high with dwarf she-oak, from which a few pale-barked gum trees grow, making it look like alpine heathland.

The track climbs out of the open forest into this heathier country, giving you an opportunity to look closely at the she-oaks. The females produce cones and shaggy red flowers, while the males produce red-brown flower spikes. As you climb, plains and neighbouring ranges show through the trees, and kilometres of valley and undulations unfold behind.

Back among taller gum trees with deeply furrowed bark, you'll come to a sign for the Big Hole, 100m, warning you to approach with caution. On reaching it you'll understand why.

This impressive sinkhole, with a maximum diameter of more than 50m and a depth of about 100m, is thought to have developed at or below the level of the Shoalhaven River, which dissolved a body of limestone, leaving a cap of sedimentary rocks. This capping then collapsed, opening the hole to the sky and, millions of years later, to human beings, some of whom venture down on ropes.

But you don't have to take up abseiling – a viewing platform looks straight down the sheer walls to the soft tree ferns at the bottom. A resident lyrebird shelters in these ferns, revealing itself to some lucky visitors. Less shy are welcome swallows that nest in the clefts and pluck insects from the air.

There's a footpad around the hole too, from which you can take good photos of friends on the platform, but keep well away from the edge. The eucalypts clinging to the rim won't break your fall.

You'll probably get wet feet whatever the height of the Shoalhaven River

Continue past the hole and fairly steeply downhill, turning left at a post with a battered white arrow on top (see point 1 on map). This walk is intermittently signed and none of the arrows are in good nick (some have worn away to bare metal), but the posts are visible and the route fairly obvious.

The track then flattens out and snakes through a damper flat inhabited by termite mounds, scribbly gums and eucalypts that litter the ground with bark streamers. Across Bettowynd Fire Trail continue through very rough-barked trees, some quite old and broad, some having fallen over, ripping up clumps of ground.

You'll probably see swamp wallabies and eastern grey kangaroos through here, and the track is often littered with elevated piles of distinctively cuboid wombat droppings.

Soon after a weathered wooden cream-on-green Marble Arch sign, the track steps steeply down a ridge (take care when it's wet), revealing a lovely view of valley and enfolding hills through the trees to the right. Swing right at the mossy post at the bottom and walk down Reedy Creek's rocky gully into a tangle of foliage. Beware the low, green,

The rock wedged at the top of Marble Arch's pointed 'doorway' is best seen from inside

serrated-leafed stinging nettles as you scramble over a fallen tree and mossy boulders between granite walls thick with moss and creepers.

This brings you to Marble Arch, a visually unimpressive cavern that narrows to a tunnel leading to a narrow ravine. The rock wedged at the top of the Arch's pointed 'doorway' is best seen from inside, so turn on your head torch and enter. Just inside on the right you'll see an opening into a smaller cave. Removing your daypack will enable you to venture about 20m beyond the main chamber to where a narrow underground stream emerges from the hill.

Return to the main cavern and walk through, noting the three distinct levels cut by water over time, the flowstone formation just below the roof, the stalactites, and the impressive red-and-white conglomerate marble (baked limestone); what a magnificent kitchen bench it would make!

Marble Arch disgorges you into a sinuous slot canyon open to the sky. The rock can be slippery, particularly when there's water in the bottom, but by wearing good-grip sandals again, or going barefoot if you prefer, you can work your way downstream with care. This brings you to a hole where deeper water turns most people back. The canyon beyond is almost overgrown anyway.

Serious canyoners will probably be underwhelmed by this as a destination, but most people could easily lose an hour or more exploring down here.

Then take a break – maybe unpack your lunch – before retracing your steps to the car.

2 THE COAST TRACK

Walk:	28.7km one-way
Time required:	2 days (or a 1-day epic)
Best time:	Mild weather (much of the track is unsheltered)
Grade:	Moderate (with some steep climbs and eroded track and a long second day)
Environment:	Eucalypt forest, cabbage palm groves, hardy coastal heath, sculpted sandstone cliffs, beaches, rocky bays, waterfalls
Best map:	*Port Hacking 9129-4N & Otford 9129-4S 1:25,000* contour maps from NSW Land & Property Information (shop.lpi.nsw.gov.au)
Toilets:	Pit toilets at North Era camping area; flushing toilets at Otford Station, at the start, in the parking areas at Garie Beach and Wattamolla on the walk, and in Bundeena at the end
Food:	You can buy hiking fare in Cronulla eateries and supermarkets; Bundeena has several cafes and a supermarket for post-walk treats
Tips:	Public transport services both ends of the Coast Track: Cronulla Ferries travel to/from Bundeena (cronullaferries.com.au/ferries-to-bundeena) and you can catch a train between Cronulla and Otford (sydneytrains.info). If you plan to use public transport to do the track as a day walk check timetables carefully to ensure you don't get stranded.

Sandstone shelving steps down to the cliffs on the Coast Track

North Era camping is restricted to 12 tents and must be pre-paid; contact NSW National Parks & Wildlife Service on 1300 072 757 Monday to Friday or book online at nationalparks.nsw.gov.au/camping-and-accommodation

Vehicle entry fees are payable for Royal National Park; you can pay a one-off fee or buy a multi-park pass; details at nationalparks.nsw.gov.au

Carry sufficient water for the entire walk. Picnic area taps are labelled unfit for drinking, North Era has no tank water and creeks along the track can't be relied on.

The Royal National Park's Coast Track is popular with groups, and in good weather, car-accessible sections heave with daytrippers. To share it with fewer folks, walk on weekdays during school term.

The park's popularity has resulted in lots of litter. It can be tempting to pick up the refuse of thoughtless hikers and picnickers and pack it out, but that's an unwelcome extra weight to carry. Just don't add to the mess!

This popular bushwalk in the world's second-oldest national park is a coastal hike like no other. Stroll remote beaches and burrow through wildflower-embroidered heath to find sculpted sandstone cliffs that plunge into crashing ocean.

Super convenient to the mega metropolis of Sydney, just across Port Hacking, Royal National Park has been a place of fun, healthy exercise and nature appreciation since its proclamation in 1879. People pour into the park over weekends and on school holidays, attracted by surf breaks, wild beaches, artistically shaped and coloured sandstone, awesome clifftop lookouts and walks. The Coast Track is the ultimate leg-stretch, a marathon day hike and a still-energetic overnight hike.

North Era Beach is the only legal camping area and its positioning results in two very uneven Coast Track 'halves'. The route described here goes north from Otford to Bundeena, giving you a short first day and a long second, with a historic ferry ride to Cronulla to finish.

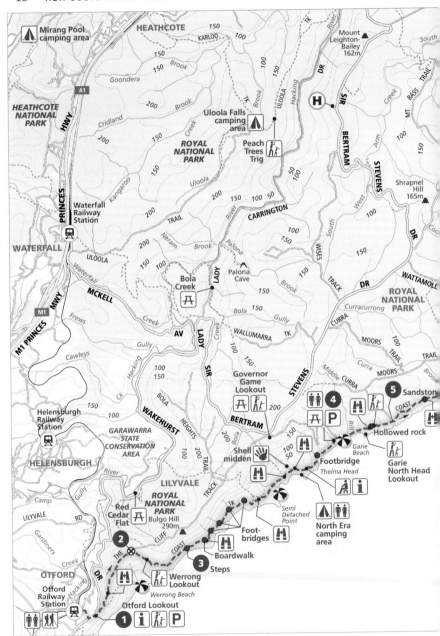

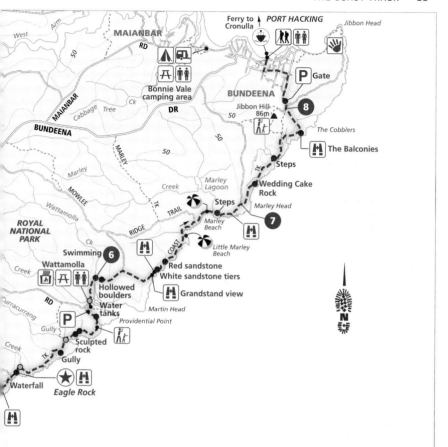

DAY 1: 8.2km (3–4 hours)

If you are catching public transport, you'll need to take two trains from Cronulla to Otford, changing lines at Sutherland. From Otford railway station, walk up the steep stairs (don't cross the tracks) and up a ramp with a handrail. Turn left onto the unsealed Station Rd fire trail and head right when it forks, following this vehicular track to bitumen Lady Wakehurst Dve, on the coast. Turn left onto the road and walk about 150m to the signed start of the Coast Track, beside a Royal National Park information board.

Those driving will start at this point (there's a roadside parking area). It's a 37km drive from Cronulla via the Princes Hwy, taking the Lawrence Hargrave Dve exit. From the national park information board, step up to a lookout (*see* point 1 on map) with views north and south, of rugged headlands, rocky shores, forested cliffs and the Pacific Ocean, which sparkles on sunny days. Then head north, up a ridge thick with banksia, she-oak, grass trees and eucalypts. Unless you're super keen to strip off, ignore the track to your right to 'swimsuit optional' Werrong Beach, and continue through Gymea lilies and cabbage tree palms, some over 10m tall. In places it will feel like you're well inland, but then you'll glimpse sheer cliffs and crashing, foaming ocean through the trees.

About 2km from the lookout you'll reach another junction (*see* point 2). Turn right onto the narrower, sandy Coast Track proper (signed 'Palm Jungle 3km') and tunnel through banksias, callistemon and broad-leaved drumsticks, which sport wiry yellow blooms from October to December. The pretty violet flowers with 'fraying' petals are fringe lilies, and the white-tipped red cylindrical blooms are fuchsia heath.

About 450m on you'll reach a more open area, where people have stepped off the track. Venture almost to the edge here for a view south, taking in a gorgeous cove and lumpy headland on serpentine coast. Continue a short way north to a second natural lookout, again off to the right, which affords a view south of the 'shack' community of Bulgo, and the Sea Cliff Bridge projecting out over the ocean. The cliffs all along this coast are great vantage points for watching migrating humpback whales from May to November; you might also

A bushwalker takes in the rugged coast from a sculpted sandstone lookout

spot southern rights, killer whales and minke whales. And in December, you might see the Sydney-to-Hobart yacht race fleet on Boxing Day.

Continuing north, you'll cross a leafy gully inhabited by an old Sydney red gum (*Angophora costata*) that's grown up and over a chunk of rock, then step down between boulders and into cabbage tree palm forest where vines twist and climb. Wend your way along the track to another creek gully, immediately beyond which log steps (*see* point 3) climb into the open, providing a fabulous view of aqua sea darkening to inky blue and dotted with fishing boats. Continue under trees pruned by wind into elongated topiary.

You'll find yourself briefly back in thick palm forest, treading a spongy carpet of fronds before emerging onto a grassy headland with views out to sea and up the escarpment rearing behind you. Note the distinct, almost straight line where palm forest ends and grassland begins. As you tread metal boardwalks over the headland – to raucous cicadas, on a warm day – soaring sea cliffs, low, tiered stonework washed by sudsy ocean, and another 'shack' community will come into view.

Keeping left – ignore smaller side tracks on the point – you'll cross a footbridge over a ferny gully and come to the top of a pretty beach. Welcome to Burning Palms shack community. Swim here with extreme caution, even if the beach is patrolled.

Listed on the NSW State Heritage Register in 2012, the Royal National Park shack/cabin communities of Burning Palms, Era and Little Garie are Australia's largest surviving group of coastal shacks. Built in the first half of the 20th century, many during the Depression, the shacks are held privately under renewable licences. You can learn more at rnpshacks.info.

The creek-fording footbridges you cross as you walk through Burning Palms are good spots to see eastern water dragons, which are handsome lizards about 60cm long.

When you reach a high-vis black-and-yellow sign turn left towards a shack and climb to an exposed hilltop junction. Keep right and head downhill (the incoming track goes to a carpark from where everything for the shacks is walked or wheeled in), and traverse another grassy headland.

On reaching South Era, just over the headland, cross a lawn-like slope and follow a sandy track down through tea-tree and more shacks to the beach, below the Era Surf Life Saving Club.

Walk along the beach then follow the obvious but eroded track at its end, which climbs over another headland to North Era Beach, visible from the top. North Era is a popular surf beach but it's not very swimmer friendly, even on a calm day. The rock shelf to the right as you step onto North Era beach is a crazy paving of different fracture and wear patterns, with bathroom-tile squares, curves, honeycomb hollows, gutters and pools awash with sea life. It's a great place to spend the afternoon.

The fenced mound just off the beach is a massive shell midden, telling stories of thousands of years of Dharawal Aboriginal life. Behind the midden is the grassy camping area, and beyond it the steps up Thelma Head, which you'll climb tomorrow.

Don't be surprised if rusa deer are grazing in the camping area (these feral animals were introduced in 1907); you'll almost certainly fall asleep to plonking frogs.

DAY 2: 20.5km (6–8 hours)

Your day starts with a fairly steep climb up Thelma Head. Some steps are high and the space between them can be boggy after rain, but keep to the track to protect against further erosion. As you crest the headland you'll have an expansive coastal view north.

Head down the other side, walking behind (mostly) more shacks. Round this small bay and follow the track along the base of the cliff, with steep, crumbly slope to your left and waves thumping into loose rocks and more crazy-paving to your right. This leads to Garie Beach picnic area (see point 4). (Another surfing spot, Garie Beach can have strong rips and currents.)

Turn left into the carpark for toilets, otherwise head along the beach, trailing boot prints to the slightly daunting headland at its end.

Now for a steep climb with several big step-ups on another obvious, fairly eroded track. Your efforts will be compensated with better and better views. The zigzag height gain will put you among callistemons, banksias, tea-tree, Gymea lilies and red-flowering mountain devils. Up top you'll find yourself treading a fairly flat, narrow track in vista-blocking heath. Ignore the wider Curra Moors Trail coming in on the left and keep north through massed *Hakea sericea* (commonly called Needlebush, for self-evident reasons), thick with curly creamy flowers from winter to spring.

Mesh walkways, which enable plants to grow beneath, cut through heath towards another creek that fans out over flat rock as it approaches the precipice. Cross over the creek – most of the time you can get across with barely a splash. This is a lovely spot for a break if you're making good time.

Down to the right, beyond the creek, you'll see the sandstone shelf from which the creek drops into the sea, and numerous footpads out to the lip. Keeping to the main track, look for Curracurrong Falls cascading off the cliffs ahead.

The Coast Track traverses curvaceous, cliff-top sandstone shelving

When you reach the point where Curra Moors Trail comes in (*see* point 5), swing right. This brings you to Eagle Rock – pale sandstone shaped like an eagle's head jutting from the cliff.

The track turns inland now and divides; keep left, along old boarding to Curracurrong Creek, well above its cliff-edge leap. You may find a board bridging a gap in its flat sandstone bed, but even without this balance beam you shouldn't get too damp.

Continue north on eroded sandy track, natural pavement and mesh boardwalk and step down to another creek that washes stone slabs before tumbling over a mini-waterfall into the sea, which will be right beside you now! You might like to have a dip in a salty pool, and then a fresh-water rinse.

Pushing on through now-familiar but still pretty heath, on your right you'll see the rocky bay into which that creek runs. To the left (north) of the bay is an undercut, layered cliff; venture out onto it and there'll be little between you and a rocky demise.

There's a hollowed and holed lump of sandstone where the track doglegs right-left, and a sandstone 'claw', another extraordinary natural artwork, in a gully on the right shortly after. A footpad going left near the top of the next headland leads to an unofficial lookout over the textural cliff-line you've just followed.

Track markers lead away from the coast now, and down to a carpark. Go right to Wattamolla picnic area. The lagoon and beach here are very popular, and the picnic area can be packed on a warm weekend. Head left towards Little Marley Beach, past the toilets and along the edge of another parking area with sand to your right. Cross a creek below a stone wall and climb to a cascade above a small dam; this is a lovely spot for a swim (see point 6).

Cross Wattamolla Creek just above the dam and climb some more, through a natural chicane of weathered boulders, Gymea lilies and gnarly banksias.

Swing right, seaward, at the next junction; there's no view, but you can smell and hear the sea. This easy track returns you to the coast at a grandstand fashioned from white sandstone over pastry-thin darker layers, commanding splendid views of the coast. Further on you'll tread curves of crumbly white sandstone; then traverse an extraordinary length of clifftop oxidised to red and yellow.

Walk on to Little Marley Beach and tread the link track along a low cliff to Marley Beach, ignoring the track coming in on the left. Beautiful Marley Beach is another popular surfing spot, but on even a mildly choppy day the peppermint waves can lose their form as they approach the beach (Little Marley Beach is usually a bit safer for a swim). Looking back from Marley Head, beyond the beach, you'll see Marley Creek snaking through marshland behind the dunes. Footpads lead to ocean-side rock slabs. There are some excellent Aboriginal engravings here, but they are not marked.

Veering right again at the next junction (see point 7) you'll come to Wedding Cake Rock, a cliff-top spectacle fenced off since May 2015 due to instability. Continue another 2km along and you can step out onto the Balconies unhindered.

Soak up the view south from this sculpted sandstone lookout, because the track now heads inland to a bitumen road. Turn right and walk along the road to another junction (see point 8). If time permits

and you're up for an extra 3km, turn right down the sandy track to
Jibbon Head and loop into Bundeena via an Aboriginal engraving site.

But if you're satisfied – or just plumb tuckered out – keep straight
on and leave the park through a gate onto Beachcomber Ave.
Follow Beachcomber to its end (it swings right), then turn left onto
Scarborough St. At the end turn right and walk down Brighton St,
through Bundeena's shops, to Bundeena Wharf, where you can catch
the ferry back to Cronulla, to train into Sydney (or pick up your car
if driving).

Clockwise from top left: *Callistemon splash red among the greenery; 'bathroom-tile' square stone shelving; wildflowers bloom all along the Coast Track; cabbage tree palm fronds interweave with shadows*

A great place to spend the afternoon, the rock shelf at North Era beach is a crazy paving of different fracture and wear patterns

3 FINCH'S LINE & DEVINE'S HILL LOOP

Walk:	11km loop
Time required:	3 hours
Best time:	Any time of year, but it can be hot in summer. Go in spring for the wildflowers.
Grade:	Moderate (rough uphill to start)
Environment:	Sandstone escarpment, 19th-century convict road, Hawkesbury River
Best map:	This one
Toilets:	Flushing toilets in the riverside car park on the Wisemans Ferry side of the Hawkesbury River
Food:	Kiosk in the park; pub and cafe food in Wisemans Ferry village
Tips:	A swag of historical and visitor information about the convict-built road is available at greatnorthroad.com.au; you can also download a free Convict Road app on iTunes to use on the walk

The combination of geology, remarkable colonial engineering and convict history on this walk tell an enthralling Australian yarn.

Constructed by convicts between 1826 and 1834, the Great Northern Road was the colony of New South Wales' largest public work and a remarkable engineering feat, even though contemporary commentators declared it a folly.

Convict stonework lines the steep Finch's Line of ascent up from the Hawkesbury River

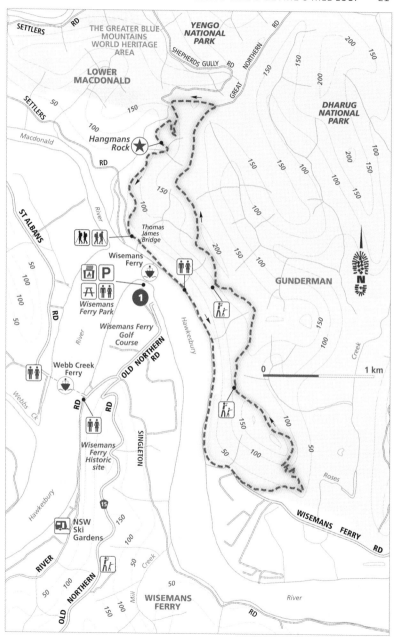

Left: *Peering over the edge of 13m high convict-built block work on Devine's Hill;* **Right:** *Magnificent Gymea lilies grow tall along the walk*

Much of the road remains in use, its colonial origins hidden by bitumen, but the most impressive section survives undisguised in Dharug National Park, on the Hawkesbury River.

Heneage Finch surveyed the road in 1825, charting an ascent from the Hawkesbury up onto its rugged sandstone escarpment. But this route was narrow, winding and precipitous and ten months after construction began, Surveyor General Major Mitchell surveyed an alternate. This walk climbs Finch's Line of ascent and descends Devine's Hill.

The walk begins at Wisemans Ferry, 75km north-west of Sydney, where Solomon Wiseman, transported to Australia for stealing timber, added inn keeper and ferry operator to his trading and shipping interests and considerable landholdings. (Wiseman was author Kate Grenville's great, great grandfather and inspiration for William Thornhill, the lead character in *The Secret River*, her brilliant and disturbing novel about the Hawkesbury's settlement.)

Parking is limited on the walk side of the river, so unless you are coming from the north or driving north after the walk (where there is plenty of interest, including Hunter Valley wineries), park in Wisemans Ferry Park (see point 1 on map) and cross the river on the oldest operational ferry (a cable ferry, or punt) in New South Wales (passage is free).

Having disembarked, turn right and walk downstream between river mangroves and fabulously fractured sandstone. There is no walking track so walk along the narrow road, keeping to the right so you face oncoming traffic.

Finch's Line goes bush on the left, about 1.9km down the road, and immediately climbs. Common wombat droppings festoon the wide trail and whip birds crack the air as you ascend, initially gently, through boulders. To your left, eucalypts perch on hollowed sandstone ledges. Here too might stand palisades of Gymea lilies, their metres-long stalks topped with flashy red flowers.

Narrower now, the track hugs sandstone cliffs as it climbs through an untidy mix of grass trees, pea-flowering shrubs and ferns ringing with bird calls.

About 700m into the climb, a hard left turn up a rocky ridge provides a sobering view back along the sandstone ridge. How a horse and cart made this ascent is a wonder – it's obvious why Finch's Line was abandoned before completion.

The track widens briefly and is stone-walled on both sides. More impressive stonewalling supports the 'road' as it zigzags up the escarpment through coarse-barked apples (angophoras).

The track finally flattens out and skirts a rocky crown, bringing you to a broad rock slab on the right, which is a natural lookout over valley folds, wetlands and the steep, treed hills behind. This is the perfect place for a break.

Continuing along the ridge, with honeycombed sandstone to the left and a beautiful, rolling valley view to the right, the track runs through eucalypts, sedge grasses and an occasional grass tree. Star flowers, beautiful daisy-shaped flannel flowers and yellow peas are common.

Finch's Line of ascent was built from both ends and left incomplete when the gangs were diverted to toil on Mitchell's alternate route.

An easy, sandy ridgeline track with only an occasional rock traverses the unfinished link, offering a view of the Hawkesbury and Wisemans Ferry. Look out for a footpad on the left; this leads down to a cliff-top rock shelf overlooking Solomon Wiseman's colonial domain and punts plying the river crossing he established. If you close your eyes you might hear an echo of convict chains and chisels on stone.

From this lookout the track moves away from the view and meanders through eucalypts, pink-flowering grevillea and she-oaks, whose needles soften your footfalls. But the cliff remains deceptively close; if pursuing the view, only leave the main track to follow obvious, well-worn side trails. Soon after the river reappears you'll see a pale, formed road through the trees; this is Devine's Hill.

Treading a grassy track now, you'll cross a massive rock slab with tree roots reaching down its face like fingers.

When you come to a junction with a sand and gravel road, turn left onto the Old Great North Road. This puts you on the infamous 43km ridge-top leg from Devine's Hill to Mt Manning that forms the boundary between neighbouring Dharug and Yengo national parks. Walkers, horseriders and wellsprung cyclists can travel this road to Clare's Bridge, reputedly mainland Australia's oldest bridge (1830), and the restored Circuit Flat Bridge (more easily reached from the other end).

A steep valley view greets walkers climbing Finch's Line of ascent

Follow the broad formed road past a restored and fenced convict-built culvert. After 500m you'll come to a junction often guarded by a phalanx of Gymea lilies. Ignore Shepherds Gully Rd on the right and continue through the gate straight ahead onto Devine's Hill, descending between tree trunks and slices of Hawkesbury River on your right and sandstone stepping uphill to your left.

The pale road surface and exposed rock can make this a warm walk in summer. And watch your footing when you stop to admire the colonial-era engineering, or you'll get ants in your pants!

The first notable example of this engineering is a splendid curved wall supporting a road bend. The sandstone blocks were cut from the adjacent hillside, and you can clearly see the distinctive marks of iron wedgers and jumpers (drill bars); you may spot some convict graffiti here too. Further down, a short side trail leads to a stockade site. Beyond another curved stone wall and quarry site you'll reach the most impressive stretch of convict stonemasonry on the Old Great North Rd.

Major Mitchell's ascent required more sophisticated engineering and stonework – and cost more money – than any other section of the Great North Rd. This included culverts and spillways, elaborate walls and support buttresses – and not just a couple of metres of precision drystone walling. In one place you can stand on the edge of 13m high block work, the rock underfoot pitted with the chisel marks of chain gangs and convict work parties. All that effort for so little use.

As you continue downhill, the river view expands and the cliffs climb. Weather and erosion have worked together to craft hollows, none more beautiful or interesting than Hangman's Rock. Folklore says this is where convicts were tried before being hanged, the rope dropped through the hole in the roof, though it is more likely that the road engineers stored blasting powder here.

From the cave you've got an easy descent past layered and cracked sandstone and leafy private property (on your right). Post-and-rail fencing runs down to a chicane beside a park gate. From here, continue a few metres more to the road along the river.

Turn left onto the road and walk along it, crossing a splendid stone bridge. The ferry is about 500m along.

4 GRAND HIGH TOPS

Walk:	12km return or 14.5km loop
Time required:	4–6 hours
Best time:	Cool, clear day; the trail is steep and exposed and can be very hot in summer
Grade:	Moderate to hard (it's a climb with lots of steps)
Environment:	Dramatic volcanic formations, panoramic views, wildflowers, woodland
Best map:	This one
Toilets:	Pit toilet in Pincham carpark
Food:	Cold drinks and snacks in the visitor centre in the main day-use and camping area; restaurants, supermarkets and takeaways in Coonabarabran, the nearest major town, a 30-minute drive east
Tips:	Help track the park's recovery from the 2013 bushfire by taking photographs at two picture points and sharing them through WarrumbungleSnap (download the app or see environment. nsw.gov.au/research/WarrumbungleSnap.htm).
	There's a mobile phone signal along this walk, so you can send boastful pics from the top to your mates.
	Ask park staff whether there is water in the tank at Balor Hut and if not, carry extra. Warm weather brings the flies out so take repellent and/or a face net.
	Vehicle entry fees are payable for Warrumbungle National Park; you can pay a one-off fee or buy a multi-park pass; details at nationalparks.nsw.gov.au.

The Warrumbungle cliffs are remnants of a massive shield volcano

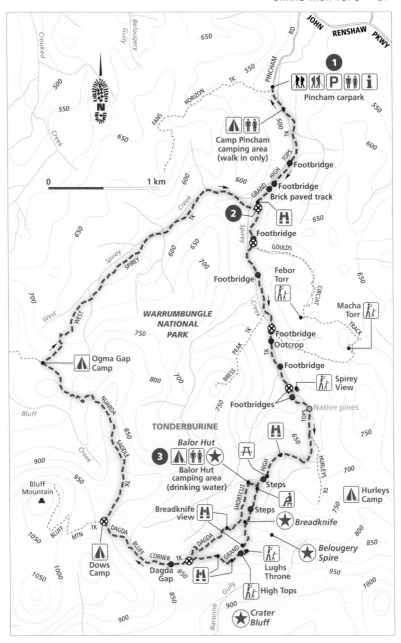

John Renshaw Pkwy

Pincham Rd

1 Pincham carpark

Camp Pincham camping area (walk in only)

Footbridge

Footbridge
Brick paved track

2

Footbridge

GOULDS

Footbridge

Febor Torr

Macha Torr

Footbridge
Outcrop

Footbridge

Spirey View

Footbridges

Native pines

Ogma Gap Camp

WARRUMBUNGLE NATIONAL PARK

TONDERBURINE

Balor Hut

3 Balor Hut camping area (drinking water)

Breadknife view

Steps

Steps

Breadknife

Hurleys Camp

Bluff Mountain

Dows Camp

Dagda Gap

Belougery Spire

Lughs Throne

High Tops

Crater Bluff

0   1 km

The distinctive 'Explore me!' spires, domes and dykes of Warrumbungle National Park are the eroded remnants of a shield volcano that was active 13–17 million years ago. These spectacular remnants are exposed for all to see on this steep, stunning Warrumbungle classic.

Warrumbungle is a Gamilaroi Aboriginal word meaning 'crooked mountains' and many of the park's 'crooked' outcrops, including the famous Breadknife, are clustered in an area called Grand High Tops. You can customise the two Grand High Tops routes, a lasso-shaped 12km return walk and 14.5km loop, with side trips.

Both routes set off from the top tier of Pincham carpark (see point 1 on map), about 35km west of Coonabarabran via John Renshaw Parkway, initially on a management vehicle track that snakes south. The track crosses Spirey Creek (which may be flowing) and passes hikers-only Camp Pincham, then meanders along the creek valley and skirts Mathgan Cone (the big hill on your right).

The January 2013 Wambelong bushfire burnt 90% of Warrumbungle National Park (and surrounding properties), destroying the visitor

Belougery Spire is a stunning volcanic plug

centre, historic woolshed and staff accommodation, killing wildlife and
severely damaging walking tracks, some of which dated back to the
1950s. Although it's relatively lush beside Spirey Creek, where you may
see nodding blue lilies, yellow bulbine lilies, pink smooth darling peas
and profusions of native wisteria's tinselly white star-flowers, there are
many burnt trees and leafy regrowth. Nesting boxes for birds, possums,
gliders and bats overhead replace hollow-bearing habitat trees lost to
the fire.

A kilometre or so along, the now-brick paved track passes the point
where the returning Grand High Tops loop walk comes in on the right
(see point 2), and soon after that the two ends, 900m apart, of Gould's
Circuit. This is a rough side loop to two great vantage points. It adds a
couple of kilometres to the walk, returning you to the creek valley down
an eroded track through cypress pine woodland.

If you didn't do Gould's Circuit, climb 140m up to Spirey View,
about 500m further on, for a tree-framed look at the Breadknife and
Belougery Spire, a much-photographed 1057m volcanic plug.

Shortly after a side trail to Hurley's Camp (closed at the time of
writing), the paved track pulls steeply away from the creek and up
Spirey Ramp through drier woodland of cypress pines and ironbarks.
As you pass a rocky rise, the saw-toothed Breadknife slices through the
view ahead.

An unmistakeable Warrumbungle landmark, the Breadknife is a
dyke formed when magma muscled into a long fissure in the rocks
under the volcano's surface, creating a cast of the fissure as it cooled.
Only 2–4m thick, 600m long and reaching 90m above the ground, it is
quite a sight. Steep wood-and-metal staircases deposit you, puffing, at
its base.

If you want to top up your water (definitely do so if you are
considering the longer walk) step right here, off the boarding, and
follow the unformed Dagda Shortcut track about 100m to Balor Hut
(see point 3) (this can be booked for overnight stays).

Then backtrack and continue left, zigzagging uphill on stairs and
boards along the Breadknife, with Belougery Spire rearing up out of
the trees beside you. Looking back, you'll see the white dome of Siding

Spring Observatory atop the hills to the east. A rocky trail then puts you flush with the Breadknife. Up this close, its vertical blockwork looks man-made, more Mayan stonemasonry than the handiwork of a volcano.

Turn left on a small saddle in the direction of a sign – 'Grand High Tops 150m' – and continue around another dyke, clambering a few metres up a goat track on the right to look back down over the Breadknife and the park. Reflectors indicate the route from here up a ridge to the top, Lugh's Throne (elevation 960m), which commands a right royal view. The 360° sweep takes in the length of the Breadknife, the once-farmed flats and the observatory; to the west stands Bluff Mountain, a 1200m high lava dome; immediately south, Crater Bluff, a huge trachyte plug, thrusts up from the plains.

Pretty pink fringed heath myrtles and phebalium shrubs grow on this exposed, rocky aerie, the latter erupting winter-into-spring into massed yellow flowers with antennae-like stamens.

This is a cracker lunch spot; just beware the local currawongs who think your food is for sharing (don't encourage them).

Once you are fed and rested, follow the reflector markers south-west along the crown, round the top of the Breadknife (less impressive here) and steeply down, enjoying the great view along the Breadknife's western face before the trail descends into dead trees and regrowth. It's surprising how soon the Grand High Tops are way above and then behind you.

It can seem like you are going the wrong way but push on west, away from the Breadknife and ignoring any lesser trails you might see. On reaching Dagda Gap you have a choice.

Most people turn hard right, towards Balor Hut, on the Dagda Shortcut. This is an easy trail through shady forest that gives you a close-up view of the swirled lava on the Breadknife's western face before ambling past the hut to the stair-top junction where you start back down the track you walked up earlier.

The longer loop has less visual oomph over its second half but by then has given you a great look at Bluff Mountain. To take this option continue straight on from Dagda Gap, through cypress pine

Post-fire regrowth greens Spirey Creek

and wattles, with the blocky mountain appearing on the left (with an early start, fit all-day hikers could add in the 2.6km return climb up Bluff Mountain). Turn right at Dow's Camp and take in three more vantage points en route to Ogma Gap, where you descend to West Spirey Creek.

An hour or so down the creek's eucalypt-lined gully – watch for koalas – the trail crosses a bridge and joins the original track. Turn left onto the track and return to the carpark.

The Breadknife, a volcanic dyke, slices through the view from the Grand High Tops

5 MOUNT KOSCIUSZKO VIA MAIN RANGE LOOP

Walk:	22.5km loop
Time required:	7–8 hours
Best time:	Autumn and early summer for wildflowers and pretty patches of late snow. The walking track is snowed under in winter and the road from Perisher to Charlotte Pass closed June to October.
Grade:	Moderate but long
Environment:	Stunning high-country ranges, exposed ridges, snow gum stands, alpine river and glacial lakes, summer wildflowers
Best map:	Rooftop's *Kosciuszko National Park Forest Activities Map Jindabyne–Khancoban*
Toilets:	Eco-toilets at Charlotte Pass trailhead and Rawson's Pass
Food:	Jindabyne, at the bottom of the mountain, has supermarkets, cafes and restaurants
Tips:	Start early and be prepared for all conditions, even snow in summer. Conditions can change suddenly and dramatically.
	Vehicle entry fees are payable for Kosciuszko National Park; you can pay a one-off fee or buy a multi-park pass; details at nationalparks.nsw.gov.au.

Stone-paved walking track snakes along the spine-like Main Range

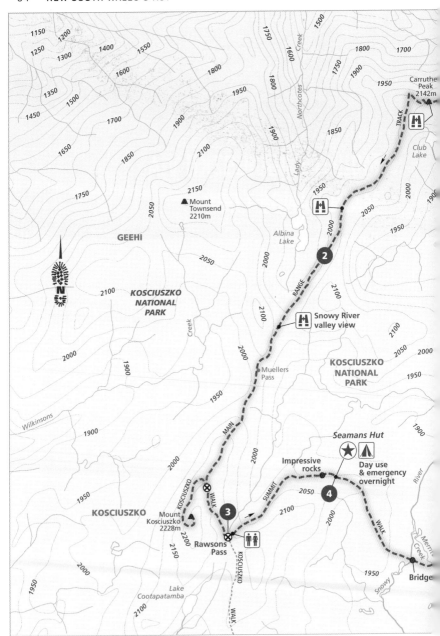

1150 1200 1250 1300 1350 1400 1450 1500 1550 1600 1650 1700 1750 1800 1900 2000 2050 2100 2150

1500 1600 1700 1750 1800 1850 1900 1950 2000 2050 2100

Creek

Northcotes

Lady

Carruthe Peak 2142m

TRACK

Club Lake

Mount Townsend 2210m

GEEHI

Albina Lake

RANGE

Snowy River valley view

KOSCIUSZKO NATIONAL PARK

KOSCIUSZKO NATIONAL PARK

Creek

Muellers Pass

MAIN

Seamans Hut

★ ⛺ Day use & emergency overnight

Impressive rocks

WALK

KOSCIUSZKO

WALK

SUMMIT

River

Merri Creek

KOSCIUSZKO

Mount Kosciuszko 2228m

Rawsons Pass

KOSCIUSZKO

WALK

Wilkinsons

Lake Cootapatamba

Snowy

Bridge

N

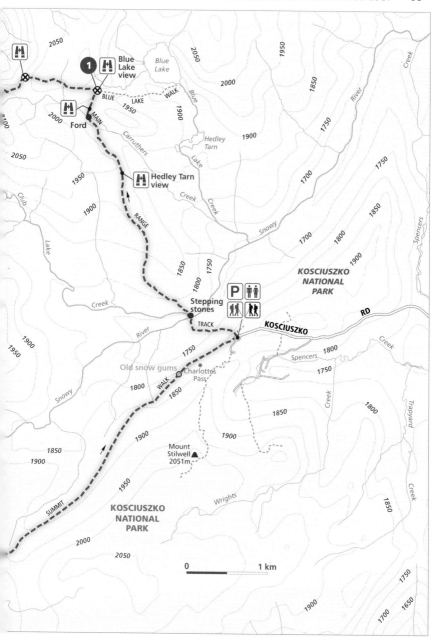

The most spectacular route to the top of the highest mountain on continental Australia, this all-day alpine experience combines multidimensional views, the country's largest and deepest glacial lake and a glorious wildflower show.

Mt Kosciuszko is no Antipodean Everest. At 2228m, it is just a quarter of the Himalayan giant's height. Nor is it even Australia's tallest peak – several peaks in Australian Antarctic and Sovereign territories dwarf it – but that's nitpicking. Kosciuszko is the highest mountain on mainland Australia, so there are boasting rights in summitting it.

The most popular route to the top, and the most popular walk in Kosciuszko National Park, is the 12km-return from Thredbo Alpine Village (hundreds of people a day walk this route over Christmas–New Year), but the more demanding loop hike from Charlotte Pass – Australia's highest resort, at 1765m – via the summit walk and Main Range packs a considerably more powerful visual punch.

Named after Charlotte Adams, believed to be the first European woman to reach Kosciuszko's summit, Charlotte Pass is a winding 40km drive from Jindabyne through small alpine villages. Park roadside near the end-of-Kosciuszko Rd turnaround area above the resort (parking within the turnaround circle is limited to about 20 minutes, for people treading the short Snow Gum boardwalk). From immediately beyond (west) of the turnaround, the clearly signed Main Range track, an initially cobble-paved path, descends quite steeply through snow gums to the Snowy River.

Stepping stones bridge the Snowy River and smaller Club Lake Creek, but crossing is dangerous when these are submerged after heavy rain or snow melt, so don't proceed if that's the case.

From here, the Main Range appears almost threadbare but low, lush gardens grow in its protected depressions and creek beds, and flowers defy the wind on its most exposed flanks and ridges. In summer, the still-cobbled track continues uphill from the river through rafts of candle heath and carpets of daisies.

A spectacular view greets you on topping Carruther's Peak

As you climb the track, Hedley Tarn appears down to your right, sparkling with sun on a perfect alpine day, and several hundred metres further on you'll come to the Blue Lake track junction (*see* point 1 on map). Blue Lake is the largest and deepest of the four cirque lakes on mainland Australia, three of which are strung along this walk. The fourth (Lake Cootapatamba, the highest lake in Australia) is on the Thredbo route. Cirque lakes are formed when a glacier digs out a basin as it pushes down a mountain face, and fill when the glacier recedes.

If you're moving well and are confident about timing, duck down to Blue Lake (about 2km return) and dip your digits in its icy water. Otherwise, turn left at this junction and continue along the Main Range proper.

Just before the track steepens up exposed Carruther's Peak you'll be blessed with a fabulous view: down sheer slopes and ridges to range upon range, each a different shade of blue, often with clouds climbing up to greet you, drifting on wind that can make eyes water, noses run and teeth ache – and that might make you query the sanity of anyone who camps overnight up here in a diaphanous hiking tent.

The view from atop Carruther's Peak (2142m) is equally fantastic: sweeps of Main Range hills, vertiginous drops to tortured crags, and blurred patches of distant farmland.

A rock-paved track brings you down Carruther's to a shaly track that snakes south along a ridge, with the ground dropping away on both sides and rearing up again to neighbouring ridges. This spectacular leg of the track can be strewn with golden everlastings, one of some 200 plant species, several of which are unique to Kosciuszko National Park, that live on the alpine plateau, thriving on cycles of snow, sun and wind.

Centuries-old mountain plum pines, a favourite hideaway of pygmy possums, hug the boulders strewn across the landscape.

Rounding a corner you'll see the track for some distance ahead, clinging to a hill that slides down to elongated Albina Lake and then winding up Mt Kosciuszko. The roughest and steepest leg of the whole hike is this next one, along the Albina Lake valley, so watch your footing as the narrow track dodges jagged rock projecting from the steep slope. This is also a great spot (see point 2) to take a breather and think about the shifting and shaping of Earth's surface. It doesn't take

Stepping out on the Main Range track

much imagination to fill the narrow-bottomed valley with the glacier that carved it.

The valley disgorges you on a wider ridge with the Snowy River valley on the left, exposed fractured granite on the right and Kosciuszko straight ahead. Ignore the footpad branching west at Mueller's Pass. The stone paving underfoot gives way to stabilising rubber mesh as you skirt a particularly rocky rise and start up the mountain.

A steady climb brings you to the summit track, which is the old road, on which walkers treading all routes meet. Continue uphill and around Kosciuszko to its crowning pile of rocks.

You are unlikely to have the summit to yourself and on picture-perfect days it can be crowded, so you might not want to linger, however it's worth framing a few photographs of the far-from-shabby view. Victoria's High Country, gathered by an unknown hand into deep, blue folds, lies to the south, while the Main Range looks like the spine of a gargantuan beast.

Follow the summit track down to Rawson's Pass (see point 3), where the mesh walkway starts south back to Thredbo and you could end your journey with a spectacular chairlift ride. This is a fun option if you can arrange a pick-up in Thredbo Village.

Otherwise, turn north-east (towards the toilets, which are cut into the hill) and follow the old summit road all the way back to Charlotte Pass, initially parallel and above Rawson's Creek. (From 1906 to 1974 people could – and did – take the easy option and drive up this road all the way to the top of Mt Kosciuszko.)

Wide and evenly surfaced, the daisy-edged road lets you step out and get up some speed. Mountain bikers are permitted along here, so beware their spinning wheels. Note the paper-thin rock layers exposed in the cutting where the road swings right. Shortly after, you'll pass a collection of impressive rocks on the right and then picturesque Seaman's Hut (see point 4) on the left. This stone day-use and emergency overnight shelter was built in 1928, after the death of two skiers.

Traversing a lunar landscape of treeless plain where you would be dangerously exposed if bad weather struck, the road crosses a very young Snowy River and Merritt's Creek on concrete bridges, then heads north-east down the Snowy River Valley.

Moss grows in moist areas along the road, and in summer billy buttons carpet the slope running down to the river. Two km from Charlotte Pass – there's a distance marker on a snow pole – you'll spot the first snow gums since this morning, on a mini-ridge below you. The walk finishes among gloriously striped, sculptural snow gums.

Clockwise from top: *Snowy River valley from the old Summit Rd leading down from Mt Kosciuszko; the Main Range track snakes upwards from the Snowy River; snow daisies grow in a fold of rock*

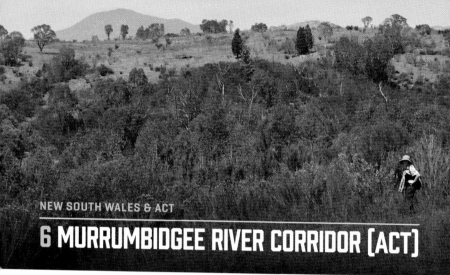

6 MURRUMBIDGEE RIVER CORRIDOR (ACT)

Walk:	12.9km one-way
Time required:	3–4 hours
Best time:	Any clear sunny day
Grade:	Easy to moderate (a few short, steep sections)
Environment:	River valley, rocky outcrops and gorges, wildflowers and mountain views
Best map:	ACT Government's *Murrumbidgee River Corridor Map and Guide*
Toilets:	Flushing toilets at Point Hut Crossing, Pine Island carparks and Kambah Pool
Food:	Canberra abounds with great food options
Tips:	Pack a picnic for lunch-with-a-view on the track, or leave food in the car at Kambah Pool. Bring your gear for a cooling swim; Kambah Pool offers multiple options for a dip, including a northern, signed section set aside for skinny dipping.

Reduce your stress levels by rambling along the wildflower-embroidered mountain-fringed Murrumbidgee River on the edge of the nation's capital.

Murrumbidgee means 'big water' in the language of the Wiradjuri, one of several Aboriginal groups through whose country Australia's third-longest river flows, and on its 1600km hook-shaped journey from the

Flowering bushes soften the rocky Murrumbidgee River corridor

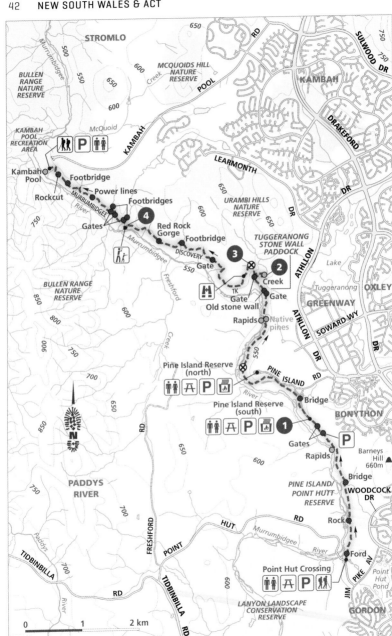

An old eucalypt frames walkers following the Murrumbidgee River downstream

Snowy Mountains to the River Murray this 'big water' meanders along Canberra's south-west boundary.

The 66km of river within the Australian Capital Territory and a narrow strip of land either side, made up of reserves, conservation zones and rural leases, are managed as the Murrumbidgee River Corridor. The walk described is the southern half of the continuous 27km Murrumbidgee Discovery Track, part of a network of walking trails along the corridor. This one-way walk – you'll need to do a car shuffle – starts at Point Hut Crossing, 30km south of Capital Hill via Tuggeranong Parkway and Point Hut Rd. Head north from the shady picnic area (there are toilets here), cross a ford over a side stream and pass through a gate to the river. The track now follows the river, wandering through wattles and snares of blackberry brambles on a good compacted track, but also stop and look back to take in the view of country rolling towards the Great Dividing Range.

Staying on the lower (Pine Island South) trail when the track divides, you'll pass through an area where lichen-covered rock reaches all the

A delicious lunch-stop view

way from your right down to tempting river pools below. European settlement dramatically changed this landscape, and 50,000 trees were planted along this stretch in 1986 in an attempt to address the effects of land clearing. Despite those efforts the track still meanders through cleared grasslands, but all along the walk you'll see, at different times of year, pretty grevilleas with furry grey-green leaves and pink-and-cream flowers, red and cream hakeas with needle-point leaves and phebalium, with massed yellow flower heads. Native river oaks line the river. The area has a lovely country feel, despite the houses behind you.

A step-through gate leads into Pine Island Reserve (toilets, barbecues, lawns and shelters). This reserve gives easy access to lovely swimming holes with sandy beaches.

The walking track resumes to the left off the northern parking area (*see* point 1 on map). Take the left fork at the next junction, walking down onto the river flats. Keep left again at the next junction (towards Kambah Pool) and enter Bullen Range Nature Reserve, where the track descends to a shady grove of river oaks beside rapids. This is a great spot to stop for a drink.

About 500m after the rapids you'll come to the Tuggeranong Stone Wall, built in 1875 in typical English drystone style (the uniquely Australian rabbit-proof fencing was added in the early 1900s). This 800m stretch is what remains of the 1800m boundary wall between the huge Lanyon and Yarralumla sheep properties.

From here you can see south, upriver, to Mt Tennent, a landmark peak with a popular, harder walking track to the top. Our track swings left and rounds the old wall, giving you a lovely river vista.

Walk on, across country sloping down to river oaks and grand old eucalypts and up eroded Tuggeranong Creek, a Murrumbidgee tributary, to a junction (*see* point 2). The track ahead leads to a bridge over the creek 500m upstream; this is the route to take if the river's running high. Otherwise, go left and down to a natural rock bridge; good steps climb up the other side to a wooden stile, over which you'll see another track sign. You'll probably also see kangaroos lounging on the grassy knoll behind it.

Follow the fenceline left and up to a gate where the high-water track comes up on the right (*see* point 3). Turn left and follow the track over a grassy hill, affording you a beautiful view of the ranges and the folded hills through which the Murrumbidgee wanders. Coming around the hill you'll see the red cliff of Red Rock Gorge, the view sometimes fringed pink with fluffy honey myrtle blooms. Raptors are often seen soaring over the cliffs.

The track now traverses an area of grassy hills dotted with eucalypts, pulling away from the river to skirt shallow gullies and descending through red grevillea and gum trees into deeper gullies.

Turn left onto an unsigned footpad immediately before a metal barrier on the river side of the track (*see* point 4). This leads to a lookout perched over rapids, which offers a sweeping view back up the gorge you've just walked down and over a large pool in which you'll often see fish. The natural shelf just in front of and below the man-made lookout is a great lunch spot, with comfy rocks.

Continuing on the lookout footpad brings you back to the main walking trail. Beyond another gate you'll briefly tread a vehicular track before the signed walking trail leaves it again. You'll come to a series of gates, some of which you can open, some of which have step-throughs. In some places you can't tell that the river is nearby, but powerlines and pylons remind you that civilisation is close.

From country almost like farmland you walk through a section where the track is cut into rock, and daphne heath grows in the hard ground. Stop and smell the roses, so to speak, if these shrubs are in bloom – their pretty, tubular white flowers with spreading lobes have a delicious honey scent.

Continue through gorgeous scribbly gums and some fabulous old burnt-out stumps to Kambah Pool parking area to finish.

7 NATIONAL PASS LOOP

Walk:	9.5km loop
Time required:	4–5 hours
Best time:	Any time. The lower half of the walk remains relatively cool on warm days, and there are opportunities for a refreshing dip; cloud can add to the drama.
Grade:	Moderate to hard (uneven ground, ladders, and lots of steps)
Environment:	Escarpment-edge lookouts, precipitous cliffs, eucalypt woodland, fern forests, waterfalls
Best map:	This one, combined with the NSW National Parks *Wentworth Falls and Valley of the Waters* map, available from national park offices
Toilets:	Flushing toilets at Wentworth Falls picnic area and partway along the walk at Conservation Hut
Food:	Breakfasts, lunches, snacks and coffee are available daily, and weekend sunset dinners during summer, at Conservation Hut (conservationhut.com.au)
Tips:	This walk can be accessed using public transport. Catch the train to Wentworth Falls railway station, then tread the Charles Darwin Walk down Jamison Creek to the falls, following in the footsteps of the naturalist who walked here in 1836 on his round-the-world expedition aboard HMS *Beagle*. This increases the walk length by 3.5km.

Views from the National Pass loop walk take in the beautiful Kedumba Valley and Kings Tableland

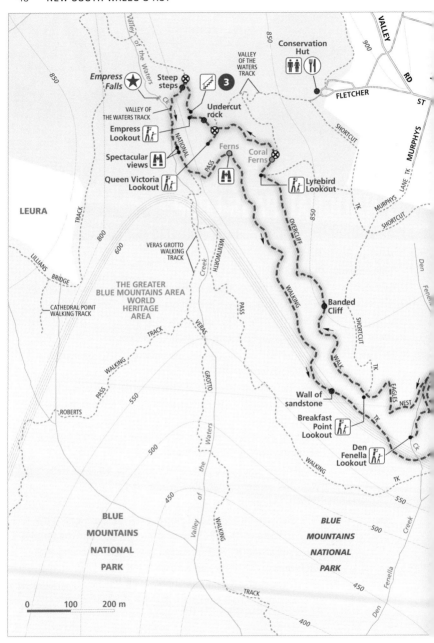

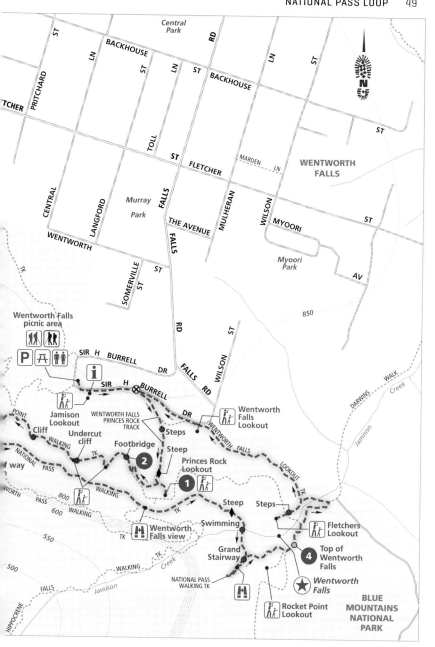

A Blue Mountains classic, this walk, on a century-old track, takes in waterfalls and ferny gullies, and travels along sheer cliffs to precipice-edge lookouts. The grand-scale vistas will take your breath away.

Part of the Great Dividing Range, which runs down Australia's east coast, the Blue Mountains are a superb example of a dissected plateau. Water, ice, wind and gravity have spent a million or so years sculpting layers of sandstone, shale and coal into valleys and escarpments that humble mere mortals. The result is a walking destination unlike any other in the country.

The popular Three Sisters at Katoomba are just the tip of the iceberg when it comes to Blue Mountains wonders, many of which are accessible only on foot. Part of an extensive network of walking trails, the National Pass, built between 1906 and 1907 using picks, shovels, crowbars and dynamite, by men sometimes suspended in a bosun's chair, headlines this awesome loop.

Starting in the Wentworth Falls picnic area, step out onto Jamison Lookout for the first of many extraordinary views, down the regal Kings Tableland. From here, head about 50m east along the footpath, then take the right-hand track down through banksias to Princes Rock Lookout [see point 1 on map].

Bask in the lookout's showy view of the Kedumba and Jamison valleys, Narrow Neck Peninsula to your right and Kings Tableland on the left. Wentworth Falls is also visible to the left, as are the steps cut into the cliff, which you'll climb later. The stand-alone flat-top seemingly thrust up through the valley floor is Mt Solitary, reachable via a challenging overnight hike; the cluster of rocks on a ridge just to its right is Ruined Castle, the end point of another fabulous day walk.

Step up from the lookout and head left, down towards the cliff edge, then turn right towards Conservation Hut and Valley of the Waters on Undercliff Track [Wentworth Falls is signed left]. Following the cliff line but offering only occasional views, this track snakes through banksias and eucalypts and along sandstone walls festooned with ferns watered

Wentworth Falls pours from the cliff edge above the walking track

by spray and trickles from the escarpment; stepping stones in damp spots keep your feet fairly dry. The track passes under an overhang, requiring anyone more than 1.5m tall to duck.

Cross a footbridge (*see* point 2) in a fern-filled creek gully (ignore the wooden steps coming in from the right) and turn off the cliff track to Den Fenella Lookout. This is a delightful detour on steep steps, footbridges and stepping stones, down a lush and leafy creek gully to another valley view.

When you've had your fill of the view, return to the cliff track. As you walk along it you'll pass trees with smooth, pink to orange-brown trunks. These beauties are *angophora costata*, commonly called smooth-barked apples (there is a rough-barked apple too). On a warm day you'll hear and probably see lots of skinks as well.

Sometimes flat and easy going, sometimes stepped and sporadically steep and uneven, the track comes up under a magnificent oxidised layered cliff where the sandstone has worn away, leaving exposed scallops of harder rock.

Beyond Lyrebird Lookout, from which you might spot one of the handsome mimics that give the lookout its name, the track cuts through an area thick with coral ferns watered by little creeks, to another junction. If you need refreshment or a toilet break, turn right for Conservation Hut (10 minutes). Otherwise turn left and head into the Valley of the Waters via Queen Victoria Lookout, which presents arguably the most majestic view so far.

To your left is an amphitheatre of striped cliff. The treed ledge partway up is the National Pass. Metal staircases drop to another track junction (see point 3) beside Valley of the Waters Creek, where over a footbridge to your right you'll see a picnic table under trees. Ignore the footbridge and go left and downstream, with falling water as your soundtrack, into a soft-lit wonderland where waterfalls weave magic as they gush and tumble over mossy stone ledges. You may be tempted to tiptoe through here lest you spook the fairies and water nymphs who surely dance across the stepping stones and slide down the handrails when you leave.

Beyond the falls, Wentworth Pass comes up steeply on the right; this harder, longer track ventures along the base of the escarpment to

Sculpted, textured sandstone is a feature of this historic walking track

Wentworth Falls. Keep left for the National Pass, zigzagging steeply up stone steps and navigating a short walkway fastened to the cliff. The track then follows the claystone ledge separating the upper and lower sandstone cliffs, pressing you close to curved rock walls and square-edged blocky bluffs.

The cliffs shelter fern gardens watered by misty veils, and yet just 10m on you find yourself standing amid grass trees and smooth-barked apples. One handsome tree, sadly scored with graffiti, has buried roots in the rock and spread them across the track.

Information plaques with black and white photographs tell the story of the National Pass, and a post at the foot of a monster sandstone wave cresting high overhead announces you are halfway along it.

Wentworth Pass comes steeply up again on the right where you swing towards the falls, which soon come into view. Pretty when it's a fine veil, the cascade is spectacular when in full flow. The track now ducks under another overhang. When you lift your head you'll see the steps cut into the opposite cliff, up which you'll shortly puff.

Wentworth Falls leaps off the escarpment and plunges to the gorge floor in two tiers. The National Pass crosses the falls between leaps, giving you a neck-cricking view of the top cascade and an opportunity for a cooling swim where the water pools before jumping again.

Whether you choose to swim or paddle or just rest, you've got only one option afterwards: climb! And the ascent starts immediately, under a leafy canopy of ferns where you'll pass a memorial to the award-winning restoration of the National Pass, completed in 2008. The pick head beside it was found during the track's restoration and is believed to be one of the tools used in its original construction.

Then it's up the Grand Stairway, Australia's tallest outdoor staircase – 173 stone-cut steps ascending 90m. The steps are steep and exposed to afternoon sun, but they catch the odd breeze and offer eagle-eye views of valleys, the pools where you crossed the falls and the National Pass track, opposite.

When you reach the top, ignore the Rocket Point circuit track on the right and ford the top of Wentworth Falls at pretty Queens Cascades [*see* point 4]. Keep left again at the next junction and follow an easy, formed track to Fletchers Lookout, a good spot for photographing rainbows on the falls.

Climb the steps opposite the lookout (the track going left leads to Princes Rock Lookout), and ignore the side track to Weeping Rock. Keep climbing through heath country dotted with pale pink orchids to Wentworth Falls Lookout for a final view (you can just see the top of the cascade), then follow the footpath west back to the carpark.

Take a breather and enjoy the view from the Grand Stairway

8 NIGHTCAP BLUFF

Walk:	16.7km return
Time required:	5–7 hours
Best time:	Mild sunny day
Grade:	Moderate
Environment:	Subtropical rainforest-clad mountain ridges and bluff lookouts
Best map:	This one
Toilets:	None
Food:	In Nimbin, 12km down the mountain, you can pick up the makings of a daypack picnic and sit down before or after the hike to assorted fare, including wood-fired pizza
Tips:	Nimbin, with its delicious food and Marijuana Museum, is just one of many reasons to spend a few days in the Northern Rivers Region

Pay homage to rainforest and the thermal forces that crafted the magnificently rugged New South Wales–Queensland border ranges on this day-long walk on the rim of a volcano.

Home to the Widjabal Aboriginal people long before European settlement, the rainforest-clad Nightcap Range forms the south-east edge of the Mt Warning erosion caldera, a massive, breached volcanic crater at the heart of the Northern Rivers Region. Part of the Gondwana

A lookout on the Historic Nightcap Track presents a view into the Mt Warning erosion caldera

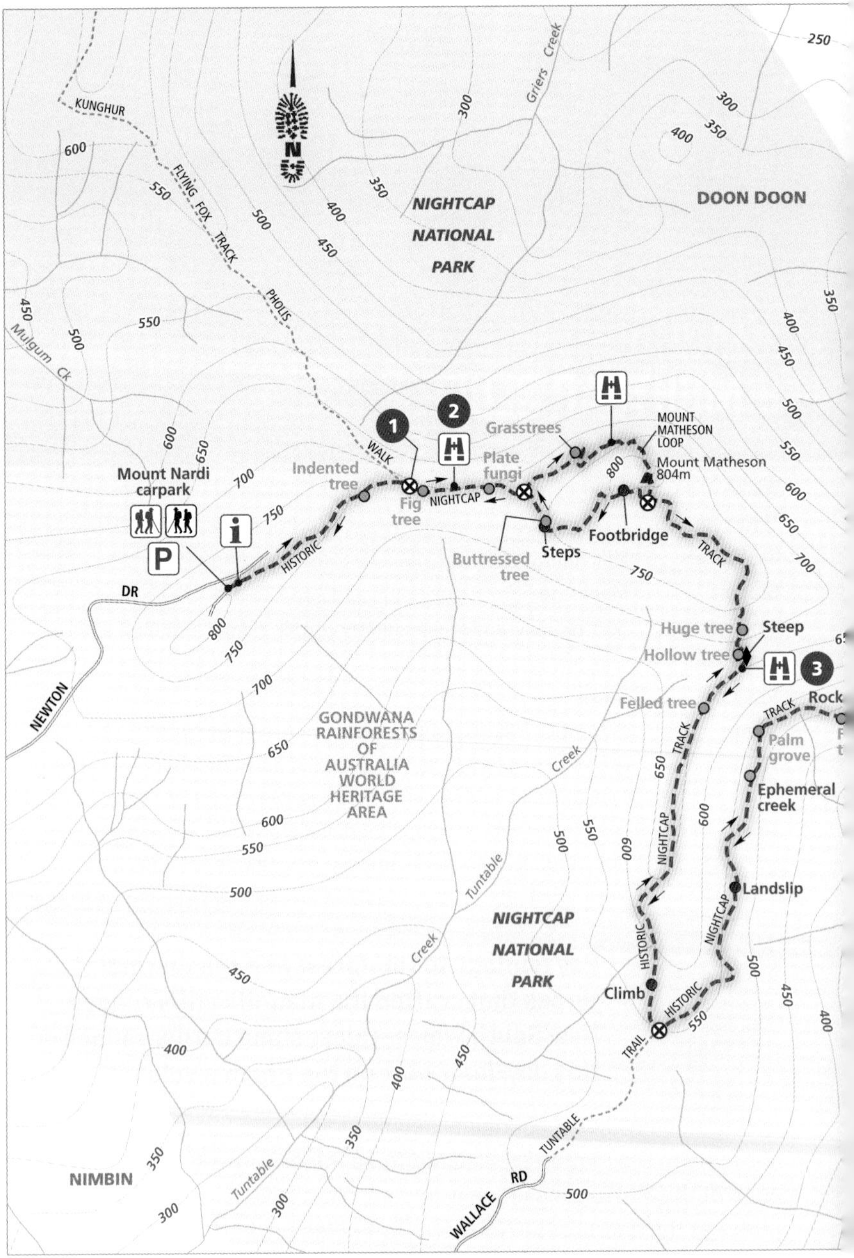

KUNGHUR

FLYING FOX TRACK

PHOLS

Mulgum Ck

600

550

450

500

550

600

650

700

750

800

250

300

350

400

350

400

450

500

550

600

650

700

750

Griers Creek

NIGHTCAP

NATIONAL

PARK

DOON DOON

Mount Nardi
carpark

Indented
tree

WALK

NIGHTCAP

HISTORIC

DR

NEWTON

Fig
tree

Plate
fungi

Grasstrees

MOUNT
MATHESON
LOOP

Mount Matheson
804m

MOUNT MATHESON LOOP

Steps

Buttressed
tree

Footbridge

TRACK

Huge tree

Hollow tree

Felled tree

Steep

Rock

Palm
grove

Ephemeral
creek

Landslip

GONDWANA
RAINFORESTS
OF
AUSTRALIA
WORLD
HERITAGE
AREA

Creek

Tuntable

Creek

500

550

600

650

700

750

800

700

650

600

550

500

450

400

350

300

NIGHTCAP

HISTORIC

NIGHTCAP

TRACK

NIGHTCAP

HISTORIC

Climb

TRAIL

NIGHTCAP

NATIONAL

PARK

NIMBIN

Tuntable

Tuntable

WALLACE   RD

500

1

2

3

① ②
③

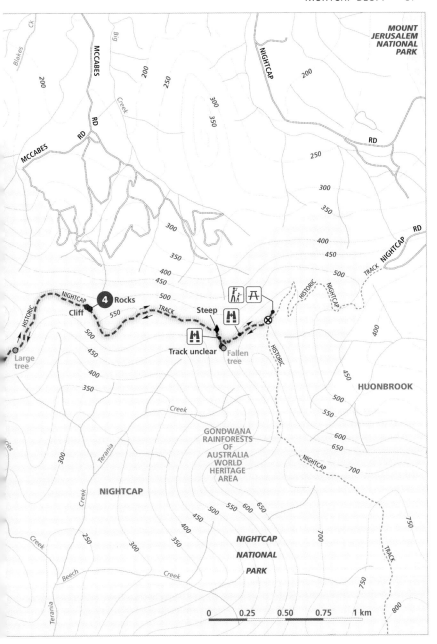

Rainforests of Australia World Heritage site, Nightcap National Park is one of 41 reserves protecting subtropical, warm temperate and Antarctic beech cool temperate rainforests dating back to when Australia was part of the Gondwanaland supercontinent. Another is Lamington National Park, a justly famous walking destination just over the Queensland border [see p. 392]. The Nightcap Range was the setting for Australia's first environmental forest blockade, in 1979, when more than 300 people camped on Terania Creek to stop the logging of 300-year-old brushbox and blackbox trees. Protesters Falls is named for their stand. That blockade, and a subsequent rally by 2000 people, led to the creation of Nightcap National Park in 1984.

The park's network of walking tracks overlaps a section of the bridle trail opened between the Richmond and Tweed valleys in 1871. You can hike this Historic Nightcap Track over two days or tread part of it on this out-and-back day walk to Nightcap Bluff from Mt Nardi. A scenic, winding 12km drive from Nimbin, the Mt Nardi carpark is basic; a bit of gravel, no toilets, and an information board. Take the footpad to the left of the information board, which plunges you into a primordial world of leafy plants that twist and strangle as they grow towards the light.

Many of the trees have buttressed roots and are patched with moss and lichen. Vines as thick as your arm hang from branches, and tree ferns and palms reach into a canopy festooned with epiphytes. Beware barbed wait-a-while and foot-entangling vines that can trip you, especially on your return if you are weary.

Early in the walk you'll see a huge stump indented with the slots for the planks on which loggers stood while cutting it down. Soon after, there's a junction [see point 1 on map], with Pholis Gap to the left. Keep straight on and downhill, towards Mt Matheson and the Nightcap Track. Old, weathered wooden junction signs suggest this is one of the less visited (and therefore less maintained) New South Wales parks, but although this track is only occasionally marked, with orange arrows, it is fairly easy to follow.

Just before the track threads between two boulders you'll pass a striking strangler fig. Born of a seed deposited by bird or animal, this parasite has strangled its host tree with a corset of roots and

Nightcap Bluff is a perfect lunch spot with a view of Mt Warning/Wollumbin and the caldera farmlands

deprived it of light with its own leaves, killing the tree and leaving a self-supporting cylinder of fig.

A lookout in the lee of a huge burnt tree stump [*see* point 2], further on, presents the first proper view into the caldera.

Turn left at the next junction, onto the Mt Matheson Loop. The prolific whippy palms at this junction are walking stick palms. The stems of this species were once used to make walking sticks, with the small knob at the base often carved into an ornate handle. In autumn the palms produce strings of red fruit, whose edible flesh leaves a peppery aftertaste.

The Mt Matheson Loop traverses steep Mt Matheson, and in places the trail is built up with mossy stone walling. You'll pass through bristling grass trees and switchback uphill, where crawling under a fallen tree will grant another view into the caldera. The conical peak in the middle is Mt Warning/Wollumbin ['cloud catcher'], the first place on mainland Australia to feel morning sun.

Around Mt Matheson's crown you rejoin the main trail. Turn left and walk on through rainforest crowded with majestic trees many metres around. Beyond these logging survivors the track zigzags steeply downhill, passing a monster hollowed tree whose exposed roots span 8m. The track then widens and runs down a ridge to a junction (*see* point 3).

The unsigned track descending to your right here is for management vehicles only, passing through endangered frog habitat. Turn hard left

Palms weave a canopy over the Historic Nightcap Track

instead and climb through palms, swinging left and downhill again in drier eucalypt forest. Palm fronds clatter as they fall through the canopy and crunch underfoot as you round a verdant palm grove with a ridgeline rising beyond. Seasonal creeks flowing out of tangles of vines and palms can make this section of track boggy.

With palms still below, the track enters more open forest of eucalypts and grass trees. Here is a NSW National Parks sign, behind which is a lookout with a sweeping vista of Mt Warning/Wollumbin and the encircling forest-clad caldera slopes.

Further on are some unsigned rocks (*see* point 4). People exploring these coarse-skinned sentinels, perhaps in search of a view (there is none from the track here), have cut footpads towards the edge; take extreme care if following these.

Walk on, your footsteps muffled by leaves, with the ridge you trod earlier briefly – and a little disconcertingly – ahead. Below a sturdy old-timer gum the trail turns hard left, immediately before a mess of fallen trees and branches. Footpads continue into this tangle but soon disappear, so you'll know if you have missed the turn.

Narrower and rocky now, the track switchbacks uphill, traversing a steep slope thick with tea-tree before depositing you on a broader track. Walkers treading the length of the Historic Nightcap Track would go right here, but we turn left.

Just around the corner you'll see a Parks and Wildlife walker symbol on a blue/green post. Step up the footpad to the left of the post onto an unfenced narrow granite promontory with an expansive view taking in the caldera, Mt Warning/Wollumbin, the caldera farmlands, and the rugged border ranges forming a green battlement to the north. This is Nightcap Bluff. Comfortable hollows worn in the rocks by other backsides make it a wonderful spot to linger over lunch.

Once refuelled, check out the sea view from the other side of the rise before heading back. Retrace your steps but ignore the Mt Matheson Loop coming in on the right, instead staying on the rooty main track and winding through palms, ferns and mighty buttressed trees back to the carpark.

9 PIGEON HOUSE MOUNTAIN (DIDTHUL)

Walk:	6km return
Time required:	3 hours
Best time:	Clear day for the views
Grade:	Moderate to hard (all uphill to the top)
Environment:	Eucalypt forest, heathland, sandstone outcrops, panoramic views, steps, steep ladders
Best map:	This one
Toilets:	Pit toilets in the parking area
Food:	None
Tips:	The walking track can be slippery and the access road can become boggy after rain; check the weather before setting out

Your climb up this landmark peak will be rewarded with panoramic views of the New South Wales south coast and the rugged Budawang Wilderness.

That this special Aboriginal women's place, long-called Didthul ('woman's breast'), reminded Captain James Cook of a square pigeon house says as much about how differently the British navigator and the local first Australians saw the land as it does about the shape of this south coast landmark. But whether you think Pigeon House Mountain

The gobsmacking panorama from atop Pigeon House Mountain (Didthul)

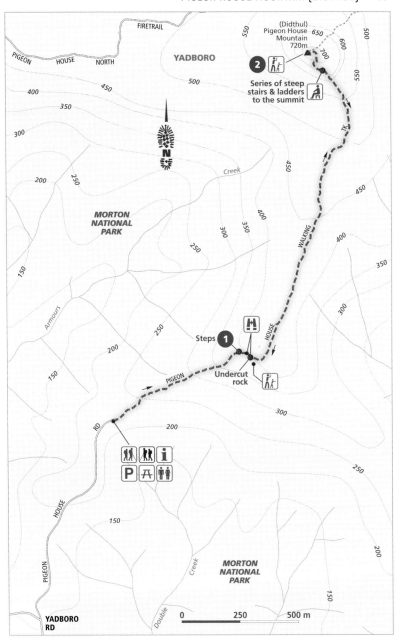

FIRETRAIL

PIGEON HOUSE NORTH

YADBORO

(Didthul)
Pigeon House
Mountain
720m

550 650 700 600 500 550

2

Series of steep
stairs & ladders
to the summit

500

400

450

350

Creek

450

300

450

200 250

MORTON
NATIONAL
PARK

400

350 300

250

450

WALKING

400

150

350

300

Armours

250

250

200

HOUSE

Steps **1**

Undercut
rock

PIGEON

200

300

150

RD

250

300

150

Creek

MORTON
NATIONAL
PARK

200

150

Double

0   250   500 m

YADBORO
RD

looks more like a dovecote or a breast, the most important thing is the view from the top – a 360° scenic blast.

Pigeon House Mountain rises out of the southern section of Morton National Park, one of the largest parks in New South Wales, which protects a maze of dissected sandstone plateaus.

The summit trail starts in a tree-ringed picnic area about 35km west of Ulladulla via Yadboro Rd, an unsealed road designed for forestry use (a sign recommends 4WD when the road is wet). Access is roughest after the last turnoff, onto Pigeon House Rd, but with care you should get through okay in a conventional vehicle in dry conditions. Watch out for wallabies and lyrebirds as you're driving through the forest.

From the picnic area the climb starts immediately, up a steep, forested ridge, initially on a wide track with occasional logs fixed across to limit erosion. Either side are banksias, scaly barked and furrowed eucalypts, and pale flowering wattles (acacias) with feathery leaves. Through the tree trunks you'll catch fragmented views of surrounding ridgetops and a tantalising glimpse of Pigeon House Mountain's sandstone 'nipple'. Mountain devil bushes produce flashy red flowers much of the year.

About 800m up, the track flattens somewhat and veers left around granite boulders (*see* point 1 on map) before clambering up wood and stone steps between rocks. Notice the stone underfoot as you climb – some of it is conglomerate, with smaller rocks naturally cemented together – and look around, enjoying more and more hints of the grandeur that lies beyond the trees.

The steps lead to a large undercut boulder with a crazy-paved floor, from which you'll glimpse ranges through the trees. But the view from the larger, flatter granite area a few steps further up is more rewarding: thickly treed valleys and ridges, steeper, rocky country that looks like it has been squeezed by hand into its flat-topped battlement formation, and Pigeon House Mountain thrust up to the north.

After the lookout you get a break from climbing and can walk along the flat through eucalypts, spiky grasses and yellow and orange flowering banksias. Here too, flowering white heath shrubs with sharply pointed leaves (*Woollsia pungens*) grow year round, along with

Clockwise from top: *A broad ocean view awaits you atop Pigeon House Mountain (Didthul); pine-leaf geebung flowers splash yellow through the greenery; steep metal staircases help you reach the top; a rocky view on the way up the mountain*

pine-leaf geebung that sport pretty, curling yellow flowers in spring and summer.

Savour the break from ascending, and the view of the top of Pigeon House Mountain, because after about 900m you'll resume climbing, and you won't stop until you reach the top. The mostly stepped second half of this walk starts amid tea-tree, continues in damper eucalypt forest carpeted with sedgy grasses, bracken and moss, then reaches drier scrub striped with stalks of red common heath.

Then it's up a series of metal staircases. If you are carrying walking poles, stow them here or leave them at the bench beside the stairs – they will be more hindrance than help now. As you climb you'll see further and further across undulated forest green. The penultimate ascent is on more metal stairs and ladders that chimney up a small canyon – it can be windy here, and the metalwork cold to touch in cool weather – and skirt a massive boulder propped up by a metal rod, beyond which awaits a broad ocean view. The trail loops left to steps [*see* point 2] that climb between sandstone boulders to the rounded stone summit.

'Wow!' is a common comment on viewing the gobsmacking panorama from atop Pigeon House Mountain. A trig station straddles its highest point [720m above sea level]; a fenced eyrie overlooks table-topped Byangee Mountain and The Castle beyond it, and the rugged cliffs and deep gorges of the Budawang Wilderness, the impressive handiwork of the Clyde River open to experienced hikers. With a little manoeuvring you can, on clear days, see the Pacific Ocean at the edge of the view. Note the multi-trunked eucalypts trailing bark streamers that crown Didthul; these are rare Pigeon House Ash.

This being both the physical and scenic high point of the walk, it's all downhill from here back to your car.

10 SPIT BRIDGE TO MANLY

Walk:	11km one-way
Time required:	4 hours (more with swimming)
Best time:	Sunny day with a sea breeze; spring for wildflowers
Grade:	Easy to moderate
Environment:	Coastal national park, sandstone cliffs, harbourside suburbs, foreshore, beaches
Best map:	This one
Toilets:	Flushing toilets at beaches and picnic areas along the way
Food:	Plonk Beach Cafe, on the city side of Spit Bridge, dishes up breakfasts (and other fare). Food of all kinds is up for grabs at Manly but stick with tradition and unwrap a parcel of fish and chips at the ocean beach – just beware thieving seagulls.
Tips:	Download the interpretive brochure and map of the Manly Scenic Walkway at www.manly.nsw.gov.au/attractions/walking-tracks/manly-scenic-walkway. Take your things for a swim along the way. Time your walk so you can catch the ferry from Manly to Circular Quay as the setting sun silhouettes Sydney Harbour Bridge.

Shallows lap a rusty anchor in a rocky bay on the run into Manly

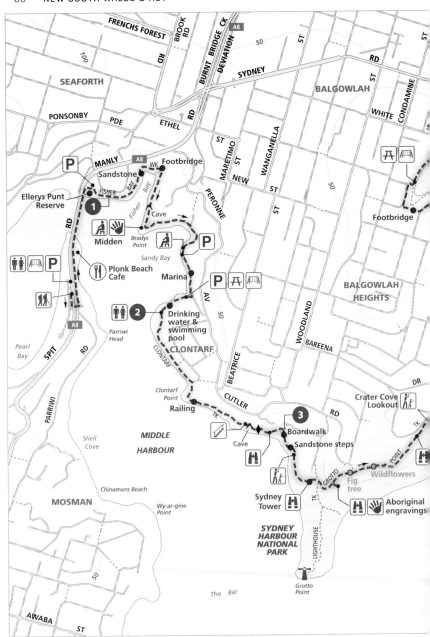

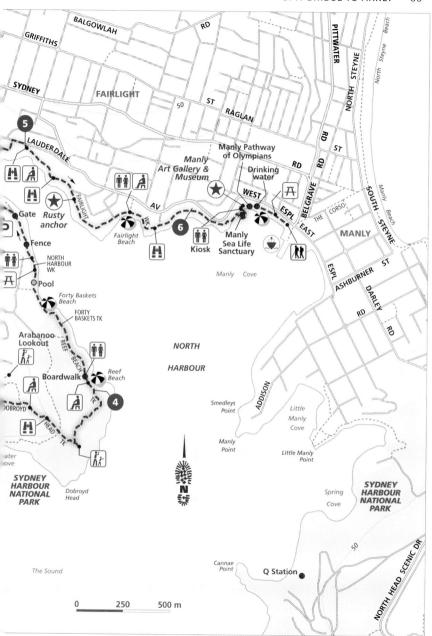

5

LAUDERDALE

SYDNEY

GRIFFITHS

BALGOWLAH   RD

FAIRLIGHT

RAGLAN   ST

50   ST

PITTWATER

NORTH STEYNE

North Steyne Beach

Manly Pathway
of Olympians

Manly
Art Gallery &
Museum

Drinking
water

RD

RD

ST

Gate   Rusty
anchor

FAIRLIGHT

AV

WK

WEST

ESPL

EAST

BELGRAVE RD

THE CORSO

Manly Beach

MANLY

SOUTH STEYNE   ST

6

Fairlight Beach

Kiosk

Manly
Sea Life
Sanctuary

Fence

NORTH
HARBOUR
WK

Pool

Forty Baskets
Beach

FORTY
BASKETS TK

Manly   Cove

ESPL

ASHBURNER   ST

DARLEY

RD

DARLEY

RD

Arabanoo
Lookout

Boardwalk

REEF BEACH

Reef
Beach

4

NORTH

HARBOUR

Smedleys
Point

Little
Manly
Cove

ADDISON

DOBROYD

HEAD TK

Manly
Point

Little Manly
Point

ater
ove

SYDNEY
HARBOUR
NATIONAL
PARK

Dobroyd
Head

N

Spring
Cove

SYDNEY
HARBOUR
NATIONAL
PARK

The Sound

Cannae
Point

Q Station

50

NORTH HEAD SCENIC DR

0   250   500 m

Is this the world's most spectacular harbour city? You decide as you explore Sydney's inland coast, walking from high-price suburb to sandy beach, from exposed cliff to sheltered marina.

The largest natural harbour on the planet is a workplace, a playground and a sought-after address. But the few Sydneysiders who can afford to live on the water share the curlicue foreshore with golden beaches, rugged, rocky coves and, surprisingly for a city, a national park. The Manly Scenic Walkway, between Spit Bridge at Seaforth and the beachside suburb of Manly, shows off this iconic corner of Australia.

More often called the Spit Bridge-to-Manly walk, the Manly Scenic Walkway is divided into seven sections. Some are suitable for wheelchairs, others steep and stony; combined, they make a leisurely few hours or day on foot (depending on how often you swim), ending with fish and chips and a ferry ride.

Trees frame yachts anchored along the Manly Scenic Walkway

Public transport is a perfect fit for this walk. Start with a bus ride from the CBD to Spit Bridge (route 178, 179 or 180 from Carrington St, behind Wynyard Station). At Spit Bridge – ask the driver where to disembark – cross at the lights (weekday morning traffic is appalling, but you'll soon escape), turn left and walk back down the opposite footpath.

Walk over the bridge and turn right down a driveway-like sealed road to Ellery's Punt Reserve. There's a map of the Manly Scenic Walkway to the left, from where you walk up a gently climbing track between moored boats and sandstone to a fenced viewing point (see point 1 on map) looking over the spit and back to the bridge.

The track continues around this sandstone point and emerges from a pocket of ferns onto a sandy bay beneath a rock overhang, its intricate natural texturing still visible despite graffiti. Boardwalk, stone steps, timber stairs and footbridges loop through this bay's fringing rainforest, passing expensive houses and hollowed sandstone. The bay ends at a tree encased in a termite mound, whose abandoned insect tunnels run like veins up the trunk.

A midden (layers of shells) beside the track is evidence that Guringai Aboriginal people cooked and ate seafood here. They probably also ate eastern water dragons, handsome lizards with black head stripes that stand their ground on the track until you are almost upon them.

The track continues along the shore to Sandy Bay and a beach where soggy canines chase sticks and balls. Beyond Clontarf Marina's floating millions is grassy Clontarf Reserve (see point 2), whose shady Norfolk Island pines were axed and poisoned in November 2014 and may not survive.

Pass the shark-netted swimming area and step onto the beach at the Art Deco Egyptian temple-style concrete building – it's a sewer siphon! When waves roll into the backyard fences along here you can keep dry on the signed high-tide road route.

Prince Alfred, Queen Victoria's second son, survived an assassination attempt on Clontarf Beach in 1868 when his India-rubber braces softened the impact of a bullet fired by Henry James O'Farrell. The Irishman was hanged forty days later.

The track resumes at the end of the sandy stretch, stepping up sandstone crusted with oysters. It then hugs the coast, climbs boulders with harbour views, ducks under lattice-like sandstone feathered with ferns, and accesses rocky bays.

An alternate route for dog-walkers goes left where ours heads into Sydney Harbour National Park [see point 3] through 6m tree ferns. Plunging cliffs are a highlight of this section of the walk, safety rails doubling as armrests as you drink in views of glistening water, and breeze-filled sails in good yachting weather.

An out-and-back side track descends to Grotto Point, where a First Fleet survey party camped on 28 Jan 1788. The squat lighthouse built here in 1911 still guides ships through the heads. Continuing on the main track you'll come to an even shorter side trail to an Aboriginal engraving site on a natural rock pavement blessed with views through Sydney Heads into the Tasman Sea. Some of the engravings are indistinct, and idiots have scratched out the sign beside the largest, but there is a suggestion of wing tips, although you might see something different.

Step up from the engraving site, through flannel flowers – a seasonal sea of white with pink fuchsia heath and red-and-green correa – and past a fig tree grown over a sandstone boulder. As you traverse coastal heath on sandstone and boardwalk, you'll see out through the heads. Soon Manly and its green-and-gold ferries will come into view; then Crater Cove's precipitous cliffs, encrusted with shacks built of stone, driftwood and corrugated iron by fishers from the 1930s.

Ignoring the trail to Arabanoo Lookout [the view is no better than along here], descend through banksias and grass trees and around Dobroyd Head, shaped by water over millions of years. The historic Quarantine Station, Sydney's isolation compound for carriers of infectious diseases from 1828 to 1984, is visible across the water from Dobroyd Track, a popular route for joggers pushing themselves to fitness.

Then suddenly you'll find yourself in taller eucalypts, one of which leans over Reef Beach's rocky shore, framing Manly. The track keeps

Reef Beach's rocky shore reaches into the shallows opposite Manly

Left: *Look out for colourful mountain devils;* **Right:** *Flannel flowers create a seasonal sea of white*

your feet clean by running along boardwalk, but what's a bit of sand?
Step onto the beach and look right, admiring a leaning gum tree
clinging to a honeycombed lip of undercut sandstone (see point 4).

This is a lovely spot to swim – though you are unlikely to be alone –
before moving on.

Approaching Forty Baskets Beach, take the high-tide route up steps
or skirt the beach on stepping stones to another netted swimming
pool. The homes here face Manly apartment blocks across the water.

Past pretty coves you'll come through a gate onto sealed Gourlay
Ave. Veer right and squeeze behind a marina building onto Reef Bay's
sandy shore to check out the yachts rocking on their moorings. (If
you don't want to wade through high-tide shallows to North Harbour
Reserve, head left through the gate and follow the road route –
Gourlay Ave and Lister St.)

The only option beyond North Harbour Reserve is a short but
claustrophobic street walk through cheek-by-jowl housing, along

King Ave into busy Lauderdale Ave. The walking track reappears 60m along Lauderdale Ave (*see* point 5) and follows linear Esplanade Park. Look out for the rusty anchor projecting from the shallows of a tiny rocky bay.

Now for a breezy amble into Manly, between apartments and benches overlooking the harbour. Stencils on the track alert you to penguins (Manly's little penguins are the only mainland colony in NSW).

Step down at a road and parking area (*see* point 6) to a wooden walkway that takes you into Manly, among crowds of people. You can shower off the salt and sand in the charming toilet pavilion, just past the kiosk and behind the Manly Art Gallery and Museum.

The last 300m to the ferry wharf follows the Manly Pathway of Olympians, which celebrates locals who have competed in summer and winter Olympic games.

The Manly Scenic Walkway has been extended with a long loop around North Head to Fairfax Lookout, at the Harbour entrance, but that's a walk for another day.

Sun worshippers relax on the edge on the run into Manly

Sunset silhouettes a walker overnighting at Wilsons Promontory lighthouse

VICTORIA

Australia's third smallest state or territory
is arguably its most diverse, encompassing
environmental extremes including deserts,
rainforests, alpine moors, eroded, wave-shaped
coast, volcanic plains and glacial lakes. Victoria
begs to be explored on foot. Hike to mainland
Australia's southernmost lighthouse; unearth
treasures in a historic gold town in a mountain
valley; work your way along a spine-like mountain
ridge; and meet centuries-old river red gums on
mallee river flats. There's so much to discover!

MELBOURNE

1	Aire River to Johanna Beach	78
2	Cathedral Range South Loop	84
3	Hollow Mountain	91
4	Lake Mournpall Loop	96
5	Mount Eccles Loop	102
6	Mount Hotham to Falls Creek	108
7	Ritchie's Hut Loop	116
8	Walhalla Train, Tram, Trail Loop	122
9	Wilsons Promontory Lighthouse Loop	130
10	Yarra Bend Loop	139

1 AIRE RIVER TO JOHANNA BEACH

Walk:	14km one-way
Time required:	6 hours
Best time:	Autumn and spring; this walk can be very hot in summer and wild in winter
Grade:	Moderate
Environment:	Ocean beach, coastal cliffs, coastal forest
Best map:	This one
Toilets:	Pit toilet at Aire River, flushing toilets at Johanna Beach
Food:	None
Tips:	There is no alternative high-tide route to the Johanna Beach walk and Johanna River crossing, so check tide times before setting out

With unpredictable ocean and tranquil river, surf beach and honeycombed cliffs, tall forest and flower-embroidered heath, this wonderful hike shows off the Great Ocean Walk's diversity of landscapes and flora and is arguably the best day walk along its length.

Where the Great Ocean Road veers inland through the Otway Ranges – 1920s impracticalities and construction difficulties be praised! – the long-distance Great Ocean Walk (GOW) remains close to the sea,

Morning sea mist drifts across Johanna Beach, on the Great Ocean Walk

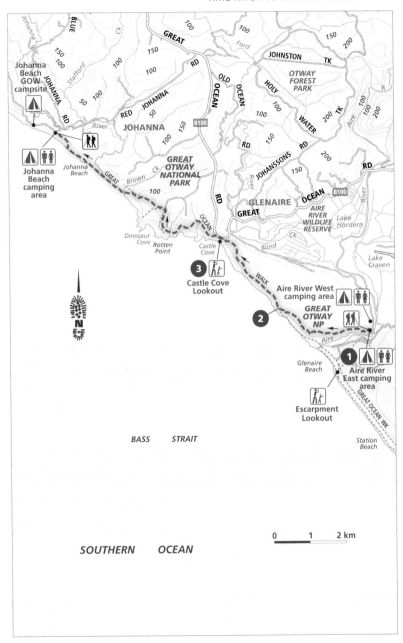

giving walkers much more than the passing acquaintance with this justly celebrated coastline that drivers enjoy. Only on foot, away from the road, can you savour the sounds, textures, tastes and smells of western Victoria's shore – and the stories of those who've lived and died along it.

But you don't have to tread the length of the trail. The walk described here is just one of the great day walks you can do on this famous stretch of coast.

A car shuffle is required for this walk, leaving one vehicle at Johanna Beach (where you'll finish) before driving to Aire River to set out. Shuttles can also be pre-booked through Timboon Taxi (0438 407 777) and Great Ocean Road Shuttle ((03) 5237 9278 or 0428 379 278).

This walk starts beside the Aire River, which snakes from the fern-filled Otways rainforest to the Southern Ocean, where it slows behind a sandbar, forming a protected estuary that's a popular feeding and nesting ground for water birds. To get there you drive about 25km west from Apollo Bay along the Great Ocean Rd and then about 5km south down unsealed Horden Vale Rd. You'll find the Johanna Beach track on

The Southern Ocean foams over coastal shelving

the estuary's west bank [see point 1 on map], which is past the main camping area and over the bridge (you may well see walkers spread-eagled on the grassy flats here).

The track goes bush beside a pit toilet, with steps climbing past a shelter. Having zigzagged up a forested ridge you get bird's eye river views as you walk through waist-high salt-loving coastal shrubs. The track then cuts through no-view forest to a cliff-top [see point 2]. The next view – drumroll, please! – is a stunning sweep of sand hills and blue-green ocean (grey-green on not-infrequent wild-weather days).

For the next 5.5km, the track undulates along an increasingly rocky shore, hugging the curves of cliffs that at times soar above you, and rising to natural lookouts from which you can watch the Southern Ocean roll/crash over the shelving rock below and nuzzle/thump the fringing sand. Late in the journey the track narrows and traverses the base of a sandstone cliff that looks like a slab of honeycomb.

A steep sandy track heading left off the GOW [see point 3] leads down to Castle Cove beach, whose wall of striped sandstone and feet-cooling shallows make it a fab lunch spot.

Beyond the Castle Cove turnoff, the GOW kisses the Great Ocean Road – you can shorten the walk by starting/finishing at the carpark here – and then ascends to a cliff-top where you walk through coastal heath crowded with grass trees sporting impressive spiky skirts. Pink common heath blooms here much of the year but spring and summer wildflowers add purple, red and yellow to the show. Look out for the white flowers and red berries of the sea box.

This pretty heath gives way to a stand of taller coarse-barked gum trees and bracken. On the other side, wash your boots at the boot-cleaning station to help stop the spread of devastating Cinnamon Fungus, which infects the roots of and kills native plants.

Along the GOW's length there are 11 'Decision Points' where hikers can take an alternative high-tide route around dangerous or just inaccessible beaches and rocky platforms. However, there is no alternative to the two-plus kilometre walk along gorgeous Johanna Beach and the un-bridged Johanna River crossing that end this walk, so check tide times, and don't rush it, especially if you are carrying a

Clockwise from top: *The trail weaves through coastal heath atop the cliffs; common heath – Victoria's floral emblem – is everywhere in spring and summer; overnight hikers tread Johanna Beach; with its sandstone cliff and cooling waters, Castle Cove beach is a fab lunch spot*

full pack and the sand is soft. Revel in the feel of the spray and taste of the ozone.

A popular surf spot known for rapid increases in break size, Johanna Beach takes its name from the schooner *Joanna*, which foundered here in 1843 on her maiden voyage between Launceston (in Tasmania) and Port Fairy (further west along the coast). Three people died in the salvage attempt (hundreds of ships were smashed along Victoria's western shore into the early 20th century, earning it the name 'Shipwreck Coast'). The most popular story about the additional 'h' in Johanna is that it was a spelling error on the replacement post-office stamp issued when the Commonwealth Government took over postal services from the colonies after Federation in 1901.

The walkers-only Johanna Beach camp (bookings essential) is a 1km uphill slog beyond the beach. So if you are continuing along the track and fancy a swim, take the plunge before heading to camp (there's also car-based camping just behind the beach).

It's worth visiting the walker's camp even if you aren't staying, because it is arguably the most spectacular spot along the GOW. Perched on a cliff high above the beach, it is the perfect place for watching the sun set and morning mist play on the sandy shore below.

The walk finishes in the Johanna Beach carpark, where you can rinse off the salt before heading home.

The walk takes you from coastal heath into a stand of taller coarse-barked gum trees and bracken

2 CATHEDRAL RANGE SOUTH LOOP

Walk:	12km loop
Time required:	5–7 hours
Best time:	Spring and autumn (summer and winter conditions can be extreme on the exposed ridge)
Grade:	Hard
Environment:	Tall eucalypt forest, fern gullies, exposed rock faces, narrow, precipitous rocky ridges
Best map:	*Vicmap Cathedral Range Special 1:25,000*, or this one
Toilets:	Pit toilets at Cooks Mill campground and Sugarloaf Saddle (no toilets on the range)
Food:	A delicious burger from the Buxton Roadhouse (about 10km south) is the closest food; there are several eateries in Marysville
Tips:	Don't be gung-ho; only take the Wells Cave Track (not described here) up Sugarloaf if you are extremely confident on exposed rock faces and have some rock-climbing experience

Arguably the best day walk in Victoria, this challenging hike along Cathedral Range's bony spine will test your vocabulary of adjectives and your head for heights.

The view unfolds as you climb Canyon Track

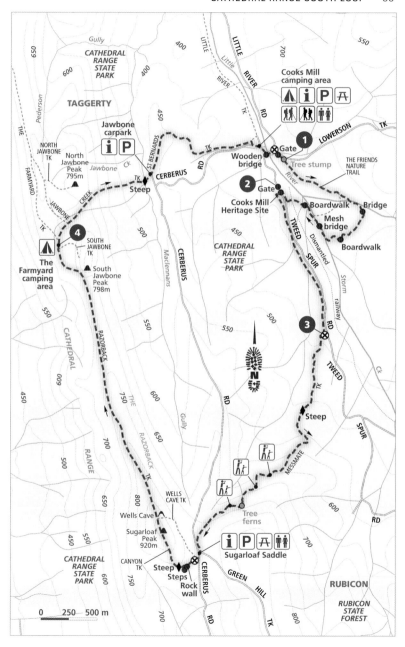

CATHEDRAL RANGE STATE PARK

Gully

TAGGERTY

Pederson

NORTH JAWBONE TK

North Jawbone Peak 795m

Jawbone carpark

Jawbone CK

Steep

ST BERNARDS

CERBERUS RD

LITTLE RIVER

LITTLE RIVER RD

Little River TK

Cooks Mill camping area

LOWERSON TK

1

Gate

Wooden bridge

Tree stump

THE FRIENDS NATURE TRAIL

2 Gate

Cooks Mill Heritage Site

Boardwalk

Bridge

Mesh bridge

Boardwalk

River

TWEED SPUR

Dismantled railway

CATHEDRAL RANGE STATE PARK

Maclennans

CERBERUS RD

THE FARMYARD TK

JAWBONE TK

4

SOUTH JAWBONE TK

South Jawbone Peak 798m

The Farmyard camping area

RAZORBACK TK

CATHEDRAL RANGE

THE RAZORBACK TK

N

3

TWEED RD

TWEED TK

Storm CK

SPUR

RD

Steep

MESSMATE

Tree ferns

WELLS CAVE TK

Wells Cave

Sugarloaf Peak 920m

CANYON TK

Steep

Steps

Rock wall

CERBERUS RD

Sugarloaf Saddle

GREEN HILL TK

RUBICON

RUBICON STATE FOREST

CATHEDRAL RANGE STATE PARK

0 250 500 m

As you emerge from Mt Sugarloaf's rocky crown, the whole Cathedral Range lies before you

More like the spine of a prehistoric beast long since turned to stone than a 7km long stand-alone ridge of steeply upturned sedimentary rock, Cathedral Range, a couple of hours' drive north-east of Melbourne, imprints itself on your memory; even at night you can sense its presence. This is one of Victoria's best hiking destinations and the ridge-top walks take your breath away.

The bushfire that almost wiped out the nearby town of Marysville on 7 February 2009 – Black Saturday – burned about 90% of Cathedral Range State Park, but both the town and the park are recovering, and it's fascinating to see how the Australian bush comes back from conflagration.

There are gorgeous strolls at the foot of the Range, but most walkers come to tread the ridge line (which is also very popular with rockclimbers). Some hike it nose-to-tail over two days, packing their gear and sleeping in tents at the Farmyard (no facilities) up on the ridge. However, if you prefer more comfort and carrying only a day pack, you can do two day walks – North and South – from a base camp at the foot of the range (there are also proper beds in nearby towns).

Uneven footing, precipitous cliffs, and lack of shelter on the range make these walks unsuitable for inexperienced hikers. But with kilometres of practice under your belt, boots with good tread and a head for heights, you are in for a challenging treat.

The North is the most popular end of the park for walking, but this more demanding southern loop, taking in Mt Sugarloaf, is top-ten material. Featuring a steep clamber up a rock 'ladder' and a walk along a ridge appropriately named the Razorback, this southern loop is the ultimate Cathedral Range experience.

Cathedral Range State Park is about 50km north of Healesville via the Maroondah Hwy and spectacular Black Spur. To begin, exit Cooks Mill campground about 5km into the park and turn left onto the road you drove in on. Cross the vehicular bridge, ignoring the gravel road with white-on-green signage on Little River's west bank. Over the bridge, where the road swings north, you'll see a sign on the right for the Friends Nature Trail. (You can shorten this walk by 2.6km by turning south at that first signed road before the bridge; however, the Friends Nature Trail is a pretty loop.)

Soon after leaving the road you'll come to an extraordinary, hollowed, burnt-out tree stump that's obviously been visited by animals and humans. Just beyond is a junction (*see* point 1 on map); go right and loop through the river flats, sometimes walking among shady tree ferns beside the river and at other times among old white-trunked manna gums trailing bark streamers. You'll cross Little River and smaller creeks and sedgy wetlands via mesh footbridges, and pass a couple of natural spas, where you might like to dip your feet, or your body, on a warm day.

Signs explain about fabulous fungi and the importance of leaf litter and other aspects of forest life. Cicadas can make the forest ring and there are also countless birds; beautiful yellow-tailed black cockatoos have a creaky call and show a fan of yellow tail feathers in flight.

The trail ends in the Cooks Mill Heritage Area, where you can find the ruins of the mill. Walk through and up onto the gravel road. On the other side of the road you'll see a four-wheel drive track heading south (*see* point 2) (gated over winter), signed for the Messmate Track. Turn hard left up this track and climb gently through messmates and coarse-barked eucalypts. Many of the trees along here look shaggy, a consequence of post-fire epicormic growth from their trunks and branches, which allows the trees to photosynthesise until the crowns regrow. There are also lots of dead trees. It's one of the marvels of the Australian bush that it can survive fire; some plants even need it in order to reproduce.

About 1200m along the track (*see* point 3), turn right onto the signed Messmate Track and follow it into tall trees and bracken. Post-fire information signs feature colourful paintings by Marysville Primary School children; the first explains that messmate is a popular wood for house framing, flooring and furniture, and that Aboriginal people traditionally use its stringy bark for weaving baskets, bags and fishing nets.

Most of the trees through here are blackened and there are few obviously old ones; however, the regrowth and the feathery leaves of the acacias soften the scene. Look for pretty white-and-purple ivy-leaf violets on the side of the track.

As the track climbs, giving you a bit of a workout, you'll start to see more of the handsome Cathedral Range; look down its length to Little Cathedral and Big Cathedral, the valley beyond and then the land rising again into more hills. Ahead of you is a great, virtually bald, grey rock face: this is Sugarloaf Peak, up which you'll climb.

Messmate Track ends in Sugarloaf carpark (you could also do the ridge walk as a one-way hike from here). Pass the toilet block, untreated rainwater tank and picnic shelter; the walking track resumes across the road.

There are two routes up Sugarloaf and both are difficult. Parks Victoria notes recommend that people uncomfortable in 'high open and exposed places' avoid the 'very hard' Wells Cave Track, and a sign emphasises this point with mentions of ropes and climbing gear. The 'hard' Canyon Track described here still provides challenges.

The walk from the road brings you to the bottom of a natural rock 'ladder' whose pitted stone and crevices and rock shelving provide grip for fingers and boots, and places to catch your breath and enjoy the broadening views on the 30-minute hand-over-hand climb to the top. (If you are at all unsure of your head for heights, don't stop on the way up or you might lose momentum.)

From the summit of Sugarloaf Peak (923m), the highest point on the range, the view extends over farmland, up the Buxton Valley to Marysville and into the ranges of the Great Divide. A few metres north the track emerges from Sugarloaf's crown of rocks and the whole Cathedral Range lies before you: the aptly named Razorback Ridge runs north towards North and South Jawbone peaks, with Cathedral and Little Cathedral peaks at the northern end. This is one of those OMG moments!

Follow the orange arrows along the Razorback Ridge, walking in the shadow of the uplifted sedimentary rock, on the ridge's sunny face and atop the stony backbone itself, where there are sometimes profusions of daisies. Loose and occasionally slippery stones, crevices, darting skinks (tiny lizards) and viciously thorned foliage make it important to watch where you put your feet and hands. Fifteen-year-old Mark L. Rothenbuecher died on the Razorback in May 1983 and a memorial plaque reminds you of the dangers.

Eventually the ridge line broadens and flattens, and you can stride out to the Farmyard, named for the lyrebirds who mimic the farm animals on the plains below, and the only place on the ridge where camping is permitted. The Black Saturday fire of 2009 stripped the forest enjoyed by the lyrebirds, but new growth will, with luck, lure them back up the mountain from the ferny creek flats below.

If you do see a lyrebird here – the males lift their delicately striped tail feathers into a lyre (harp) shape when displaying – stop and enjoy the show. These beautiful birds can have dozens of bird calls in their repertoire, and it's a privilege to watch, listen and try to identify the different calls.

At the Farmyard, turn right (east) onto the Jawbone Track (see point 4) and walk down Jawbone Creek. The track is very steep to start but moderates, allowing you to appreciate the wildflowers – orchids can be found here – and curlicue fern fronds. The track crosses the creek several times on stepping stones before easing through grassy creek flats. On reaching the bottom of the creek gully, the track turns left and climbs to Jawbone carpark, from where you take the Saint Bernard's Walking Track (at the north of the carpark) back to Cooks Mill.

Marysville (top left, in the valley) comes into view as you climb Mt Sugarloaf

3 HOLLOW MOUNTAIN

Walk:	3.4km return
Time required:	2 hours
Best time:	Any time, but avoid wild weather – there is little protection up top
Grade:	Moderate
Environment:	Sandstone outcrop
Best map:	This one
Toilets:	Pit toilets in carpark
Food:	None
Tips:	Wear loose clothing or you might rip your pants asunder

On a scale of 1–10 for adventure and scenery this walk scores top marks with outdoor fun-lovers of all ages. Part walk, part rock climb, part grandstand, this is the most enjoyable short walk in the Grampians, if not Victoria.

The Great Dividing Range ends its run down Australia's east coast on Victoria's volcanic Western Plains in a breathtaking series of north-south-running razor-tooth ranges. Known as Gariwerd to the Jardwadjali and Djab wurrung Aboriginal people, for whom the ranges have great cultural significance, the Grampians are a natural and geological wonder that brings bushwalkers back time and again.

Sculpted rock atop Hollow Mountain frames a view over farmed plains and ranges

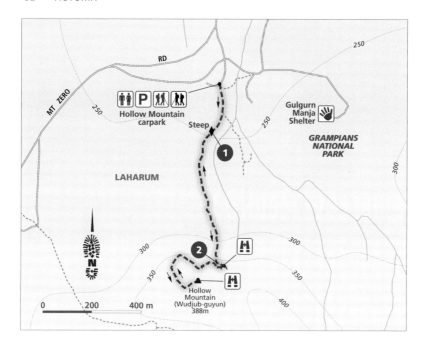

One of several walks in the northern Grampians, far from the crowd-pulling Wonderland area and Halls Gap, the short Hollow Mountain climb is just that: a climb, with pitches ranging from gentle to hand-over-hand, and little flat ground. Which is why children love it, often getting up and down at mountain-goat speed and with a surefootedness that embarrasses (and sometimes terrifies) more cautious mature walkers. Lots of adults can and do get to the top, but this walk is not recommended for anyone with vertigo or dodgy knees, or who is uncomfortable clambering up rocks.

The fun begins in Hollow Mountain carpark (where there are pit toilets), off unsealed Mt Zero Rd, about 36km north of Halls Gap via unsealed Mt Zero Halls Gap Rd. From the carpark the walking track heads south towards lumpy red and grey natural stonework.

The Disneyesque brown and yellow orchids sometimes seen just near the carpark are leopard orchids, one of more than 900 indigenous flowers identified in the Grampians, 20 of which are found nowhere else. The shrubs among the desert banksias along the first section of the walk, whose tiny cup-shaped white flowers give the impression of a dusting of snow, are Grampians thryptomene.

After a brief warm up through thryptomene, grass trees, desert banksias and eucalypts, on a sandy track with occasional steps, the real climbing starts, initially up a rocky spine to the foot of a sandstone cliff (see point 1 on map), stained with iron and cracked and undercut by time. From here you clamber up, over and between great lumps of stone tucked against the leaning cliff. Navigating these giant stepping stones is when your clothes are most at risk, either from ripping when stretching a leg or from rubbing on coarse stone, if you're more comfortable traversing rocky slopes on your backside.

Above here the going is easier, but still far from flat. Stepping up the mountain's rocky face brings you ever closer to a monumental wall of layered ochre rock, which is eventually right in front of you. To the left of the wall is a separate, massive cracked rock – or two rocks – at

Left: *Part walk, part climb, this is great fun for kids and the young at heart (and knee);* **Right:** *Pretty Grampians thryptomene give the impression of a dusting of snow*

The hollow that gives Hollow Mountain its name frames an expansive view of the Wimmera Plains

the base of which is a dark opening (*see* point 2). This is the 'hollow' that gives the mountain its non-Aboriginal name (Hollow Mountain's indigenous name is Wudjub-guyan or 'spear in the middle', so perhaps the cave is a gaping wound).

From inside the cavern you get a fabulous view, framed by the cave mouth, of Mt Zero, another hill you can climb, and the Wimmera Plains, their rows of olive trees and fields of canola stretching to the horizon. Out of the cavern and around this rock to the left, you enter an often windy stone-walled corridor leading to a sudden drop off. From the edge you can see along the cliff and down to a rocky demise.

Turning back, walk along the rock wall, passing the hollow rock and the track down to the carpark, and instead following a trail of arrows painted on the rough stone.

As you descend to the wall's end, look left and you'll see sky through a window in the wall – you might also see silhouetted figures, often hanging upside down from the ceiling. These are not bats! They're boulderers, mostly-young men and women who rock climb without ropes, seeming to defy gravity as they crab across walls and low ceilings of caves. Walkers in the Grampians often see groups of people to-ing and fro-ing from bouldering sites with climbing mats on their backs.

The arrows lead around the end of the wall and up a rock slope with a crazy-paving pattern, past the entrance to the cave you looked through from below (stopping to watch the boulderers gives you a good rest/drink stop). You might also see other groups of climbers working on stone overhangs further up. At the top of the rock slide the track loops left and up more rocky tiers.

Up top, 300m above the carpark and well clear of any protective trees, the rock has been – and continues to be – worked by wind and water into extraordinary shapes, often with sharp edges, and hollowed to depressions that collect rainwater, which reflects the sky.

Mt Difficult Range (great walks) reaches to the south of you; to the west and north are plains.

From here you retrace your steps, around the wall, down the natural shelving and over the boulders, for a cruise back through a sea of thryptomene.

Boulderers defy gravity as they crab across the ceiling of a cave on Hollow Mountain

4 LAKE MOURNPALL LOOP

Walk:	9.6km loop
Time required:	2–3 hours
Best time:	Spring or autumn; temperatures soar in summer, and in winter flooding can close the tracks
Grade:	Easy
Environment:	Mallee dunes, red gum floodplains, permanent and ephemeral lakes
Best map:	This one
Toilets:	Pit toilets at Lake Mournpall camping area
Food:	None
Tips:	Walk early morning or late afternoon for the best light. After long or particularly heavy wet weather, check road and walking track conditions with Parks Victoria (13 1963).

Marvel at the sculptural beauty of sand dunes and ancient river red gums and the complex relationship between plants and animals – humans included – as you meander through the Mallee.

Wedged between the mighty Murray River and the Calder Hwy, in Victoria's north-west Mallee–Sunraysia region, Hattah–Kulkyne National Park protects a network of freshwater lakes and billabongs

Lake Konardin waters some majestic old river red gums

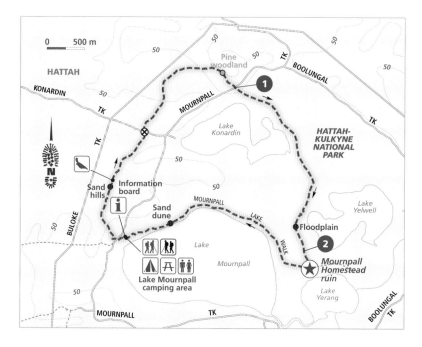

filled every few years or so by Chalka Creek, a Murray anabranch. The national park, together with Murray–Kulkyne Regional Park, on the river, covers nearly 50,000ha of flood plains.

The parks are registered as a Biosphere Reserve under UNESCO's Man and the Biosphere Programme, which studies the impact of humans on natural environments and how changed environment impacts on humans. The lakes are also a Wetland of International Importance, with many birds breeding here or dropping in on continental migrations. So this is a fascinating as well as a beautiful walk.

Kulkyne is the local Aboriginal word for a wood or wooded area (Hattah is believed to be a Scottish name). This loop walk showcases the dramatic changes in flora over a few metres of altitude and with proximity to water. It also gives you close encounters with old-man river gums full of character.

The walk begins in the Lake Mournpall campground. To get there, drive 9km north of Lake Hattah Visitor Centre on Mournpall Track, a good, sandy road that's generally fine for 2WD vehicles. (Where the road turns hard left, park and visit the final resting place of James Mahon, who drowned crossing flooded Chalka Creek in 1923; there could be few more beautiful gravesites than this waterside one at the foot of a sandhill.)

There's a sign marking the start of the track (Mournpall Lake Walk 9.6km) between the road and the river gum saplings crowding the lake shore and in line with the pit toilets. Marked with orange arrows, the track crosses Mournpall Track and meanders through twisted rough-barked eucalypts and feathery cypress pines towards red dunes. You are unlikely to cover this 300m or so without being serenaded by birds. Chattering apostle birds and squabbling white winged choughs, noisy miners and many others frequent the campground; magnificent pink and white Major Mitchell cockatoos often snack in the trees and flotillas of pelicans can be seen overhead.

At a track junction, with the lookout tower 3.5km to the left, turn right and within metres you'll be climbing low red dunes that can be powdery soft in dry weather and greened with foliage after rain. The huge, spiky rings, some 5m in diameter, are porcupine grass; animals like resting in the hollowed centres of old grasses and you'll often see their telltale scat.

Animal tracks decorate the sand too; you'll likely see kangaroo and emu prints and, particularly early morning, the embroidery-like spoor of lizards and insects. Abundant ground animals mean good feeding for raptors, so look up. Harriers, wedge-tailed eagles and white-bellied sea eagles patrol these skies, as do whistling kites, with their distinctive, high-pitched whistle.

The dominant tree in the dunes is the mallee, a eucalypt family whose multiple branches grow from a gnarly underground root, so they have no trunk. Some of these mallees are hundreds of years old. Despite being stinking hot in summer, this country supports a year-round bird population and the mallees are not particularly dense, so it is easy to spot nests. Mallee leaf-scale insects feed the spotted pardalote, a gorgeous little bird with a blunt beak and distinctive white spots on its crown and black wings.

River red gums need to be inundated on occasion for healthy growth

The track takes you on a gentle roller-coaster ride through the
dunes, the ups giving sweeping views of the Murray River plains and
tall-treed watercourses. You then veer right and down the rim of a
broad depression on the left, through young domes of porcupine grass,
more mallees and precious remnant pine and buloke woodlands.

About 3.75km into the walk, you cross back over Mournpall Track
(*see* point 1 on map) into scaly barked black box trees, and with the
change from red sand to beige underfoot you'll find yourself on the
flood plain proper, domain of the river red gum. These medium-sized
trees with blotched white, red, silver and grey trunks can grow to
metres in diameter, and each one is a slightly different size, shape,
texture and profile.

To the right as you go, about 30m off the track on the edge of
Lake Konardin (north of Mournpall), is a stand of particularly gnarly
gums. Some are covered in burls and one is nearly dead, with only a
few branches, yet they're still splendid – survivors of the stock grazing
and clearing that followed European settlement and persisted until a
national park was created in 1960.

The river red gum requires regular inundation to thrive and reproduce, and it's worth wandering over for a close look at these ones before continuing. On the water you might spot white-faced herons, black swans, grebes, cormorants, geese, swamphens and several duck varieties.

Line-of-sight orange arrows mark the walking track, so watch for them if you do leave the track to look at something or detour around water.

As you continue through the sandy flats between semi-permanent water (even the main lakes can shrink dramatically in long dry spells) and ephemeral swamps, note the difference between the fat river gums and their strappy saplings on the flood plains, and the drier forest with the odd mallee on even marginally higher ground.

About 4.8km into the walk the country to the left opens out into a less treed expanse of grass and succulents, and you briefly walk along a mini-ridge between two lakes/depressions, which may or may not contain water. Another kilometre on, you'll find yourself in the

Multi-trunked mallee trees dominate the dunes abutting the flood plains

middle of the flood plain, among old-man gums that have witnessed centuries of cycles of flooding and drying. A red grassy weed commonly grows on and around the lakes, and the masses of almost woven woody stalks around the shore are tangled lignum.

Climbing slightly, you enter a broad clearing (see point 2) with a stand of pepper trees ahead, a splash of more intense green indicating that there is, or has been, a settlement here. This was the second homestead site of the Mournpall squatters run (1847), and while there is little left of the building, the shady trees and the Mallee ringneck parrots that you can see here make this spot, overlooking Lake Yerang, an excellent place for a break.

On the move again, cross the clearing at right angles to the track you came in on, noting how water and insufficient ground cover have produced gullies to the left. Then you're back among river gums on a distinct sandy track with Lake Mournpall ahead (you can usually see water through the shoreline saplings). The track veers right and follows the shore about 30m inland, winding through some truly splendid old eucalypts.

The last leg of the walk is stunningly beautiful, an amble between Mournpall's north shore and a metres-high red dune, through a colonnade of ancient river red gums at their best in late afternoon light. Any members of your party who only want a short walk could meet you along here from the campground.

Partway along the dune there is an obvious track on the right where people have climbed up onto the sand, but the track proper remains on lower ground until it veers away from the lake and towards your car.

5 MOUNT ECCLES LOOP

Walk:	8.6km loop
Time required:	3 hours
Best time:	Any season
Grade:	Easy to moderate
Environment:	Volcanic lake rim and open lava tunnel
Best map:	This one
Toilets:	Flushing toilets in main parking area
Food:	None
Tips:	Take a torch for looking at the rock structure within the caves on this walk

Walk through a history of volcanic cataclysm now prettily camouflaged by leafy forest, mossy man-made rock walls, and tranquil lake waters paddled by ducks.

As a name, Mt Eccles doesn't have the same impact as Krakatau, Etna or Vesuvius; however, Mt Eccles, in south-west Victoria, was born of one of the state's last volcanic eruptions. Just 10,000 years ago, fissures opened, the earth shook, clouds of ash and dust rose into the air and lava reached 50km towards the sea.

Such violence is difficult to imagine when watching ducks paddle the rush-fringed crater lake at the heart of Mt Eccles National Park.

Watch your step!

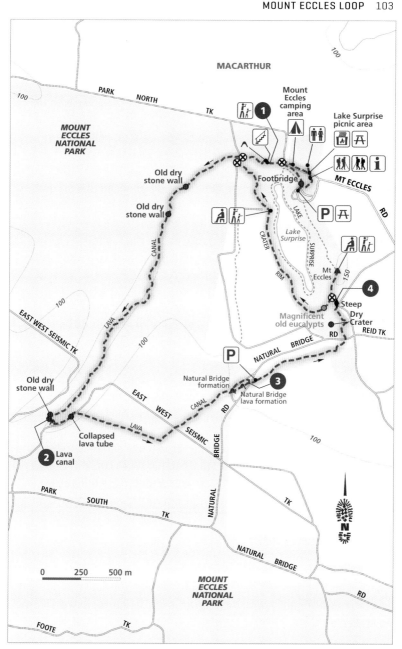

Tucked away at the south-west end of Victoria's vast volcanic plains, this park is best reached by driving the Hamilton–Port Fairy Rd to Macarthur and there turning west along the sealed Mt Eccles Rd.

This walk combines the Lava Canal and Canal Rim walks, leaving the third walk, a 2km stroll around the lake shoreline, for people with the time and inclination for more.

The walk begins at the main (lower) parking area, which has gas barbecues, picnic tables and flushing toilets. The visitor centre here has information boards and self-serve park notes. To stay in the camping area (through the trees to the right) you need to book and prepay at parkstay.vic.gov.au.

Climb the wooden steps up the bank to the left of the visitor centre and, ignoring two walking tracks on the right, stroll anticlockwise around the top carpark and picnic area to a wood-and-metal lookout. From here you can see that Lake Surprise is not one but three crater lakes joined together. The layered structure of the crater's granite walls is also obvious; the man-made stone wall on the crater rim directly opposite is a lookout on the Rim Walk you come to later.

Mt Eccles is just visible to your left, behind a splendid manna gum. This eucalypt tree, with smooth, spread-wide white branches that peel in long ribbons, is the favourite food of koalas and these too-cute marsupials are sometimes seen sleeping in forks only metres from the lookout platform.

Retrace your steps along the picnic area fence and take the second walking track, signed Lava Canal Walk and Rim Walk track. This sealed track strewn with bark and leaves crosses a footbridge and takes you through mixed forest on the crater rim with glimpses of lake water through the thick trees on the left. Superb fairy-wrens are common here and throughout this park.

Ignoring the track coming up on the left a few hundred metres along, you'll come to another junction (see point 1 on map) with Lava Canal signed to the right and Lookout to the left. This lookout, rimmed with stonewalling thick with moss, gives a full-length view over the lake to Mt Eccles.

Left: *Watch for kangaroos as you walk down the collapsed lava tunnel;* **Right:** *Natural Bridge was formed when faster, more turbulent lava formed levees that met*

The Lava Canal track (right) slips between two rocks and descends wooden stairs running down a rock wall cloaked in almost luminescent green moss. The stairs drop you outside a cave the size of a small house; venture inside with your torch and have a look at the silvery sparkles on the ceiling.

An unsealed trail continues through bracken to a grassy vehicle-wide track. You want the incorrectly signed 'Larva Canal Walk' pad going left off the road immediately beyond the Crater Rim Walk, which goes up a wide grassy ramp.

For about 2.4km you walk down a collapsed lava canal on a track that's loosely lined with small basalt rocks and/or indented, so it's easy to see, even where it's grassy, but it is rough and rocky underfoot in places. The track winds between the canal's walls, which for most of the walk are topped with dry-stone walling built to restrict the movement of grazing stock in the century before the park was declared in 1960. Clearly visible beneath the man-made walls are the layers deposited by subsequent lava flows.

Further down the canal its walls are naturally cracked into building blocks, some quite neatly laid, others more higgledy piggledy, and manna gums cling to the edge with their roots. Crimson rosellas splash colour through here.

Twice along the way you pass through breaks in the stone walling erected across the canal, the black rocks now thick with moss, and soon after the second break the track turns hard left (see point 2), with orange arrows showing the way up the canal wall. Almost at the top is a cave, the top lip of which supports a handsome 20m manna gum. Crouching down in the cave mouth you'll see metres of cracked rock that looks as if it is barely holding on; this might just deter you from going inside (although it is safe to do so).

Arrows direct you across the cave mouth and onto the top of the canal wall, where a sign points left to Mt Eccles via Natural Bridge. Walking along this grassy track is considerably easier than down in the canal. About 130m along on the right, a tunnel collapse has formed a big hole, just beyond which the track turns right and runs along a mossy wall away from the canal and through open forest of bracken and gum trees, where eastern grey kangaroos graze.

Keep on the track to a fork at a wooden frame signed Natural Bridge, beneath which, through a hole in the ground, you can see steps and cave walls. Follow the left fork to a road and turn right and then

The rim track offers the best view of Lake Surprise and Mt Eccles

right again onto a foot pad along another, narrow open lava canal (*see* point 3). About 100m along is the entrance to a stone cathedral formed by faster and more turbulent lava, building levees that sagged to meet each other, forming a natural bridge or roof. Torchlight reveals the patterns in the rock either side of you as you descend the stairs into the chamber.

Back at the road, cross over and continue along the canal, following it upstream to the tree-filled crater (Dry Crater) from which that lava flowed.

Up the canal wall to the left of the crater and down the other side, you cross a road, skirt another crater and enter a gully before looping right to the road and back to steep steps (*see* point 4) that climb to the rim of Lake Surprise. You are ultimately going left, on the Canal Rim Walk, but first turn right and walk around the rim and up Mt Eccles; it's steep but short and the views are worth it.

Mt Eccles (178m) is a cone of scoria, the holey, reddish rock that forms when frothy lava cools quickly, and it was raised on the crater's eastern rim by the prevailing westerly wind. From the top, on a clear day, you can see to the Southern Ocean and Grampians. It can, however, be extremely windy up here so you might appreciate a jacket.

Return to the track junction and continue clockwise around the crater, navigating several notable ups and downs before the track flattens out, giving you expansive views through trees, over the lake and of Mt Eccles' rough, precipitous lakeside face. The lava canal down which you walked earlier is beyond the pasture and grazing cows immediately on your left.

Soon you'll reach the stone-walled lookout visible from the upper picnic area, now directly opposite, atop the block-like crater wall. This lookout is a great spot for lunch or a snack, and a bit of koala spotting.

The walking track continues around the crater rim and takes you down a grassy ramp beside the misspelled 'Larva Canal Walk' sign. Turn right and retrace your earlier steps to the cave and up the wooden staircase.

The left track at the next junction takes you past the camping area and back to the main carpark.

6 MOUNT HOTHAM TO FALLS CREEK

Walk:	23.5km one-way
Time required:	Full day
Best time:	Summer (for the wildflowers and best weather)
Grade:	Hard
Environment:	Alpine peaks, moors and lakes; snow gum and mountain ash forest
Best map:	*SV Maps Bogong Alpine Area 1:50,000* or this one
Toilets:	None
Food:	The nearest food to the start is in Hotham Heights ski village, or Falls Creek before boarding the bus
Tips:	Even when Melbourne's temperatures soar, the Australian Alps can be cool and even cold, with occasional summer snowfalls. Whatever the forecast, take warm clothing and be prepared for sudden and dramatic changes in weather.

With its towering mountain ash and striped snow gums, expansive high plains, massed spring–summer wildflowers and jaw-dropping mountain vistas, this all-day walk between two of Victoria's most popular ski resorts is becoming a classic high-country hike.

Paper daisies carpet the slopes between the walking track and Mount Hotham Village

Whichever way you tackle it, this big hike is unsuited to novices. It is also stunningly beautiful and gives you a taste of some of the diverse environments within Victoria's Alpine National Park. It is written up here as a one-way day walk, but you could camp en route at Parks Victoria sites; the really keen could walk one way and then back again after spending a night at Falls Creek.

The walk described requires a summer shuttle bus ride from Falls Creek to Hotham (pre-book and pay through Falls Creek Information Centre, ph (03) 5758 1202, fallscreek.com.au), or you could set up your own car shuffle. You also need to organise a pre-walk car drop at Pretty Valley Pondage, 6km from Falls Creek village; without this you'll be covering that distance on foot at day's end.

The walk begins with a 2-hour shuttle bus ride down from Falls Creek, through the towns of Mt Beauty and Harrietville, and up the Great Alpine Rd to Mt Loch carpark, about 2km shy of Mt Hotham Resort. From there you follow the gravel Machinery Hi Track around to the left (west) of the Mt Loch water storage.

Descending gently, the track skirts ski lifts and downhill runs and gives a grandstand view south to Hotham Village before entering Alpine National Park, where you are unlikely to have eyes for anything other than the Razorback, to the west, a spine-like mountain ridge running north from Great Alpine Rd to Mt Feathertop, Victoria's second-highest peak after Mt Bogong. The Razorback walk to Feathertop is another fantastic hike.

After two warm-up descents and climbs, each of about 50m altitude, over 2.8km, you reach a track junction (*see* point 1 on map). Keep left, on Machinery Hi Track. The right-hand track descends Swindlers Spur to Dibbins Hut in the lush Cobungra Valley and is the official route of the 650km-long Australian Alps Walking Track (AAWT) between the heritage-listed gold town of Walhalla, in Gippsland, and Namadgi National Park near Canberra, Australia's capital. This alternative route to the one described here descends and climbs less, and is about 3.5km shorter (although this difference is reduced by some 1.5km with a recommended detour to Mt Loch). The two routes merge at Cobungra Gap.

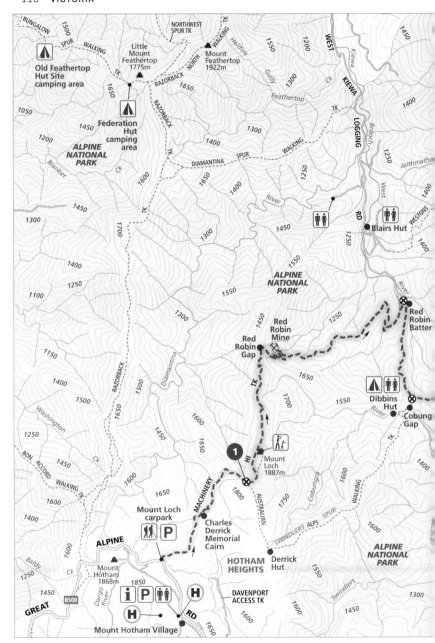

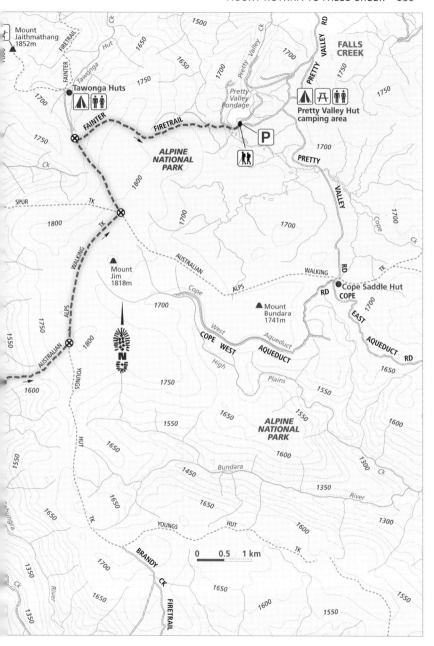

Mt Loch offers one of the best views on this classic alpine walk

A grey snow-gum stubble across the slopes and along the ridges is the legacy of the 2006–2007 summer bushfires that burnt millions of hectares of Australia's high country. Like most eucalypts, snow gums can regenerate after fire; however, unlike most eucalypts, they reshoot from their roots rather than their trunks. Covered in grey branches poking from dense green regrowth, the mountains up here look like a gargantuan silverback gorilla, a resemblance only increased with the few extra metres of elevation gained by making the short detour up Mt Loch (1887m). Obvious everywhere you look are the subtle variations in shades of blue mountain ridges.

Back down off Mt Loch, continue north along Machinery Spur on a wide track edged with snow gums and often, in summer, yellow drifts of paper daisies and billy buttons and other beautiful alpine flowers.

About 2km north of Mt Loch you come to Red Robin Gap, from where a dirt road switchbacks steeply downhill. This is the beginning of a 650m altitude loss you'll later make up to rejoin the AAWT! About 1km down you come to a corrugated iron hut nestled against the hill, with narrow-gauge tracks running from a corrugated-iron door in the hillside across the road to a platform projecting over a truck parked on a branch track below. This is the Victorian Heritage-listed Red Robin Mine.

The discovery of Red Robin reef by prospector Bill Spargo in 1940 caused a gold rush to the high country, and this mine, once billed as Victoria's highest and richest, has operated almost continuously since.

Continue down the road into beautiful mountain ash forest with trees soaring skyward from tangled greenery. Three kilometres or so beyond the mine you come to the Red Robin Battery (this is a private property, and you can't see the battery). Here the road continues downhill, and our broad walking track heads south, up a ridge. There are prettier places further on for lunch, but you might want a drink and a snack here before beginning the ascent, which is about two hours of climbing, sometimes steeply.

Tall timbers are giving way to snow gums by the time you reach Cobungra Gap, where the AAWT emerges from Cobungra Valley. On the valley floor below is Dibbins Hut, the latest shelter erected at the head of the Cobungra River since the Dibbins brothers, from Freeburgh, near Bright, established a cattle run here in 1900.

Turning east now, climb up through snow-gum forest inhabited by magnificently striped old trees, some with twisted trunks and wide-reaching branches. Distract yourself from the steepness of the slope by looking for wildflowers (over 1100 native plants have been recorded in Alpine National Park). Aside from rafts of everlastings and golden billy-buttons, you might see royal bluebells, strings of pale-vanilla lilies and stalks of grass trigger-plants, whose pink flowers have a 'tongue' to daub pollen on visiting insects.

About 3km up from Cobungra Gap you step from snow-gum forest onto plains of native herbs and grasses crowned with big sky. Enjoy the space and, perhaps, a sense of your own insignificance, as you traverse the most exposed country on the walk.

You may well see brumbies (wild horses) up here, usually a stallion and his brood. Efforts are underway to reduce the numbers of these introduced animals, but they are a wonderful sight galloping across the plains. Also look for Mueller's snow gentians, white flowers with purple veins that bloom in snow-like drifts.

Less obvious among the snow gums, numbered snow poles march in single file across the high plains. Follow them from the first junction out of the snow gums (turn left) 2.5km to another junction, where the AAWT continues right. Turn left towards Tawonga Huts, continuing through grassy plains strewn with occasional rocky rises, and at the next track junction, about 1.5km further on, turn right towards Pretty Valley Pondage.

The steady 1.2km climb before the final descent on this walk can be dispiriting but the countryside is no less beautiful, with shallow, treeless valleys resting in the folds of rolling hills and dramatic ridgelines. The sight of Pretty Valley Pondage – this reservoir was built as part of the Kiewa hydroelectric scheme and is a popular angling site – and then your car, helps you down the final 2.2km to the finishing line.

Drifts of mountain gentians decorate the high plains

Numbered snow poles march single file across the plains

7 RITCHIE'S HUT LOOP

Walk:	12km loop
Time required:	1 day or easy overnight
Best time:	Late spring to late autumn (winter conditions can be extreme)
Grade:	Easy to moderate
Environment:	Mountain river
Best map:	This one
Toilets:	Pit toilets at 8 Mile Flat and Ritchie's Hut
Food:	Mansfield, 38km away, is the closest major town for all supplies
Tips:	Howqua River camping areas attract lots of people in the summer school holidays and on warmer long weekends, so try to visit at other times.
	Waterproof walking sandals are the ideal footwear for the lower section of this walk; some people might find them adequate for the whole hike too, even if carrying a pack.
	The Howqua River can rise suddenly after heavy rain, making crossings dangerous, and authorities sometimes close the low route. Before setting out check conditions on the Parks Victoria website – parkweb.com.au – or phone 13 1963.

Sandwich a night under the stars between two easy walks or make a one-day round trip to timber-slab Ritchie's Hut; whichever way you go, you'll fall in love with the Howqua River.

Rebuilt slab-plank Ritchie's Hut is the halfway point – a lovely place to lunch or camp

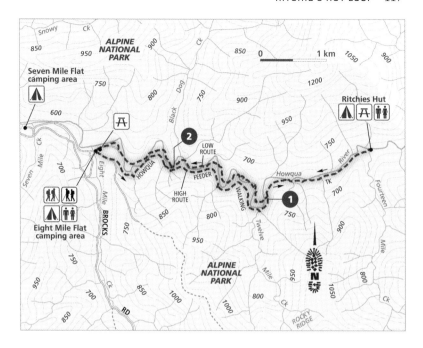

The spectacular valley that the Howqua River has carved – and continues to shape – on its 66km run from Mt Howitt, in Victoria's Alps, to Lake Eildon via Alpine National Park, was a major trade and war route for the central Victorian Taungurung (Daung wurrung) people, and a source of the hard Cambrian greenstone from which they made tools and weapons. Yet 'Howqua' is not an Indigenous word.

Consensus is that this beautiful river took the moniker of a pastoral run named for John 'Howqua/Houqua' Hunter, whose nickname was a product of trade with Canton Hong merchants, among whom Howqua/Houqua was synonymous with tycoon.

This 12km loop walk to Ritchie's Hut shows off the splendour of the Howqua River and the valley embracing it. An enjoyable day walk, it is an ideal introduction to overnight hiking or an easy outing for more experienced hikers. There are high and low walking routes from 8 Mile Flat. Heavy rain and flooding can close the low track, forcing you to walk in and back on the High Track, but you still get wet feet when the Low Track is open.

The walk begins at 8 Mile Flat camping area, 38km from Mansfield. To get there, head east out of Mansfield towards Merrijig on sealed Mt Buller Tourist Rd, in winter a busy thoroughfare of alpine enthusiasts headed to mounts Buller and Stirling. On the right, 2km beyond the Merrijig hotel, actually the Hunt Club Hotel (c. 1873), is Howqua Track; generally okay for conventional vehicles but narrow in places with steep drops, this gravel road winds 15km through farmland and treed hills to Sheepyard Flat, a popular camping spot in the Howqua Hills Historic Area.

Four decades of on-again off-again alluvial and reef gold mining centred on this area from the 1860s. One relic of those noisier times is the red-brick smelter chimney on the easy self-guided Heritage Walk between Sheepyard Flat and Frys Flat. Another is the 100m long tunnel that Chinese miners cut in 1884 to send water along a hand-dug race to the gold treatment works; you can see their handiwork at Tunnel Bend, several kilometres further along Howqua Track.

Keep on the main valley road to 8 Mile Flat, turning left and steeply downhill to this popular camping area and fishing base. These notes describe the loop walk in an anticlockwise direction, which gives you grandstand views of the river and Mt Buller range from the High Track going in, and a dozen river crossings coming out on the Low Track.

The Low Track crosses the beautiful Howqua River a dozen times

DAY 1: 6KM

The High Route goes bush from the south-east corner of 8 Mile Flat parking/camping area. It immediately climbs through towering manna gums and peppermint trees reaching skyward from a dense understorey of prickly bush pea that becomes a sea of yellow and red flowers in spring. Golden everlastings (also called paper daisies because of their papery petals), delicate purple-and-white ivy-leaf violets and Australian buttercups also grow here.

In about 300m the track flattens out. Ignore the side trail coming in on your right (from a ridge to the south), instead staying on the riverside trail for the next 4.5km. The track remains well above the Howqua, crossing grassy, gum-treed slopes (you'll see an old gold mining shaft beside the track) and occasionally ducking into fern gullies watered by tiny streams headed for the Howqua. Along here there are changing but always impressive aerial vistas of river straights, U-bends, rocky rapids and deep pools dotted with trout (the barred Galaxias, an endangered native fish, inhabits a few of the river's trout-free tributaries). Crimson rosellas, with their flashy red and blue plumage, are also seen hereabouts.

The Howqua River makes two particularly impressive bends about 2.5km and a further kilometre from the track junction. About 4.5km into the walk (see point 1 on map), the High Route drops to the verdant, leafy river flats to meet the Low Route, which comes up from the river on your left.

It's 1.5km from here to Ritchie's Hut, with a few more ups and downs and a run of a couple of hundred metres along the river's rocky shore. Fed by mountain rivers and snowmelt, the Howqua is never warm, even in summer, so this straight stretch is perfect for an invigorating dip on a warm day.

Corrugated iron and timber show through the trees 5.8km (by GPS) from the walk start. Cross 14 Mile Creek by stepping stones just above where it pours over a natural fallen-log dam into the Howqua, and climb a few steep steps to stand on the verandah of Ritchie's Hut.

The 2006/2007 Great Divide fires, which ravaged Australia's Alps, destroyed the original hut built here in the 1940s by Bob Ritchie and

Fred Fry, a local fly-fishing identity who inspired the character Billy Slim in Nevil Shute's 1952 novel *The Far Country*. (Fry's name is perpetuated in the hut that he lived in and the flat on which he built it, which can be visited in the Howqua Hills Historic Park.) Parks Victoria staff and volunteers completed this faithful reconstruction, with its axe-cut drop-slab walls and corrugated iron chimney, in April 2010.

The hut has a large open fire place, a wooden table and wooden benches on which you can unroll a sleeping bag on a rainy night, but there are good tent sites and a fireplace with fallen-log seats in the grassy clearing outside. Campfires are permitted, except on days of Total Fire Ban, as is gathering fallen timber to burn. There is also a post-and-rail horse corral, albeit in need of repair (horseriding is permitted on the Low Route and to here).

If you dare, take a pre-dinner dip in the Howqua, which burbles noisily past the hut; follow one of the foot pads 10m or so through the leafy tangle between the hut and river and find a natural spa-seat among the rocks. Superb fairy-wrens are common along the river and the dawn bird chorus is loud.

DAY 2: 6KM

Retrace your steps to the High–Low route junction on the river flats and take the right (Low) track through a colonnade of towering trees to the Howqua for the first of 12 crossings. If you feel uncomfortable on this first crossing, turn back and return to your car via the High Route.

Some of the crossings are only a few metres wide, others 15m or so; few are deeper than your knees and all are generally well marked. The best footwear is waterproof walking sandals with a good grip, which are also fine for the High Route. If you wear hiking boots, you'll have to take them off for each crossing or walk with wet boots. Walking poles can be useful.

Allow three hours to enjoy the trees that tower over you and the beautifully coloured, rounded river rocks underfoot as you work your way downstream to 8 Mile Flat.

A rocky shelf with a stony beach immediately downstream of the ninth crossing (*see* point 2) (the fourth up from 8 Mile Flat, if walking clockwise) is a wonderful spot for a picnic lunch and a swim in a deep pool between a small cascade and some gentle rapids.

Afterwards, you've got only 1.5km or so to your car.

Whichever way you go – High Track or Low – you'll fall in love with the Howqua River

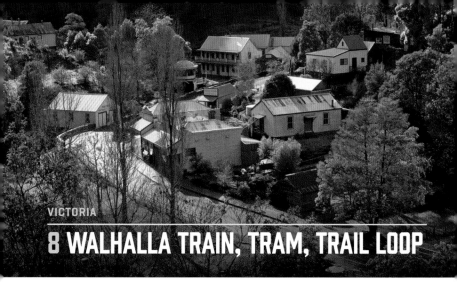

8 WALHALLA TRAIN, TRAM, TRAIL LOOP

Walk:	16km loop
Time required:	4–5 hours
Best time:	Year-round (increased water flow in winter, wildflowers in spring and summer, brilliant hues in autumn)
Grade:	Moderate (long but fairly flat)
Environment:	Historic gold town, mine ruins, river gorge
Best map:	*Vicmap Walhalla South 8122-2-S* or this one
Toilets:	Flushing toilets at both railway stations and in the day visitor area and main carpark, opposite the information centre, in Walhalla
Food:	The Walhalla Lodge Hotel (Wally Pub) dishes up good counter meals Wednesday to Sunday; Grey Horse Cafe is open most days for pies, cakes and coffee; Walhalla Lolly Shoppe has a large choice of bushwalking snacks
Tips:	This walk description includes the steam train journey into Walhalla (timetable: walhallarail.com.au), without which you'll need to add additional kilometres of road walking or organise a car shuffle. With visits to shops and museums and a mine tour, you could spend considerably longer doing this walk than the estimated time.

The pretty gold town of Walhalla nestles in a steep, forested valley

Ride a train, tread a tramway route and walk along a river in the footsteps of the men and women who poured into north Gippsland's rugged valleys in search of gold.

When news got out in early 1863 that former convict Edward 'Ned' Stringer's party had found alluvial gold in the foothills of the Baw Baw Plateau, other prospectors soon followed, and when John Hinchcliffe discovered a quartz reef, which he named Cohen's, the rush to Walhalla (as the Stringer's Creek settlement was renamed) was on.

Fortune hunters were not put off by early reports of the country having '... a most fearfully precipitous character'. Walhalla boomed until around 1900. Cohen's Reef yielded more than 55 tonnes of gold over 50 years, during which time the town's population peaked at around 2500 people (now about 20) and the number of hotels reached 15.

This walk begins with a train ride on the line that reached Walhalla from Moe in 1910 – the first motor vehicle only arrived in Walhalla two years earlier – in time to witness the town's decline. Much of the line was ripped up from 1954, but the last 5km was restored by volunteers and reopened in 2002.

Despite the original train transporting more people away from than to the gold town, the 30-minute Walhalla Goldfields Railway journey (a steam engine when fire risk allows; no services on days of Total Fire Ban) up steep, narrow Stringer's Creek gorge, over six lovely trestle bridges, is the perfect way to enter Walhalla. A 48km drive from Morwell, via the town of Tyers and Walhalla-Tyers Rd, brings you to the Thomson Station, where the restored rail line begins.

Disembarking the train at Walhalla, walk north out of the station and up the main bitumen road (ignore unsealed Happy Go Lucky Rd on your right) to the Walhalla Day Visitor area (with toilets, gas barbecues and parking) on the site of the old Walhalla Tennis Club. From here you can see the white picket fence of Walhalla Cemetery, up the valley's steep east bank. Access is via a marked track on the right-hand side of the road (beside an interesting timber eco-house), which climbs up a creek and swings right through tree ferns to the pickets.

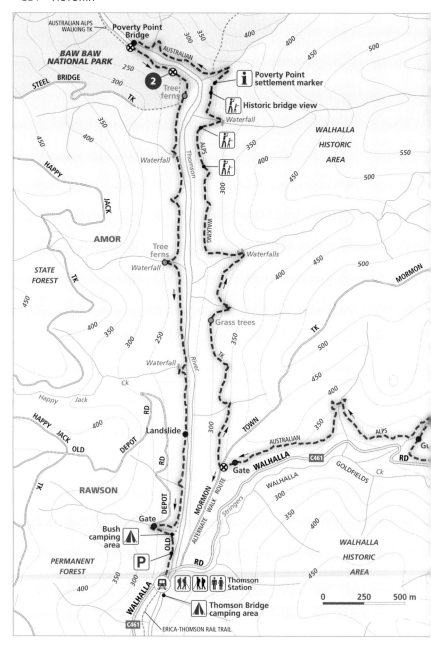

AUSTRALIAN ALPS
WALKING TK

Poverty Point
Bridge

BAW BAW
NATIONAL PARK

STEEL

BRIDGE

TK

300

250

AUSTRALIAN

300

350

400

400

450

500

2

Tree
ferns

Poverty Point
settlement marker

Historic bridge view

Waterfall

WALHALLA

HISTORIC

AREA

550

500

HAPPY

JACK

AMOR

STATE
FOREST

450

400

350

450

400

350

Waterfall

Thomson

ALPS

350

400

500

450

Tree
ferns

Waterfall

300

250

WALKING

Waterfalls

400

450

500

MORMON

TK

500

River

Grass trees

350

450

Waterfall

Ck

Happy

Jack

TK

300

250

400

TK

450

TOWN

400

350

AUSTRALIAN

ALPS

Gu

HAPPY

JACK

OLD

RD

DEPOT

RD

400

Landslide

300

DEPOT

Gate WALHALLA

C461

GOLDFIELDS

RD

Ck

TK

RAWSON

Gate

OLD

MORMON

WALK ROUTE

ALTERNATE

Stringers

WALHALLA

300

350

WALHALLA

HISTORIC

AREA

450

Bush
camping
area

P

PERMANENT
FOREST

350

300

WALHALLA

400

RD

Thomson
Station

Thomson Bridge
camping area

0   250   500 m

C461

ERICA-THOMSON RAIL TRAIL

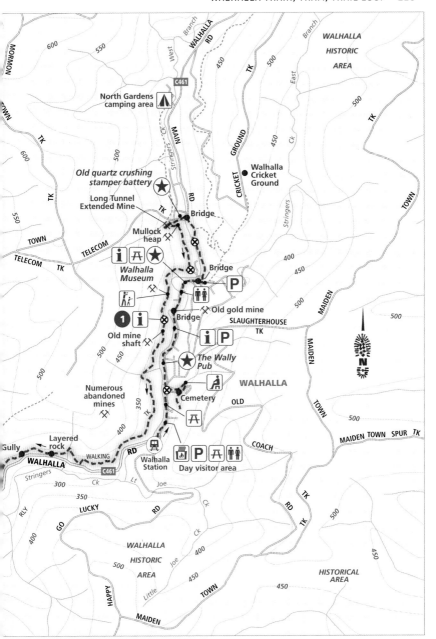

The walk passes rusty stamper batteries and climbs the Long Tunnel Extended Gold Mine mullock heap

Walhalla's steep and rocky terrain made residents inventive; they sliced the top off a hill to make a sports field and terraced a hillside to accommodate the graves of those killed in accidents and childbirth and by disease. Have a wander and read some of the old headstones.

Back down on the road walk into town, passing the Walhalla Lodge Hotel, an old-fashioned establishment better known as the Wally Pub, and a mining tunnel with a metal grille to your left, on the opposite bank of Stringer's Creek.

Strolling through town, check out the post office (157,000 items were sent from here in 1868), the fire station, which straddles Stringer's Creek, and the Bank of Victoria vault (only the vault survives). Look in the Museum & Corner Store window for an advertisement for tawny cocaine port, a cure for drunks 'who will almost instantly lose their want and need for alcohol and will gain a new want for life and fun'!

Continue up the road, past the beautiful old rotunda on the left and the Star Hotel on the right, and with great mullock heaps on the opposite side of the creek now, turn left about 400m beyond the rotunda, onto a road signed for the Long Tunnel Extended Gold Mine [on Cohen's Reef]. Walk up this sealed road past a massive mullock heap and a collection of rusty stamper batteries and mine machinery.

Excellent daily mine tours take you deep underground through the timbered entrance on your right at the top of the hill, and through the gap in the corrugated iron fence directly ahead you'll see another shaft. Continue around to your left, past corrugated iron buildings, to the top of the mullock heap.

At the height of the gold rush, Walhalla mines consumed about 70,000 tonnes of timber a year for steam boilers, timbering mines and construction, an appetite that quickly denuded the hills around the town. From here you follow the routes of horse-drawn tramways (a few used diesel engines) built to transport timber from further and further afield.

Walk downstream on a good track about 30m above the valley floor, ignoring the steps going down to the Star Hotel and rotunda. Just beyond, the track slips into damp forest with ferns and moss only to emerge into drier forest with no ferns at all. Perched partway up the opposite valley wall you'll see the lovely old hospital building.

Beyond another mine site you'll come to signs and information about the Australian Alps Walking Track (AAWT) (see Mount Hotham to Falls Creek, p. 108). Walhalla is the start/end point of this 650km trail, which traverses the remote and rugged mountain spine running through Victoria, NSW and the ACT; this is a demanding trail and hikers must be experienced, self-reliant and have good navigation skills.

Veer right (yellow AAWT marker) at the next junction (see point 1 on map) and pass another mine. Descending gently now, on a track hugging the valley's curves, you walk through tall eucalypts and occasional pine trees. The forest is awash with yellow acacia blossoms in late winter and early spring and common heath bells festoon the hard rocky ground. Imagine the valley stripped of its trees.

About 500m after the track turns west you pass, on your right, a natural wall of very thinly layered slate, upended to vertical, some of the layers only millimetres thick. Down to your left you can see the road and occasionally glimpse the train if your timing works. The track ducks into two fabulously lush gullies where you cross creeks by stepping stones under umbrellas of tree ferns. The water is deliciously clear but may well not run in summer.

Through a gate the AAWT crosses unsealed Mormon Town Track, which descends from the right and continues down another 600m or so to the Thomson River bridge and station. Heading down the track will shorten this walk by about 8km, but it's worth doing the extra to see and cross Poverty Point Bridge.

There is some discrepancy between the track distances on the signs here and in Walhalla, but by GPS it is 4km downhill (and upriver) to the bridge, through another gate and along the wider, deeper Thomson River valley on a good, shaly track.

This is a beautiful walk, with rock faces and hills treed with elegant eucalypts on your right and a steep drop to your left. Some of the trees have been blackened by fire but the ground is green with regrowth.

You cross ferny gullies watered by little, probably ephemeral, creeks and pass along a bank festooned with grass trees, their spikes shimmying in the slightest breeze. Then the track turns hard left and the grass-treed bank slams into a slope covered in ferns. Coming out of another fern gully with a natural water feature you can see the Thomson River, a serpent of green water between steep, rocky banks and tree ferns descending to the water's edge.

After a couple more mini waterfalls, which are probably dry in summer, you'll see historic Poverty Point Bridge spanning the Thomson, along with the swathe cut down the west wall of the gorge by the Black Saturday fire. This blaze then roared up the other side to threaten Walhalla, which fortunately escaped unscathed.

Constructed for the Long Tunnel Mine Company for the transport of boiler fuel and construction timbers to its Walhalla mines, Poverty Point Bridge was completed in 1900, but the handrail was only fitted in 1976! Think about that as you cross the National Trust-listed metal bridge and stop to look down 15-odd metres to the water.

On the opposite side, ignore the AAWT heading right and walk left, downstream, on an initially grassy track. Because it is not part of the AAWT, this track is walked far less than the earlier ones and it was also damaged in the fires. About 300m along (see point 2) it appears as if the track heads down to the left but keep going straight on a seemingly much more minor track running into trees. This 'upper' track is not actually blocked and the lower one just takes you down to the river.

The track crosses several waterfalls, one of them plunging perhaps 40m through tree ferns above and below the track. Either side of these dense, damp folds, the country is drier, with lots of tangled grasses and wattles. (Australia is fortunate that its most successful post-fire recolonising plant produces such beautiful flowers.)

The walking track ends at a gate, beyond which you turn left onto a sometimes-muddy road (with a broken sign) and walk 300 metres along the road to the Thomson River station parking area.

Down the valley, the track passes through fabulously lush fern gullies

9 WILSONS PROMONTORY LIGHTHOUSE LOOP

Walk:	44.4km loop
Time required:	2 or 3 days
Best time:	Year-round, although winter weather can be wild
Grade:	Hard (long days)
Environment:	Beaches, heathland, sea cliffs, historic lighthouse
Best map:	*Vicmap Wilsons Promontory Special 1:50,000 Topographic* or this one
Toilets:	Flushing toilets at Telegraph Saddle, lightstation and Tidal River visitor centre; pit toilets at Roaring Meg junction and Oberon Bay
Food:	The store at Tidal River sells takeaway food and drinks
Tips:	If you can afford the time and money, book two nights at the lighthouse to allow a rest day at the historic site with a (free) lighthouse tour. Hire a doona for your stay to lighten your pack.

Pristine beaches, granite sculptures, wildflowers and the chance to watch a storm from a lighthouse keeper's cottage make this one of Victoria's most memorable overnight walks.

At different times an island and part of the land bridge that once joined Tasmania to mainland Australia, Wilsons Promontory is Victoria's oldest national park. Declared in July 1898, it has attracted visitors ever since.

Wilsons Promontory Lighthouse perches on a knob of land jutting into Bass Strait

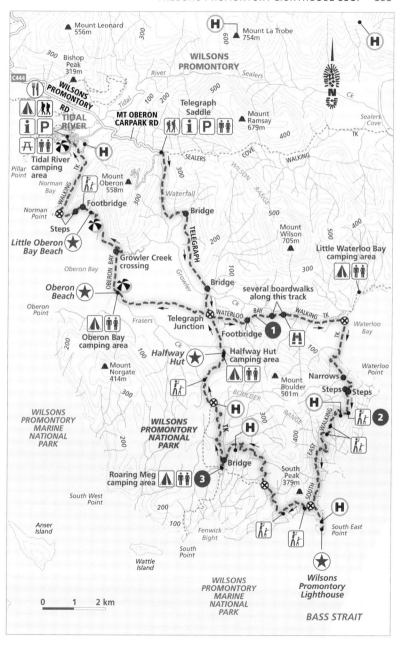

Its rugged granite hills and headlands, diverse flora and fauna, and pristine bays and beaches make it one of the state's most popular parks, with summer camping balloted. Fondly called the Prom, this knobby peninsula is fiercely protected when anyone raises the issue of commercial development in national parks.

Crisscrossed with trails close to Tidal River and into wilderness areas, the Prom has a walk to suit everyone, from short ambles through fern gullies to overnight hikes such as this one.

Lighthouses by their nature are almost without exception situated on geologically spectacular land, and mainland Australia's southernmost lighthouse is no exception. Built in 1859 from local granite and still operational, though now automated, Wilsons Promontory lighthouse crowns a knuckly stone finger thrust into Bass Strait. The only access is by boat or foot (and helicopter in an emergency).

Joggers have been known to run to the lighthouse and back in a day down the midline Telegraph Track (about 38km return), but there are more scenic permutations and combinations of ways to and from. You could make the journey over more, shorter days by camping, but the route described here sandwiches a night in a self-contained restored keepers' cottage managed by Parks Victoria (bookings essential) between two long day walks.

You'll leave boot prints on the beautiful Waterloo Bay beach

At 44.4km this best suits hikers with previous backpacking experience; however, fit, well-prepared first-time pack carriers will love it too; the rewards for your efforts will leave you open-mouthed.

DAY 1: 20.3KM

The walk begins at Telegraph Saddle, about a 3.5km drive out from Tidal River, the Prom's main camping area. Parks Victoria operates shuttles to the saddle carpark at peak holiday times; otherwise you need to car shuffle. Hikes up Mt Oberon (562m) and down to Sealers Cove also start from the saddle, but leave the summit view of Tidal River and the beautiful, yellow-sand east coast beach for another time and head south from the Saddle information board on the well-marked route to Waterloo Bay, the Lighthouse and Oberon Bay.

The first 6.3km of this walk is on Telegraph Track, the unsealed management road running almost to the lighthouse. The first hour is downhill and much of the walk is through an attractively scruffy forest of eucalypt and banksia trees, with Mt Oberon on your right.

Early on you pass two new track-edge fences with boulder bollards erected since the destructive 2011 floods (the second overlooks a pretty creek) and cross a post-flood concrete bridge over Growler Creek, which is littered with fallen and cut timbers. Acacias – commonly called wattles – are proficient recolonisers and the immature ones along here probably germinated after the April 2005 fire, which necessitated helicopter evacuations of campers and hikers. Look for spotted pardalotes in the trees, gorgeous little birds with profuse white spots and red rumps.

Telegraph Track eventually flattens out amid banksias and spiky, spherical green grass trees. A couple of hours into the walk you pass a right-branching side track to Oberon Bay and Tidal River; 75m further on turn left to Waterloo Bay.

The Waterloo Bay track undulates eastward over sandy ridges thick with tea-tree and through stands of wattle and banksia, crossing boardwalks through wetlands that can run with water. (If using walking poles, watch you don't lose their rubber tips in the gaps on the boardwalks.] At high points, look north to Mt Oberon and behind you to sand dunes and offshore islands.

The track skirts a hilltop crowned with what, from a distance, look like standing stones [see point 1 on map]. When you get closer you'll see that these fantastic natural sculptures take the shapes of a pig, an Easter Island head, and a bottom complete with cellulite. And to think that wind, rain and time shaped them!

Then you get your first glimpse of Waterloo Bay, stunning turquoise on a sunny day. The water comes and goes from sight as you continue east on track and boardwalk, through tea-tree forest and knee-high coastal heathland embroidered with colourful wildflowers in spring. Looking south, the lighthouse track is a fine scar across the face of the steep hill at the end of the bay.

Lunch spots don't get prettier than Waterloo Bay. Offload your pack, remove your boots and go for a paddle, remembering that the 9km hike to the lighthouse can take longer than you expect and is a challenge in the dark!

The track leaves Waterloo Bay a couple of hundred metres before sand becomes rocks – look for a sign and people appearing and disappearing – and climbs about 320m in the next 2.5km. Squeeze between boulders, dip into tree-fern gullies padded with rain-holding moss, and amble through drier forest, taking advantage of the frequent viewpoints to catch your breath.

Just after the track finally starts downhill again, a huge boulder on the left [see point 2] gives you your first view of the lighthouse, gilded with sun if the Prom weather gods are kind. Don't dwell on the demoralisingly steep driveway, which looks more like a slippery slide than a track suitable for pack-carrying hikers.

Having climbed and climbed, you descend and descend through bracken forest and occasional taller eucalypts, and more aromatic creek gullies roofed with tree ferns. Lighthouse views encourage you uphill and down through fire-blackened tall gum trees, like charcoal stripes against green regrowth. Late in the day there can seem to be more headlands between you and the lighthouse than on the map, but at last you reach the lighthouse junction. Follow the track going ahead

Left: *View the lightstation from the lighthouse external walkway.* **Right:** *Afternoon sun gilds the granite lighthouse*

and down to the left of a granite boulder, watching for roots that can trip weary feet.

Coming out of a tea-tree tunnel opposite two fabulous boulders, enjoy a few metres of flat walking before starting up a concrete path to the rocks. Catch your breath among these extraordinary hollowed, water-carved, stone-lipped sculptures before summitting: you have 300m on foot and an altitude gain of about 55m before a hot shower and a cup of tea in your cottage.

DAY 2: 24.1KM

Starting with a walk down the lighthouse driveway that leaves some knees wobbling, today's route is longer but less hilly than coming in and ends with a lovely beach walk into Tidal River.

Retrace your steps to the lighthouse track junction and turn left. Then, with the ocean below and the lighthouse over your left shoulder, walk uphill through banksias, tea-tree and, in spring-summer, swathes of red, pink and white common heath bells suggestive of a cottage

Granite hills rise behind rocky Oberon Bay

garden. A rocky outcrop on the left soon after the track starts downhill provides the last lightstation view.

Beyond here you wind inland through tea-tree and whispering she-oaks to Telegraph Track, 700m north up which there is a foot pad on the left to Roaring Meg campsite. This westward side trail is hillier but shorter (2.3km) and prettier than the Telegraph Track (3.4km).

There is a welcome pit toilet at the Roaring Meg–Telegraph Track junction (*see* point 3). If you are super keen and fit you could do a 7.4km return walk from here to the Australian mainland's southernmost point.

There are two options for continuing north: remain on Telegraph Track or tread a prettier parallel walking track along the old telegraph line through heathland. The two meet about 2.5km north atop Martins Hill.

Descending the hill you pass Halfway Hut, a stone shelter midway between Telegraph Saddle and the Lighthouse, before coming first to the Waterloo Bay track junction and then the Oberon Bay turnoff, both on fairly flat heathland unrolled at the feet of ranges whose multiple peaks look like the heads of spectators. Turn left to Oberon Bay, and enjoy an easy 3.4km walk, in places through tea-tree tunnels.

As you walk north along gorgeous Oberon Bay beach to Growler Creek, whose golden water snakes through the sand to the bay, look for sooty oyster catchers with their enamel-red beaks, and for the convict-arrow footprints they leave on the sand. Depending on the tide, you might get across the creek dry footed or opt to go barefoot and replace your boots on the other side.

About 100m upstream, past granite boulders orange with lichen, stone steps climb from the beach to a track heading around a small headland. Gullies along here, carved by water pouring down the stony slopes during the 2011 flood, are testimony to the damage done and why it took two years to reopen some tracks. Yet the flood scars are only momentary distractions from the elevated view of Oberon Bay's broad beach and aqua water. The track out of Oberon is one long lookout.

Little Oberon Bay, immediately north, is shorter and cupped by magnificent granite sloping into water that rolls ashore in five parallel breaking waves. A landslide looks like an open wound on the hill behind the beach and the walking track detours around the deep gully it sliced through the shoreline.

A trail of footprints is the easiest marker for where you leave Little Oberon beach but there is also an orange arrow. Veer right about 50m before the sand runs out and head between two huge rocks, then walk steeply up a few metres of soft sand to a sign that says 'Tidal River 3.9km'.

Immediately off the beach a wooden footbridge crosses a washout and another fords a gully. The track then burrows through tea-tree and wattles, giving glimpses of sea and land. Look back when you reach rock steps leading down a massive granite slab: above where you've come from is a fabulous striped rock wall.

Another climb puts you atop the last headland. If your feet are willing, follow the side track 300m out to Norman Point for another splendid view. Otherwise continue around the headland into relatively protected Norman Bay.

From May to October listen for noisy exhalations indicating the presence of whales. Humpbacks and southern rights sometimes venture into the bay and this walking track is an excellent vantage point. From here you also get a close-up view of waves washing against the boulder-strewn shore below with percussive thumps.

Having dropped you onto Norman Bay beach, the walking track crosses a creek and heads inland through tea-treed hills to the Tidal River Visitor Centre. A more enjoyable way to finish is to stroll along Norman Bay beach and then up through the camping area to the visitor centre carpark.

The walk takes you through granite boulders strewn across Oberon Bay beach

10 YARRA BEND LOOP

Walk:	11.2km loop
Time required:	3–4 hours
Best time:	Year-round
Grade:	Easy to moderate; the track is uneven in places
Environment:	Riverside eucalypt forest, parkland
Best map:	This one
Toilets:	Flushing toilets in carparks at Studley Park Boathouse, Fairfield Park Boathouse and Bellbird Picnic Area
Food:	Delicious fare is available at both boathouses. Fairfield is open daily for breakfast, lunch and afternoon tea. At Studley Park, the kiosk serves snacks, hot food and scones daily; the cafe does lunch and afternoon tea daily and breakfast on weekends and public holidays; and the restaurant is open for dinner on Friday and Saturday and lunch on Sunday (bookings essential).
Tips:	You could start this walk at the Fairfield end, however, there is less parking. Allow time for a paddle on the river.

Take two historic boathouses, one upside-down river, in-your-face geology, countless birds, tens of thousands of flying foxes and quiet places for contemplation and you have a loop for the whole family, only 4km from Melbourne's CBD.

Coming up from Dight's Falls you get a great view of Melbourne's CBD

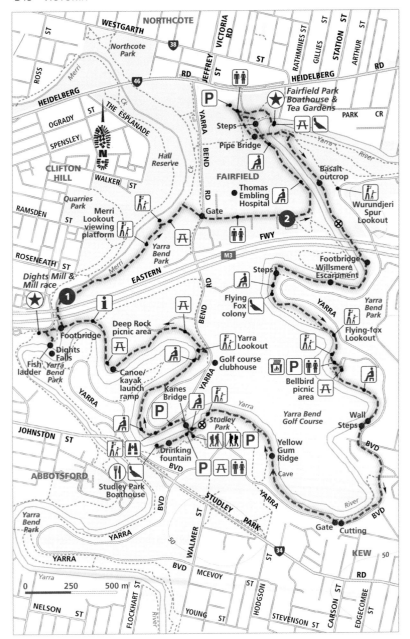

The naming of the much-loved and fondly mocked 'upside-down' Yarra River, which flows through the city of Melbourne, is attributed to a historic miscommunication. Apparently, when surveyor John Wedge, a companion of John Batman on his 1835 exploration of Port Phillip Bay, asked local Aboriginal people what they called the lower river's cascading waters they answered 'yarro yarro', meaning 'it flows'. However, the Wurundjeri name for the river, a ceremonial place that also provided food and water and fibres for weaving, was (and still is) Birrarung ('place of mists and shadows'). Morning mists and shadows abound on this loop walk through Yarra Bend Park, near the end of the Yarra River's 242km journey from Mt Baw Baw and almost within cooee of Melbourne's CBD.

The walk begins with a coffee or cake at Studley Park Boathouse, where Melburnians have bought refreshments and hired paddle boats since 1863. Even on weekdays the riverfront kiosk here can be busy (with people and plump white geese), but quick service gets you fed and on your way.

Back near the carpark, veer left over Kanes Bridge, a landmark wooden suspension bridge erected in 1935 after floods swept away its predecessor. Turn left on the opposite bank (don't go up the steps) onto a wide, flat gravel track that skirts another parking area and meanders past ancient river red gums on grassy flats perfect for picnicking and flinging a frisbee.

After a few hundred metres the track narrows and continues through denser riparian scrub to a concrete canoe launching pad. Push up a short, sharp climb to a lookout with no view, beyond which the track runs into Yarra Bend Rd opposite the Yarra Bend Golf Course clubhouse. Turn left and follow the signs to Deep Rock Picnic Area (700m).

Home to the Deep Rock Swimming Club from 1905, the broad brown river here was the setting for recreational and competitive swimming until the 1940s. In 1918, an estimated 70,000 spectators watched Alick Wickham make a world-record dive of 62.7m from the sheer cliff opposite.

The going is easy now, flat through wattles and eucalypts to where the Yarra meets Merri Creek. The pretty chimes along here are the

Crossing Kanes Bridge, a landmark wooden suspension bridge, puts you on track to Fairfield Boathouse

calls of bell miner birds, small green choristers that can be difficult to see amid the foliage. Before turning right at Merri Creek, cross the footbridge to Dight's Falls.

These falls were a natural crossing point for the Wurundjeri people before John Dight built a stone weir in the 1840s to channel water to his flour mill. Step down into the mill ruins, now covered in graffiti, and follow the red brick path to the restored weir and new fish ladder.

Back over Merri Creek, turn left under the Eastern Fwy. You are now on the shared cycling-walking Main Yarra Trail, so watch out for lycra lizards! As you ascend gently through parkland with pink flowering gums (see point 1 on map), look back over your left shoulder for an eyeful of inner-city suburbs and Melbourne's CBD skyline; the signed 'viewing platform' through the trees gives an even better view of the city and Merri Creek, way below.

As you approach buildings to the right, veer off the track, go through a pedestrian gate, cross Yarra Bend Rd and walk along Fairlea Rd, directly opposite, between twin soccer ovals and the Thomas Embling Hospital, a forensic mental-health facility. The road ends at a fly-fishing pool, from the south-east corner of which (see point 2) a walking track descends to the Yarra. Follow a good walking track north along the river to Fairfield Park Boathouse, an early 20th century establishment saved from sliding into the Yarra in 1985, where you can fuel up on scones with cream and jam.

You now cross the Meccano-like yellow Pipe Bridge visible from the boathouse. Get there by walking up the bluestone-lined road towards the carpark and then turning left (don't take the Main Yarra Trail to the right). Where the descending road U-turns, keep going straight onto the bridge, which gives fabulous views up to the Boathouse and down the green–brown river flowing through a tunnel of river red gums spreading their great limbs over the water.

Back on solid ground, turn hard right off the bitumen, go through a timber chicane, veer left at a fork and keep the river on your right. Narrow in places, with interesting rocks underfoot, this track can get muddy after rain but the going remains fairly easy with mostly gentle ups and downs. Watch out for mountain bikers. A wall of basalt, upended so its many layers now run vertically, is one of several geological exhibits along here. The trees attract red-rumped parrots.

About 1.5km from Pipe Bridge you come to a massive colony of chattering grey-headed flying foxes more commonly known as fruit bats. Relocated from Melbourne's Royal Botanic Gardens in 2003, the colony numbers more than 10,000 (volunteers can join the monthly count; bookings through rvdr@unimelb.edu.au are essential). The animals hang from the trees along a 500m stretch of river like an excess of Christmas baubles. Australia's largest bat species, with a wingspan of up to 1m, these flying foxes are surprisingly cute, which makes up for their smell.

You are now on the Flying Fox Wetland Walk, an easy short alternative to the full loop, which has information boards about these animals' habits. Bellbird Picnic Area, with lawns, barbecues and parking, marks the end of the colony. Take either of the two sealed tracks down to the river from Bellbird and keep walking downstream, but look up for your first glimpse of the prime real estate along Yarra Blvd; steps take you up to the road.

There's only 1.5km to go from here, the first 600m along the Boulevard footpath. Just past a striated cliff sliced through to make the road, go through a pedestrian gate on the right and down a rocky path and wooden steps to the river. Watch and listen for paddlers on the water as you hug the riverbank back to Studley Park Boathouse for afternoon tea.

Clockwise from top: *Enjoy the country feel in the suburbs; a handsome goose poses for the camera at Studley Park Boathouse; Melbourne's upside-down Yarra reflects the gums trees lining its banks; allow time for a paddle on the river in a wooden boat*

The summit of Mt Ohlssen-Bagge presents hikers with a panorama of steeply upended rock

SOUTH AUSTRALIA

Forget about renowned wine regions, for a little while at least, and sample some bushwalks instead! Whether you want to embark on a multi-day hike in honour of a famous landscape artist; walk through geological history writ large on ancient, weathered rock; tread from Adelaide's summit to the sea; stand on the edge of plunging sea cliffs where sea eagles nest, or climb a Dutchman's stern, South Australia's got a trail to suit your palate.

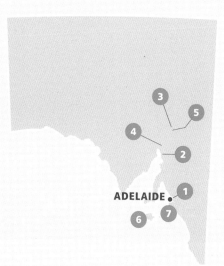

ADELAIDE

1	Adelaide 'Summit to Sea'	148
2	Alligator Gorge Loop	160
3	Bunyeroo Gorge	166
4	Dutchmans Stern Loop	171
5	Mount Ohlssen-Bagge	177
6	Rocky River to Sea	183
7	Waitpinga Cliffs	189

1 ADELAIDE 'SUMMIT TO SEA'

Walk:	35km one-way
Time required:	2 days
Best time:	Cool, clear day
Grade:	Moderate (easy sections, but long)
Environment:	Hills, suburban streets, national parks, linear parks, beach
Best map:	This one; also helpful is the downloadable *Belair National Park map* (environment.sa.gov.au) and the *Sea to Summit* brochure
Toilets:	Flushing toilets atop Mt Lofty and in parks along the way
Food:	You can tuck into a delicious breakfast at the Summit cafe on Mt Lofty; assorted fast food is available at the Main South Rd– Flagstaff Rd junction on day 2; ice-creams and cold drinks await at Kingston Park Beach kiosk
Tips:	This walk can be done using public transport. Visit adelaidemetro.com.au for Adelaide bus and train timetables. Several of the parks visited may be closed on days of extreme fire danger; check conditions at environment.sa.gov.au.

Over two days, walk from a scenic lookout atop Adelaide to the city's sandy shore, treading a route through scruffy native forest, manicured linear parks and leafy suburbs.

A sea and city view spreads out at the feet of a walker treading the 'Summit to Sea' walk

'The dark green round the town I proposed to be reserved as park grounds,' wrote Colonel William Light, first Surveyor-General of the then Colony of South Australia, on an early sketch of Adelaide, and the city still abounds with parks.

The George Driscoll Sea to Summit Walk, named by Tim McCartney Snape after the keen local hiker who plotted it, celebrates this open space, tracking a linear route between Gulf St Vincent and Mt Lofty. Driscoll designed it as a challenging day walk, but how you tackle it depends on why you hike.

Some folks walk it boot camp-style, from sea to summit in one hard day as described in the *Sea to Summit* brochure (available from the Friends of the Heysen Trail at heysentrail.asn.au). The walk described here takes you in the easier reverse direction, with sea views encouraging you much of the way, and is spread over two days.

DAY 1: 19KM – Mt Lofty to Coromandel Railway Station

The walk begins atop Mt Lofty, in Cleland Conservation Park, 18km south-east of Adelaide's CBD. The summit is easily accessed by car, but then you'd have to come back for it afterwards. Instead, arrange a drop off or take a taxi. You can also travel by public transport, riding two buses from the city.

However you arrive, allow time for coffee and/or breakfast in the Summit cafe, often full of lycra-clad cyclists who ride up the mountain for fun, and to take in the panorama of Adelaide Hills, park-ringed city and Gulf St Vincent waters. Information boards explain that sedimentation, uplift and erosion crafted this sweep, but that in the Dreaming of the Kaurna, the first people of the Adelaide Plains and surrounding ranges, Mt Lofty is the body of ancestral being Nganno, who died after battle.

This walk is a composite of walking trails, shared-use tracks and footpaths with no specific track markers. Unclear and inadequate signage can cause confusion in several places, so these points are detailed.

Step off Mt Lofty summit onto the well-marked Heysen Trail, which runs 1200km north from Cape Jervis on Fleurieu Peninsula to

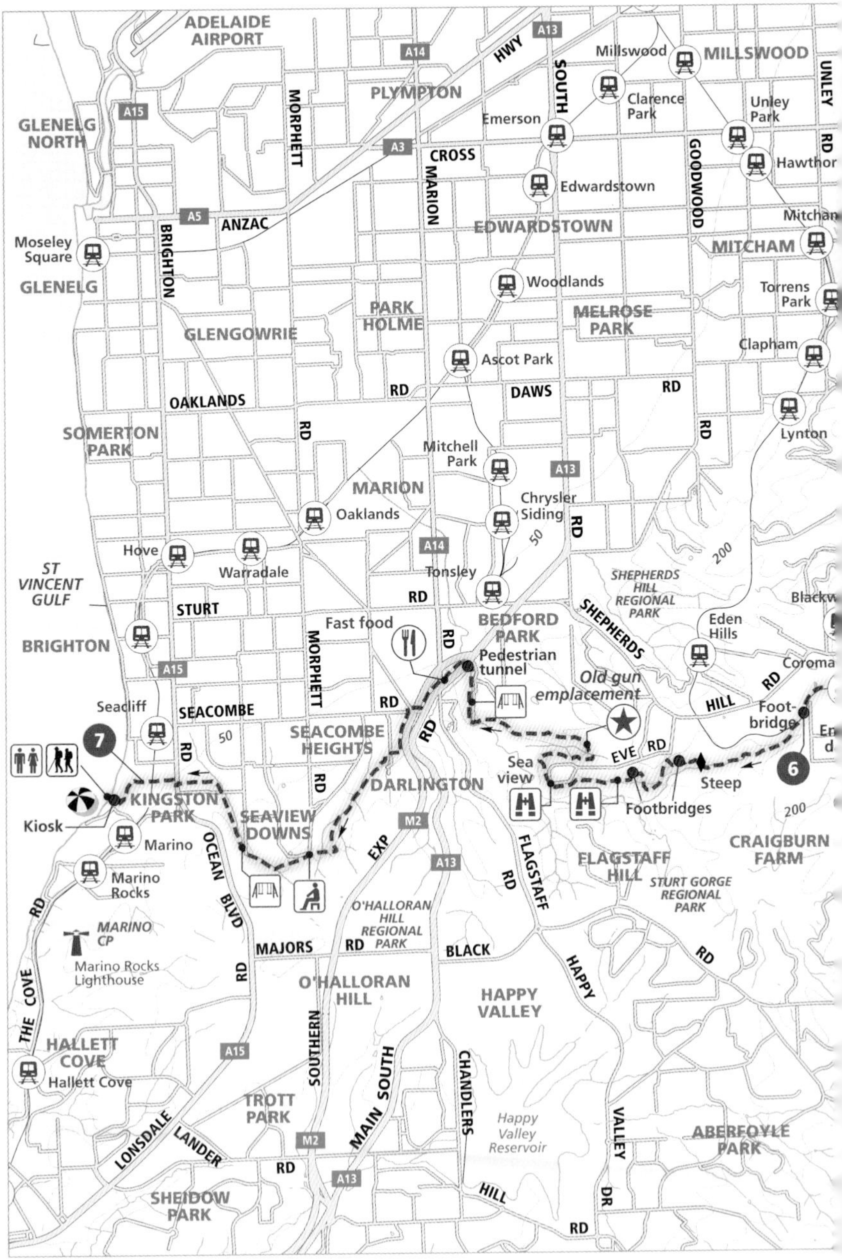
ADELAIDE AIRPORT
GLENELG NORTH
PLYMPTON
MILLSWOOD
Millswood
Clarence Park
Emerson
Unley Park
Hawthorn
Edwardstown
EDWARDSTOWN
MITCHAM
Mitcham
Moseley Square
GLENELG
Woodlands
Torrens Park
PARK HOLME
GLENGOWRIE
MELROSE PARK
Clapham
Ascot Park
OAKLANDS
DAWS
SOMERTON PARK
Lynton
Mitchell Park
MARION
Oaklands
Chrysler Siding
Hove
Warradale
Tonsley
ST VINCENT GULF
STURT
SHEPHERDS HILL REGIONAL PARK
BRIGHTON
Fast food
BEDFORD PARK
Pedestrian tunnel
Eden Hills
Seacliff
SEACOMBE
SEACOMBE HEIGHTS
Old gun emplacement
Foot-bridge
DARLINGTON
Sea view
Steep
Kiosk
KINGSTON PARK
SEAVIEW DOWNS
Footbridges
Marino
Marino Rocks
CRAIGBURN FARM
FLAGSTAFF HILL
STURT GORGE REGIONAL PARK
O'HALLORAN HILL REGIONAL PARK
MARINO CP
Marino Rocks Lighthouse
MAJORS
BLACK
O'HALLORAN HILL
HAPPY VALLEY
HALLETT COVE
Hallett Cove
TROTT PARK
Happy Valley Reservoir
ABERFOYLE PARK
SHEIDOW PARK
THE COVE RD
LONSDALE
LANDER RD
MAIN SOUTH RD
SOUTHERN EXP
CHANDLERS HILL RD
VALLEY DR
HAPPY VALLEY
FLAGSTAFF RD
OCEAN BLVD
BRIGHTON RD
MORPHETT RD
MARION RD
SOUTH RD
GOODWOOD RD
UNLEY RD
CROSS RD
ANZAC HWY
SHEPHERDS HILL RD
EVE RD
A15
A14
A13
A3
A5
M2
50
200
7
6

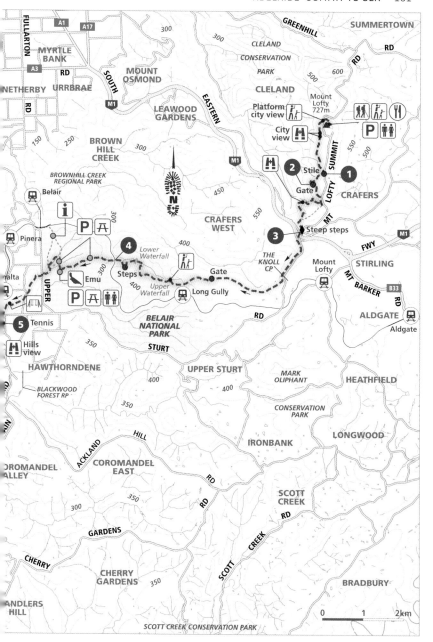

Parachilna in the South Australian outback (*also see* p. 189). Follow the
Heysen and, initially, signs for the Waterfall Gully walk, down through a
mix of dusty green eucalypts and darker cypress pines. Cross Mt Lofty
Summit Rd, watching for cars and fast-descending cyclists, and enjoy
the city view through the trees from the safety of the metal stairs on
the far side.

Ignore the first cross track and veer left at the next junction, past
Mt Lofty YHA, a stone shepherd's hut built in the 1880s. Glimpsing
coast through the trees as you go, continue gently downhill, on a
wide trail now marked as Nangare Track, through forest cracking with
whip bird calls and answers, and echoing with the manic laughter of
kookaburras.

Having crossed Attunga Track and entered a 'heritage area' (note
the different banksia species and assorted groundcovers), veer right
at each of the next two track junctions and then again over a stile (*see*
point 1 on map). Walk down gravel Reynolds Dve and re-enter Cleland
Conservation Park at Gate 21. Follow Carro Track to another gate
(*see* point 2), through which you ascend Summerhill Dve, admiring
the expansive views over the Adelaide Plains and city. On reaching

Water pours over this rock lip after heavy rain

Lofty Summit Rd, turn right and, keeping in the bicycle lane and watching for cyclists, walk about 50m down to an arrow on the safety barrier directing you right to Crafers Trail.

Turn off the road here into Blackburn Dve, turning right again almost immediately down a laneway between house fences with a gate visible at the end. Take the short, steep goat track immediately before the gate, which scrabbles down to Gate 19, and climb over a stile onto Cleland Conservation Park Spa Track.

The track ambles through tall stringybarks, hugging the contours of a steep slope topped with houses and bottoming in a gully. Spring and summer wildflowers festoon the hill (look out for pretty pink hyacinth orchids), but you may see gorgeous orange-and-green correas year round. The city view through a gap widens as you climb towards a gate, through which you turn right and walk down Shurdington Rd.

Go left into Mount St, marked with a black Crafers Circuit arrow, and walk past the beautiful sandstone Church of the Epiphany. Stone steps put you on busy Crafers roundabout (see point 3).

The next half hour is noisy and unpleasant. Cross the road bridge over the Princes Fwy, turn left towards Belair National Park and tread the footpath along Waverley Ridge Rd. About 1km along on the right, Sheoak Rd provides an escape from hills traffic and an entry to South Australia's oldest national park.

Enter Belair National Park (1891) and swing right onto a vehicle-wide track signed as shared use. Called the Tom Roberts Horse Trail on the information board as you enter the park, this track undulates through scruffy eucalypt forest lumpy with termite mounds and decorated with butterflies and seasonal wildflowers.

Leave this wide track at a sign for the Waterfall Hike (the longest walk in the national park, and a loop). Go right and keep right, heading steeply down to the Upper Waterfall, an unfenced natural wall over which Workanda Creek can pour in winter; there's a small cave and a tangle of blackberries at its foot.

The view of Spencer Gulf's blue water, to the west, improves as you follow a rocky-in-places trail along the left-hand creek cliff-line (parallel to a wider shared-use track). Some of the rock through here is shot with quartz, and beautiful old, peeling gum trees grow from it. Turn right at the next junction for a short, sharp, slippery-when-wet descent.

Turn right onto a wider gravel track and then left for the Waterfall Hike, staying this side of a creek, and wander through wattles and yellow daisies to the Lower Waterfall viewing platform. A fenced boardwalk crosses the creek to cascade-viewing platforms.

Continue downstream through acacias to the mouth of Echo Tunnel, which burrows under the rail line (see point 4). Walk through – mind your head – and note the fabulously lumpy gum tree where you emerge. She-oaks give the scrub at this end of the tunnel a very different look from the area through which you just walked.

Turn left onto Echo Track and walk south to Old Government House, the Colony of South Australia's first official vice-regal summer residence, on Queens Jubilee Dve (open to the public 1–4pm on Sundays and public holidays only). Opposite Old Government House is State Flora, one of South Australia's original plant nurseries. Backtrack a short way and then walk north-west (anticlockwise) on the Lorikeet Loop Walk, returning to the creek.

Several park walks share the next half kilometre or so of track along the creek and through eucalypts. Turn right for the Yurrebilla Trail (which runs 54km from Belair to the River Torrens) and cross sealed Gooch Rd. Loop around tranquil Playford Lake on the Wood Duck Walk and back to Gooch Rd. (Yurrebilla Trail continues north of Playford Lake to historic Belair Station, on the Adelaide line. The Sea to Summit brochure suggests you break the walk here, but doing so makes one day considerably longer than the other.)

Follow Gooch Rd out of the park, through metal gates and past stone Western Lodge, the old head ranger's house.

Walk about 50m south on Upper Sturt Rd, then turn right into Pine Lodge Dve, just before Workanda Creek, and left into Bermuda Way, with the creek appearing again to your left. Now you essentially follow and crisscross a small creek through leafy hills suburbs, treading sealed bike track in linear parks and footpaths along streets of elegant houses with handsome front-yard eucalypts. There are also some beautiful smooth gum trees whose orange bark peels to a pale

The walk finishes on the rippled sand in front of the Kingston Park Caravan Park

lemon-lime trunk. Occasional hand-painted white arrows indicate the route, but you can't rely on these.

Just past tennis courts (*see* point 5), turn right into Forrest Dve and zigzag: left into Acacia Rd, right into Acorn Rd, left into East Tce. About 200m along, walk right up a laneway to the rail line.

Walk left through the railway carpark to Main Rd and cross next to the railway crossing. Follow the train tracks through Davies Thomas Reserve and along Johnson Pde to Coromandel Railway Station, at Brighton Pde. Day one ends with a train ride into the city (or you could stay locally).

DAY 2: 16KM – Coromandel Railway Station to Kingston Park Beach

Catch the train back to Coromandel Station and walk west on the bitumen walking–cycling track north of the line. This passes fenced Wittunga Botanic Garden, originally a private homestead established in 1902 and opened to the public in 1975. You can't enter the garden from here, but it's worth coming back to see the extensive plantings of waterwise Australian and South African plants. The adjoining grounds of Blackwood High School resemble a park, too.

Through a childproof gate (*see* point 6), cross the rail line on a red metal footbridge into grey box woodland. Follow the rough track along the lip of the rail cutting and then descend steeply to narrow Magpie Creek Gully.

Ford this Sturt River tributary and stay on the lower footpad on the opposite bank. Beautiful gum trees grow here and it feels remote, despite the nearby houses. Ignore Magpie Gully Trail veering left and keep to the lower track, criss-crossing the creek to small rock pools between steep gorge walls.

These pools can dry up at summer's height but if there's water, watch for lizards swimming. This is also good red-bellied black snake country, so be alert (but not alarmed).

Quite rough underfoot, the track runs into an unsealed vehicular track, which is now closed to cars, to your left. Turn right, past a parking area to a junction of vehicular tracks, there heading left down to and over the creek. Pick up a footpad on the right, where the vehicle track swings left; cross a side creek and keep right when this rocky track divides, essentially doing a dogleg.

You are now in Sturt Gorge Recreation Park, which conserves an area of the nationally threatened Greybox Grassy Woodland vegetation once abundant across southern Australia. The gorge was cut by the Sturt River (also called Sturt Creek), which the Kaurna people used as a link between the hills and the sea. Colonel William Light's initial rough sketch of Adelaide (1836) put the city on the Sturt, rather than the River Torrens.

An eroded track leads through spiky acacias; turn right at the next junction and traverse a series of gullies, then work your way steeply uphill, with the main gorge on your left.

Go left at the T-junction up top, where houses and an embankment suggest a road on your right, and follow the hill's contours, through gum trees and wattles, to a vehicular track running along backyard fences. Descend again, away from the fence line but still along the slope, ignoring occasional tracks coming up from the gorge.

Quite suddenly you'll get an eyeful of hillside houses and see down into the gorge from which you've just climbed. Visible behind and below is the Sturt River flood-control dam. Keep left at each of the next two forks, heading generally downhill, with more houses coming into view. The trail runs into a wider vehicular track that descends gently, and you'll see the sea as it swings around the hill.

Walk on, past a gate and a green wooden sign (the first) for Sturt Gorge Recreation Park, and through she-oaks and fluffy grasses. The trail now does a huge backward S-bend, up a side valley that has no trees to provide shade on a hot day.

Continue along the upper gorge on a mix of walking trail and vehicular track, going under powerlines, in and out of gullies and past the concrete base of a gun emplacement, which was part of WW II defences. (General Kitchener staged a mock battle in Sturt Gorge during WW I.)

Come under more powerlines and veer left, joining a vehicular track that runs on through eucalypt woodland and grasses bleached yellow in summer to end at a sealed road beside Flinders University. Hook left back into grasses on a foot trail paralleling the road and head seaward through stands of olive-like native trees with leathery leaves.

A factory comes into view on the gorge floor, with a spectacular, angular modern house jutting from the cliff above. Look for a rough track on the left, almost in line with the factory and towards houses; this takes you down a grassy slope along backyards to river flats.

Head downstream between houses and river, passing a magnificent grey-barked gum tree on the bank and a beautiful cream-and-red striped eucalypt where the track swings right into Riverside Dve.

Tread the gravel footpath north to linear Bedford Park and walk through the park to its end on Main South Rd, Adelaide's major southern arterial. Turn left onto the footpath and then left again before McDonald's, going under the road through a graffiti-covered tunnel shared by pedestrians, bikes and creek.

Walk south on Main South Rd towards traffic lights and fast-food outlets. Cross Flagstaff Rd and turn right, about 400m south along Flagstaff Rd, into Seacombe Rd, which spans the Southern Expressway, offering a great CBD view. Swing left onto the pedestrian track beside the rust-red expressway fence.

Enter the fifth cul-de-sac and then, with a lovely sea breeze now in your face, take the first road left and then walk diagonally through a small hilly park to its top. Seaward and right from here you'll see Glenelg's high-rise waterfront apartments, and behind you, the Mount Lofty Ranges where you started out.

This park sits in a horseshoe of look-at-me houses. Walk west and downhill to the end of the development. Clamber over a stile into lightly-timbered O'Halloran Hill Recreation Reserve, proclaimed in 1989 as part of a state government strategy to create a second ring of parklands outside those that Colonel William Light annotated on that early city plan.

Motor along the vehicular track around the hill's lower contours to the base of a shallow, treed creek gully. Make your way up the gully to the power pylons ahead (perhaps too snake-friendly in summer), or continue up the vehicular track and down a walking track into the creek gully, climbing up the other side to the power pylons. The latter option offers better views; both take you under the powerlines to a row of houses facing the reserve. Turn left along the road here and then right behind the last house, relishing the sea view and breeze.

Follow the backyard fence line down to a gate. Turn right onto a road and then left at the roundabout, into a park. Ramble through this park almost to its end, following a creek gully and passing eucalypts that produce flashy bright yellow flowers.

On footpath now, swing left on Thomas St and along to Ocean Blvd. Cross at the lights and dogleg right and down Pine Ave (you can get refreshments at the corner IGA if you can't wait the few minutes to the beach kiosk).

Walk Pine Ave's length, crossing the rail line that will take you back into Adelaide, and where the avenue turns right, continue down a gravel laneway between houses (*see* point 7). Keep west on a footpad that brings you to concrete steps leading down to a beach. Ignore that tempting descent and instead take the gravel footpath 20m to the left, which zigzags downhill along treed coastal cliffs (Pine Valley) above bowling-green neat Kingston Park Caravan Park. Concrete and stone steps lead down to Kingston Park Beach's rippled sand.

Toes wriggling in the foam, turn around and look back up those steps. Why would anyone do this walk in the reverse direction?

The obelisk atop Mt Lofty commemorates Matthew Flinders' sighting and naming of the hill in 1802

2 ALLIGATOR GORGE LOOP

Walk:	9.3km loop
Time required:	3–4 hours
Best time:	Mild, sunny day during autumn or spring; summer temperatures can soar
Grade:	Moderate; uneven and loose gorge floor
Environment:	Deep, blocky creek gorge, treed escarpment, hill and plains views
Best map:	This one
Toilets:	Pit toilet in Blue Gum Flat picnic area
Food:	The closest food is in Wilmington, where you can get an excellent coffee in the old general store and a counter meal at the pub opposite
Tips:	Walking poles come in handy on this walk, especially when there's water and you need to rock-hop through the Narrows.
	Vehicle entry fees are payable for Mt Remarkable National Park; you can purchase a single-park or multi-park pass: details environment.sa.gov.au/parks/entry-fees.

Walkers pause while descending the management vehicle track from the top of Alligator Gorge

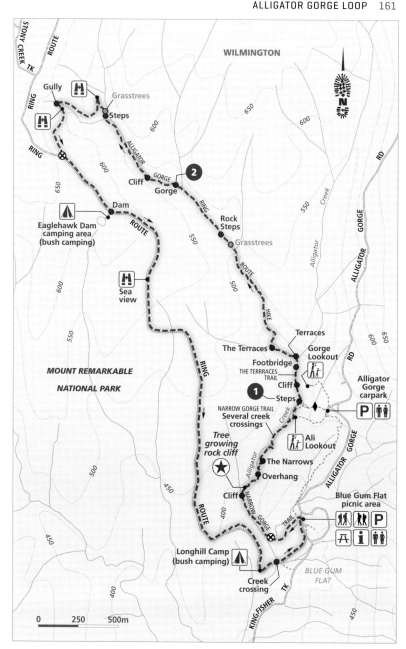

WILMINGTON

N

STONY CREEK TK

ROUTE

RING

Gully

Grasstrees

RING

Steps

RING

ALLIGATOR

600

ROUTE

GORGE

Cliff

Gorge

2

Dam

Eaglehawk Dam
camping area
(bush camping)

ROUTE

RING

Rock
Steps

Grasstrees

ROUTE

Sea
view

HIKE

Terraces

The Terraces

Gorge Lookout

MOUNT REMARKABLE

Footbridge

THE TERRRACES
TRAIL

Alligator
Gorge
carpark

NATIONAL PARK

Cliff

Steps

NARROW GORGE TRAIL
Several creek
crossings

P

Creek

RING

Tree
growing
rock cliff

Ali
Lookout

The Narrows

Overhang

Alligator

ALLIGATOR GORGE

RD

Cliff

ROUTE

NARROW GORGE

Blue Gum Flat
picnic area

TRAIL

P

Longhill Camp
(bush camping)

Creek
crossing

KINGFISHER TK

BLUE GUM
FLAT

0   250   500m

An adventure for all ages, this walk travels the length of a gorge burrowed through ancient rock and ends with an easy run through forest festooned with wildflowers in spring.

Fear not! There are no alligators on this walk. The reason for its name is uncertain, but Alligator Gorge, in Mt Remarkable National Park, is a prehistoric creature of huge appeal. Reaching east from the coastal plain of Spencer Gulf across the southern Flinders Ranges to the edge of the Willochra Plain, Mt Remarkable National Park shelters an interesting mix of flora and fauna from South Australia's arid north and wetter south.

One of a dozen hikes across three areas of the park, this walk starts from Blue Gum Flat picnic area, a scenic but winding (unsuitable for caravans and buses) 15-minute drive from the historic town of Wilmington.

The Alligator Gorge Ring Route Circuit is shown on the colour-coded walks map in the picnic area information shelter as a 7km loop, but this is well short (other signage and park brochures give the correct length). No direction is suggested either, but doing it anticlockwise, as described here, towards the Narrows first, gives you a long, steady descent with views to finish, rather than a boring climb to start.

Water reflects red rock and white gums within Alligator Gorge

The anticlockwise loop starts at the information shelter, on a track that becomes rocky as it snakes through acacias, she-oaks and eucalypts, towards the gorge rim. If Alligator Creek is running you'll hear water as you descend. Cross a feeder creek (or dry gully) to stand between stacked red rock with she-oaks and centuries-old river red gums; about 400m up the gorge you can walk under a eucalypt that's fused, sucker-like, to the right-hand wall.

This walk involves numerous creek crossings and you might have to rock-hop in a few places to stay dry footed; on the other hand, you might encounter little water. (Some people have walked many times in the Flinders Ranges and the only running water they've seen is what comes out of their drink bottles!)

Alligator Gorge is prettiest when there's some water to reflect the red-rock walls, trees and sky. The layered cliffs glisten and drip after rain, and rafts of moss glow bright green in hollows where moisture settles. Look out for morel mushrooms and other interesting fungi tucked here and there. The young at heart might also enjoy tadpole spotting in the pools.

The gorge narrows and widens several times as you work upstream, with the walls rearing above you and the trees atop them leaning out into space; but there is no mistaking The Narrows, where the quartzite cliffs come within 2m of each other, cutting a ribbon of sky overhead. This is a stepping-stone section when the creek's running, but an easy walk on gravel in drier conditions. If you're not concentrating on your foot placement, check out the detail in the stonework either side; aeons of sedimentation and compression are writ large on the red rock.

Emerging from The Narrows you'll see a set of steep steps on the right (*see* point 1 on map); these lead to Alligator Gorge carpark (an alternative place to start this walk).

Continue upstream on a flatter, easier track beside the creek, passing squared, almost sharp-edged red quartzite cliffs on the left and fallen rocks, a river of lichen-covered stones, on the right. This brings you to an area of cross-gorge shelving called The Terraces. See the rippled rock underfoot? This was a seabed way back when.

A wooden footbridge fords the creek here, even though it's one of the easiest crossings so far; it's probably slippery when water washes over the horizontal rock layers.

Walk on, passing through a sea of grass trees that bristle up the rocky slope to your left and atop the cliff. The gorge then steepens and you'll traverse an area of broken stone, small pieces rough with lichen and great slabs carpeted in mosses and lichens.

There are few trail markers, because you just follow the gorge; but on occasions you'll need to look well ahead to work out the best way around rocks. Where there's a choice of footpads on either side of the creek, stick to the most obvious, better-worn option.

The gorge narrows again and the cliffs become shallower as you climb, but just past a side gorge on the right [see point 2] the track runs along the foot of one last momentous cliff, comprised of multiple extremely thin layers, like a magazine stack.

Soon after more grass trees, the track starts up the left-hand gorge wall. Stone steps climb from leafier creek into acacias and pea shrubs and pretty pink grevilleas. As you turn sharp left at a lovely old gum with a hollow underneath [logs block a side footpad] you'll get a view over the top of the gorge to the hills beyond.

The track brings you out on a management vehicle track. Turn left towards Blue Gum Flat [5km] and descend through eucalypt forest with the southern Flinders Ranges – and, briefly, Spencer Gulf – on show through the trees ahead. A vista of treed ranges encourages you down the hill for much of these last few kilometres.

There's an occasional small clearing beside the track but the ground is predominantly scruffy with yellow-flowering ground cover. Purple orchids often bloom along the verges, as does Early Nancy [pretty pink or white flowers with a distinguishing red/purple ring around the stamens]. Western grey kangaroos are often seen through here too, but you'll need a bit of luck to spot an echidna trundling along.

The track swings left at Long Hill Camp [a hike-in overnight area on the right] and returns you to Blue Gum Flat, where you could have a snack and a drink among wattles and multi-trunked eucalypts and, commonly, lazing western grey kangaroos, before heading out.

Clockwise from top left: *Walkers step from stone to stone in The Narrows; Alligator Creek has cut a spectacular route through multi-layered cliffs; red, white and blue are the primary colours of Alligator Gorge; geological processes are writ large everywhere you look*

3 BUNYEROO GORGE

Walk:	8.2km return
Time required:	2–3 hours
Best time:	Year round, but check water levels with rangers after rain
Grade:	Easy to moderate (the track is unformed and rocky in places)
Environment:	River gorge, cliffs, centuries-old river gums, plains
Best map:	This one
Toilets:	None
Food:	Coffee, treats, takeaway food and lunch supplies available at Wilpena Pound General Store, beside the visitor information centre; Wilpena Pound Resort for sit-down restaurant meals
Tips:	Before setting out, download the Bunyeroo Gorge information sheet from walkingtrailssupportgroup.org.au (click Bush and Geology Walks in the Flinders Ranges), which numbers and describes different formations along the Bunyeroo Creek drive and walk.
	Vehicle entry fees are payable for Flinders Ranges National Park; you can purchase a single-park or multi-park pass; details environment.sa.gov.au/parks/entry-fees

 Follow an outback creek on its serpentine journey through hundreds of millions of years of geological history writ large.

Take in a jaw-dropping view of Bunyeroo Valley and saw-tooth ranges from the lookout on the drive to Bunyeroo Gorge

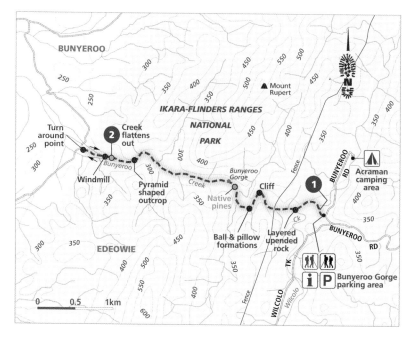

The Flinders Ranges are prehistoric mountains, dating back to when Australia and Antarctica were still one continent and formed by roughly 850 million years of marine sedimentation, compression, upthrust and erosion. Nowhere is this timeline more obvious than in Bunyeroo Gorge, which slices through the Heysen Range. Information posts along this out-and-back walk identify the different geological formations, but it's far more than just educational; it's also a fascinating walk, suited to rock-hounds of all ages.

The walk starts at the Bunyeroo Gorge parking area (no toilets), 18km north of Wilpena Pound resort and camping area. Getting there is a scenic drive of the highest order – but then, all Flinders Ranges drives are – with a jaw-dropping lookout view of Bunyeroo Valley and saw-tooth ranges, best in afternoon light and prettiest when the rocky slopes are dusted mauve with silver mulla mulla. The unsealed road then drops into the valley and snakes through the ABC Range, where the gorge walls close to within metres of your car. Soon after popping out the other end you'll see the gorge parking area on the left. The road continues north between the ABC and Heysen ranges to Brachina Gorge, another geological timeline, and the Aroona homestead ruins.

From the car park follow the very obvious black-and-yellow signs for the Bunyeroo Gorge Geology Walk. A horizontal plaque at the start of the walk explains how the gorge came into being, and numbered information posts along the walk name and describe the different formations, including Rawnsley Quartzite and Red Bonney Sandstone, which also tell stories of climate changes.

The track, which is initially formed, with fine red shale underfoot, sets off through native cypress pines along Bunyeroo Creek, whose rocky bed is home to both immature and centuries-old river gums. The opposite gorge wall is a multitude of thin stripes, once-horizontal sedimentary layers compressed by unimaginable forces into a snaking line. Lichen looks like pale green icing on the rocks.

As the track runs down into the creek bed (see point 1 on map), note more fantastic, upended layering to your left in a smaller side gorge. The walk crosses the creek, passing a fabulously gnarly gum, then crosses an area of upended, almost slate-thin layers of red rock shot through with other coloured rock.

About 1km into the walk the creek bed swings left along an impeding cliff of limey siltstones and limestones, part of the Wonoka Formation, to find a fault line. Walking through that long-since widened crack, you pass another area of dramatically upended layering.

This walk crosses the creek several times, with the route marked by yellow-backed black walking figures on blue posts. Each time you cross, note the different coloured and textured rocks in the creek bed; the mixed assortment of red, blue, pink, grey and white is testimony to the multiple geological layers in the Flinders Ranges. Think too about the bullock teams and coaches that rocked and rattled through this gorge in the 19th century, transporting copper, mail and produce to the western plains.

Continuing through the gorge you pass some particularly high, steep cliffs on the right; and then on the left another area where a section of cliff juts upwards and outwards, forming what from below

Some 850 million years of sedimentation, compression, upthrust and erosion are on show in Bunyeroo Gorge

looks like a red rock pyramid. At its base there's a small cave, and a river gum whose roots reach across the creek.

The long-distance Heysen Trail [see p. 189], named in honour of famous landscape artist Sir Hans Heysen, does not pass through Bunyeroo Gorge, but the range through which it cuts bears his name and this is very much his country. He wrote in a letter, 'The Flinders region has held a "spell" over me ever since I first went to Quorn and Hawker looking for new material for brush and pencil ... The great Red Gums in the creek beds fill me with wonder; their feeling of strength of limb, of vigour and life, suggest the very spirit of endurance.' Spot on, Mr Heysen!

2.5km into the walk the gorge walls come down to a plain [see point 2] where Bunyeroo Creek broadens and straightens towards Lake Torrens, a vast salt lake to the west. The creek bed ahead of you can look pinkish brown, but that's an optical illusion because you still have multi-coloured rocks underfoot.

The walk ends at a gate guarded by another handsome old river gum. Retrace your steps from here, admiring the gorge and creek from the reverse perspective.

Note the different coloured and textured rocks in the creek bed

4 DUTCHMANS STERN LOOP

Walk:	10.8km loop
Time required:	3–4 hours
Best time:	Mild sunny day; spring for the best wildflowers, although there is something in bloom year round
Grade:	Moderate
Environment:	Grassland, rocky uplift, cliff edges, gorge
Best map:	This one
Toilets:	None
Food:	In Quorn you can tuck into quandong (native plum) pies, cakes, coffee and spiders in cafes and sit down to counter meals in historic hotels
Tips:	Cloud cover can obscure the views and hide the cliff edges, so reconsider if bad weather is forecast or if conditions change for the worse while you are on the track

Cliff-top vistas reaching from Wilpena Pound to Spencer Gulf reward those who tackle this family-friendly walk in the southern Flinders Ranges.

The impressive bluff anchored in green pastures north of Quorn, in the southern Flinders Ranges, was named by Captain Matthew Flinders in 1802 for its similarity not to a European gentleman's backside but to

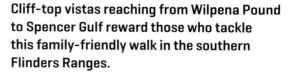

Dutchmans Stern presents many long-distance views

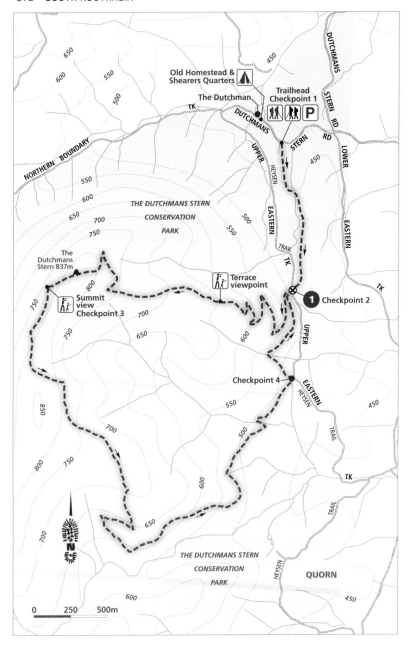

the stern of the Dutch sailing ships that plied the world's oceans in the 18th century. Flinders perceived this likeness from Spencer Gulf, about 30km south-west, and from the foot of the bluff its quartzite cap does indeed look a bit like a railed ship's deck.

The fun and far-from-taxing walk up this local landmark leaves from a small parking area in the Dutchmans Stern Conservation Park, 9.5km north of the historic railway town of Quorn, via Arden Vale Rd and unsealed Dutchmans Stern Rd. A locked gate in the parking area gives vehicular access to the Dutchman Homestead and shearers' quarters that, combined, provide self-contained accommodation for up to 15 people and can be booked online at environment.sa.gov.au.

High-vis yellow trail marker posts every 200m – unnecessarily frequent on the walk's easiest stretches – lead past an information board, through a paddock and along a fenced area protecting plants required by the rare white-spot skipper butterfly, at the extreme west of its range and vulnerable in South Australia.

Climbing through open woodland of blue gums, Christmas bush and drooping she-oak, with unfurling views of neighbouring hills, the track traverses a slope sliding into a creek lined with gums. You'll probably

The summit view reaches north to Wilpena Pound

Fluffy clouds often drift by the rocky summit, briefly blocking the view

see western grey kangaroos reclining in the grass along here, or bounding away.

The vehicular track behind the small dam that comes into view is the Heysen Trail (*see* p. 189), the long-distance shared-use trail named after landscape artist Hans Heysen, which runs between Cape Jervis, on Fleurieu Peninsula, and Parachilna in the Flinders Ranges. Cross the Heysen Trail (red-and-white trail markers) and veer right at the fork in our narrower track (*see* point 1 on map) to start up the bluff (you come out on the left at the end of the walk).

Yellow and brown daisies, acacias and a swag of other flowering plants adorn Dutchmans Stern at different times of year: silver mulla mulla, with their fluffy pink-and-white flower heads; pink, star-like common fringe myrtle; carnivorous tall sundews; tubular red flame heath; herbaceous Early Nancy, whose six-petal white flowers have a distinguishing purple ring around their yellow-tipped stamen. The attractive stalky purple flowers are Salvation Jane (called Paterson's Curse outside of South Australia), an invasive weed that's poisonous to grazing stock, introduced from Europe in the 19th century.

An unformed but well-worn track provides easy passage across the Stern's face, zigzagging past sloping rocks and overhangs as it climbs towards layered red stonework. The view just gets better and better, but there are quite a few ants' nests along the track so take care where you stop for photographs, or you might end up crawling with ants!

Rockier now, the track climbs an easy ridge, through grass trees, sugar gums and she-oaks, putting you on The Terrace viewpoint, overlooking the parking area, homestead and rolling, almost treeless hills. The cradle-like formation on the north-east horizon is Wilpena Pound (see p. 177), at the heart of the Flinders Ranges.

The 12km Devil's Peak and 22km Mt Brown Summit walks are marked going left from here, but the track is not obvious. Our trail zigzags uphill and across a river of rocks.

And then you are up top (820m), on the ship's deck, so to speak, with a captain's view sweeping clockwise from the Port Augusta coal-fired power plant, closed in 2016, and Spencer Gulf south-west, through salt-bush coastal plain and the dry expanse of Lake Torrens, to Wilpena Pound and round to cliffs thrust upward beside you. (A horizontal plaque on a plinth identifies the landmarks.)

Refreshment spots don't get much more scenic, so poke around for a while, watching fluffy clouds drift by, sometimes at eye level, or a peregrine falcon if you are really lucky, before moving on refuelled. Past the plaque and heading down the bluff's spine, the encircling summit panorama is replaced by a Quorn valley vista cut into pieces by tree trunks.

About 2km from the top you emerge from sugar gums and she-oaks onto a hillside flooded with grass trees. Swing right, past a fabulously gnarly old gum that begs to be hugged, and continue riding the ridge, down through taller eucalypts and Quorn wattles with acid yellow flower balls. Navigate narrow rock slides and dip into a folded gully before swinging left towards a wall of weather-resistant quartzite edged with plain.

Clinging to a slope running steeply down into Stony Creek gorge, the track fords several scree slopes, the largest extending to the creek bed, all mirrored by others flowing down the opposite gorge wall.

Alert walkers might glimpse a yellow-footed rock wallaby along here but there's no missing Quorn, which comes into view again through the branches of another old-man gum tree.

Putting the gorge behind you, the track swings left again, flattens out and undulates along the base of the bluff, now sitting high on your left shoulder.

Having traversed small clearings and shaly siltstone, walked through blue gums and crossed ephemeral creek gullies, you'll reach an information plinth. Ignore the vehicle-wide Heysen Trail on your right and keep to the narrower walking trail closer to Dutchmans Stern, crossing a couple more creeks before returning to the junction where you started uphill earlier. Turn right here and follow the track back to your car.

You can see for many kilometres from the top

5 MOUNT OHLSSEN-BAGGE

Walk:	7.6km return
Time required:	3 hours
Best time:	Mild sunny day; the Pound can be dangerously hot in summer
Grade:	Hard
Environment:	Gum-tree lined creek and steep, rocky cliffs
Best map:	This one
Toilets:	Flushing toilets at Wilpena Pound visitor centre
Food:	Coffee, treats, takeaway food and lunch supplies available at Wilpena Pound General Store, beside the visitor information centre; sit-down restaurant meals at adjoining Wilpena Pound Resort
Tips:	For the ultimate view of Wilpena Pound, splash out on a scenic flight over the remarkable formation. These can be booked at the Wilpena Pound visitor centre or through Wilpena Pound Resort.
	Vehicle entry fees are payable for Flinders Ranges National Park; you can purchase a single-park or multi-park pass; details at environment.sa.gov.au/parks/entry-fees.

Summiteers bask in the view from the top of Mt Ohlssen-Bagge

Part walk, part climb (no ropes required), this fun fitness test rewards participants with an eagle's-eye view of South Australian geology and mythology.

Geologists have a tough job in Australia, because Aboriginal creation stories frequently transcend even the most fascinating and intriguing tales of geological goings-on. There is no better example of this professional disadvantage than Wilpena Pound, the public face of Flinders Ranges National Park. How can 1500 million years of sedimentation, uplift and erosion compare with the Adnyamathanha story that the natural amphitheatre's walls are the petrified nose-to-tail bodies of two akurras (Dreaming serpents) that encircled an important corroboree and ate the participants?

Whatever its origins, Wilpena Pound is a remarkable creation. Viewing it from its rocky ramparts is bettered only by viewing it from above, on a scenic flight; and climbing Mt Ohlssen-Bagge is one of the most spectacular of 17 walks in and around the Pound. Rocky and very steep, Mt Ohlssen-Bagge suits sound-kneed adventurers of all ages, but the drops are precipitous and unfenced, so children should be closely supervised.

Like all Wilpena Pound walks, the Ohlssen-Bagge ascent starts at the trailhead behind the visitor information centre and flows west along Wilpena Creek on a formed track. Following posts rainbow-striped with track markers (Mt Ohlssen-Bagge is orange), cross the river-gum lined creek bed opposite the Wilpena Pound Resort buildings and turn left (west) onto a vehicular track beside a massive eucalypt many metres around its base.

Watch for green-and-yellow flashes of Mallee ringnecks (parrots) in the dense, dark creek-bed greenery as you pass the St Mary Peak track and an outcrop of red rock, both on the right, soon after which our walk veers left and crosses the creek again. Enjoy the flatness and shade along here because there'll be little of either from here on.

Climbing almost immediately, you'll pass the Drought Busters Walk on the right (this is also confusingly called the Boom and Bust Walk),

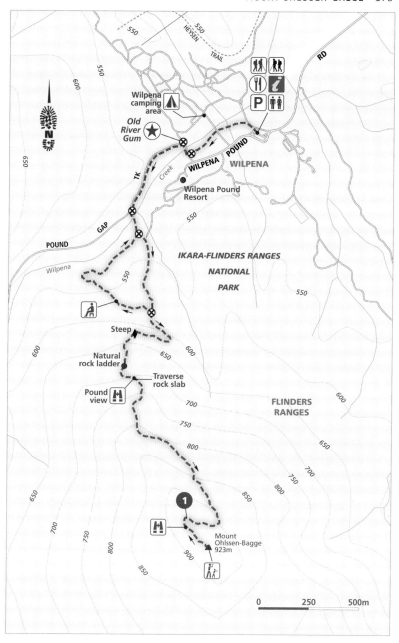

and emerge from leafy riparian cover below an intimidating yet inviting cliff of blocky red rock. Look up; your destination is right up there at the top.

Continuing through eucalypts, grass trees and other hardy plants, the rocky route climbs, levels out, climbs some more, and passes the other end of the Drought Busters Walk. It then swings left and down and around cliff-face through drooping she-oaks blackened by fire. With the change in direction comes an expansive view of the ABC Range to the east, often referred to as the backbone of the Flinders Ranges, and here you might also glimpse a light plane, or a wedge-tailed eagle surveying its hunting grounds from on high.

Stone steps clamber up to a false summit, reflectors showing the way to those who climb in the dark to witness dawn over the Flinders Ranges, or to descend after sunset. As you go you'll see Wilpena Pound Resort below, the access road winding through the plain and the narrow gap through which Wilpena Creek escapes and visitors enter the Pound.

Beyond the false summit, a natural rock ladder climbs steeply up the Pound wall; stone stained black by water can be slippery, even when there is no obvious wetness, so watch your step. To the west you can now see the Pound floor, tweedy-brown in the dry, greened with grass after good rains, and often patched with wildflowers. Still climbing, the track veers to the right of an angular jutting outcrop.

Enjoy a brief break from climbing as you hug the bluff's contours, with two rock tiers stepping up to your right and the ground dropping left to sprawling plains.

The grass trees, eucalypts and she-oaks here appear pruned – perhaps by the wind, or the heat.

You can tell male from female she-oaks by their winter–spring flowers. Females produce hairy, tufty red flowers while males grow cylindrical spikes that lend the shrubs a red hue. One of the acacia varieties here produces great spherical balls of yellow blossom 1.5cm in diameter.

Around the bluff, another steep climb marked with reflectors, black-and-yellow marker posts and occasional white arrows ends at a sign directing you left to Mt Ohlssen-Bagge (400m) (*see* point 1 on map).

The walk takes you up through rugged, weathered rock

The Pound floor and walls, and the Red Range beyond, come into view as you climb

This last stretch is uneven and traverses sloping rock, some of it crazed, some pimply, some wearing away in thin layers, but each step improving your view of the Pound's sawtooth encircling cliffs and the distinctively banded Red Range beyond the western wall.

There's no formal lookout up top, just rocks on which to sit or stand while appreciating the geological – and mythical – masterpiece wrapped around you; the ABC Range to the east; the Pound walls, rising to St Mary Peak – the head of one of the akurras and the highest point in the Flinders Ranges – and sloping down to a variegated plain; and the four ramparts of the Red Range. All drawn in the blues, purples, reds and greens that landscape artist Hans Heysen made famous.

When you've had enough of the view or just accept that you need to start back, retrace your steps to the top Drought Busters Track and follow this left. Read about this country's boom and bust life-cycles on interpretation panels as you descend through softer foliage to the creek's shady stands of river gums and cypress.

This interesting detour puts you back on the Ohlssen-Bagge track, where you swing left and head for home.

6 ROCKY RIVER TO SEA

Walk:	16.5km one-way
Time required:	5–6 hours
Best time:	Clear day; wildflowers are best in winter–spring, but there is usually something in bloom year round
Grade:	Moderate (a few hills, and uneven footing near the river mouth)
Environment:	Flowering heath, waterholes, cascades, eucalypt forest, river, gorge, ocean beach
Best map:	This one
Toilets:	Flushing toilets at Flinders Chase National Park visitor centre at the start of the walk; pit toilets in Snake Lagoon campground
Food:	Snacks, light fare and coffee are available from Chase Cafe in the park visitor centre; the nearest Kangaroo Island town for a range of food and supplies is Kingscote, 100km north-east
Tips:	You can fly to Kangaroo Island from Adelaide in a small plane (rex.com.au) and explore the island in a hire car, or take your own wheels on the ferry. SeaLink operates vehicular ferries between Cape Jervis, about 1.5 hrs' drive south of Adelaide, and Penneshaw, on Kangaroo Island's east coast. Passage must be booked (sealink.com.au). Travelling companions preferring less of a leg-stretch could meet you at the Snake Lagoon parking area for the wonderful short final leg of the walk; this would also save you doing a car shuffle.

Rocky River nears the sea

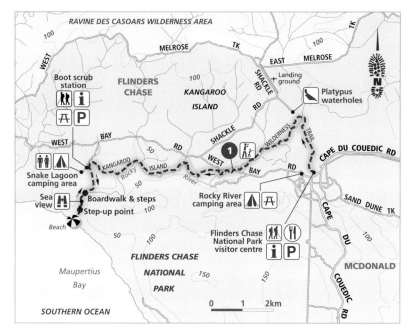

Follow the toffee-coloured Rocky River from tranquil waterholes where platypus paddle to a Southern Ocean beach where rogue waves lurk.

Wildlife haven, gourmet food destination, and simply gorgeous, Kangaroo Island – KI to its friends – is a wonderful place to walk. The latest addition to the network of trails to historic lighthouses, beaches and feature rocks is the Kangaroo Island Wilderness Trail. This multi-day hike takes in Admiral's Arch and the truly Remarkable Rocks on its 65km journey through national and conservation parks, wilderness and private property.

The day walk described here traces the first leg of the Wilderness Trail, which begins by following the Rocky River to its mouth. (The return Snake Lagoon Hike at the end, so-called even though there is no lagoon and snake encounters are rare – remain alert though! – is one of Australia's best short walks, and great fun on its own.)

The trail sets off from the trailhead information board behind the Flinders Chase National Park visitor centre, 100km southwest of Kingscote, the island's main town. Through a picket gate and past outdoor cafe tables you'll pick up the Rocky River Hike, which leads into leaf-littered eucalypt forest.

One of many interpretive signs early on suggests you search the tree tops for koalas. If you're lucky you might also spot an echidna trundling through the leaf litter as you tread a sealed track down to a lookout over Black Swamp. Ignoring side trails left and right, keep to boardwalk and gravel track through the swamp, which is often not very swampy but usually green, and dotted with beautiful grey Cape Barren geese. Many other birds frequent the reedy grasses and eucalypts, including cute scarlet robins.

The viciously spiked acacia (wattle) where the boardwalk ends are commonly called bugger bush! Continue through untidy eucalypts, tea-tree and bugger bush, stopping to clean your boots at a scrub station to limit the spread of cinnamon fungus. Amble on through yakkas (the South Australian name for grass trees), gum trees and orange flowering showy parrot pea bushes. You'll almost certainly see stalks of red common heath.

A massive bushfire ravaged this part of Flinders Chase National Park in 2007, and signs alert you to the regrowth since.

On reaching a junction decorated with delightful platypus sculptures, turn right and loop anticlockwise around the Platypus Waterhole Walk. Platypus are more easily glimpsed in the early morning and at dusk, but can show themselves at any time, so stand quietly for a while on the over-water lookouts watching for telltale bubbles, and a duck-billed head breaking the surface.

After crossing the main waterhole by footbridge you come to another junction, with Shackle Rd carpark to the right (to your left the old road is closed with a fence and beautiful rusty metal cut-out insect panel). Continue straight ahead through yakkas to another junction. Turn right off gravel onto the leafy Rocky River Hike trail, which meanders through melaleucas (paperbarks) – it can be a bit slippery in places – then steps from scruffy forest onto the edge of Black Swamp.

Clockwise from top: *Sculpted rock litters the beach where the Rocky River snakes into the sea; an echidna ambles through leaf litter along the Rocky River track; the track follows the river to the beach; yakkas grow tall along the Rocky River walk*

Across the river again – you'll see or hear it for much of this walk – continue through massed pea flowers, boronias, grevilleas, and other heath plants with spiky, serrated, elongated and furry leaves; through regrowth sapling gums; through damper eucalypt forest.

Turn right for Rocky River Hike at the next junction and follow the track through tall eucalypts to the Rocky River Bridge carpark. Turn right and walk over the vehicular bridge and immediately left back onto a foot track soft with compacted leaves. Walk on, with the river right beside you now, looking out for orchids and high-vis jelly fungi. (You'll see different types of fungi all along this walk.)

Having zigzagged – don't make or take short cuts! – up through old gums and many immature ones into yakkas, the track flattens out and becomes slightly rockier, but the walking is still easy. The tallest trees up here are only about 5m or so – it's as if they're not game to poke their heads any higher!

The track brings you to a lookout (see point 1 on map) perched on a limestone cliff high above the river. From this aerie you've got an easy descent into tall striped gums and through yakkas on fire-blackened trunks, many of which have miniature moss gardens growing on them. The track then traverses a hill dropping away to the river. This section is particularly pretty after rain, when the assorted leaves are very green and the birds twitter.

Descending again, you'll hear the river and cross a rock shelf; detour left along it to where Rocky River rushes down a slippery slope into a chicane. Then walk on through a guard of honour of prickly wattle.

After crossing a footbridge you've got a choice: left (dry season track) or right (wet season track). You can usually get through on the former, and the two options merge about 100m further on, so it's not far if you have to come back.

Moving away from the river now, you'll meander through flowering heath, eucalypts and yakkas to another junction, with the carpark and campground on the right. You'll return to this carpark, but for now turn left onto the Snake Lagoon Hike, and walk through some beautiful big sugar gums (the grassy area through the trees is the now-dry lagoon after which this walk is named).

A short, slightly rocky climb through mixed-age eucalypts and into massed acacias becomes a descent on a track growing lumpy with exposed limestone, through eucalypts with multiple trunks that almost look like they have been coppiced. Correas splash red through here in autumn and winter. Limestone gives way to compacted sand as you near the river.

The descent brings you to a crossing, a rocky area spanned with footbridges. A sign warning against crossing if there's water over the bridge seems to be stating the obvious! Cross if safe to do so – you can see down the river gorge towards the mouth as you slalom on rock and bridge – then climb the stone and wooden steps opposite.

Looking up, you might spot magnificent wedge-tailed eagles on the wing. Looking back, you'll see a cave in the limestone gorge wall you've just descended; limestone and greened sand dunes line the far bank.

Having climbed about 10m, the track returns to the river's edge and continues along the rocky shore through dense flowering shrubbery and succulent pigface that opens pink flowers to the sun. Black arrows and yellow markers show the way over grey rock slabs decorated with orange lichen; as you continue, you'll see the Southern Ocean and the natural chicane of upended stone ledges through, over and around which the river works its way seaward. The track skirts these rugged rapids, giving you a good look at the narrow bay where it runs into the sea and the limestone cliff opposite, which looks like it's dripping stone.

The track lands you on white sand between a honeycomb cliff and a pile of rocks, where the golden river – tea-tree tannin gives the water this gorgeous hue – snakes through another barrage of teeth-like rock to mix with blue ocean water. A sign warns of freak waves, and out-of-the-blue waves do rush up this beautiful bay, dumping unwary folk and cameras, so take care if you go further. It's worth it, though, to see the sculpted rock (points and curves shot through with quartz) further down the beach up close.

Have fun puddling around the river mouth before heading back up the hill to the parking area to finish.

7 WAITPINGA CLIFFS

Walk:	12.6km one-way
Time required:	4 hours
Best time:	Mild, sunny day; a stormy sky adds drama, but most of the walk is exposed and offers no protection, so it is much more challenging in wild weather
Grade:	Moderate
Environment:	Heath-capped sea cliffs, rocky bays, beaches
Best map:	*Heysen Trail Southern Guide (Book 1)*, available from Friends of Heysen [heysentrail.asn.au]; and this one
Toilets:	Waitpinga Beach carpark and Waitpinga campground
Food:	None
Tips:	For an all-day coastal experience, start further west, at Parsons Beach carpark, and walk about 1.5km along Waitpinga Beach to start, then continue beyond King Beach to Rosetta Head to finish

Live life on the edge for a few hours, walking along the heath-moustachioed lip of sea cliffs that plunge into Southern Ocean wash.

Early in its serpentine 1200km journey from the Fleurieu Peninsula to outback South Australia, the Heysen Trail navigates awesome sea cliffs, and this exhilarating one-way day walk on the trail follows the cliff-line from thumping surf beach to boulder-strewn bay.

Waitpinga Beach – a popular but unpatrolled surfing destination

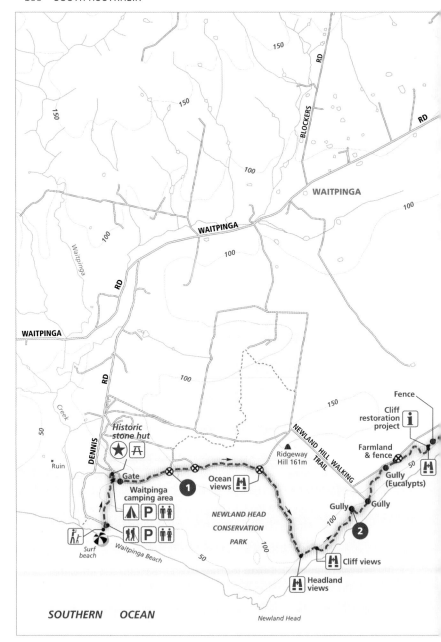

150

RD

150

BLOCKERS

RD

150

100

WAITPINGA

100

WAITPINGA

100

100

Waitpinga

100

RD

WAITPINGA

RD

100

150

NEWLAND HILL WALKING TRAIL

Fence

Cliff restoration project

ℹ️

Creek

Historic stone hut

★ 🅰

Ridgeway Hill 161m

Farmland & fence ⊗

50

50

Ruin

DENNIS

RD

Gate ⊗ ⊗

Ocean views 🔭

Gully (Eucalypts)

🔭

1

Waitpinga camping area

⛺ 🅿 🚻

NEWLAND HEAD

Gully

Gully

⊗

⚏ 🅿 🚻

CONSERVATION

100

2

50

🔭

Surf beach

Waitpinga Beach

PARK

100

Cliff views

50

Headland views

🔭

SOUTHERN   OCEAN

Newland Head

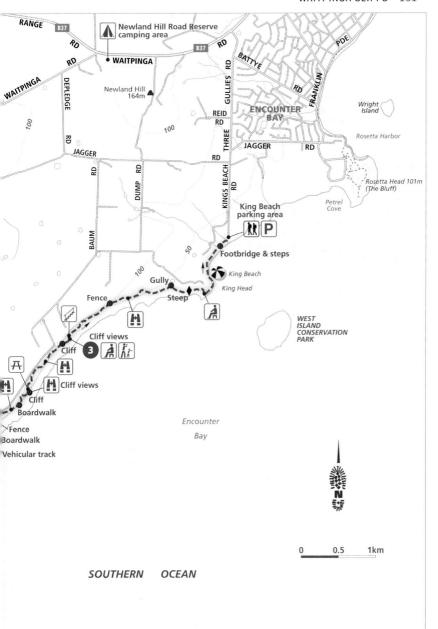

RANGE B37

RD

WAITPINGA   RD

DEPLEDGE   RD

Newland Hill Road Reserve
camping area

WAITPINGA

B37   RD

GULLIES   RD

BATTYE   RD

FRANKLIN   RD

PDE

Wright
Island

Newland Hill
164m

REID
RD

THREE   RD

ENCOUNTER
BAY

Rosetta Harbor

JAGGER   RD

JAGGER

RD

100

100

100

KINGS BEACH   RD

Rosetta Head 101m
(The Bluff)

DUMP   RD

BAUM

King Beach
parking area

Petrel
Cove

50

Footbridge & steps

Gully

King Beach

Fence

Steep

King Head

Cliff views   3

WEST
ISLAND
CONSERVATION
PARK

Cliff

Cliff views

Cliff

Boardwalk

Fence

Boardwalk

Vehicular track

Encounter

Bay

N

0   0.5   1km

SOUTHERN   OCEAN

The walking track snakes along the coast beyond the Waitpinga Cliffs

The adventure begins at Waitpinga Beach carpark, 16km west of Victor Harbor via Waitpinga Rd and Dennis Rd (both sealed), and ends at King Beach, 1km south of Encounter Bay, so you'll need to car shuffle or organise to be dropped off and picked up.

Waitpinga is a popular but hazardous unpatrolled surf beach, unsafe for swimming. Before starting up the walking track, on the landward side of the carpark, step out onto the elevated wooden walkway and take in the salty scene of swell, board riders, white sand and surf fishers casting for salmon, mulloway and mullet.

Then turn your back on the water, for now, and step up onto the narrow walking trail, at the top of the carpark, that noses through ground-hugging plants, including red-and-green Running Postman. The track becomes sandier as it climbs through taller shrubbery, but chained planks provide firmer footing through the dunes to Waitpinga campground.

The Heysen Trail (red-and-white markers) heads east a short way along bitumen through the campground, but first detour left to the two-room limestone 'hut' built in 1890 by the Dennis family, early settlers in the area. Off-road walking resumes at the eastern end of the campground, beyond a gate, in Newland Head Conservation Park, on a broad gravel track that climbs through mallee eucalypts, grass trees and broad-leaf grasses. Here the Heysen Trail overlaps the Ridgeway Hill and Coastal Cliffs loop walks.

Veer right onto a sandy track when the gravel swings left (see point 1 on map) and ignore another track coming in on an angle further up, still climbing through heath awash with native wisteria (*hardenbergia*), red-and-yellow bush pea, spidery red grevilleas, several shades of yellow wattle blossoms and massed, fairy floss-froths of common fringe myrtle late winter into spring.

Keep right on the Heysen Trail (and Coastal Cliffs walking trail) at the next junction, high enough now to see the ocean again. The blue stripe lengthens along the horizon as you tread a compacted red sand track seaward through eucalypts coming back from fire, their skeletal grey top branches reaching up from leafy saplings.

Forced left by a precipitous drop, the trail hugs the coast. Rising and falling, steeply in places but never for long, rocky in spots but not ankle-threateningly so, the track meanders east, slowing your feet with views down rock slopes to foaming water and along black-rock cliffs. From June to November keep watch for southern right whales on their annual migration.

The track barrels through areas of grass trees and gum trees, some laced with purple-pea climbers, but you are mostly in knee-high flowering heath on a trail that can be lined with gorgeous donkey orchids.

About 5.5km into the walk the trail dips into a gully (see point 2) thick with wattle and often humming with bees, soon after which the Coastal Cliffs Walking Trail loops left via the Ridgeway. Remain on the east-bound Heysen Trail, which threads inland and up through spread-limbed eucalypts to follow a farm fence for 100m or so.

Back near the cliff edge, you can read about the ongoing Waitpinga Cliffs Restoration Project. This involves replanting and anti-erosion measures along a strip of land between farmland and cliff that you traverse on walking trail, vehicular track and boardwalks. The last, short boardwalk runs directly towards a pace-slowing view of headlands, beach and Victor Harbor.

Beyond the restoration area (another sign marks its end) the track drops into a narrow gully down which registered rock climbers access the cliffs. Climbing out again puts you on the brink, with the ground plunging to the sea at your feet and near-vertical black cliffs ahead: millions of years of deposition and compression upended and seemingly leant against the shore by some great hand. This impressive defensive wall ends in a beach and a grassy headland topped with houses, just off which sits West Island (Conservation Park).

The Heysen Trail runs along the length of this most dramatic section of the Waitpinga Cliffs, often near the edge but sometimes pulling back for safety, and snaking through grassed areas, wattles and stands of eucalypts all twisted and bent over, their arm-like branches reaching out and low, as if for balance in a gale.

Watch for parrots in the trees and wedge-tailed eagles, nankeen kestrels and peregrine falcons patrolling the cliffs. If the bird-watching gods are feeling especially benevolent you might even see white-bellied sea eagles. The only breeding pair of these majestic aerial hunters on the Australian mainland between the Eyre Peninsula and central Victoria nest on the Waitpinga Cliffs.

Further on you come to arguably the best sited bench in Australia (see point 3). Ignore the footpad going left here (to a house that plays peek-a-boo through the trees) and continue down fenced steps and east, among more shapely gums and along the cliff. The track is narrow and rocky so take your time and enjoy the long-distance views and close-up heath details.

Exit Newland Head Conservation Park over a stile and keep along land's edge, following a fence steeply down to a small rock-strewn bay. You could easily lose an hour checking out the orange lichen-covered boulders, upended black rock and other stonework here.

The bench atop the next headland is a great spot to sit for a while, looking back along the cliff-line you trod, out to sea, and down at the linear rock beached below, like shipwreck timbers. It's an easy walk from here around the headland and down to King Beach, named after

English settler Eli King. Your car (or pickup) is now within easy reach, so how long you spend exploring this pretty beach is up to you – and your schedule.

Rosetta Head (The Bluff), from where Sir Hans Heysen did the sketches for his magnificent oil painting *The South Coast* (1926), is another 1.5km or so on foot along the coast, but the long-distance hiking trail named in honour of the famed landscape artist goes inland from the King Beach parking area, where this walk ends.

Clockwise from top: *Waves roll ashore on Waitpinga Beach; orange and yellow lichen embroiders rocks on King Beach; the spectacular Waitpinga Cliffs rear out of the ocean*

Coming down from on high on the Bibbulmun Track: the track parts a sea of wildflowers between Sullivan Rock and Monadnocks camping area

WESTERN AUSTRALIA

As well as headlining wildflower extravaganzas across the country, Australia's largest state shows off in other ways. Covering a staggering 2.6 million square kilometres, from the time-carved Kimberley region to damp forests along the Southern Ocean coast, it delivers hours of fun on foot. Stroll among some of the world's tallest trees, step out in goldfields history and delve into Earth's crust.

PERTH

1	Bluff Knoll	198
2	Cape to Cape Day Out	204
3	Cathedral Gorge Loop	212
4	Coalmine Beach to Treetops	217
5	Hellfire Bay to Lucky Bay	226
6	The Loop	234
7	Sullivan Rock to Monadnocks Campsite Loop	240
8	Wadjemup Walk Trail Loop	246
9	Warren River Loop	257
10	Weano & Hancock Gorges	262
11	Weir & Wildflowers	269

1 BLUFF KNOLL

Walk:	6.3km return
Time required:	3–4 hours
Best time:	Mild sunny day year round for views; August to November for wildflowers. Do not climb in wet and windy conditions.
Grade:	Moderate to hard (short but continuous climb)
Environment:	Flower-studded heathland, hardy montane forest, rocky slopes, precipitous cliffs, breathtaking views
Best map:	This one
Toilets:	Flushing toilets in carpark
Food:	None
Tips:	This walk is short but energetic, so carry drinking water and a snack. It also takes longer than the distance suggests, so allow time to descend before dark. Carry a torch if you intend to remain up top for sunset.
	Vehicle entry fees are payable at Stirling Range National Park; you can purchase a day entry pass (more than one park in a day) or multi-park pass; details at parks.dpaw.wa.gov.au/know/fees.

Rugged mountains make way for a glimpse of plain from Bluff Knoll

An extravagant array of wildflowers, rugged mountains and patchwork plains reward your efforts on this short, sharp climb to the highest point in southern Western Australia.

Western Australia's annual wildflower extravaganzas attract travellers from across Australia and overseas. One of the state's many floral hot spots is Stirling Range National Park, home to 1500 flowering plant species, some 80 of which are unique to this area.

Scaling Bluff Knoll (1095m), the easternmost of 20 or so jagged peaks in the uplifted and buckled sedimentary Stirling Range, provides an opportunity to tick off a few more blooms while enjoying gobsmacking views of the Great Southern region.

The summit assault begins in a carpark that doubles as a lookout and picnic area, atop a rise at the foot of the Bluff, 90km north of Albany via Chester Pass Rd. Metal and stone steps lead down from a

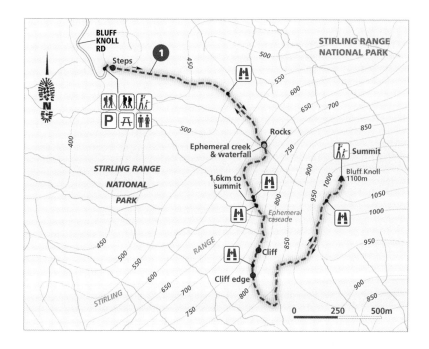

shady information shelter with benches on which the less adventurous could sit and admire the mountain while others climb it.

The track initially descends, a sealed red ribbon threaded through tea-tree, grass trees and gravel bottlebrush with spiky leaf stalks and elegantly drooping red bottlebrush flowers. Mountain bells may put on a show too. [Ten species of darwinias grow in Western Australia, only one of which is found outside the Stirling Range.] Gently rub one of

Drooping red bottlebrush frame the crown of Bluff Knoll

the smooth-barked eucalypts with a powdery white finish and you'll uncover beautifully coppery bark beneath.

The bitumen ends where a well-formed unsealed track starts climbing (see point 1 on map), with steeply sloping rock above and below. Gaining height gives you increasingly spectacular views of other park peaks, including the chipped pyramidal Mt Toolbrunup (another great walk), and glimpses of Bluff Knoll's jagged crown through the trees.

Stopping to look over the park is a legitimate excuse to catch your breath on the unrelenting climb, but don't follow any rough footpads off the main trail – the cliff edges threaten limb and life.

A kilometre into the walk the track clambers up a cascade of grey rock to an ephemeral waterfall, the way marked with yellow boot prints on blue metal triangles. If there's water, you may see birds splashing about in the pools. Trees up to 10m tall make this one of few shady spots on the walk.

Climbing a little less steeply now, you cross below a layered red cliff, with the top of Bluff Knoll over your left shoulder and views unfurling to your right. It can feel like you have walked much further, but you soon come to a sign marking 1.6km to the summit.

A rock slide has cleared plants here, opening a grandstand view of sharp peaks, saddles and layered, upended bluffs rising from patchworked plains. On a clear day you'll see the granite domes of the Porongorups to the south-west. Cars on the rise below look like Matchbox toys.

The track now does a sweeping U-bend up man-made and natural steps, passing mossy grey rock sometimes trickling with water and an overhanging rock face studded with quartz and patched with shale. This manoeuvre takes you up into fragile montane forest and to the very edge of the cliffs. About 1km from the top you come to a sign warning you to stop and check the weather.

The local Aboriginal name for the Stirling Range, Koi Kyenunu-ruff, approximates to 'mist rolling around the mountains', and it often does. Rapid, unexpected deteriorations in conditions are common up here, with dramatic drops in temperature, rain, hail and reduced visibility catching out the unwary and unprepared. Bluff Knoll is one of the few

The car park is a tiny dot with a tail when seen from the precipitous edge of Bluff Knoll

places in Western Australia to receive snowfalls. If in any doubt, don't proceed any further.

The steepness of the track lessens as it swings around to the left, through a saddle, and presents you with your first proper view south, over farmland to the Southern Ocean. Explorer Matthew Flinders was sailing along that coast, early in 1802, when he made the first recorded European sighting of the Stirling Ranges, a chain of rugged mountains eight leagues (44km) inland. He named the easternmost peak, also the tallest, Mount Rugged, subsequently renamed Bluff Knoll.

Rocky now, with natural steps, the track scrabbles through exposed, domed rocks peering out of montane forest, a shallow sea of plants equipped to survive the climatic extremes at this altitude. In spring these hardy plants burst into yellow, orange, white and red flowers, almost as if celebrating having survived winter. There's even a dwarf banksia.

Dieback (cinnamon fungus), fires and grazing have contributed to the loss of several montane species once common on Bluff Knoll. The small fenced area you pass is part of restoration research, and keeps native quokkas and introduced rabbits from grazing on plants.

A few hundred metres more of rocky ridgeline and you are up top, taking in a jaw-dropping 360° view of mountains, ocean and plain. Only from up here do you realise that the Stirling Range is a rocky island thrust up from a sea of productive farmland, patchworked with high-vis yellow canola in late winter–spring. A refuge for indigenous flora and fauna – and walkers with the legs for it.

The return hike to the carpark is quicker than the ascent, but a knee trembler.

The Stirling Range is a rocky island thrust up from a sea of productive farmland

2 CAPE TO CAPE DAY OUT

Walk:	26.7km one-way
Time required:	8–10 hours
Best time:	Any time; spring for a wildflower spectacular
Grade:	Moderate to hard (very long, with a few steep climbs)
Environment:	White ocean beaches, surf, heath-capped sea cliffs, coastal town, cave, wildflowers, river mouth
Best map:	WA's Department of Environment and Conservation's *Walk the Cape to Cape Track #1 map*, 1:50,000, available from the Friends of the Cape to Cape Track (capetocapetrack.com.au)
Toilets:	Pit toilets at Conto Field and Redgate Beach; flushing loos at Prevelly (walk's end)
Food:	The Margaret River region is foodie heaven – indulge!
Tips:	*The Cape to Cape Track Guidebook* is as invaluable to day walkers as end-to-enders; it details the walk north to south, but also gives hints for those walking in reverse. Copies are available online at Friends of the Cape to Cape Track (capetocape.com.au).
	You'll need to car shuffle to do this walk, or book a Margaret River taxi to take you from Pevelly to the start. Take binoculars, especially in whale-watching season.

The Indian Ocean pounds Western Australia's south-west shoreline

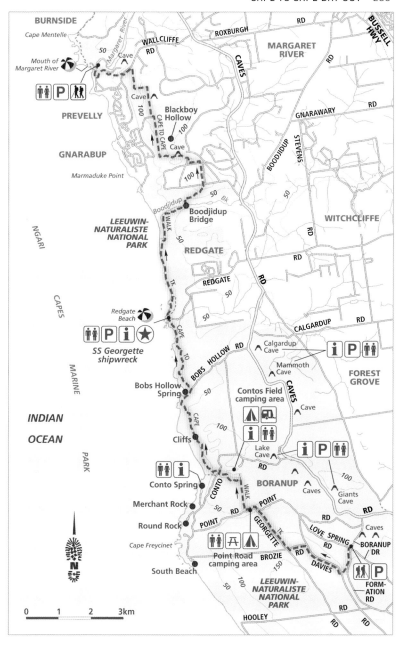

BURNSIDE

Cape Mentelle

Mouth of
Margaret River

WALLCLIFFE
RD

Cave

ROXBURGH
RD

RD

BUSSELL
HWY

CAVES

MARGARET
RIVER

50

Margaret River

PREVELLY

Cave

Blackboy
Hollow

CAPE TO CAPE

100

GNARAWARY

RD

GNARABUP

Cave

BOODJIDUP

STEVENS

RD

Marmaduke Point

100

Boodjidup
Bridge

50 Bk

50

WITCHCLIFFE

LEEUWIN-
NATURALISTE
NATIONAL
PARK

Boodjidup

WALK

50

REDGATE

RD

NGARI

CAPES

Redgate

RD

RD

50

TK

CALGARDUP   RD

Redgate
Beach

CAPE

SS Georgette
shipwreck

TO

BOBS HOLLOW   RD

Calgardup
Cave

Mammoth
Cave

i P

FOREST
GROVE

MARINE

Bobs Hollow
Spring

50

Contos Field
camping area

CAVES

Cave

INDIAN

OCEAN

100

CAPE

Cliffs

TO

Lake Cave

i P

PARK

Conto Spring

CONTO

RD

Merchant Rock

Round Rock

POINT

50

RD

POINT

WALK

POINT

Lake
Cave
RD

Caves

BORANUP

100

Giants
Cave

RD

Cape Freycinet

Point Road
camping area

South Beach

GEORGETTE

TK

BROZIE

RD

LEEUWIN-
NATURALISTE
NATIONAL
PARK

50   100

150

LOVE SPRING
RD

DAVIES

RD

RD

Caves

BORANUP
DR

P

FORM-
ATION
RD

HOOLEY

RD

RD

N

0   1   2   3km

Catch the Cape to Cape Track bug by treading from tall timbers to river mouth along this gorgeous coast on a big – and great – day out.

Strung along Western Australia's south-west coast, between the Margaret River wine region and the equally famous surf that breaks off gorgeous beaches and plunging cliffs, the Cape to Cape Track is one of Australia's great multi-day walking trails.

Some people feast on the track, treading the full 135km from Cape Naturaliste to Cape Leeuwin, where the Indian and Southern oceans collide, over a week; others savour the remote beaches, heath-capped headlands, tall timbers and coastal towns along the track in smaller helpings, doing shorter overnight hikes and day walks down the spine

This cave, one of many in the limestone that caps the ridge, frames a very blue ocean view

of Leeuwin-Naturaliste National Park. You can also do guided or self-guided accommodated walks with private outfits; there are links on the Friends of the Cape to Cape Track website.

This long day walk, from regrowth karri forest to the mouth of the Margaret River, showcases the diversity of the Cape to Cape Track (C2C).

The walk starts at a junction tucked into karri forest about 25km south-west of Margaret River town. Turn west off Caves Rd onto unsealed Boranup Rd about 3km south of Conto Rd, and park where Boranup Rd turns hard left (south-east). You're on foot from here, walking south-west and slightly uphill along 4WD-only Formation Rd, passing Love Spring Rd on the right.

Continue for almost 1km through regrowth karris often noisy with ringneck parrots, turning right at the first junction. A short and slight descent lands you on Davies Rd, which here doubles as the C2C. Walk north through forest striped with shadows on sunny days. The bull banksias – they're the ones with thick, saw-toothed leaves – produce cylindrical pale yellow flowers up to 40cm long in spring and summer.

After passing through Point Road Campsite, in a shady peppermint grove, you'll reach a four-way junction. Take the gated 4WD track on the right and follow it for about 1km uphill before stepping left off it again onto a foot track. (The vehicular track continues into Conto Campground, where you should begin this walk if you don't fancy the tall timber warm up; this shortens the hike by about 6km.)

Turn left at the next junction, about 500m along, onto another 4WD track (Conto Campground is signed right) and follow this to wide, unsealed Conto Rd, which accesses Cape Freycinet cliffs and beaches. The C2C continues about 60m to the right, along Conto Rd. Follow this well-signed narrow foot track through coastal heath made up of as many shades of green as there are shapes and sizes of leaves, to a cliff-edge high above the Indian Ocean. This is a great whale-watching spot from June to early December, the best time being October–November, when the wildflowers are also out.

Humpback whales cruise this coast on their annual migration north from Antarctica to breed. You might also see southern right whales closer in. Dolphins are seen year round, often travelling in large pods and sometimes surfing the waves – a real treat!

No distracting whales? You've still got gorgeous rocky bays below, edged with footprint-free sand and water that's a dozen shades of blue, lifting into perfect rollers.

Continue along the coast through heath that in spring is stitched pink, red, white, yellow and purple; something flowers here most times of the year. In places along the C2C the shrubbery is so tightly interwoven you'd struggle to push through it if you had to make a new trail. Look out for splendid and red-winged fairy-wrens and stumpy tail lizards.

Check out the rocks on your left where the track becomes rougher and rockier; you might spot bolts and other climbing paraphernalia. You get a view of these popular rock-climbing cliffs as you start down steps towards the beach.

This brings you to a broad, shallow cave whose mouth frames an ocean view, and which echoes with the *thwump* of unseen waves into the rocks below. This is one of many caves (both open and underground) in the limestone that caps the Leeuwin-Naturaliste Ridge's granite base; you shouldn't leave the Margaret River region without visiting nearby Lake Cave, even if you've been to lots of limestone caves. Few sights compare with this cave's 'suspended table' formation reflected in permanent water.

The track descends to another set of rocks below the cave, at the base of which is the now dry Bob's Hollow Spring.

Follow the track to a lovely grove of melaleucas (paperbarks). You might see long-billed Baudin's black-cockatoos (white cheeks and white tail detail) and red-tailed black cockatoos as you clamber up layered rock.

On top you'll enter a maze of sandy 4WD tracks that demands watchfulness for track markers (these are maintained by the Friends of the Cape to Cape Track). Essentially, you need to hug the coast, so if you come to an unsigned junction, keep left. Safely through, on a clear day you'll see Redgate Beach carpark ahead.

Clockwise from top: *Dangers await off the coast at the Margaret River mouth; pink sea urchin shells litter Redgate Beach; grass trees poke flower stalks skyward on the cliff-top walk towards the river mouth; the ocean has carved fantastic rock formations along this coast*

Turn left at the next T-intersection (there's a C2C sign) and walk down towards the sea on a 4WD track that becomes quite steep. Again, there are multiple tracks, so keep to the main one here and look for markers.

You'll have fabulous views and pass a shady informal camping area (C2C hikers are permitted to camp anywhere along the track so long as it is well away from road/vehicular access) as you tread a narrow trail through dunes to the beach. Walk north to the end of the sand and follow a walking trail to the carpark (there are toilets here). You're over halfway into the walk now.

In 1876, the leaking SS *Georgette* drifted into Calgardup Bay and started breaking up off Redgate Beach. Alerted by her family's indigenous stockman, Sam Yebbie Isaacs, 16-year-old Grace Bussell offered to help, and the pair rode their horses repeatedly into the surf to rescue survivors. Their efforts earned them bravery medals and Grace the nickname 'Australia's Grace Darling'. (England's Grace rescued shipwreck victims in the Farne Islands in 1838.)

The C2C drops onto the main beach from the top end of the carpark. Walk north along the sand and over rocks onto a long sweep of sloping sand. You'll stay on the beach for the next 2.5km or so, and it's lovely on a sunny day; just hope (or plan) for low tide, because it can be a bit of a slog treading the soft sand higher up.

Cockies Tongues splash red along the Cape to Cape in spring

Redgate Beach can be littered with pink sea urchin shells: red and furry when fresh from the water; hard, pink and hairless after longer exposure.

As you stroll north, with any luck you'll see Boodjidup Brook coming through the dunes ahead (sometimes barely a trickle in summer). Don't cross the brook. Leave the beach before the brook on a sandy footpad (there's a sign); this climbs steeply into the dunes to overlook the brook and sea, then slogs up another hill. Easier walking on a firmer track takes you up the brook's lush valley to Boodjidup Bridge.

Cross the bridge and catch your breath on the shaded bench here, for the track now climbs steeply, up 350 steps. (There's another bench, with a view, part way up.) From the top you can look out to sea and over a handful of houses nestled in the hills' green thatch.

The track continues more gently uphill and then down to cross a 4WD track (Blackboy Hollow Rd). Continue on a narrow foot track through massed grass trees, particularly spectacular when sporting flower spikes pointing skyward, turning 90° from vertical and coiling like corkscrews. You'll probably also see kangaroo paw, Western Australia's floral emblem.

Work your way through Blackboy Hollow, looping left, behind a ridge, on foot track and 4WD management tracks (you'll really appreciate the official map for this section). Then turn right onto a track running north, up a ridge to a communications tower.

It's late in the day and you're nearly there so take it easy on this 1.2km climb; stop to catch your breath and enjoy the spectacular view south to Cape Freycinet. The holiday village of Prevelly lounges between you and the sea now.

The track doglegs at the tower and continues north, then turns hard left and right again, bringing you to Wallcliffe Rd, which enters Pevelly. Swing left onto a cycle path and cross the road, taking the narrow track going right off the cycle path; this is Pevelly Old Rd.

You get beautiful views of river and ocean on this final descent to the mouth of the Margaret River, where the walk ends.

3 CATHEDRAL GORGE LOOP

Walk:	4.5km loop
Time required:	3 hours
Best time:	Mild winter's day; the park is open only in the dry (winter) season, usually April to November but dates vary with weather conditions. Daytime winter temperatures can still reach 40°C, which dictates what you do and when, and nights drop below 0°C.
Grade:	Easy to moderate (mostly flat, but with a couple of short ladders)
Environment:	Dome formations and rocky corridors; exposed, dry river bed; cool, shady cavern
Best map:	This one
Toilets:	Pit toilet at Piccaninny Creek carpark
Food:	Soft drinks, bottled water and packet snacks at visitor centre at park entry
Tips:	Visitors must carry in food and water, as in-park supplies are extremely limited.
Vehicle entry fees are payable for Purnululu National Park; you can purchase a day entry pass (more than one park in a day) or multi-park pass; details at parks.dpaw.wa.gov.au/know/fees/
Splurge on a helicopter flight over the deeply incised Bungle Bungle Range (helispirit.com.au); it's money well spent, and the extra thrill of flying without a door is free!

Nothing says 'the Kimberley' as unambiguously as the striped beehive domes in Purnululu National Park

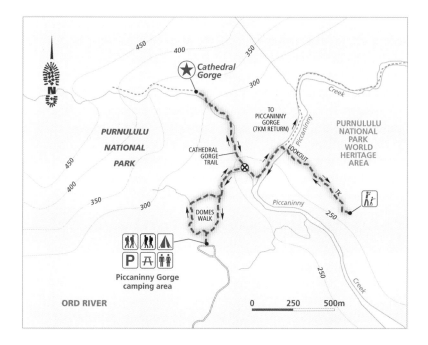

A Kimberley degustation, this remote walk will give you a taste for beehive domes, sinuous gullies, monolithic natural sculptures and sun-loving flora and fauna.

Nothing says 'the Kimberley' more unambiguously than the towering, striped beehive domes of the Bungle Bungle Range, in Purnululu National Park. The Bungle Bungles, as most people call the range, is a mass of these sandstone and conglomerate formations, a product of aeons of deposition, weathering, erosion and cracking, stowed well off the bitumen. They stand shoulder to shoulder or separated by fantastic gorges, most of which funnel summer flood waters and some of which only a few Aboriginal men are permitted to enter. (The park is jointly managed by WA's Department of Parks and Wildlife and Kimberley Aboriginal people, whose Dreaming includes stories about these ancient rocks.)

This walk, combining three shorter trails, reveals the extraordinary physicality, and hints at the spirituality, of this natural artwork.

Purnululu National Park is about 300km south of Kununurra. The last 53km in from the Great Northern Hwy are rocky, sandy and corrugated, and navigable only by high-clearance 4WD vehicles and off-road trailers. This stretch can take a measly 90 minutes, but yarns about journeys of more than three hours are campfire classics.

Purnululu was a cattle property before it was gazetted a national park in 1987 – World Heritage listing came in 2003 – and the access track winds through private stations, traversing and rounding lower hills to reach the range hidden behind.

The walk starts at Piccaninny Creek carpark, 27km from the park visitor centre and ranger station, and 15km beyond Walardi Campground, the southernmost of two public camping areas. (You can glamp in the park at APT's Bungle Bungle Wilderness Lodge, kimberleywilderness.com.au, and East Kimberley Tours' Bungle Bungle Bush Camp, eastkimberleytours.com.au.) The drive to the creek carpark is stunning and will often tempt you to stop roadside, outside the designated pull-over spots, for photographs.

Leave the parking area on the signed Cathedral Gorge Trail but turn off it a short way along onto the Domes Walk. This easy 1km detour loops through mounds of spinifex and iconic sandstone beehive domes, so close you could touch the individual sedimentary layers and distinctive red and black stripes – but don't!

The dark rock has a higher clay content, so better retains moisture, which suits cyanobacteria, primitive organisms that colonise the surface, forming a thin protective crust that reduces erosion. More porous, so too dry for cyanobacteria, the paler bands are more exposed to the oxidisation – or 'rusting' – that gives Bungle Bungle sandstone its red colour.

You'll probably see fittingly striped peaceful doves and double barred finches as you wander through here.

Turn left when the loop runs back into the Cathedral Gorge Trail. Follow this longer trail through water-sculpted dry creek beds, past perfect beehive domes usually crowned with boastfully blue sky, and along the foot of sandstone cliffs weathered into honeycomb slabs. It's fairly easy walking most of the way, but sandy rock slopes can be slippery.

The track funnels you down a narrowing corridor between twin walls of rounded red rock, where you'll climb two short ladders. Then it opens into a lofty natural amphitheatre carved out of the range.

The sculptor is the waterfall that pours down the wall in the wet season, and trickles in winter, painting a broad stripe on the sandstone suggestive of a retablo. The gorges and pieces of sky framed by the cathedral 'door' look like stained glass, too, so don't be surprised if you find yourself whispering!

For much of the walk here you are in full sun, and Cathedral Gorge provides welcome refuge from the heat on warm days. It's a beautiful place to linger for quiet contemplation, or to test the acoustics with a song.

Emerging from the shade, backtrack down the sandstone corridor into more open spinifex country. Pass the Domes Walk track and ignore the track heading back to the carpark, instead following signs

Cathedral Gorge is a lofty natural amphitheatre carved out of the Bungle Bungle Range

Piccaninny Creek dries to a wide crazy paving of creased stone

to Piccaninny Creek Lookout. These lead to Piccaninny Creek, a wet-season torrent that dries to a wide crazy paving of creased, almost finger-like pink-grey sandstone that reflects sunlight back at you.

A moderate all-day 7km return hike up the creek would bring you to the entrance to Piccaninny Gorge. Adventurous, well-prepared hikers with navigational skills – there is no marked track – can venture deeper into the heart of the Bungle Bungle Range and explore the gorge over several days.

Resisting this temptation – minimal in hot weather – turn right onto the Lookout Track about 300m upstream and follow it about 700m through striped stonework to an elevated vantage point. The sandstone here bookends a pastel-hued vista of Piccaninny Creek snaking south across the plain towards a standalone colony of beehive domes.

You won't miss flashy enamel-red Sturt's desert peas blooming along here, but look out for less flamboyant Sturt's desert roses (pink with a dark red centre). Beautiful rainbow bee-eaters gleam like bronze darts as they pluck insects from the air.

Retrace your steps to Piccaninny Creek, then follow the signs back to the carpark.

4 COALMINE BEACH TO TREETOPS

Walk:	27.8km one-way
Time required:	2 days
Best time:	Any time; the wettest months are May to August, when temperatures can drop to single figures
Grade:	Moderate
Environment:	Coastal heath, red tingle forest, mountain river
Best map:	WA's Department of Environment and Conservation *Bibbulmun Track Map 7 Walpole*; purchase at bibbulmuntrack.org.au
Toilets:	Flushing toilets in Coalmine Beach carpark and Treetops Walk; composting toilet at Frankland River
Food:	Supplies, snacks and meals in Walpole; cold drinks, ice-creams and treats in the Valley of the Giants Tree Tops Walk cafe
Tips:	You can lengthen day one of this walk by starting at the visitor centre in Walpole, and following the Bibbulmun from there to Coalmine Beach via Walpole Inlet; this adds a flat, 3km warm-up through the pretty Collier Creek Wetlands, which flood with wildflowers winter into spring.
	Book a trail transfer at naturallywalpole.com.au to save a car shuffle; cars can be left in the Tree Tops Walk carpark.
	The distances shown on the profile diagram are less accurate than the distance table on the official map; the distance on day one recorded by the author with GPS and given here differs by about 1.5km from the official map.

This walk is all about the trees that tower over you

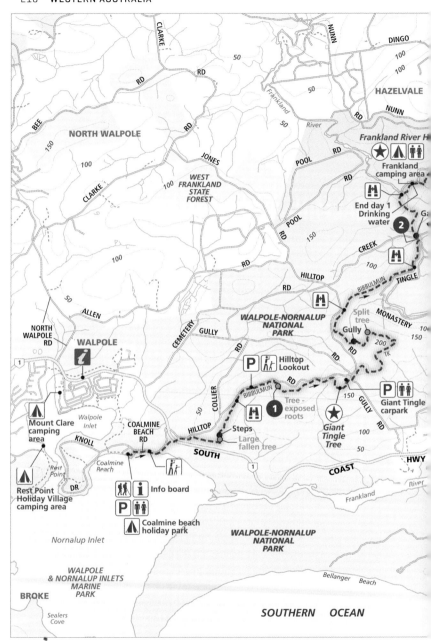

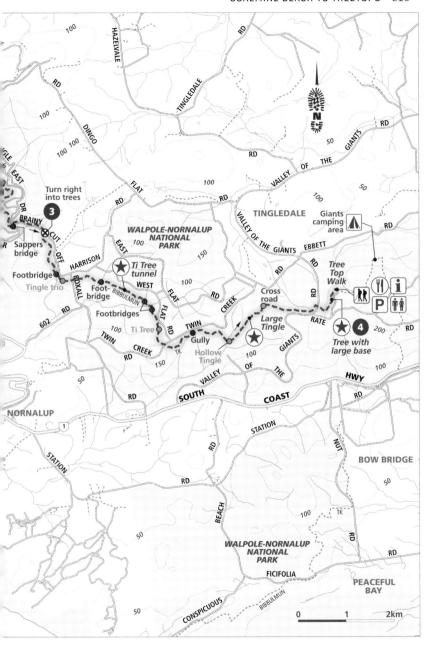

This two-day pack walk from tranquil inlet to forest canopy is all about Western Australia's tall timbers, none more imposing than the colossal red tingle.

Reaching heights of 70m and girths of 24m, red tingles are not just any old trees. One of Australia's 700-plus varieties of eucalypt, these colossi look like they could up-root and walk: the inspiration for J.R.R. Tolkien's *Lord of the Rings*, perhaps, although their rough, furrowed and stringy bark is more suggestive of Chewbacca from *Star Wars*. This two-day leg of the 1000km Bibbulmun Track, in Walpole-Nornalup National Park, immerses you in the fantastical world of *Eucalyptus jacksonii*.

DAY 1: 14.8KM – 4–5 hours

The walk starts at the eastern end of Coalmine Beach carpark, 3.5km south of Walpole, via South Coast Hwy and Coalmine Beach Rd, where a well-signed trail burrows into oft-flowering coastal scrub beside the ramp road to Nornalup Inlet jetty. Having welcomed you to the Bibbulmun Track with a view of the inlet and the dunes that shelter it from the Southern Ocean, the trail goes bush again through the information shelter in the Delaney Lookout layby.

Swing away from the shore and dogleg left and right at two well-marked adjacent junctions amid rough-trunked eucalypts and grass trees. Then turn right at the next junction onto a gravel track leading to the South Coast Hwy. Cross with care and enter thick, green forest on a track spongy with leaf litter and often festooned with the creamy flowers of karri, the tall, elegant eucalypts that surround you here. Reaching heights of 80m, the karri is one of the world's tallest trees.

Ignoring a marginally wider track on the right, descend through mature karri, some of them several metres around, as well as younger specimens.

Here, you are treading both the Bibbulmun Track and the Munda Biddi Trail, an off-road cycling trail running 1000km from Mundaring Weir (*see* p. 269), in the Perth hills, to Albany, on WA's south coast.

Moss and lichen cloaks the rocks along the Frankland River

The Bibbulmun soon breaks left off the cycling trail and starts climbing. Just around a corner you'll meet your first red tingle.

There are both troll-like tingles and elegant karris through here, and the first of many fallen giants breaking down under attack by pretty mosses, lichens and fungi. The tingles darken the forest atmosphere.

The steepest climb on the walk takes you 1.5km up to Hilltop Lookout, which presents a spectacular view of Nornalup Inlet and the ocean. There's a road to the lookout, so you may have to share the view with people who've taken the easier option!

Walk on, uphill, passing a rotten, hollow tree balanced on a few remnants of bark but still alive. The Bibbulmun then flattens slightly through eucalypt saplings and elders; some have lost their tops, others fallen and started to rot away. The forest is noisy with birds.

Walk the length of a fallen tingle (see point 1 on map), then swing around its base, a natural roomy amphitheatre of ripped-out roots blackened inside by fire. A smaller fallen tree further on, sawn to clear the track, is covered in leathery grey and yellow shelf fungi.

Walk through a junction, where a carpark is marked 200m to the left, and continue to a boardwalk (slippery after rain) around a pair of huge tingles. The first is a great lump, trunk and branches bumpy with burls. The second is the Giant Tingle, estimated to be centuries old and standing tall on widespread buttresses. Historic photographs

Even the signs go green in this damp forest

show cars parked inside, but compaction of the soil damages the trees' shallow roots, so that is no longer permitted. You can still walk through the cavernous hollow, though.

From the bottom of the boardwalk, zigzag up a sealed track to the Hollow Butte Tree (on the right). A hundred metres or so further up the sealed track to your left there are toilets in the Giant Tingle carpark. About 40m to the right, off the main track, on a rougher trail that burrows into the forest beside the hollow tree, you come to a reassuring Bibbulmun marker. Cross a gravel road and follow the track through karris and tingles – one unusual specimen has twin trunks.

On reaching a vehicle-wide track, turn right and follow it down and up through more open forest. Some of the older trees are hollowed and blackened, some have lost their tops, some lift twisted branches above the lower canopy or reach over the track. Most of these old timers are tingles, but there are also karris, she-oaks and other trees, many entwined with a star-like white climber.

Be prepared to divert around, duck under, step over and push through fallen trees and branches as you head down the side of a hill, on a track whose edges are softened with maidenhair fern. Going straight on where an equally wide track comes up on the right – here you again share the route with the Munda Biddi cycling trail – you'll glimpse a creek below to the right, reflecting blue sky on a sunny day. You'll hear and then see a small cascade.

Just before the road swings right and crosses over the creek, follow the Bibbulmun left and up. It climbs briefly, then snakes through forest, crossing an unsealed road and coming to a gate (*see* point 2). The track continues through she-oaks, eucalypts and the day's first grass trees and then you're back among mixed-age tingles.

An encouraging view of river, through trees, eases your passage down the final descent to the Frankland River hut and camping area, the favourite of many Bibbulmun Track hikers – as you'll discover reading the visitor book.

When the river is low you can rock-hop up and downstream and have a refreshing swim, but when it's running you've got a sudden drop-off into the water just below the hut. And if the river is thick with foam and looks like someone has emptied washing powder into it, don't despair at humankind's thoughtlessness. This is a natural phenomenon, resulting when decaying organic matter releases surfactants that break the surface tension, allowing more air to mix with the water and produce froth.

A hundred metres or so beyond the hut, where the Bibbulmun swings right, away from the water, footpads through the riparian scrub lead to rapids and natural pavements patchworked with moss. This is a lovely spot to sit and watch last light on the river before dinner.

DAY 2: 13KM – 3–5 hours

On day two you'll ford creeks and cross and dogleg over vehicular tracks, but not every junction is signed. Keep going in the direction you are heading on the trail/track you are following unless a Bibbulmun sign directs you elsewhere.

Start by heading downstream again, but this time ignore the footpads to the rapids and instead climb away from the river. There can be lots of spiders' webs early morning here, so send the tallest member of your party ahead to clear the way! The climbing shrub with flashy red and orange pea flowers all through here is heart-leaf flame pea.

You've got ups and downs early on today, through eucalypt forest, tea-tree and clusters of grass trees. About 3km in, wooden log steps and wooden planks lead down to an unsealed road and Sappers Bridge, a vehicle-wide wooden bridge over the Frankland River open only to hikers and cyclists.

Cross the bridge and turn right onto Brainy Cut Off, a compacted track that climbs, but only just, through red tingles, their branches forming an open yet still cathedral-like canopy; the going is easy after the earlier undulations.

About 700m up from the bridge, turn right off the road onto a walking track (see point 3) that descends through native pines to the tinkle of a creek you cross by a footbridge. Across another gravel road, the track weaves through a trio of adjacent tingles, and repeats this morning's ups and downs. The forest twitters with birds, so stop and watch for movement and splashes of colour.

Enjoy the views over Nornalup Inlet from Coalmine Beach before plunging into the forest

Over another unsealed road – there are more roads than are marked on the official Bibbulmun map, so working out where you are can be confusing – you'll pass a fallen red tingle with a massive root ball. The track then navigates two gullies separated by yet another vehicular track; a creek runs through the second, wider gully, so your feet might get wet here.

After a long steady ascent through remarkable trees and a couple more track and road crossings, you're on the last leg of the walk, the star of which is a remarkable tree (*see* point 4), lumpy and burnt about 4m up and then narrower and smooth, so it looks almost like an arboreal telescope.

Ignore the side trail going left down to a picnic area and carpark and continue through trees offering between-trunk glimpses of road signs (you'll be able to hear cars too). A formed gravel track comes out into the Treetops Walk carpark beside a tingle hollowed with age – because you haven't had enough of these giants!

Want even more? Do the Tree Tops Walk before heading off, for a canopy-level perspective on Western Australia's arboreal giants.

5 HELLFIRE BAY TO LUCKY BAY

Walk:	7.7km one-way
Time required:	3 hours
Best time:	Dry weather (rock can be slippery when wet)
Grade:	Moderate
Environment:	Granite domes and slopes, costal heath, wildflowers, rocky bays, white sand beaches
Best map:	This one
Toilets:	Pit toilets at Hellfire Bay and Lucky Bay
Food:	None
Tips:	Allow time for beachcombing at both ends of the walk, and perhaps to cook up a barbecue breakfast at Hellfire Bay before starting.
	You need to car shuffle, and have a vehicle at both bays, or arrange a drop-off and pick-up to do this walk as described.
	Vehicle entry fees are payable for Cape Le Grand National Park; you can purchase a day entry pass (more than one park in a day) or multi-park pass; details at parks.dpaw.wa.gov.au

Clamber over granite domes and leave footprints on pristine white beaches on this land's-end walk along Western Australia's spectacular and sometimes wild southern coast.

Rocky rises and bays are strung along this striking length of coast

The granite peaks and domes of Cape Le Grand National Park, Cape Arid National Park (further east) and the Recherche Archipelago are the exposed core of an alpine mountain range formed about one billion years ago and long since reduced from any boastful height.

These rocky rises and the bays and beaches separating and linking them make this one of Australia's most striking lengths of coast, and this through walk, which is the central section of the full-day 15km Cape Le Grand Coastal Trail, is a salty sampler of the Park's wonders.

The walk starts at Hellfire Bay, 60km east of Esperance, one of the most beautiful bays in the park and a popular spot for picnics and refreshing dips in calm weather. (This coast is even more stirring under a stormy sky, but the walk is exposed and there is no protection if bad weather rolls in.)

With Hellfire Bay's curved white sand beach and azure waters at your back, exit the carpark via steps and follow a trail of brown posts tipped with white paint and red reflectors east over a granite rise, passing a huge elongated granite slab on the right and piled boulders. A wide, crushed gravel track meanders up through coastal scrub and down through massed cycads, banksia, acacia and eucalypts to Little Hellfire Bay, a crescent of white beach and two-tone blue water tucked among enfolding stone.

That's the last of wide, formed track for a while, and the marker poles no longer wear red reflectors. White-tipped posts show the way up the granite dome east of the bay, initially on almost bare rock and then between bands of shrubbery, including red-and-yellow flowering grevillea concinna (red combs). Take a close look at the miniature gardens flourishing in depressions in the stone, and watch out for echidnas, western grey kangaroos and basking lizards.

As the track climbs, Hellfire Bay emerges beyond Little Hellfire Bay behind you. Rocky headlands and dozens of granite islands, some of the 100 inundated granite domes that comprise the Recherche Archipelago, greet you as the track crests (see point 1 on map) and starts down the other side.

Marker posts clamber across and steeply down a granite slope decorated with black water stripes that are slippery when wet, but

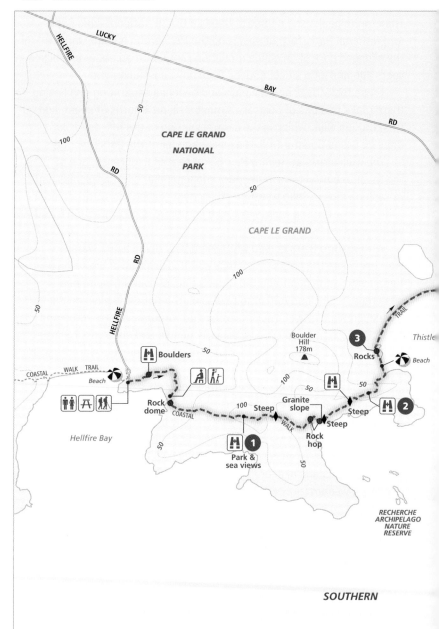

HELLFIRE

LUCKY

BAY

RD

CAPE LE GRAND
NATIONAL
PARK

CAPE LE GRAND

50

100

RD

HELLFIRE

RD

50

50

100

TRAIL

Boulder
Hill
178m

3
Rocks

Thistle

Beach

H Boulders

50

COASTAL WALK TRAIL

Beach

Rock
dome

COASTAL

100 Steep

Granite
slope

H

Steep

H **2**

50

Steep

Hellfire Bay

50

WALK

Rock
hop

H **1**
Park &
sea views

100

50

RECHERCHE
ARCHIPELAGO
NATURE
RESERVE

SOUTHERN

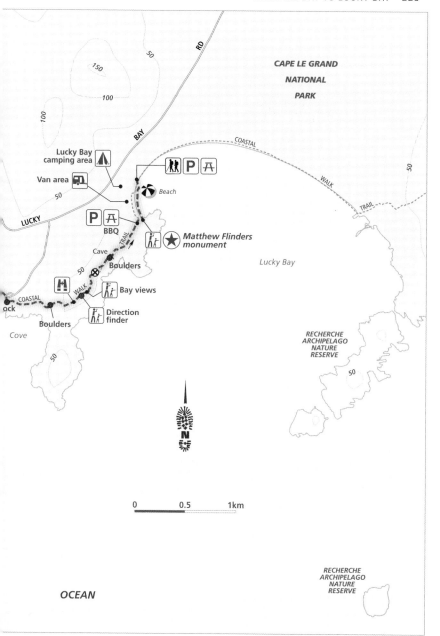

CAPE LE GRAND
NATIONAL
PARK

Lucky Bay
camping area

Van area

LUCKY

BAY

RD

50

150

100

100

50

COASTAL

WALK

TRAIL

50

Beach

P   A

P   A
BBQ

Matthew Flinders
monument

Cave

Boulders

Bay views

Direction
finder

Lucky Bay

RECHERCHE
ARCHIPELAGO
NATURE
RESERVE

50

COASTAL

WALK

TRAIL

50

50

ock

Boulders

Cove

N

0   0.5   1km

RECHERCHE
ARCHIPELAGO
NATURE
RESERVE

OCEAN

Left: *Rounded rock noses into turquoise water;* **Right:** *Afternoon sun casts a walker's shadow onto beautiful Thistle Cove beach*

the posts then disappear. Continue down the slope towards a 2m-tall diamond-shaped boulder on the edge of the scrub. The track continues just above that distinctive rock, and the next post comes into view as you descend.

Keep to the rock-greenery junction, still descending sharply, and step into the bush at a small cairn, following a sandy track through thick scrub of every degree of coarseness and prickliness to a pretty little bay. The walking track edging around the bay can be overgrown, but it's a fairly easy rock-hop to the other side, where the posts resume.

Cross another gulch, round another dome, navigate another gully opening into a rocky bay, and climb more granite sloping down to the sea. The remarkable 'horned' red and yellow flowers growing from the rafts of moss on the stone are redcoats, a member of the carnivorous bladderwort family.

Roughly 3km into the walk you pass a cluster of eroded and sculpted boulders, one with a Pac Man profile, shortly after which you reach a lumpy natural viewpoint (*see* point 2). From here, the slope you just ascended looks like it was formed by two rock layers meeting and one running over the top of the other. There's a distinct crack between the two.

From the next rise you can see the white sand and blue waters of Thistle Cove and beyond it, through a saddle, more expansive Lucky Bay. The track slaloms down to the cove, traversing steep granite shot through and striped with other rock types. This lands you on a white beach but you've got another gentle climb, over an outcrop (*see* point 3), to the main cove beach for a 1km stroll between low dunes and lapping shallows, where pied and sooty oystercatchers probe the sand for food with long red beaks.

A geological enigma of Cape Le Grand – a mystery even – is that the composite crystals of quartz, feldspar and other minerals making up the granite are relatively large and should weather to coarse sand, yet the beaches are fine and uniformly grained, and every step squeaks.

The beach ends at a rounded granite rise to the right of which the walking track resumes (white sign). As you step up from the sand you'll see another track marker below some boulders, and find yourself on a 2m-wide sealed trail working up through scrub. This brings you to Thistle Cove carpark. Detour right and explore the fabulously sculpted rocks – one looks like a whale head – that 'whistle' in the right conditions. Then continue along the coast on a sandy track that meanders uphill through knee-high heath, then taller scrub, towards a splendid headland and over a granite rise with boulders between you and the sea. Lizards dash everywhere here on mild days.

The track heads inland around a bay whose huge granite boulders have been drilled with holes by time, and brings you to the first notable track junction on the walk. Footpads continue along the shoreline towards another great lump of rock teetering on the edge, but the official walking track veers left, uphill. Follow this track, sandy in places and sometimes a bit soft, through heath to some standalone boulders on which beautiful nankeen kestrels sometimes perch. Look for pretty pink rice flowers and donkey orchids as you go.

As you descend from there, look back at those standalone boulders and you'll see that the biggest, closer to the sea, has been hollowed into a cave.

The view east is now dominated by a massive headland thrust into the ocean from a neck of land, a saddle, over which you can see Lucky Bay's long, sandy sweep and intense blue water. The walking track is clearly visible snaking ahead, and rock and sand soon disappear under a footpath of compacted gravel that climbs that saddle and presents the best view yet of Lucky Bay.

The glorious view looking west, back along Thistle Cove beach

Two-tone water and white sand separate rocky headlands along Cape Le Grand's shoreline

This track leads to a parking area with a picnic area and barbecue on the right, and continues towards the beach. Turn right at the next track junction, towards the Flinders Monument, then right again, on a footpad to a cairn. Matthew Flinders named Lucky Bay after he sheltered his ship HMS *Investigator* from a summer storm here in 1802.

Return to the previous junction and go right and down onto Lucky Bay beach – via one last lump of granite! If the tide is high or the sand here piled deeply with seaweed, you can backtrack to that first junction and follow the walking track to the carpark, but it's more fun to finish this walk on the beach.

The parking area is a few hundred metres along, past a picnic area with tables and up a track where 4WDs come down onto the sand, but there's no rush. You could easily spend hours here swimming, snorkelling, fishing, or just lounging on the beach with the local kangaroos.

6 THE LOOP

Walk:	9.4km loop
Time required:	3–4 hours
Best time:	Mild sunny day; late winter and spring for the wildflowers. The entire walk is exposed, with little shade from scorching summer sun.
Grade:	Moderate with a couple of hard spots
Environment:	High cliffs, wide, snaking gorge, sandy river bank
Best map:	This one
Toilets:	Pit toilets at The Loop carpark
Food:	Picnic lunch ingredients are available at the supermarket in Kalbarri, on the coast. The town also has cafes and restaurants, and you can watch the sun set while tucking into scrumptious local fish and chips at The Jetty's outdoor tables.
Tips:	Allow extra time to explore Kalbarri's coastal reaches and appreciate the national park's renowned annual spring wildflower spectaculars.
	Vehicle entry fees are payable at Kalbarri National Park; you can purchase a day entry pass (more than one park in a day) or multi-park pass; details at parks.dpaw.wa.gov.au/know/fees.

The Murchison River snakes through fossil-rich banded sandstone

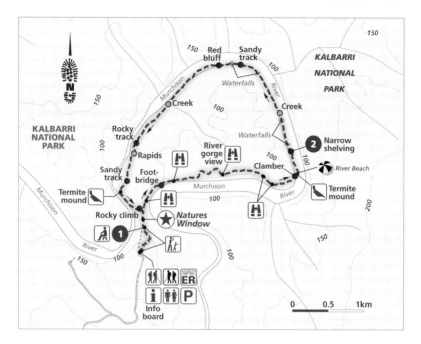

Behold the erosive and artistic powers of water as you explore the highs and lows of the Murchison River gorge.

Towards the end of its 800km-plus journey from the state's mid-west to the Indian Ocean, Western Australia's second longest river performs a series of switchbacks and loops as it works its way through fossil-rich banded sandstone to the sea. The dramatic Murchison River gorge is the centrepiece of Kalbarri National Park, which also protects coastal cliffs and sculptural formations. The Loop walk, in the gorge, takes you back through geological time.

The walk starts in The Loop car park, 39km from the holiday town of Kalbarri, at the river mouth. The last 25km of this journey is on a compacted sandy road sometimes closed after heavy rain – check at the visitor centre in town.

The first of many breathtaking vistas on this walk is from the carpark-edge information board about Kalbarri geology. The Loop/ Nature's Window trail is to the right, down metal stairs and along a sealed walking track through hardy heath splashed in winter–spring with *Grevillea petrophiloides* (pink pokers).

As the track swings left you'll see a huge loop of river. The gorge rim is undercut and the bottom a long way down, so resist the temptation to leave the formed track for an even better view! The track soon arrives at a natural lookout (*see* point 1 on map) above a big U-bend; to your right here is a banded striated cliff, all crumbly and worn away, and directly below is the shelved riverbed.

Follow the white arrows down a ridge, noting the ripples underfoot, formed in ancient times, when this rock was under a shallow sea, and the distinct sedimentary stripes in the sandstone as you round areas of undercut rock. You have river on both sides at Nature's Window, a hole drilled by time through the red-and-white banded Tumblagooda sandstone.

Many people go no further than this natural picture frame; some continue down the tiered ridge but turn back at a sign warning that completing The Loop involves navigating deep sand and rocks.

Undercut rock near Nature's Window frames a sweep of Murchison River and the stony country through which it has cut its path

Keep descending the ridge beyond that sign, stopping to look back at the rock formations and down at the river beach; sometimes you can see animal tracks in the sand, but not what kind. The track follows a ridge with gorge on alternating sides, its rockiness softened at different times of year by pink pokers, purple daisies, pink starflowers, several shades of wattles and many more flowers.

More than 1000 plants have been identified in and around Kalbarri, about a fifth of which are at the northern extremes of their range, and the national park is a showstopper on spring wildflower tours.

The trail swings right to the gorge rim and you can see all the way back to the carpark. From here you basically follow the cliff-line, diverting occasionally away from the precipitous drop around side gorges.

Bleating alerts you to the presence of feral goats, but spotting them amid the rock can be more difficult. Wedge-tailed eagles wheeling over the gorge exhibit no such shyness.

Walking down into the gorge is like treading a geological timeline. As you step down banded natural shelving, you'll see that the far side of the gorge is rocky and tiered, while this side is edged with sand.

Where rock meets beach there is a huge termite mound, and a sign warning that this walk becomes increasingly difficult from here, and you should turn back if unprepared and/or carrying inadequate drinking water. Yes, the next kilometres are remote and there is no drinking water, so you do need to be prepared, but the walk doesn't become harder. After clambering along several hundred metres of steep rock shelving the route flattens out and the going becomes easier.

Amble downstream a short way on the beach, then start along the gorge wall. Water spray drifts over you from rock lips after rain – refreshing, but it also makes the stone slippery, so take care, especially near the edge. Looking up you can see the layers of sediment lain down and compressed over millions of years, and how time and water have combined to sculpt, erode and undercut.

The banded shelving then becomes extremely narrow (*see* point 2), with only foot-wide ledges. You may need to traverse this section on hands and knees. Keep your group together along here in case anyone needs help, or just encouragement. When the river is very low there may be an easier route.

Track markers direct you several tiers up beside an ephemeral waterfall, after which the shelving widens in places, making walking easier. Daisies bloom in hollows here and gums, clinging to the rock with buried roots, lean over the water.

With 4km to go the trail drops to river level and you tread sand and rock through handsome old eucalypts.

Moving between patterned and textured rock shelves and sand, which can be soft, the track wends its way downstream and through immature river gums (these eucalypts are adapted to inundation). Cross a creek, up which is another striped undercut cliff, then step up rocky tiers and around rapids that roar after rain.

Gorgeous splendid fairy-wrens – the males sport several shades of blue plumage – add interest to a sandy section through acacias, immediately after which the track swings left along a stretch of water frequented by black swans, and Nature's Window comes back into view up ahead.

Go left on a sandy track where the Murchison River loops right towards the Indian Ocean. Soft sand gives way to loose rock as you zigzag up the ridge below Nature's Window. Compare the view it frames with what you saw in earlier light before walking back to your car.

Clockwise from top: *Nature's Window; a cloud-streaked spring sky caps a stunning spread of wildflowers; down beside the river you get a full-frontal view of the layered sandstone; pretty blooms flower among the rocks*

7 SULLIVAN ROCK TO MONADNOCKS CAMPSITE LOOP

Walk:	14.6km loop
Time required:	4–5 hours
Best time:	Year round (but beware hot and cold extremes)
Grade:	Moderate
Environment:	Granite domes, tall timber forest, wildflowers
Best map:	This one, combined with *Bibbulmun Track: Map 1 Darling Range* (bibbulmuntrack.org.au)
Toilets:	Pit toilet at Monadnocks campsite
Food:	None
Tips:	There is little protection from sun and storms on this walk, and you are completely at the mercy of the weather on the exposed granite hills, so check the forecast beforehand.

Get high on granite domes and wildflowers on this fantastic one-dayer on the famous Bibbulmun Track.

While some people approach the Bibbulmun Track with a pilgrim's fervour, and tread its 1000km on epic end-to-end hikes from the Perth hills to the historic south-coast town of Albany, Western Australia's long-distance walking trail wasn't designed with only endurance hikers in mind. There are assorted shorter overnight hikes [see p. 217] and many day walks along its route.

A vista of valleys and forested hills unfurls as you climb the granite domes

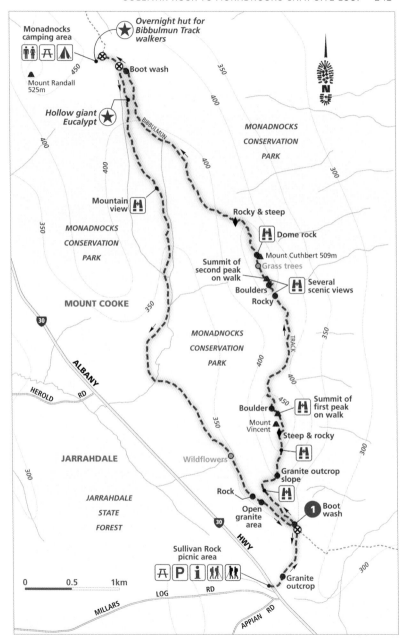

Monadnocks
camping area

Mount Randall
525m

*Overnight hut for
Bibbulmun Track
walkers*

Boot wash

**Hollow giant
Eucalypt**

BIBBULMUN

Mountain
view

MONADNOCKS
CONSERVATION
PARK

Rocky & steep

Dome rock

Mount Cuthbert 509m

Grass trees

Summit of
second peak
on walk

Several
scenic views

Boulders

Rocky

MOUNT COOKE

MONADNOCKS
CONSERVATION
PARK

TRACK

ALBANY

HEROLD   RD

Boulder

Mount
Vincent

Summit of
first peak
on walk

Steep & rocky

JARRAHDALE

Wildflowers

Granite outcrop
slope

Rock

Open
granite
area

Boot wash

JARRAHDALE
STATE
FOREST

Sullivan Rock
picnic area

0   0.5   1km

HWY

Granite
outcrop

LOG   RD

MILLARS

APPIAN   RD

N

The bald granite domes give an uninterrupted view of approaching rain

One of the most popular Bibbulmun day walks – and no, that doesn't
mean crowded – is from Sullivan Rock to Monadnocks campsite,
in Monadnocks Conservation Reserve (proposed Monadnocks
National Park).

This cracker hike goes off from Sullivan Rock picnic and parking
area, about 80 minutes' drive from Perth's CBD. (From Armadale,
south of Perth, drive south-east on Albany Hwy for about 37km; the
pine treed parking area is on the right opposite a brown-and-yellow
Bibbulmun Track sign, shortly after a bend in the highway and just
before Millars Log Rd.)

From the parking area, cross the highway and step from gravel
verge into mixed forest packed with grass trees, through whose spiky
spheres the bald granite dome of Sullivan Rock soon comes into view.
Cairns show the way up and over the rock, between rivers of moss
and other ground-hugging plants, with the Darling Range (or Scarp)
revealing itself as you climb. The hill to the left at about 10 o'clock
is Mount Vincent, the first of two monadnocks (isolated rock hills,
knobs, ridges or small mountains rising abruptly from gently sloping or
virtually level eroded country) scaled on this walk.

A larger cairn shows where you step from Sullivan Rock into an attractive combo of eucalypts, grass trees, grevilleas and wattles entwined with purple pea-flowering native wisteria (*hardenbergia*). You might also see yellow and purple-brown donkey orchids with pricked 'ears' and pink fairies (another orchid) here in spring.

This narrow trail runs into a wider, gravel track. Turning right would put you on the Bibbulmun heading south for Albany, so dogleg left and right and follow it north, scrubbing your boots at the wash station (*see* point 1 on map) to reduce the spread of cinnamon fungus.

Climbing slightly, with another granite rise on one side and broadening views of hills and plains on the other, you'll pass old gums blackened and hollowed by fire.

The track comes to Mt Vincent's granite-slope base. The rock can be slippery when wet, so take care as you follow a line of cairns up through boulders, with views opening up around you.

This walk is spectacular even if the views come and go behind drifting cloud. The hills are festooned not just with cycads, grass trees and eucalypts but also massed shrubs that burst into colour in winter and spring. Mt Vincent's smooth lower slope is another great place to see orchids, the delicate flowers seeming to find all they need in tiny cracks.

A large cairn crowns the summit of Mt Vincent (515m by GPS), from where you can have a good look at Mt Cuthbert (520m by GPS), the second peak on this walk.

Rocky track zigzags steeply down Mt Vincent and flattens out through post burn-off regeneration. Then you're climbing again, on good gravel footing, with boulders both sides, to open granite with a fabulous view over the ranges.

Rather than the footpad at the top of this natural lookout, you want the trail stepping off it to the left (marked with a small cairn). Keep watch for soaring wedge-tailed eagles as you weave through flowering shrubs and boulders to the foot of a bigger, steeper granite slope patched with moss. Enjoy the view, over ranges clad in native forest (and some pine plantations), as you work right and around this slope. Then focus on your feet as you scale it.

Pause to take in the stonking good view from here before pressing on: up through more rocks, down a ridge where the ground drops away on either side of you, and up again, more sedately. As you near the top you'll pass a remarkable grass tree with five heads coming off three main branches.

Mt Cuthbert's summit provides a grandstand view of the Darling Range that really pops on a clear day. And then there's the summit itself, a broad bald granite dome fringed with grass trees and scattered with mossy mats embedded with insectivorous sundews.

Follow the cairns over Cuthbert's crown, then descend the mountain on a narrow, winding trail through rocks and eucalypts, some with white trunks, some with mosaic-like bark. The trail gets rockier and steeper here, before flattening out again.

Leaves and she-oak needles will muffle your footfalls through woodland populated by some seriously old trees, most still standing but one, just past another boot wash station, a fallen monster. Cross an eroded fire trail and follow the Bibbulmun another 300m to Monadnocks hut and camping area. With a pit toilet, tank water, shelter and forest frontage, this is a great lunch spot.

Refuelled, backtrack to the fire trail you just crossed. You could return to your car the way you came, summitting Mts Cuthbert and Vincent again; however, the fire trail (unsigned Herold Rd) is a less energetic but very pleasant alternative.

Turn right onto the trail and start the pretty easy run home, mostly downhill on a track that soon becomes less eroded, past an old eucalypt hollowed and burnt out but still living, through stands of banksias and grass trees and open forest with Mts Cuthbert and Vincent on your left.

Because it's less important where you put your feet, and you're no longer distracted by grand views, you can now concentrate on the flora, for which Western Australia is justly famous. In late winter–spring you might see couch honeypot (a dryandra with full-cup-shaped yellow flowers) and more donkey orchids.

About 3.5km after lunch, the 'road' forks on either side of a burnt tree stump sporting a BT (Bibbulmun Track) arrow pointing left. At the time of writing there was also an arrow in logs on the left track. The right track runs west about 600m to the Albany Hwy and you'll probably be able to hear cars again by now.

Take the left track, which heads towards Mt Vincent and swings along below it, through the best wildflower area on this lower route. As you walk south-east through granite and eucalypts, look for spidery red grevillea with forking needle-like leaves (sometimes called native fuchsia) and pretty pink and blue foxtails – you'll be surprised at what you find growing if you stop and look around a small area for a few minutes. And some of the grass trees here are 6m tall!

Before you know it you'll reach the track junction where you crossed this road earlier. Turn right and retrace your steps over Sullivan Rock to your car.

Left: *Moss carpets the rounded granite slopes;* **Right:** *The grass trees along this walk grow weird antennae*

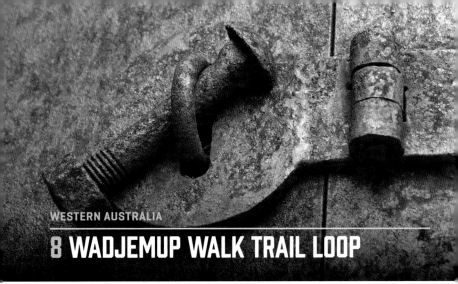

8 WADJEMUP WALK TRAIL LOOP

Walk:	16km loop
Time required:	5 hours
Best time:	Mild sunny day
Grade:	Easy to moderate (long)
Environment:	Sandy beaches, coastal cliffs, salt lakes, heathlands, mainland views, colonial history and WW II installations
Best map:	This one
Toilets:	Flushing toilets in the village and at Oliver Hill
Food:	Assorted sit-down and takeaway food, snacks and picnic supplies are available from Thomson Bay settlement shops
Tips:	Ferry transfers to Rottnest Island from Perth and Fremantle can be booked through Rottnest Express (rottnestexpress.com.au) and Rottnest Island Ferries (rottnestfastferries.com.au). Another option is to fly to the island from Perth by air taxi (rottnestairtaxi.com.au).
	Coordinate your walk with the Oliver Hill Gun and Tunnels Tour (several times daily, tickets on site) and Wadjemup Lighthouse Tour (hourly, tickets on site). You can do this loop walk in either direction.

A rusty door fitting is one of many WW II relics on Rottnest Island

This long but easy walk around Perth's island playground dishes up exquisitely beautiful beaches and bays, too-cute native animals, and colonial and military history.

Named by Willem de Vlamingh in 1696 for its abundant quokkas, native marsupials that the Dutch sea-captain thought were giant rodents, Rottnest Island is much more than a 'rat's nest'. De Vlamingh described it in his journal as a paradise on earth, '… where it seems to me that nature has denied nothing to make it pleasurable beyond all islands I have ever seen.'

Known as Wadjemup to Aboriginal people, for whom it was a place of celebration and healing before becoming a place of incarceration and spiritual and physical deprivation, Rottnest Island is simply Rotto to the thousands of folk who arrive by ferry each year.

The five integrated sections of the Wadjemup Walk Trail (due for completion in 2018) explore the island's wildlife, natural beauty and maritime, penal and military history. The walk described here combines lengths of three sections into an all-day outing.

Starting at Rottnest Island visitor centre, at the top of the ferry jetty, head south towards Thomson Bay, walking along the beach, or on the foreshore, past a playground, cafes, old Cypress pines and low-rise holiday accommodation, and following the blue-bordered Bickley Bay track markers. Perth's finger-like CBD is to the north-east.

Leave the beach at Army Jetty (ablutions block) (*see* point 1 on map) and continue on a sealed track above the sand, watching for birds of prey. Pulling away from the water, tread undulations to Kingstown, which accommodated Australian Army personnel during WW II (the red-brick barracks now operate as bunkroom accommodation for school groups). Kingstown is also the railhead for the train ride to Oliver Hill Battery.

Swing right across the barracks and follow rail tracks through a tree tunnel (*see* point 2) framing the Bickley (gun) Battery. The ground to your left drops away, revealing the sea, soon after which a salt lake comes into view on the right.

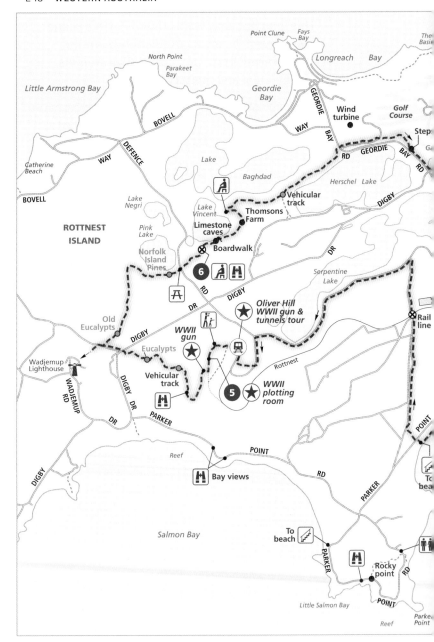

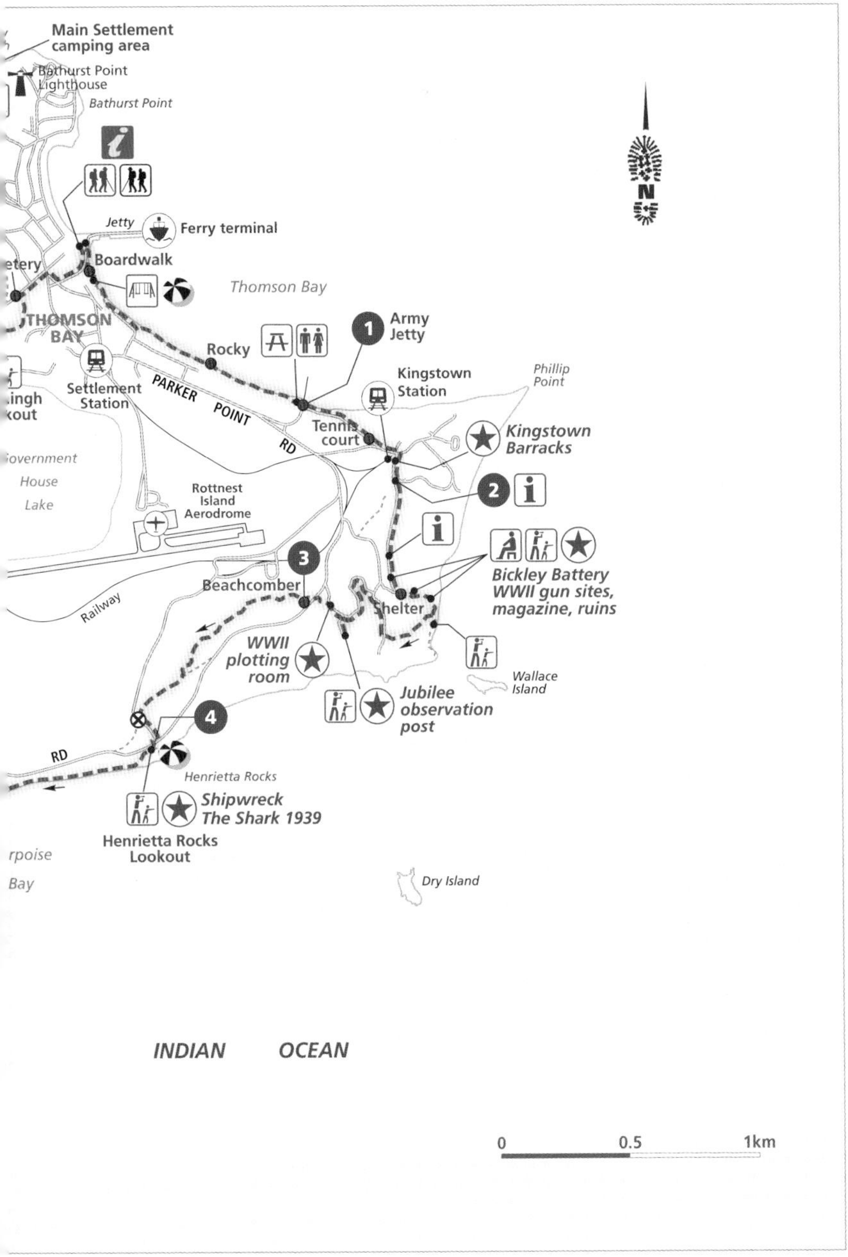

Main Settlement
camping area

Bathurst Point
Lighthouse

Bathurst Point

Jetty Ferry terminal

Boardwalk

etery

Thomson Bay

**THOMSON
BAY**

Rocky

1 Army
Jetty

*Phillip
Point*

Kingstown
Station

Settlement
Station

PARKER POINT

ingh
kout

RD

Tennis
court

Kingstown
Barracks

*Government
House*

Lake

Rottnest
Island
Aerodrome

2 i

i

Railway

Beachcomber

3

Shelter

Bickley Battery
WWII gun sites,
magazine, ruins

*Wallace
Island*

WWII
plotting
room

Jubilee
observation
post

RD

4

Henrietta Rocks

Shipwreck
The Shark 1939

Henrietta Rocks
Lookout

rpoise

Bay

Dry Island

INDIAN   OCEAN

0   0.5   1km

Read about the Bickley Battery and women at war in the khaki and yellow shed with rusty shutters abutting the railway track. Then roll along the tracks to wooden steps, immediately past a wire-mesh clad ruin.

Climb the steps to Bickley Battery, the site of two 6-inch guns that were installed in 1938 to defend the Port of Fremantle from enemy ships and decommissioned and dismantled in 1963. The historic gun site enjoys a view of islands and turquoise bays and the Kingston barracks. The battery observation post's slit window fashions a panoramic vista reaching north-west to Bathurst Lighthouse, beyond the Thomson Bay settlement.

Retreat down the steps and follow the railway tracks to the bombproof magazine. Descend the wooden steps here and tread a sandy track through the dunes towards the water. Detour left at the next junction to overlook Rottnest's southern bays. Then return to the main trail and continue along what becomes a compacted track,

Wadjemup Lighthouse is Australia's fourth-oldest, and was the country's first rotating beam

through grassed dunes and an old parade ground where soldiers played cricket. You can just see the end of the concrete pitch to the right and behind the information board.

Go left at the next junction for a beach swim, or right to keep walking uphill to another junction. Turn left and walk past rusty metal water tanks for a wide view of Rottnest's interior salt lakes.

Beyond more rusted water tanks, there's another observation post from which you might see fishers standing on the rocks. Soon after, you pass the red-brick plotting room.

Cross the sealed island road (Parker Point Rd), alert for cyclists, and climb to Fleur Marron's sculpture *Beachcomber* (*see* point 3), inspired by Rottnest's ospreys and their stacks (nests) and the importance of waste management. The track continues north-west from the sculpture rise, traversing an area of natural grey rock that looks like it was poured over the ground from a concrete truck. The grass here attracts quokkas that often pose for close-up photos.

All along this walk you'll see revegetation, in clearings and on footpads and old vehicular tracks. Part of the Wadjemup Walk Trail project, this is to reduce the environmental impact of ad-hoc and informal access tracks.

Turn left at a vehicular track and then right onto Parker Point Rd (sealed), then stop at Henrietta Rocks lookout. Projecting from the ridiculously blue water are the rusty remains of The Shark, a hopper barge wrecked here in 1939. (At least 12 wrecks have foundered on or just off Rottnest since 1842; the main wrecks are marked with underwater information plaques for snorkellers and divers.)

Now you've got 1km of beach walking to Porpoise Bay, where de Vlamingh is thought to have landed in 1696. Venture out onto the undercut limestone shelf at the base of the steps (*see* point 4) for a great view along the coast and into the water. A well-worn track steps over another low limestone rise about 100m west, but you can usually get around dry-footed. It's a lovely stroll from there, often with cruising pelicans for company.

Climb the metal stairs at Porpoise Bay to Parker Point Rd. From here, you can go west on the purple-marked Salmon Bay section of the Wadjemup Walk Trail for more bays and beach, or inland to the salt lakes.

We're going inland, so cross the road and walk through a grove of eucalypts to traverse Rottnest's central plain. Having crossed the Oliver Hill train track and passed the fenced airport (scenic flights only) you land on Serpentine Lake's salty shore. Turn left and walk towards Oliver Hill and Wadjemup Lighthouse (both visible) on a flat track between two-tone grasses and woody old tea-trees (left). The edible succulent samphire reddening the lake shore has an interesting link-like structure.

From Serpentine Lake's western end the track works through eucalypts towards Oliver Hill and its crowning gun battery. Go left at the next junction onto sealed road, then step off again onto the sandy walking track heading right part way up a steep hill. Steps put you back on the road for a short walk up to the first gun. If your timing's right, you can take a guided tour of the restored 9.2 inch WW II gun and maze of underground tunnels (tickets on site); this is Australia's most intact 9.2 inch gun placement.

Head down the blue-arrow marked stairs (Oliver Hill loop walk), and right again to a picnic table under shady trees. Continue along the track beyond the picnic area, detouring up more steps to the right to a lookout with near 360° views of Rottnest and the mainland, as well as a series of information panels. Walk further along the main track to the second Oliver Hill gun, on the right.

Follow the train tracks to an information sign, from which steps descend to another plotting room, dug into the hill (*see* point 5). Continue on the footworn but unformed track beyond this war relic, winding through sand hills and ignoring the purple-signed Salmon Bay section of Wadjemup Walk Trail coming up on the left. From the next rise you'll see rocky bays and a small lake, and Wadjemup Lighthouse on the island's highpoint.

The track to the light tower rides sand ridges, drops into another grove of eucalypts trailing bark streamers, and climbs through native pines and tea-tree woodland patched with moss. There are so many quokkas you risk tripping over one.

Perth CBD pokes its head over a rocky headland on Rottnest Island

Cross the sealed island road and continue on the Bore Fields North fire trail opposite, now following beige-bordered Lakes Section track markers. Ignore the walking track going right and walk up to the lighthouse.

Built in 1896 to replace the original, smaller limestone tower constructed by Aboriginal prisoners incarcerated on Rottnest, Wadjemup is Western Australia's fourth oldest extant lighthouse and was Australia's first rotating beam. The now computerised lighthouse's magnificent glass lens still turns on a bed of mercury.

Take a volunteer-led tour (hourly) up the 155 internal steps to the lens and external balcony. Information boards in the 1849 tower's square base (all that survives) tell the tower's story.

Also on Wadjemup Hill are an early 20th century maritime signal station, red-brick World War II battery observation post and weatherboard house that accommodated WRANS (Women's Royal Australian Navy Service) personnel during the war.

Take the same route back down the hill to the Lakes Section turnoff and head north-east, following beige-bordered track markers (and ignoring side tracks) through mature eucalypts whose multiple

Rottnest Island's main settlement nestles among Norfolk Island Pines, on the shores of salt lakes

branches reach down to the ground. You get a great view back to the lighthouse as you crest a hill.

The track lands you beside Pink Lake, an almost meditatively tranquil spot on a still afternoon. Follow its southern shore to a sealed road, where The Lakes walk goes both left (this slightly longer option returns to the settlement via north coast bays and beaches) and straight on.

Cross the road and continue straight ahead. Turn left onto a vehicular track parallel to a fence and step off it again (see point 6) down rough rock and concrete steps to Lake Vincent.

Permanent and ephemeral salt lakes cover a tenth of Rottnest Island. In summer they are up to seven times saltier than sea water, yet insects and crustaceans breed in the lakes; these feed resident and migratory birds, including the magnificent Mountain Duck.

Swing right along Lake Vincent's samphire shore, walking between long-legged waders in the shallows and fallen trees that have lost their grip on the rocky rise to your right.

Tread the boardwalk that hugs the lake's shore and rounds honeycombed limestone undercut into small caves. Then traverse what was once the Thomson family farm. Robert Thomson, after whom the settlement bay is named, became a major landholder – town lots and pastureland – after Rottnest was surveyed in 1830.

Parallel to the lake shore but above it now, the track climbs another limestone outcrop. Walk out to a point and take a seat on a bench perfectly positioned for birdwatching, with the lighthouse standing tall beyond the water. Then continue along the track towards the settlement's dark green pine trees.

It's easy walking now, on a hard limestone track, to and between lakes Herschel and Baghdad, with rock shelves stepping down to water that mirrors the sky on still days.

Cross a sealed road that follows the lake shore, and climb the unsealed track over another limestone bluff, passing Rotto's wind turbine and golf course and enjoying another restful lake view.

Step down again to the road and follow it between lakes, turning left around tiny Garden Lake. Stop at the historic cemetery about

400m along Digby Dve on the right. The volunteer-manned Rottnest Island Museum, in the Old Mill and Hay Store on the corner of Kitson St, shines a light on the island's history, including its dark chapters as an Aboriginal prison.

Continue past the shops (left) to the waterfront and return to the visitor centre.

Clockwise from top left: *Rottnest Island was named by a Dutch sea captain for its abundant quokkas; sharp-edged stone juts out from the island's shore; afternoon light softens the island's hard edges*

9 WARREN RIVER LOOP

Walk:	11.3km loop
Time required:	3–4 hours
Best time:	Any time
Grade:	Moderate (steady climbs and descents)
Environment:	Bird filled tall-timber forest, lush river reaches, fire lookout tree
Best map:	This one
Toilets:	Pit toilets in carpark and camping areas along the river
Food:	None
Tips:	Take binoculars for identifying the forest birds.
	Vehicle entry fees are payable at Warren National Park; you can purchase a day entry pass (more than one park in a day) or multi-park pass; details at parks.dpaw.wa.gov.au/know/fees.

Appreciate just how small you are on this leafy loop through old-growth forest inhabited by some of the tallest trees on Earth.

Karri (*Eucalyptus diversicolor*) is Western Australia's tallest tree species, reaching 80m and living for centuries. Warren National Park, in the state's south, protects thousands of hectares of virgin karri forest, and the Warren River Loop walk immerses you in the world of these majestic arboreal leviathans.

Time for some quiet contemplation beside the Warren River

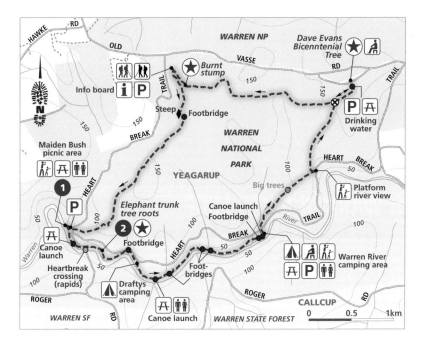

The walk starts in a small, forest-ringed parking area off unsealed Old Vasse Rd, about 13km south-west of the historic timber town of Pemberton. Pick up a park pamphlet in the picnic shelter among the trees and from there tread south and downhill to a junction, where the Bicentennial Tree is signed to the left.

Keep straight on towards Maiden Bush, so you're walking the loop anticlockwise; going in reverse leaves you a steeper climb to finish. The trail marker is a white tree on a black background.

The track is wide and fairly flat early on, and carpeted with leaves and bark that soften your footfalls when damp with rain. Moss grows thickly on standing trees and fallen ones that have ripped their roots from the ground and toppled onto the dark soil.

Several different species make up this forest but none are more impressive than the karris, with their elongated trunks and skirts of peeling bark; some are four or more metres around their bases. In contrast, the native pines have thick, fissured bark suggestive of cork.

An enthusiastic bird chorus, featuring kookaburra solos, is the soundtrack for your descent, gently and then more steeply to a footbridge over a creek. The track then undulates through the forest before descending steadily to the music of running water.

Cross the unsealed Heartbreak Trail, built by hand to give firefighters access to Warren River water, which is now a 12km one-way scenic drive, into Maiden Bush picnic area, where there are tables and toilets. This is the first of several riverside picnic and camping spots accessible from the scenic drive and walking track.

Head upstream, past a metal viewing platform and canoe launch (*see* point 1 on map) (the Warren River has some small rapids, white water grade 2, and is a moderate paddle). A much narrower trail along the riverbank, where reeds grow in thick clumps and red coral vine and white clematis entwine fallen timbers, leads to another picnic area, beyond which you come to a vehicular track that disappears into the river at low rocky rapids. This is Heartbreak Crossing. A very steep vehicular track climbs out of the water up the opposite bank, but a sign warns drivers against crossing and reminds them that vehicle recovery is very expensive.

It's a long way up – and down – the Dave Evans Bicentennial Tree

All is quiet beside the Warren River

Cross the vehicular track and keep going upstream, occasionally climbing away from the river around overgrown and thickly treed areas. On one ascent you'll pass a fallen tree (*see* point 2) with a mossy exposed root that rears up like an elephant's trunk. The trail meanders through shady camping and picnic areas with viewing platforms and canoe launches (there are toilets too, up from the water) and fords creeks on footbridges.

About 3km upstream from where you joined the river you leave it, at a picnic spot with a bench on its viewing platform for watching the river roll by. Walk through the parking area and up an unsealed road towards a one-way sign – there's a toilet on the left and a camping registration station on the right. Cross the scenic drive and head towards Warren River Lookout, up a vehicle-wide walking track through tall timbers and cycads. Many of the oldest trees have lost their crowns but are still impressive, and part way up there's a pair of huge old karris, the larger one 2m fatter and wearing a mossy collar.

Birdwatching is a good excuse for stops on this climb; black, white and yellow honeyeaters, purple-crowned lorikeets (their rapid shrill calls can be almost deafening) and tiny spotted pardalotes, identified by the white dots on their wings, are often seen. The even spottier red-eared firetail and the white-breasted robin inhabit these forests too.

On coming to a junction where the walking track goes left, turn right across the scenic drive to Warren River Lookout. The towering karris standing sentinel here are sadly, but perhaps predictably, scored with the names of some of the people who've stood here before you, looking down at the river far below and the steep treed hills through which it winds.

Cross back to the walking track and start downhill towards the Bicentennial Tree. At the next junction, with a management access-only track ahead, turn right – you'll come back to this point – and follow a wide, effectively flat track to the Dave Evans Bicentennial Tree picnic area (barbecues and tank water).

The first fire lookout tower was constructed in a towering karri tree in 1938, and by 1952 there were eight in the network. Forest fires were pinpointed by cross-referencing bearings on smoke from two towers until 1972, when light planes took over bushfire surveillance, but fire spotters still climb the trees in some extreme weather conditions.

At 75m, the Dave Evans Bicentennial Tree, constructed in 1988 and named after a retired teacher and politician, and local resident, is the tallest of three in the Pemberton area open to the public. It's a nerve-testing climb up more than 150 metal spikes to the top, but the 360° forest and farmland view, with glimpses of the Yeagarup Dunes and ocean, can still trembling knees and slow a racing heart. The top platform can sway 1.5m side to side in high winds; the lower platform, 25m up, has no views but is a good spot for taking photographs of those who remain on terra firma.

Return to the last track junction and walk west on a wide track that leads most of the way back to the carpark, going gently downhill before steadily climbing. A tree-silhouette track marker about 2km along directs you right, onto a narrower track, which skirts a burnt-out moss-covered tree stump that's home to a host of fungi as it snakes the last 300m through towering karris to your starting point.

10 WEANO & HANCOCK GORGES

Walk:	3.7km
Time required:	3–4 hours
Best time:	Sunny day late autumn to spring (temperatures soar in summer, when wet-season rains can close roads and gorges)
Grade:	Moderate (but requires some agility)
Environment:	Timeworn mountains, vertiginous lookouts into deep chasms, steep shoulder-wide gorges, bone-chilling pools
Best map:	This one
Toilets:	Pit toilets in Weano Gorge Day Use Area, with large bowl of disinfectant to scrub after use!
Food:	Restaurant meals (bookings essential), cold drinks, coffee and treats available at Karijini Eco Retreat (karijiniecoretreat.com.au), on the approach to Weano & Hancock gorges; cold drinks and ice-creams at the visitor centre
Tips:	Karijini gorges can flash flood; don't enter if there is significant rain locally, and leave promptly if rain starts falling. Take a waterproof camera or dry bag. Carry a towel for drying your feet or wear good-gripping walking sandals that drain well. And don't be daunted; exploring these gorges is easier than it first appears, and more than worth the effort!

Vehicle entry fees are payable at Karijini National Park; you can purchase a day entry pass (more than one park in a day) or multi-park pass; details at parks.dpaw.wa.gov.au/know/fees. |

Awesome chasms and sinuous gorges dissect the aeons-old mountains of Karijini National Park

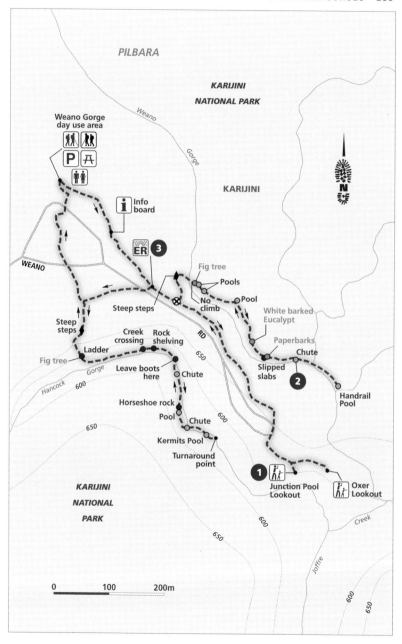

PILBARA

KARIJINI
NATIONAL PARK

KARIJINI

N

Weano Gorge
day use area

P

Info
board

ER 3

Fig tree

Pools

No
climb

Pool

White barked
Eucalypt

Steep steps

Paperbarks

Steep
steps

Creek
crossing

Rock
shelving

Chute

Ladder

Fig tree

Leave boots
here

Slipped
slabs

Chute

Horseshoe rock

Handrail
Pool

Pool

Chute

Kermits Pool

Turnaround
point

KARIJINI

NATIONAL

PARK

Junction Pool
Lookout

Oxer
Lookout

1

2

Creek

Joffre

Weano

Gorge

WEANO

Hancock   Gorge

600

650

650

650

650

600

600

600

RD

600

650

0   100   200m

Weano Gorge's banded walls converge to form a metre-wide chute

Delve into cracks in Earth's crust and come face-to-face with ancient geology on this extraordinary adventure walk in the heart of the Pilbara.

The names Hamersley Range and Lang Hancock will forever be linked, and continue to prompt reflections on the tragic human cost of blue asbestos mining. But Karijini, the range's traditional name, has very different connotations. More than 20,000 years of Aboriginal culture and the wildflowers that festoon the high plateau add to Karijini National Park experiences, but most people come for the awesome chasms and sinuous gorges that dissect the aeons-old mountains, which culminate in the state's highest point (Mt Meharry, 1253m).

Three hours' drive south of Port Hedland in Western Australia's Pilbara, Karijini National Park is cliché country, and this walk combines three of the 17 walks in its eight accessible gorges. The walk departs from the Weano Gorge day use area, 38km from the park's western entrance and 85km from the visitor centre. A shorter route from the visitor centre includes an unsealed stretch recommended for 4WD only.

From the information shelter, just past a monster termite mound at the eastern end of the day use area, walk parallel with the road, on rocky ground textured with spinifex mounds and daubed with white-stripe snappy gums, ignoring for now the Weano Gorge track going left.

The track rocks along the ridge to a smaller carpark, beyond which a good trail winds down to Junction Pool lookout (*see* point 1 on map). This metal platform boasts an awesome view down red-rock battlements into Joffre and Red gorges, two 100m-deep chasms sliced through the Hamersley Range. A cross beside the lookout commemorates SES volunteer Jimmy Regan, who drowned in a flash flood in April 2004 while rescuing a British tourist injured while rock climbing.

A rougher, narrower trail ventures about 80m further to Oxer Lookout, which oversees the confluence of Weano, Hancock, Joffre and Red gorges. There's no denying though that the view has lost a bit of punch since the lookout was pulled back from the small crumbly knoll further down!

More than 100 bird species have been identified in Karijini. Look and listen for crested spinifex pigeons scuttling about like wind-up toys as you return from the brink. Acacias, northern bluebells and fluffy mauve mulla mullas can add colour to the walk.

Back up the track, turn right for Weano Gorge and descend rock and concrete steps into the ravine. Turn right at the bottom – another walk loops up the gorge past the pool on your left – and head downstream, following a trail of yellow-disc (Grade 4) track markers on stepping stones. The curvy white trunk of a splendid fig tree contrasts the blocky red gorge wall.

How wet you get on this walk – to the ankles or thighs – depends on recent rain. If you are unwilling to dampen your digits you shouldn't go any further (do not climb the gorge walls to keep dry). At the first pool, start left but wade right at an upended rock slab, keeping right thereafter along a rock shelf that can be dry or underwater. Emerging from that pool, cross an area of trickling water and flat rocks to a second pool, where you might stay completely dry in late winter.

Karijini's characteristic banded rock originated as sediments on an ancient sea bed. Over millions of years the pressure of subsequent deposits transformed deeper layers into rock, which buckled and cracked before surfacing. Then a sharp drop in sea level caused the rivers to slice down rapidly, creating sheer-sided gorges. The water-polished rock down here is striped blue, mauve, burgundy and brown and is very different from the iron-rich red crust up top.

Weano's banded walls now converge, forming a metre-wide chute (see point 2) that spits you out into a cylindrical cavern open to the sky, with a wading pool and natural tiered rock seating. Skirt around to the even narrower gap through which the water escapes and work down this sinuous corridor, spidering between banded walls, to where the water and ground nose-dive into Handrail Pool. (This section of the walk is marked with blue discs, Grade 5.)

Drilled and rounded by countless wet season floods, this beautiful permanent pool rarely feels the sun, so is always cold, and sometimes bone-chilling; swim with caution. Bolted footholds and a handrail take you down to the rock shelf beside the water.

Massed wildflowers, including the spectacular Sturt desert pea, carpet the approaches to the park in spring

It is possible to explore Weano Gorge below this pool, but you should first inform the rangers. (A great way to delve deeper into Karijini is on a guided multi-day walk with Willis's Walkabouts: bushwalkingholidays.com.au.)

Retrace your steps to the ridge then start back towards your car, then cross the road at the emergency radio (see point 3) for part two of the adventure.

The Hancock Gorge walk roughs through white-on-red snappy gums to the cliff, where two ladders descend into Hancock Gorge. At the bottom go downstream, following blue marker discs (Grade 5) between striped gorge walls and navigating pools whose size is determined by recent rainfall.

Now for the fun bit!

Not far from the ladders, the gorge narrows and the water forms a lap pool of sorts, albeit in a setting no architect could best. Here you have a choice: swim (only recommended in warm weather, when there's sun to dry you) or clamber along the polished, layered rock to the right (the most popular option, and the marked route).

The latter demands some agility and sure-footedness, but it's easier than it looks, and doable with care by people of all ages. The hardest part can be taking the first step – coming back you'll wonder what the fuss was about. Bare feet, non-slip water sandals or surf booties are more suitable than stiff-soled hiking boots.

Exploring Hancock Gorge is sometimes described as journeying 'to the centre of the Earth', and now it becomes obvious why. The gorge narrows even further beyond the lap pool, funnelling you between shapely walls that cut the Pilbara sky to a sliver. Some people spider through here but the floor is wide enough for feet, and not too slippery, despite the running water. A wedged rock creates a miniature cascade over which you have to clamber.

This brings you to a rope strung across the gorge above the rock slide down which water pours into Kermit's Pool, another geological sculpture. Permission from park authorities is required to explore further.

Take time to savour this remarkable place as you walk back into the light. At the top of the ladders, head left to the carpark.

Clockwise from top left: Crested spinifex pigeons saunter about the rocky ridge between the gorges; sinuous Weano Gorge is an adventure for all ages; how wet you get on this walk depends on recent rains

11 WEIR & WILDFLOWERS

Walk:	9.6km one-way
Time required:	3 hours
Best time:	Any time; wildflowers best September to November
Grade:	Easy to moderate; there are some short steep sections and steps in and around the weir
Environment:	Suburban park, eucalypt forest, dam wall and environment, industrial museum
Best map:	This one
Toilets:	Flushing toilets in Mundaring Park and at Mundaring Weir
Food:	Supermarket and cafes in Mundaring; daily counter meals, weekend breakfasts and Sunday carvery roast at Mundaring Weir Hotel
Tips:	Take a camera with a macro setting or lens to photograph the flowers

A ramble through Perth hills scrub that finishes with a blast of industrial history, this walk is an easy day out from the CBD.

Critics and cynics called Charles Yelverton (C.Y.) O'Connor's turn-of-the-19th-century plan to pump fresh water from the Perth hills to the arid Kalgoorlie-Boulder goldfields 'a scheme of madness'. Water had never been pumped uphill so far (true), and it wouldn't work (false) – because

Spring turns this ramble into a wildflower extravaganza that's pretty even in the rain

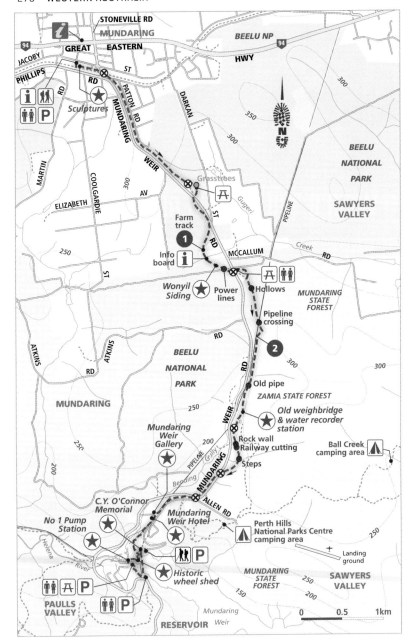

STONEVILLE RD
MUNDARING
BEELU NP
94
GREAT EASTERN
JACOBY
HWY
94
PHILLIPS
RD
PATTON RD
ST
300
MUNDARING
350
Sculptures
BEELU
MARTIN
WEIR
DARKAN
NATIONAL
COOLGARDIE
300
N
PARK
ELIZABETH
AV
Grasstrees
SAWYERS
VALLEY
250
ST
Gugeri
Creek
300
Farm
track
1
RD
ST
MCCALLUM
RD
Info
board
MUNDARING
Wonyil
Siding
Power
lines
Hollows
STATE
FOREST
Pipeline
crossing
RD
ATKINS
BEELU
2
300
300
NATIONAL
RD
MUNDARING
250
PARK
Old pipe
ZAMIA STATE FOREST
WEIR
Old weighbridge
Mundaring
& water recorder
Weir
200
station
Gully
Gallery
Rock wall
Ball Creek
PIPELINE
Railway cutting
camping area
250
Bending
Steps
MUNDARING
200
ALLEN RD
250
C.Y. O'Connor
Memorial
Mundaring
No 1 Pump
Weir Hotel
Perth Hills
Station
National Parks Centre
camping area
Helena
Landing
ground
River
MUNDARING
250
SAWYERS
Historic
STATE
200
VALLEY
wheel shed
FOREST
150
PAULLS
VALLEY
Mundaring
0   0.5   1km
RESERVOIR
Weir

rather than trying to raise water 340m (vertical) over 560km in one go, Western Australia's visionary Engineer-in-Chief designed a pipeline with eight separate sections and eight pump stations.

In January 1903, ten months after O'Connor committed suicide, his spirit broken by slander, public ridicule and unfounded accusations of cronyism and corruption, the Goldfields Water Supply Scheme was officially opened. And it remains open, with an average of 90 million litres of water a day pumped through the pipelines (a second pipe now irrigates wheatbelt towns along the route to the goldfields town).

Part of the multi-day self-drive Golden Pipeline Heritage Trail, the 75km multi-use Kep Track (named from the Noongar word for water, gep) traces pipeline history along the rail formation between Mundaring Weir and Northam. This weir-and-wildflowers walk is the first leg of the Kep Track.

You could walk it both ways, but to do it as a one-way walk you'll need to pre-arrange a car shuffle or have someone drop you off and pick you up.

Our starting point is Mundaring Sculpture Park, 40km east of Perth CBD via the Great Eastern Hwy and two blocks south of Mundaring shopping centre. An open-air exhibition space for sculptures commissioned as part of Australia's bicentennial celebrations, this grassy picnic area is the site of the old Mundaring Railway Station.

The park is also the departure point for the Munda Biddi Trail, an off-road bike trail wheeling 1000km south to Albany. Our walk begins on the gravel Munda Biddi (blue and yellow markers) track disappearing into trees to the left of the tap sculpture.

Munda Biddi means 'path through the forest' in the Noongar language – you are walking a path through a linear eucalypt forest with cars and houses either side.

Shortly after crossing Hodgson St the track forks. The bike trail and ours (the Kep Track marker is cut-out metal with attached information board) go right, through dense scrub, where it crosses another road.

Late winter into early summer this patch of bush is a wildflower wonderland, with wattles and grevilleas and tea-tree and several varieties of pea shrubs, and it feels like remote bush, despite the overhead powerlines and traffic on the Mundaring Weir Rd, about 30m to the right, early in the walk.

And if you hear a croaky sound, like a creaking gate, look up. You'll probably see black cockatoos high in the gum trees, or the leaves they're pruning falling to the ground.

Stroll on through eucalypts, grass trees and show-off wildflowers, passing a picnic area and crossing Mundaring Weir Rd with care. Beyond a greened railway cutting you pass a cedar-plank farm house (see point 1 on map). In the pipeline's infancy a vineyard and a timber mill operated in the sheep paddocks opposite, and there was a railway siding a short way along on the right.

After crossing a vehicular track following powerlines and the main road, mosey through forest inhabited by an occasional huge old gum trees that survived the timber cutters.

And then you come to O'Connor's pipeline – or at least, the modern incarnation of the engineer's vision. Over the twin pipes the track swings away into the bush, where it divides, and markers lead you back down to the pipeline. Walk between the mossy, overgrown old pipe bed and relict concrete pipe cradles on your left and the twin pipes dropping lower to your right.

Swinging hard right and down at a huge pine tree just before a water tank, you have two old pipes covered in graffiti directly ahead (see point 2). Turn right again into the grassy stand of wattles and check out the remains of the recorder cabin that measured the flow of water from number two pump station.

The trail continues past the water tank and the site of number two pump station. The pine trees here were the only shelter for people waiting at the railway platform.

The track divides again, with Munda Biddi bike trail going left and uphill. Stay on the lower track, with the anti-bike chicane, walking through cuttings and a fairly steep, rocky gully.

Cross Munwaring Weir Rd and walk along the other side – do not go into Fred Jacoby Park, although you may want to see one of Western Australia's largest English oak trees. Then veer right at the roundabout, keeping left on Mundaring Weir Rd, in a lovely ribbon woodland bristling

More than 110 years after the Goldfields Water Supply Scheme opened, the pipeline still carries water more than 550km to Kalgoorlie

with grass trees and bursting with loopy grevilleas blooms, wattle baubles and other wildflowers in season. Here you are on the long-distance Bibbulmun Track (*see* pp. 217 and 240), so you can say you walked the Bibbulmun!

Then the pipeline is beside you again and you enter the weir precinct.

The 1908 red-brick Mechanics Institute ahead is now the Mundaring Weir Gallery, which exhibits and sells works by local craftspeople on weekends and public holidays. Past the Mundaring Weir Hotel on the right, step up concrete steps and turn right between the parallel pipes.

Here the track is rougher than anywhere else on the walk so far, so take care as you descend between the now-diverging pipes. Step up and over the left pipe into a rocky area crowded with grass trees and down rough steps, beyond a huge granite boulder, and back to the descending water pipe (you can see its twin down a very rocky gully).

As you zigzag steeply downhill, think about the children who ran along this steep section of pipe with their fathers' lunches!

The track then leaves the pipeline and crosses a clearing to a U-bend in a gravel road. Keep right on the lower road, the dam wall looming into view as you come through a rocky cutting.

Work down steps and fence to the base of the dam wall, following a section of the zigzag train line that carried dam wall construction equipment and heading towards a magnificent red brick industrial building with a tall chimney.

This is Number One Pump Station, where static displays and enthusiastic volunteers bring the fascinating story of the pipeline alive. You could easily spend an hour here reading and listening.

On emerging, cross the footbridge over the outlet channel to a chorus of plonking frogs, and wend your way to the top left of the barbecue area and carpark. Stairs lead to another parking area (there are toilets here too), through which you access the dam wall.

Walk over the dam, atop which sits a lovely old cream-and-white valve station house, and on the far side go left and up to the C.Y. O'Connor Memorial.

The parking area to the right is a good place to end this walk, although there are others further up the hill.

This walk is a wildflower wonderland in spring

Water lilies float on Crystal Creek, one of the waterholes on the Jatbula Trail

NORTHERN TERRITORY

Eroded, prehistoric mountains, expanses of old red desert, and a monolithic rock with deep spiritual significance are the heart and soul of the Northern Territory, and the bushwalks on offer here are spectacularly raw and often rocky. Hike between permanent waterholes strung along a Top End escarpment; delve into the history of Central Australia and the country's telecommunications; and make what is arguably Australia's most famous ascent – in chiffon if you dare!

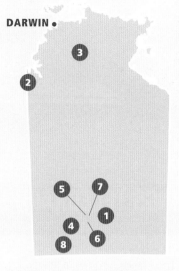

1	Alice Springs Telegraph Station	278
2	Jarnem Loop	284
3	Jatbula Trail	290
4	Kings Canyon Loop	304
5	Mount Sonder	311
6	Mpulungkinya Walk (Palm Valley) Loop	316
7	Ormiston Pound Loop	321
8	Uluru Base Walk	327

1 ALICE SPRINGS TELEGRAPH STATION

Walk:	5.5km one-way or 9km return
Time required:	2 hours (plus Telegraph Station time)
Best time:	Mild sunny day
Grade:	Easy (one short climb)
Environment:	Town, riverside shared track, historic precinct, desert scrub, low rocky outcrops
Best map:	This one
Toilets:	Flushing toilets on riverbank early in walk and at Telegraph Station
Food:	Snacks, drinks and light meals at Trail Station at Telegraph Station; diverse range of food across Alice Springs restaurants and cafes
Tips:	The Telegraph Station is open daily (except Christmas Day) 9am–5pm; the surrounding reserve is open 8am–9pm, giving you time for a picnic or barbecue after the walk

Step back in time through telecommunication history on this riverside stroll from city streets to desert scrub.

Alice Springs, in Australia's Red Centre, owes its existence and name to an engineering and technology feat that revolutionised communication across the colonies and between Australia and the world: the Overland

The telegraph station was a vital part of early Australian telecommunication

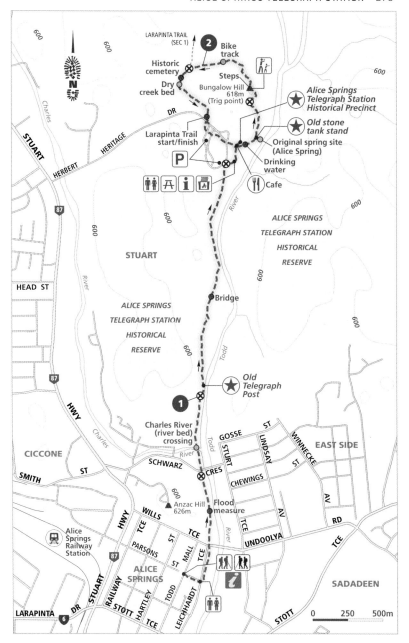

LARAPINTA TRAIL
(SEC 1)

2 Bike
track

Historic
cemetery

Steps

Dry
creek bed

Bungalow Hill
618m
(Trig point)

*Alice Springs
Telegraph Station
Historical Precinct*

DR

*Old stone
tank stand*

Larapinta Trail
start/finish

Original spring site
(Alice Spring)

P

Drinking
water

Cafe

River

ALICE SPRINGS
TELEGRAPH STATION
HISTORICAL
RESERVE

STUART

HEAD ST

River

ALICE SPRINGS
TELEGRAPH STATION
HISTORICAL
RESERVE

Bridge

Todd

*Old
Telegraph
Post*

1

Charles River
(river bed)
crossing

River

GOSSE   ST

EAST SIDE

SCHWARZ

STURT

LINDSAY

WINNECKE

ST

CRES

CHEWINGS

HWY

CICCONE

Charles

SMITH

ST

AV

RD

Anzac Hill
626m

Flood
measure

TCE

TCE

TCE

AV

WILLS

Alice
Springs
Railway
Station

HWY

TCE

PARSONS

ST

MALL

River

UNDOOLYA

TCE

SADADEEN

87

ST

ALICE
SPRINGS

ST

i

RAILWAY

STOTT

TODD

HARTLEY

TCE

LEICHHARDT

TCE

STOTT

LARAPINTA

DR

STUART

6

0   250   500m

Charles

STUART

HERBERT

HERITAGE

87

Telegraph Line, strung from Adelaide to Darwin. This walk follows the Todd River north from 'new' Alice Springs, called Stuart from its proclamation in 1888 until 1933, to the Telegraph Station opened on Alice Spring in 1872.

Starting at Alice Springs visitor information centre on the corner of Todd Mall and Parsons St, walk one block east on Parsons to the river, passing some funky seats with interesting sun shades, and the city's excellent YHA in the old Alice Springs cinema. Note the mural of Australian wildlife on the rear wall of the carpark opposite.

Cross Leichhardt Tce and turn left onto a sealed walking-cycling track on the riverbank, following it past beautiful old red gums.

The usually dry Todd River is the setting for the annual Henley on Todd Regatta, in August, when teams race bottomless boats. The wide, sandy riverbed is also where the annual Camel Cup race meeting, held each July, began in 1970, when Noel Fullerton challenged his mate and friendly rival Keith Mooney-Smith to a duel, with camels as weapons.

The Todd does sometimes flow, however, and that flow can become flood, so there's a gate on the red metal footbridge spanning the river

A gum leans over the dry Todd River

to close it when water covers the foot bed. Further on you'll pass a flood measure.

Cross Wills Tce and continue past a footy oval on your left. The rocky hill rising behind it is Anzac Hill; detour to the top, either now or on the way back, for a great view over the city and MacDonnell Ranges. The galahs along here are unafraid of people, and you can often get close enough for great photographs of these rambunctious pink-and-grey cockatoos.

This next section of shared-use track is a commemorative walk for Australians at War, with embedded plaques for different conflicts and military groups. These finish at a trail junction, with the Discovering Alice Springs Trail 'Communications' (Telegraph Station) 3km ahead. Walk on, crossing another road dipping into the Todd and passing a map of Alice Springs' mountain bike track network.

Staying with the river, and leaving housing behind, you come to an unsigned track on the left (see point 1 on map) climbing a low rocky rise. Climb this for a look at an old telegraph post, otherwise remain on the lower path into Alice Springs Telegraph Station Historical Reserve. All along here are mature and immature gum trees and coarse grass bleached pale gold. The green-and-yellow melons are a naturalised introduced bitter melon commonly called paddy melons.

On a blue-sky day you'll soon catch flashes of sun reflected off vehicles ahead in the Telegraph Station carpark, and then reach the grassy picnic area (free barbecues).

The Trail Station here is cafe, souvenir shop and Telegraph Station entrance. Go in now (fee payable) or turn right, along the fence in the direction of the arrowed Trig Hill walk, for a taste of Red Centre desert.

Where Trig Hill is marked left, go right, down to a sign on the river bank. It looks unlikely when the river is dry, but the depression here is the original Alice Spring (not a spring but a waterhole) named after Mrs Alice Todd, wife of Superintendent of Telegraphs, Charles Todd, in 1871.

Back on the walking track, follow arrows towards a rocky rise crowned with a trig point, winding slightly uphill to a wider bike track. Veer right and up stone steps, climbing to the trig point and a great view: beyond the Telegraph Station is the northern edge of Alice; to the right, the road to Alice Springs Desert Park and mesa-like Mt Gillen rising behind the award-winning wildlife park.

Head down the other side of Trig Hill, on the Cemetery Walk, which snakes between rocky rises and through thorny wattles and fluffy mauve mulla mulla. You may see kangaroos or a dingo. If you do spot a wild dog, do not panic and do not approach. Just retreat slowly out of sight and let it pass.

Cross another mountain bike track and follow signs for the Cemetery and Telegraph Station (1km), across a flat area (see point 2) scruffy with mulga and another old telegraph pole.

This track then runs into the Larapinta Trail (larapintatrail.com.au), the 223km walk that snakes through the West MacDonnell Range to Mt Sonder (see p. 311). Turn left and tread the Larapinta to a tiny stone-walled cemetery. One of the five people buried here is Ernie Bradshaw, younger brother of telegraph stationmaster T.A. Bradshaw, who died of tuberculosis just six months after coming here from Melbourne in the hope the dry climate would improve his health.

Wander along the wide, flat track to the left of the cemetery towards another pile of rock topped with gums and wattles. Watch for flocks of pretty zebra finches as you skirt clockwise around the rocks and amble through the carpark to the Telegraph Station.

Allow at least an hour to explore the restored stone buildings and read about the Overland Telegraph Line and life at the Alice Springs Station, one of 12 stations strung along the 3000km line. You'll also discover its later incarnations as a home and education centre for 'half-caste' children (Charles Perkins, one of Australia's most influential Aboriginal activists, was born here in 1936), WW II army base, and Aboriginal reserve.

The easiest return route to Alice Springs is back along the river. A slightly hillier option is the Spencer Hill Walk, which takes you down the other side of the Todd River and joins the Riverside Walk near Anzac Hill.

The walking track runs between the Todd River and rocky rises

2 JARNEM LOOP

Walk:	7.7km loop
Time required:	3 hours
Best time:	May to August (summer months can be hot and wet)
Grade:	Easy to moderate (one short climb)
Environment:	Savanna, palm-filled gullies, red-rock hills, beehive domes, Aboriginal art
Best map:	This one
Toilets:	Pit toilet in Jarnem campground
Food:	None
Tips:	Start early to see this country at its best, with the hills turning purple to brown to red in the morning sun

Changes in landforms and perspective make this walk an outback treasure: see the country from above and among the textures and colours.

Keep River National Park, just short of the WA border, is a wonderful spot for a stopover on the big lap around Australia. Spend a lazy night under the stars, eating the food you can't take through the quarantine checkpoint into WA, perhaps even sharing the prohibited fruits,

Beehive domes are the backdrop to fan palms and rough barked eucalypts in Keep River National Park

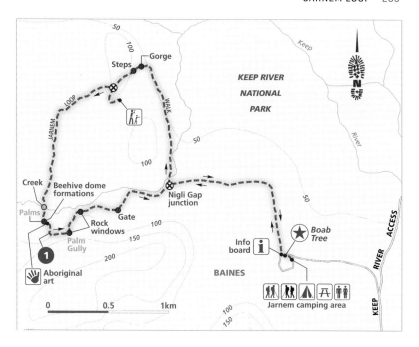

vegetables, honey, etc. with others staying longer or travelling in the
other direction.

The longest and most diverse walk in the park is the 8km Jarnem
Loop, from Jarnem campsite (pit toilets and tank water), 31km north
of the Victoria Hwy on 2WD gravel (the roads can be closed due to
wet season flooding; closures are listed at parksandwildlife.nt.gov.au/
parks/find/keepriver). The flat, red-sand walking track sets off from the
northern corner of the camping area, beside a bulbous boab tree, and
saunters across golden floodplain savanna studded with bloodwoods,
kapok trees and boabs.

A few hundred metres along, the track swings left around a low
rocky rise trimmed with palm forest and reveals, ahead through Nigli
Gap, the beehive domes through which you'll later weave. Changing
from red sand to pale sand as you pass from savanna into dense
riparian pandanus and peeling paperbarks, the track can be soft when

very dry. Just slow down and take your time; don't walk wide in search of firmer ground because this damages the grass, leading to erosion.

Turn right at the Nigli Gap junction in this greener, cooler forest and walk along the base of a great red caterpillar of rock with feeler-like livistona palms up top, strolling from pandanus into more open forest of acacias, white-barked gums and palms growing from pink-tinged grass.

The track then swings left into an open gorge and steps up between undercut walls of worn conglomerate and, higher up, an area of near-vertical rock revealing its multiple-layered construction.

You've got a great view already from the saddle – west to another ancient range and south, across spinifex-dotted bloodwood savanna to Jarnem escarpment – but turn left at the track junction and walk the extra 150m to the lookout. Note the layering in the rock as you tread this rougher track to time-worn high ground that drops away just metres beyond your toes. At your feet now lies a quintessential NT vista of beehive domes, yellow grasses, white-trunked trees and countless greens beneath too-blue sky.

Retrace your steps to the junction, turn left and work your way down to the plain. Back on the flat, the track parts a sea of spinifex on which ride countless bloodwoods, quinine trees sometimes laden with cumquat-like fruit, and turkey bush (also called fringe myrtle); the latter is readily identified in winter when it bursts into frothy shows of pink star flowers. Darwin woollybutts litter the ground with bright orange blossoms (these eucalypts also grow in the Jarnem campground, attracting flocks of noisy rainbow lorikeets). Look out for leopard-spotted small pond dragonflies perched, lacy wings shimmering like gold thread, on single stalks of grass.

Well-marked with blue arrows, the track rounds an area of standalone rock, the chunky stone appearing to have been placed by hand, then continues through cabbage palms and pale termite mounds. Watch for tiny black and white butterflies and green flashes of red-collared lorikeets as you weave through spiralling pandanus and fern leaf grevillea to the base of a mass of conjoined sandstone domes.

Like the considerably more famous and larger Bungle Bungle formations in Purnululu National Park, about 150km south (*see* p. 212)

Towering livistona palms reach skyward

in WA, these domes are the creation of sedimentation, uplift, cracking, weathering and erosion. The darker contrasting horizontal stripes indicate the presence of cyanobacteria, which are supported by layers of higher clay-content rock that retain more moisture than the drier, red layers.

The track swings left along the base of these weathered domes, many of them undercut, to an Aboriginal art site. The ochre emu and

Top: *At your feet lies a quintessential NT vista of beehive domes, yellow grasses, white-trunked trees and countless greens beneath too-blue sky;* **Bottom:** *The beehive domes take shape as you approach across the plain*

Left: *A silver leaf grevillea flowers against the winter sky;* **Right:** *A boab tree leans away from an Aboriginal art site tucked under the cliff*

serpent are only just visible on the rock, but this is a beautiful spot framed by boab trees and palms that provide welcome shade on warm days.

From here you swing right, around the art site into a horseshoe of rock [*see* point 1 on map], a natural amphitheatre populated with towering livistona palms. Those on the plain are a few metres tall, but these sweep skywards like elongated parasols.

The track cuts across the amphitheatre to another section of domes and continues along their base, passing narrow erosion gullies crammed with palms. The stone all along here has been severely weathered over time and small caves have formed in places. Look for a window worn through the rock fairly high up; and a narrower one like an arrow slit further on.

The track follows the escarpment to a gate, just beyond which it pulls left, away from the domes and a fenced sacred site into thick pandanus. Follow the fence line through Nigli Gap to the track you trod earlier, there turning right to walk back to your car.

3 JATBULA TRAIL

Walk:	63km one-way
Time required:	6 days
Best time:	The recommended Jatbula Trail walking season is 1 June to 30 September. Only experienced walkers who are aware of and prepared for extremes in temperature and humidity and the strong possibility of flooding should walk outside this time.
Grade:	Moderate, although the trail is officially graded challenging. This is less to do with the terrain than the length and remoteness, and the need to carry a full pack.
Environment:	Sandstone plateau, waterholes and waterfalls, woodland, riverine landscapes, savanna and Aboriginal art
Best map:	This one
Toilets:	Flushing toilets at the start (Nitmiluk Centre) and end (Leliyn/ Edith Falls); pit toilets in each camping area
Food:	Tuck into delicious breakfasts and lunches on the outdoor deck at licensed Sugarbag Cafe, adjoining the Visitor Centre at Nitmiluk/Katherine Gorge; celebrate finishing the walk with barra (barramundi) and buffalo burgers, ice-creams, great coffee and more from Edith Falls Kiosk
Tips:	Jatbula Trail bookings commence 1 November at 9am (Australian Central Standard Time) for the following year. A maximum of 15 walkers are permitted to set out each

A rocky view down the gorge greets you from 17 Mile Camp, where the creek plummets over the cliff

day. You can book online for the recommended season at parksandwildlife.nt.gov.au or contact the Parks Information Desk at Nitmiluk Visitor Centre on (08) 8972 1886 (8am–4pm) or parks.desk@nitmiluktours.com.au. A camping fee of $3.30 per person per night is required to secure your booking. You'll also need to book a ferry ride across the Katherine River at the same time. Transfers between Katherine and the start and/ or end of the walk can be booked with Gecko Canoeing and Trekking on (08) 8972 2224 or email gecko@nttours.com. There are emergency radios (and nearby helicopter pads) along the trail, but it's best to carry an emergency personal locator beacon anyway.

Follow in the footsteps of generations of Jawoyn people between Nitmiluk (Katherine Gorge) and Leliyn (Edith Falls), immersing yourself in country, culture, waterfalls and tranquil lagoons as you traverse the Arnhem Land escarpment.

Named after Jawoyn traditional owner Peter Jatbula, who fought for the return of this land to his people during the 1970s and 1980s (it was handed back in 1989) and walked the route with his family, the Jatbula Trail snakes along the western edge of the Arnhem Land escarpment in the south-west corner of Nitmiluk National Park. An Aboriginal songline and old stock route, Jatbula is also an escape route, from the crowds who swarm around the well-known sites at either end of the trail, and from the salties (estuarine crocodiles) that frequent many NT waters.

And it's the salty-free swimming holes that make Jatbula so special, jewels strung along the walking track!

Many people do Jatbula in five days, rolling the fifth and sixth days described here into one, but while this facilitates doing the walk over a week off work, travelling on the weekends at either end, it limits your time at Sweetwater Pool, the last swimming hole before Edith Falls. If you have the time, allow six days and spend all of the fifth afternoon at Sweetwater Pool.

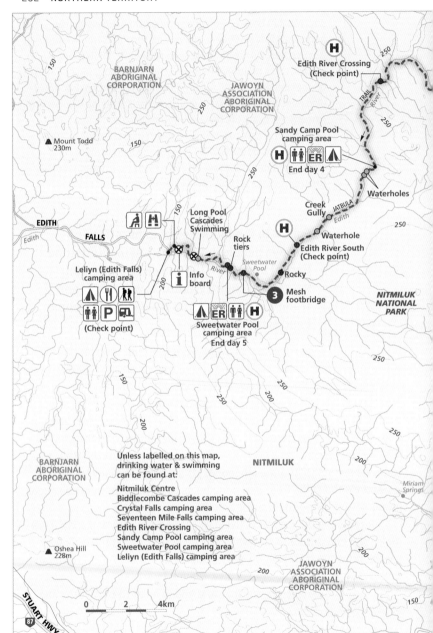

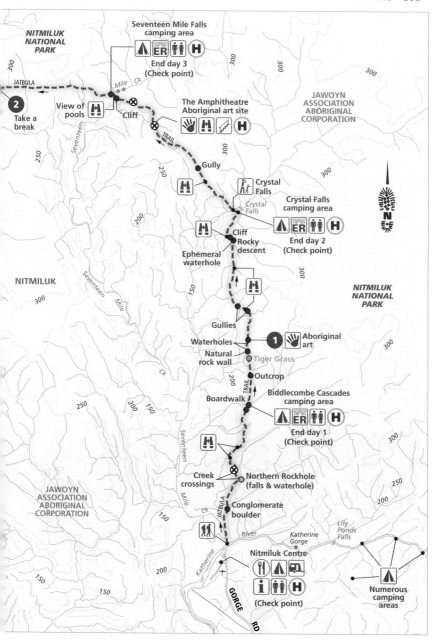

NITMILUK
NATIONAL
PARK

Seventeen Mile Falls
camping area

End day 3
(Check point)

JATBULA

2
Take a
break

View of
pools

Cliff

The Amphitheatre
Aboriginal art site

JAWOYN
ASSOCIATION
ABORIGINAL
CORPORATION

TRAIL

Gully

Crystal
Falls

Crystal
Falls

Crystal Falls
camping area

End day 2
(Check point)

Cliff
Rocky
descent

Ephemeral
waterhole

NITMILUK

N

NITMILUK
NATIONAL
PARK

Gullies

Waterholes

Natural
rock wall

1

Aboriginal
art

Tiger Grass

Outcrop

TRAIL

Biddlecombe Cascades
camping area

Boardwalk

End day 1
(Check point)

Creek
crossings

Northern Rockhole
(falls & waterhole)

JATBULA

Conglomerate
boulder

JAWOYN
ASSOCIATION
ABORIGINAL
CORPORATION

River

Katherine
Gorge

Lily
Ponds
Falls

Nitmiluk Centre

i

(Check point)

GORGE RD

Numerous
camping
areas

DAY 1: 8.2KM – 2.5 hours

The Jatbula Trail starts, at Nitmiluk/Katherine Gorge, with a ferry ride –
a ridiculously short one, for your $7; it's about 20m directly across the
Katherine River to a steep bank up which you scramble, farewelling
those ferry passengers embarking on a gorge cruise.

Marked by blue triangles suspended from trees, the track heads
north through coarse grass between 17 Mile Creek and the Arnhem
Land escarpment's south-western flank. This is a popular hangout for
red-tailed black cockatoos, and one of the highlights of the walk for
many people is encountering a huge flock of these beautiful birds, their
tails fanning flame-red as they fly from eucalypt to eucalypt ahead
of you.

Fairly flat for the first 4km, the trail navigates seas of fine grass
tinged pink and green and dips into and follows ephemeral creeks lined
with spiky spiral screwpines (a pandanus species) and kapok trees.
The kapok is a calendar plant for Jawoyn people: blousy yellow flowers
indicate that freshwater crocodiles and turtles are carrying eggs, while
green fruits indicate it's time to dig up eggs to eat. Also look out for –
they're hard to miss – the fern-leaved grevillea's vivid orange flowers.

Crystal Creek foams through rocks just below the camp on night two

Park management involves fuel reduction burns, so you'll likely pass through areas blackened by fire.

In places the trail becomes less distinct, but blue arrows guide the way to the sand and screwpine-fringed Northern Rockhole, which is fed by a waterfall that usually flows during December and January. Cascading water has painted a black stripe down the horseshoe of cliff above you. Head left across the front of the rockhole and rockhop across the creek trickling out of the waterhole – and watch your step; the footing is very uneven. When there's a breeze there's a lovely papery sound through here from the palms rubbing against each other.

Having followed the creek north-west and scaled a low saddle crowned with gums, you come to a sign warning against proceeding unless you're doing the long-distance Jatbula Trail. Continue to a creek crossing among paperbarks. This can be boggy or deep enough to wet feet and boots, in which case you might like to go barefoot.

The trail now runs into a 4WD maintenance track; turn right and follow this uphill, enjoying a view back down to the plains beyond the gorge and, as you crest the rise, plain and neighbouring ridge to the left and creek gully to the right. If you're lucky, the turkey bush will be at its best, producing clouds of starry fairy-floss pink.

The vehicular track is fairly rocky in places so it's difficult to get up any speed, but you'll have sand underfoot as you come through grassy scrub to your first campsite. Biddlecombe Cascades camping area is not the world's most scenic campsite but it is flat, and a short walk from the waterfall.

Tent pitched, follow the signs towards Leliyn/Edith Falls, over a granite slab. The track swings right, over a footbridge to the top of the swamp-fed falls, but an unmarked footpad going left leads to the plunge pool into which the creek pours before racing down a sluice.

DAY 2: 11.6KM – 3–4 hours
Continue towards Leliyn, this time crossing the footbridge to the top of the cascades; this is a good place to fill up your water bottles, and comes with a view down into the valley to the west.

The red rosette-like plants flat to the ground in damp areas here are insectivorous sundews.

Rocky to start and boggy in places, the trail wanders upstream through tropical banksia trees with small, tubular yellow flowers (in winter) and serrated leaves and grassy forest to a creek crossing. It's about 5m wide, with stepping stones, but you may still get wet feet.

Safely across, swing away from the water into savannah grassland lumpy with termite mounds and sometimes dotted with buffalo droppings. Staff warn you about buffalos when you register for the walk at Nitmiluk; these feral pests will usually avoid you but if you do see one, stop and remain quiet.

The trail meanders through outcrops and tunnels through swathes of tiger-stripe two-tone grasses. It follows a creek (walk in the creek bed when it's dry, or follow the track to the right) lined with salmon gums peeling snake-skin outer bark to smooth pink beneath, and clambers up rock beside another ephemeral waterhole.

About 4km into the walk the trail approaches a pile of rocks shaped like an easy chair (see point 1 on map). At its base, just off the main trail, you'll see a tall, red humanoid figure with spiky hair painted on the rock. There are several smaller Aboriginal artworks tucked higher up around the back of this formation. (To date, more than 400 Aboriginal art sites have been recorded in Nitmiluk National Park.)

Continuing north, with a few lazy twists and turns, the trail traverses rocky slopes and pushes through sedgy grasses, climbs hills to viewpoints over the 17 Mile Creek valley and dips into lush gullies lined with screwpines and paperbarks. (The Jawoyn people used large sheets of paperbark to make shelters, beds and rafts, and flavoured meat and fish with paperbark leaves.) Watch for drifts of apricot bladderworts, another carnivorous plant with flowers like a pea-orchid cross.

The going alternates between rocky and sandy and littered with palm fronds, but mostly you're on a flat dusty track through savanna where grey termite mounds form concrete boots around the assorted eucalypts.

Then you're walking over red rock where the termite mounds are red and you've got more views into 17 Mile Creek Valley. Cross several

Left: *A trail marker frames a hiker traversing savannah;* **Right:** *A eucalypt clings to a cliff with finger-like roots*

creeks (often dry) and navigate more gullies before following a creek through lush stands of screwpines. A rocky climb then puts you atop a ridge for another terrific valley view.

The day's final descent isn't steep, but the loose rock can be slippery. You'll pass a pit toilet on the right as you head down to camp number two, under the shady trees beside beautiful Crystal Creek.

The choice is yours: subside into a one-person spa among the rapids or walk a few metres upstream to a large waterhole and swim among the waterlilies. Why not do both?

DAY 3: 10.6KM – 3–4 hours

You have to cross Crystal Creek to continue on the trail, and the combination of your nimbleness and the height of the creek will determine whether you reach the far side dry of foot or dripping. If you are not confident about rockhopping with a pack, the creek is usually shallow enough to walk through during the recommended walking season, but hikers have been known to wade through chest-deep water after a late wet season.

Safely across, you'll climb to some rocks overlooking the waterhole below the rapids where you camped. Continue through a gully then you'll see the top of Crystal Falls and the chute through which they foam before going over the edge. A short, signed detour takes you left to a spectacular lookout above the twin plunges.

You'll find a checkpoint station at the lookout junction, where you should put your name and permit number in the book.

Having climbed up from the checkpoint, listen and watch for red-tailed black cockatoos (creaking call) and spinifex doves (like a wind-up toy) as you walk through restful grassland. Note the termite tunnels running up the tree trunks.

About 4km from tonight's camp there's a track junction with Leliyn/Edith Falls ahead and the Amphitheatre to the left. Leave your pack here and follow the left-hand track along the rim of a gorge, watching for the bronze flashes of rainbow bee-eaters in the trees.

A metal staircase descends to a footpad that doubles back along the artistically striped cliff to two art sites. You'll see animals and figures at the first, but an unusual creature awaits you at the second (also a quarry for weapons rock and ochre). The main figure here is a

Camping among the scrub beside Biddlecombe Cascades

Jawoyn woman, painted in red, white and yellow, dressed in a breast girdle, bracelets, wrist and knee bands, her face distorted by a nose bone, ready to dance all night to get the man she wanted, perhaps to lure him to his doom. Because this is women's business (although approved for visitors of both sexes), getting details is more difficult.

From the stairs you may glimpse Aboriginal art on the opposite gorge wall, but there are also sacred sites down here, so respect the Jawoyn people's wishes and don't venture deeper into the gorge. Just retrace your steps to the stairs and your pack.

Pack back on, continue along a 4WD management track until a blue arrow on a tree directs you left, into yellow grass. This trail returns you to the lip of the escarpment and presents a fabulous view of the multiple tiers of narrow 17 Mile Falls plummeting from the escarpment into a large pool way below.

Moving clear of the edge beyond the lookout, the trail traverses rocky slabs before climbing a natural staircase of tiered rock and revealing a lovely upstream waterhole. Arrows point over rock and across 17 Mile Creek, where the water has drilled holes and polished rock between two falls.

The track up the other side, leading to the campsite, can be boggy. If you must keep your boots clean, walk downstream on the same side of the falls but on the rock; this takes you steeply down to the first plunge pool, from where you've got a short climb to camp. (The toilet is a concealed 100m walk up from the campsite, safe from flood waters.)

You've got several options for swimming in and around these top pools, with easy ascents from the camping area. But don't leave without following the cliff-line south-west from camp for a dramatic view of the fractured, layered rock through which 17 Mile Creek works in the lead-up to its precipitous plunge.

DAY 4: 17.3KM – 4–6 hours

The longest day on the Jatbula Trail begins with a short, rocky climb out of camp. Start early to bask in pastel morning light on the escarpment and so you can spend the afternoon lolling, floating and splashing about in Sandy Camp Pool.

Although much of the country seems similar to yesterday, and the day before, it doesn't get boring. Because it changes, both dramatically – from grassy woodland to screwpine-filled gully in a few steps – and subtly. The walking isn't hard either, so you can push on while noting the different-coloured termite mounds and the nesting holes drilled into them by birds (you might even see one fly out).

Exposed rocks on a slight crest about 6km from the previous camp (see point 2) make great seats for a snack break. The track now snakes through rocky country, climbing and descending just enough for you to notice, sometimes with large pieces of stone underfoot, sometimes gravel.

Then you traverse a broad grassy valley between natural low stone walls thick with fern-leaved grevillea and small stands of screwpines; many of the latter have grown along the ground before heading skyward, and put down roots along their trunk, so they look like weird giant woody caterpillars.

With rock coming in on both sides, the trail wanders through dense stands of screwpines and beautiful paperbarks. Be aware of occasional roots as you tread this section. Then you're walking through tall eucalypts with smooth, white trunks escaping from coarse bark collars, and acacias that sport cylindrical yellow flowers in winter and runner bean-like seed pods up to 20cm long.

About 10km into the day you'll start following the Edith River (on your right). Keeping right of a natural wall and climbing over stone pavement brings you to a natural ford over the Edith River. Again, conditions will vary depending on time of year and recent rain. Mid-winter, the crossing will likely be dry.

The trail continues down the opposite river bank but the sloping rock and shading trees at the crossing make it a good spot for lunch, and perhaps a swim.

At first threading along the river, the trail then pulls away and tunnels through tall grass towards layered, almost dome-like formations unlike anything you've seen before on the walk. Skirt this outcrop and scale low rocky rises, continuing through coarse, mallee-like bushes.

Past a wooden sign for the Channels Waterhole (you could take a look), stay right of another natural wall. Then, with the river on your left, cross several rocky areas before escaping their reflected heat, into a grassy stand of salmon gums. You may see water buffalo wallows as you tunnel through sometimes chest-high grasses.

The trail now enters leafier riparian forest, crossing a creek and passing a beautiful waterhole covered in waterlilies. It's easy to lose sight of the trail among the screwpines here, but the suspended arrows are high enough to keep you on the correct heading.

Back in banksias, grevilleas and coarse-barked eucalypts, the trail climbs a rise and you're looking down at a circular lagoon. Cross the feeding stream, where it's drilled a two-person plunge pool, and walk along the shore to Sandy Pool Camp, among the paperbarks.

DAY 5: 11KM – 3 hours

With your back to the delicious water that washed off yesterday's dust, head left along the base of the rocks behind the sandy camping area. There's a shortage of track markers early on day 5, but essentially you start by following the river, treading a rocky-then-sandy route past smaller waterholes framed by paperbarks.

Then you're in savanna again, where you'll stay for a while, walking parallel to a greener, leafier riparian strip to your left, with red and green parrots darting everywhere. Beyond a pretty beach on your left and pools and rock shelving to your right you'll come to the Edith River South checkpoint (sign in again here).

The trail continues through white gums, massed grevilleas, and showy turkey bush; then areas of assorted plants. After slowing you down through another rocky section the trail traverses a marshy area (*see* point 3) where hikers have cut wider and wider tracks to keep out of the mud, creating a web of boggy tracks.

Visible from atop the next rise are shallow tiered rapids in the river just down to your left. Follow the river downstream, treading natural pavements of gently sloping, layered shelving and occasional patches of soft sand; thick grevilleas separate you and the water, and paperbarks stand majestically over everything and everyone else.

Traversing the rocks before Sandy Pool Camp

Ahead now is a large waterhole and the trail drops down onto rock that shelves bleacher-like into the water. This is the top end of Sweetwater Pool, where many hikers have a cooling dip before pressing on to Leliyn/Edith Falls.

The track steps down and works around the edge of those tiers then presses on another 200m or so down the lagoon to the camping area. It's an easy walk back to these rock-rimmed pools, so pitch your tent and then spend the afternoon immersed in the beauty of this spot. You may have to share the pools with day hikers from Leliyn/Edith Falls, but you'll probably have the camp to yourself.

DAY 6: 4.4KM – 1.5 hours

Go with the flow, downstream but clambering over the base of the rocks that create the camp backdrop; past more rapids to another big waterhole, beside which the trail pulls away from the water, only to return. Having crossed creek gullies and cut through an untidily treed plain, you'll find yourself on a sandy track often scored with insect and animal tracks as well as human ones, beside a beach and shelving falls.

And shortly after, you'll be gazing down the length of Long Pool, which reaches as far as you can see.

By now very familiar blue-arrow trail markers direct you uphill on a rocky track, where you might meet day walkers heading the other way to Long Pool or Sweetwater Pool for a swim. You can see for kilometres through the trees from here.

From twin signs about the Jatbula Trail and the Jawoyn people, a rocky track descends to a junction. Turn left for a swim in Upper Pool (300m) on the Leliyn Loop Trail (orange markers) and right for a barra burger at the Edith Falls Kiosk.

Sweetwater Pool, where hikers with the time spend an extra night, is a beautiful place to swim and relax

4 KINGS CANYON LOOP

Walk:	6.7km loop
Time required:	3–4 hours
Best time:	Mild sunny day; temperatures can soar from October to April, so you'll need to set out early (access to the walk can be restricted during extreme weather)
Grade:	Moderate, with a challenging but short early climb
Environment:	Beehive dome formations, precipitous red-rock cliffs, palm-filled creek gully, perched waterhole
Best map:	This one
Toilets:	Flushing toilets in carpark
Food:	Lunch supplies, takeaways, drinks, snacks, and evening meals available at Kings Canyon Resort
Tips:	Spoil yourself with a scenic helicopter flight for a bird's-eye view of Kings Canyon and George Gill Range; book at kingscanyonresort.com.au or through Professional Helicopter Services (phs.com.au)

Navigating a labyrinth of beehive domes and putting you on toe-curling cliff edges, this outback loop finishes well ahead of most starters in the scenery and geology stakes.

Weathered timber frames red rock on the Kings Canyon Rim Walk

Centrepiece of Watarrka National Park, home of the Luritja Aboriginal people for over 20,000 years and a refuge for plants and animals from the harsher plains, Kings Canyon is a breathtaking chasm sliced into the red rock of the George Gill Range by water, erosion and time. This 6km loop walk around its rim is a desert classic.

The walk starts from Kings Canyon picnic and parking area, about 300km north of Uluṟu and 450km south-west of Alice Springs. The most scenic route to the gorge is via West MacDonnell National Park, the Mereenie Loop (4WD recommended and permit required) and Lasseter and Stuart highways, but you can drive all the way on bitumen via the highways and Luritja Rd.

Head east on a sealed track with smooth, white-barked gums and a lumpy ridge of red rock to your right (behind which the rim walk returns to the carpark). Past an information shelter with complimentary wifi and signs encouraging you to post your pics to promote NT tourism, and a separate safety information shelter and toilets (left), the track forks, with the 2.6km return Kings Creek Walk (orange arrow) going straight ahead. Turn left for the Kings Canyon Rim Walk and follow the blue arrows steeply uphill on rock steps.

This is arguably the most famous climb in Australia, thanks to the international cinematic hit *The Adventures of Priscilla, Queen of the Desert*. But while you might be tempted to recreate the scene and climb in chiffon and ostrich feathers, it is safer and more comfortable in less flamboyant walking attire. Hiking boots fit the bill, but are not essential on this walk; sandals or runners work fine.

You'll pass through a couple of flat areas with bench seats before the track tops out on a roomy natural lookout presenting grandstand views up the canyon and down to people walking its treed floor. An easy track of cemented rocks continues through massed spinifex and eucalypts towards a cluster of rock domes (*see* point 1 on map), with a short rocky climb landing you among them. A landmark geological feature of Kings Canyon, these rock stacks were originally the lower layers of sand dunes, compacted and compressed by the deposition of more sand and cemented together by water rich in silica. Wind and rain eroding a grid of vertical cracks produce these clustered domes separated by natural walkways, a 'lost city' of sorts.

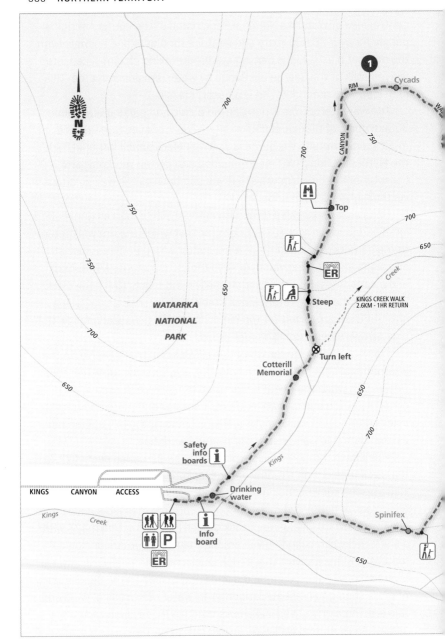

N

1

Cycads

RIM

WA

CANYON

700

750

Top

ER

Steep

Creek

KINGS CREEK WALK
2.6KM – 1HR RETURN

Turn left

Cotterill
Memorial

WATARRKA

NATIONAL

PARK

700

650

650

Safety
info
boards

Kings

Drinking
water

KINGS CANYON ACCESS

Kings   Creek

Spinifex

P

Info
board

ER

650

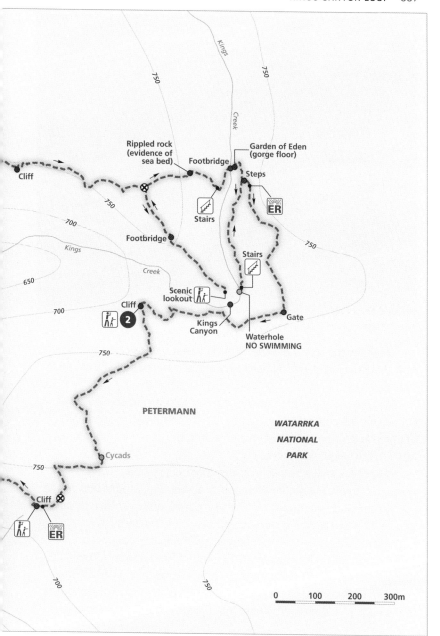

Natural walkways lead through a 'lost city' of striped domes

Note how the layers wear differently, resulting in stone shelving, and how the crusty oxidised exposed sandstone is much darker than the rock beneath.

The trail takes you to the brink of a cliff with an awesome view of the plains, the canyon and its extraordinary south wall, a great slab of holed and 'dripping' toffee-like rock atop which you'll probably see walkers further along the track.

As you follow blue arrows over the lower slopes of domes and through spinifex to another stomach-dropping cliff, stop to look at the pretty tubular cream flowers, with hairy, purply-brown striped throats, of a twining and climbing shrub commonly called spearbush.

Heading away from the cliff now you come to a track junction. Turn right to Cotterill's Lookout (600m return) and walk over and through domes to a footbridge accessing a dome facing the canyon's southern cliff. Continue through cracked and crazed natural stonework to the edge of a sheer wall, where the brave/foolhardy lie down and

peer into the void; then press on to the final lookout, above the Garden
of Eden waterhole.

Back on the main track you'll come to an area where the rock
shelving underfoot is rippled. Follow the trail across this old lake bed
and through more domes and descent a timber staircase, down under
a wave-like rock and into a deep gully. A refuge for rare and relict plants
dating back to when Central Australia was wetter and snaked with
rivers, and a haven for birds and aquatic wildlife, including two species
of frog, this is the Garden of Eden.

A footbridge spanning the gully leads to a ladder up an undercut.
Scale the ladder and duck under the larger timber staircase climbing
out of the Garden of Eden and walk downstream to a waterhole nestled
between undercut cliffs. The traditional owners of Watarrka National
Park request that visitors help keep the water healthy by not swimming
here, but you are welcome to splash the cool water on your face and
sit on the flood-polished rocks, watching birds dart about and water-
reflected sunlight dance on the stone walls.

Retracing your steps to the staircases and climbing out of the gully
puts you back on the escarpment, with the canyon on your right.

Through a metal gate, end point of the 4.8km South Wall Return
Walk, the trail hugs and clambers between domes as it ventures to
the lip of the south wall (see point 2). To the Luritja people, these
domes are young 'kuninga' men who travelled through here during the
Tjukurpa (the Dreaming). You are now one of those ant-like figures you
saw earlier from the opposite precipice. All the cliffs on the Rim Walk
have warning signs, but few people can resist standing or even sitting
on the edge, and this spot is no exception.

The track pulls away from the canyon wall here. It heads south and
across the escarpment and works down a corridor of slow-growing
prehistoric cycads, great balls of stiff green leaves, some of which are
centuries old. Cycads are one of 17 plant species in the park that date
back to when dinosaurs inhabited this country.

The trail now descends steadily, behind a row of domes separating
you from Kings Canyon proper, and along the lip of a smaller side
canyon, through eucalypts, cypress pines and holly grevilleas with curly

red flowers. Just past a sign indicating that it's 1km to the carpark you'll pass the Giles Track going left; this two-day 22km walk snakes along the George Gill Range to Kathleen Springs.

As if you haven't had enough jaw-dropping moments already, you come to a lookout over another canyon where nankeen kestrels nest and Kestrel Falls pours after heavy rain. The head of the canyon is a massive chunk of crazed rock dotted with spinifex and the odd tree, seemingly growing out of nothing.

The trail climbs briefly along a crescent of domes before looping left for a full-frontal view of Kestrel Falls cliff (turn around and you can see the carpark). Then you're on the downhill run home, on sealed track traversing a hill covered in spinifex mounds, like an Aboriginal dot painting.

Across Kings Creek (often dry) you run into the main canyon walking track, which takes you back to the parking area.

Walkers get toe-curlingly close to the edge of the monumental South Wall

5 MOUNT SONDER

Walk:	15.6km return
Time required:	6–7 hours
Best time:	Mild sunny day (the track is exposed and unsuitable for walking in summer, when temperatures soar)
Grade:	Moderate to hard (long and continuously up then down on rocky track)
Environment:	Ancient outback mountain range, unfenced cliffs, spectacular clifftop views
Best map:	This one
Toilets:	Pit toilet in Redbank Gorge carpark
Food:	Snacks and sit-down meals are available at Glen Helen Resort, 19km east of the Redbank Gorge turnoff, along Namatjira Drive, the main road to Alice Springs
Tips:	If you're feeling flush, take a scenic helicopter flight over the ranges from Glen Helen Resort (glenhelen.com.au)

Climb to the highest point on the long-distance Larapinta Trail for eagle-eye views of the ancient West MacDonnell Ranges.

Rwetyepme to the local Arrernte Aboriginal people, for whom it has spiritual significance, but commonly called 'the pregnant lady' because

The ancient MacDonnell Range sprawls at your feet

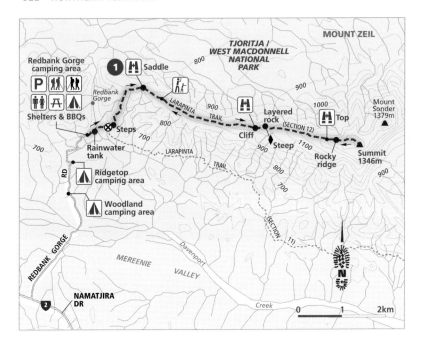

its twin-peaked profile looks like an expectant woman lying on her back, Mt Sonder is a West MacDonnell Ranges landmark. It's also the highest point on, and the final leg (Section 12) of, the 223km Larapinta Trail; or the first, for those bucking the trend and hiking west–east, to the Alice Springs Telegraph Station (see p. 278). Some people climb the mountain by torchlight in morning darkness, so they are up top for sunrise, which adds another degree of difficulty to the moderately hard ascent.

But before heading out, you need to know that Mt Sonder is not the highest peak in the West Macs – that honour goes to Mt Zeil (1531m) – nor is the end point of this walk the highest point on Mt Sonder, so it's a minor fraud to call it the top. But, while some people make their way off-track to the true summit, the walk is cut short for safety reasons and most hikers find the spectacle from the false summit enough of a reward for the almost unremitting climb to the 'top'.

The walk leaves from Redbank Gorge carpark, in West MacDonnell National Park, about 5km off the bitumen and 156km all up from Alice

Springs. The unsealed access road can be rough, is steep in places and crosses two creek beds, so all-wheel-drive is recommended. But it's scenic, too, offering a wonderful view of the mountain ridge you have come to conquer, so you won't want to speed.

The track heads downhill from the eastern end of the parking area and forks a short way in. Take the right-hand track marked for Larapinta sections 11 and 12, leaving beautiful Redbank Gorge for later. There's a water tank on the right near the bottom. A NT Parks and Wildlife sign warns that the water is untreated and should be boiled, sterilised or filtered, although many people drink it as is.

As you cross the sandy creek bed, you may spot hiking tents among the majestic river red gums; Larapinta Trail hikers are permitted to camp in the creek, while all other visitors have a choice of woodland and ridge camping areas a few minutes' drive back up the access road.

Walking through the red rocky country beyond the river soon knocks the sand off your boots, coating them instead with dust when it's very dry. Ignoring the track to Glen Helen (Gorge) – this 25km two-day walk is section 11 of the Larapinta – head left to Mt Sonder summit 16km (the sign suggests eight hours return), climbing slightly through mulga and spinifex.

The view from atop Mt Sonder stretches many kilometres across Australia's arid heart

The rocky Mt Sonder track heads down the range towards the gorge and camping areas

Now the track becomes rockier and zigzags uphill through slate-fine layers. As you climb, a range, eroded to scallop-like curves and drawn in pastel shades in early light, lengthens to your right and then behind you. Height gain is rapid and within about 45 minutes you'll see the carpark below and, beyond it, any tents and vans perched on the ridge-top camping area.

Having climbed steeply you get a brief respite on a saddle (see point 1 on map) before more gently continuing up a ridge. Your destination is the first of Mt Sonder's twin saw-tooth peaks, clearly visible ahead now but even more impressive from the Summit Lookout, a short way through a sea of spinifex and stubby eucalypts.

A map here identifies all the landmarks and a sign warns that the track beyond is only for well-prepared walkers. Looking along the ridge you'll see that the track descends again before making the final push to the top. Behind you now is the rounded hill over which you walked and, to its right, at about one o'clock, is Mt Zeil (1531m), the highest mountain in the MacDonnell Ranges and the highest mainland Australian mountain west of the Great Dividing Range. The standalone, ragged edged red formation at about nine o'clock is Tnorala (Gosse Bluff), the eroded impact crater of a massive comet that crashed into Earth about 140 million years ago; this remarkable formation is accessible by high-clearance 4WD vehicle.

The track beyond the lookout is a mix of loose shaly rock and larger, sturdy, embedded stone, and the going is fairly good. The ridge then narrows, forcing the track nearer the cliff edge, where sloping rock juts out over an abrupt drop.

From here you zigzag steeply down a rugged red-rock bluff made of countless, almost filo-pastry thin layers of sedimentation. Depending on your perspective, this is either one of several welcome flat areas and descents that give you a break from climbing, or one of too many dispiriting descents that rob you of hard-won altitude! However you view it, this bluff presents you with a great view of the track winding up the last ridge – and of the top, although you can't yet see the cairn.

Within the cairn there's a visitors' book and pen for recording your comments about the walk and the panorama, which may test your adjectival vocabulary.

Easily identifiable is Glen Helen Gorge, a V in the scalloped range through which the Finke River flows; to the south-east are the walls of Ormiston Pound (*see* p. 321). Stepping towards the north of the summit – not too near the edge! – note the ridges fanning off this peak. Tufts of greenery grow defiantly atop these extremely narrow walls like mohawk hairdos.

The true Mt Sonder summit is the next peak, with the trig point. It's about 20m higher, but there is no walking track, and you're asked not to climb it. When you've recovered from being short-changed, and caught your breath, head back down (with a few ups) the way you came.

6 MPULUNGKINYA WALK (PALM VALLEY) LOOP

Walk:	5km loop
Time required:	2 hours
Best time:	Mild sunny day; the cooler months are April to October, summer can be extremely hot
Grade:	Easy to moderate (short climb and some sandy sections)
Environment:	Rocky escarpment, rocky and sandy river bed, rare palm grove
Best map:	This one
Toilets:	Pit toilets in Finke Gorge National Park day-use area and campground
Food:	Supermarket and cafes in Hermannsburg, on Larapinta Dve, just outside the park
Tips:	Palm Valley is the most popular place in Finke Gorge National Park and is visited by all independent travellers and commercial tours coming to the park. Try to come outside Northern Territory and South Australian school holidays, and get in and out early to avoid the crowds.

Red rock, Central Australia's only palms, and one hell of a fun access drive make this loop much more than just another Red Centre walk.

Often cited as 'the oldest river on Earth', the Finke flows some 600km from the West MacDonnell Ranges south-east to the edge of the

A ghost gum frames Palm Valley

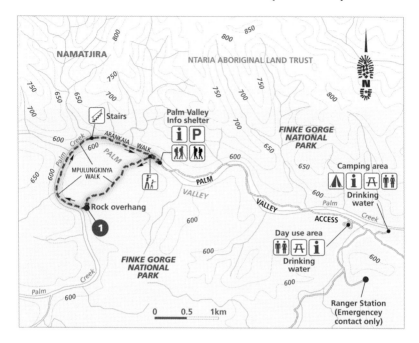

Simpson Desert, where it soaks into the dunes. The river has followed this route for over 100 million years, and some sections of its course are three times that age, so even if others are older, the Finke is certainly no whippersnapper!

On its journey from prehistoric mountains to inland sea (of sand), the Finke (local Aboriginal people call it Larapinta, the name given to the long-distance walking track through the West MacDonnell Ranges) snakes and loops, forming lazy waterholes frequented by wildlife and travellers. It also waters thousands of red cabbage palms, an isolated stand of these rare plants tucked between Finke Gorge's serpentine sandstone walls.

Palm Valley is the most popular part of remote Finke Gorge National Park, and the Mpulungkinya Walk a great way to get a feel for this extraordinary part of the world.

The national park is 138km south-west of Alice Springs, the last 16km following the Finke River's sandy bed and navigable only by high-clearance 4WD vehicles. [The park is open year round, but heavy rain and flooding can make access impossible; if in doubt check road conditions by phoning 1800 246 199.]

The walk starts from the Palm Valley parking area, three-or-so spectacular and rocky kilometres further west along the gorge.

Clockwise from top: *Walking back down Palm Valley; swirled red rock climbs skyward; red cabbage palms tower over walkers treading the valley floor.*

Park notes recommend you tread the Mpulungkinya Walk anticlockwise, but we're bucking the trend because this way you get great gorge views before wending your way back down it. So from the shady information shelter in the parking area, welcome on a warm day, turn left and clamber up the tiered sandstone and walk parallel with the gorge rim, with riverbed, rock walls and your first sight of red cabbage palms below you now.

A majestic ghost gum clings to the edge here, its white trunk against a backdrop of red rock and blue sky like a Namatjira painting.

The track now steps away from the cliff edge and veers slightly higher, but it's still fairly easy going. Keep left at a junction marked with two arrows (the shorter Arankaia Loop goes right) and cross the escarpment, walking through white-stripe ghost gums and cypress pines and dodging mounds of spinifex. Some of the spinifex is very old and has formed bristling doughnut rings. Blue arrows direct you up broad tiers of red rock to the top for a fabulous view to the neighbouring sandstone plateau.

Oxidisation and weathering have fashioned circular patterns in the stone underfoot here, and its thin crust is peeling away in places. Note, too, the sparkling specks of silica in the sandy patches between the rock as you follow arrows and small cairns to the edge of the escarpment. From here you can see the riverbed and palms, plains and beehive-like formations.

Follow the cliff edge left around a side gully with the broad rocky gorge floor now sharply below. The track zigzags under a huge overhanging rock (see point 1 on map) whose ceiling is festooned with tiny mud nests; you might like to take a breather from the sun in the rock's shade before descending.

Down in the riverbed, turn right and keep right, with a fabulously layered red cliff stepping up on your right and expanses of grey stone to your left, almost crater-like with indentations where water has pooled. One larger dry 'pool' is ringed with reeds and has a great red rock in the middle, like an altar.

The riverbed becomes rocky and uneven as you approach the first cabbage palms, and the middle of the gorge becomes thick with their greenery as you continue. The geology ups its game too, and you'll pass a cliff of extremely fine layering.

Palm Valley is home to a diverse mix of plants, lots of which are unique to the area. These include the aforementioned red cabbage palms, many several hundred years old and over 20m tall.

Genetic testing recently disproved the long-held and oft-repeated theory that the palms are botanic remnants of a time when Central Australia was lush with tropical forests, rather than red desert. But how the palms got here remains a mystery – their nearest close relative is 1000km away. Aboriginal legend tells of gods from the north bringing the seeds to Palm Valley.

Whatever their story, the palms are precious and warrant protection. Juveniles, which are red, hence the name, are vulnerable to trampling, so don't wander too far off track for photographs, and watch where you tread.

Continue down the gorge, between a host of interwoven cycads and shaggy headed palms and a wall of undercut, layered rock to which ghost gums cling. Past another side gorge, coming in on the left, and water pooled in hollows in the river's rocky bed, you'll squeeze between undercut rock and a large bed of reeds with fluffy seed heads.

Patches of sand alternate with rock, but walking's still pretty easy. Look out for the single lines of pebbles embedded in the red sandstone 'paving', and another area where conglomerate rock overlays the sandstone like a concrete pour.

Beyond a set of stairs coming down on the right from the shorter Arankaia Walk, you'll find yourself on a swirly natural footpath with palms and ghost gums left (we are leaving the massed palms behind) and a rampart of red rock to the right. Ascend the next stairs and wander along the ledge at its base, passing massive chunks of stone that have sheared off the cliff above.

A rail gives some reassurance as you descend sloping sandstone back onto the riverbed, and rubber mesh makes it easier to walk through a particularly sandy reach. Mesh continues along rounded, undercut cliff streaked white with ghost gums and most of the way back to the information shelter and carpark.

7 ORMISTON POUND LOOP

Walk:	9.3km loop
Time required:	3–4 hours
Best time:	Mild sunny day; the pound is open year round but can be extremely hot in summer. After high rainfall you might have to wade or even swim through waterholes in the gorge.
Grade:	Moderate (very rough walking on rocky gorge floor)
Environment:	Ancient hills, broad pound, stony rim lookouts, ephemeral desert creek, deep and rocky gorge
Best map:	This one
Toilets:	Flushing toilets in carpark
Food:	The kiosk in the picnic and camping area sells great coffee, ice-creams, toasties, BBQ packs and fresh-made pizza (selected nights during winter season)
Tips:	This walk can be done in either direction but has far more impact walked anticlockwise, as described, which heightens the impact on entering the pound and the gorge

Geology is front and centre on this spectacular Red Centre loop from the broad expanse of Ormiston Pound down Ormiston Creek's narrow stone-walled gorge.

A walker takes in the view from the pound rim

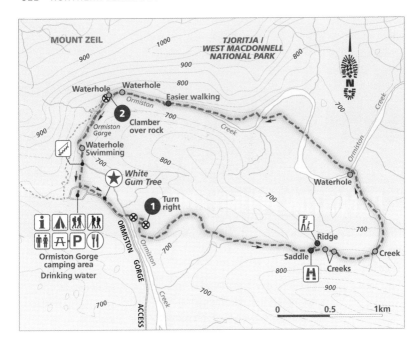

From a plane, the timeworn mountains reaching east and west of Alice Springs look like the fossilised remains of gargantuan creatures and in Arrernte Aboriginal mythology, giant caterpillars created this country. But the paired arms of the MacDonnell Ranges are neither monstrous nor dead, and beg to be explored on foot, with little effort required to reach a spot deep in their folds where enamel-red dragonflies flit about waterholes and dripping water marks time's slow passing.

One of the best day walks in Australia, and a popular add-on for hikers treading the Larapinta Trail through East MacDonnell National Park, the Ormiston Pound loop departs from the Pound parking area, 135km west of Alice Springs via Namatjira Dve. Follow the signs for Larapinta Trail Section 9 (blue triangle) and Pound Walk (orange arrows), which means turning your back on the gorge and the great pyramid of red rock guarding its mouth.

The rocky trail wanders through ghost gum woodland softened with fluffy pink and white mulla mulla flowers, runs along the pound access road for about 20m and then ducks left, crossing Ormiston Creek. Bark and branches piled in the forks of river gums testify to the force of the water that storms down the creek in occasional flood events. Also note the pink, grey, blue and other coloured and textured rocks underfoot.

Turning left where the Larapinta Trail heads right, walk through long-leafed corkwood trees, with very coarse trunks and curlicue green-yellow flowers.

Past a cutaway cliff with tile-like patterning, the track zigzags uphill through spinifex mounds and curry wattles. Beware the distracting flowers though, because at one point footpads continue across a shaly hill where the walking track swings hard right; a stacked jumble of red rock (see point 1 on map) is a good marker for this turn.

The track swings around so Ormiston Creek and the pound access road are steeply below on your right, and looking back over your shoulder here you can see Mt Sonder between the neighbouring range and the gorge mouth guardian.

Swinging up another hill robs you of that view, but it's visible again when you reach the next ridge. From here, a rocky trail meanders up

A permanent waterhole reflects the walls of Ormiston Gorge

and down through hills thick with spinifex, bloodwoods and holly-leaf grevillea bushes with splashy red flowers. Then it hoists you up onto a saddle, giving a wide-angle view back down the valley up which you've climbed.

Follow the side track on the saddle up onto a narrow ridge crowned with ghost gums for a breathtaking view over Ormiston Pound. To your right this broad, natural bowl is rimmed with a splendid wall of serpentine rock, while opposite it rises gently, ramp like, to a sheer-walled tabletop. And through the pound snakes often-dry Ormiston Creek, its sandy bed disappearing between rock folds into the gorge, to the west.

Back down from that rocky aerie, descend from the saddle, noting how the stone clinks underfoot, almost as if the hill is hollow. The track crests another rise, rounds a smaller pyramid of rock, fords several ephemeral creeks, clambers over eroded sawtooth layering and deposits you in the pound.

The track then traverses the pound floor, dodging exposed chunks of red rock shot with quartz as it weaves through bloodwoods, wattles, spinifex mounds and mulla mulla, twice crossing the creek. Detour downstream on the first crossing to a string of rock pools and companionable old gum trees that have witnessed many floods. The second crossing is sandy and soft, and from the shade of an ancient gum in the river bed you get your first good view of Ormiston Pound's east wall.

Continue through red rock and quartz towards stone battlements with thick flat tops resting upon lesser slopes dotted with spinifex; white ghost gums grow in the margin where the layers meet. A third river crossing lands you on a grassy bank beside three graceful mature ghost gums.

As you follow the creek into the gorge the mesa-like top layers slope down either side to almost meet, and you are walking through the lowest point, the weak point, between two descending plains of deposition. The stonework underfoot here is red, orange and grey; from pebbles up to great slabs, some rounded, some sharp-edged. And beside you rears a jaw-dropping red wall. Further in, the gorge is lined

Left: *Remarkable red-and-white striped red rock decorates the gorge;* **Right:** *Mauve rock meets red cliff climbing up from the river bed*

with deep pink rock fashioned into blocks and slabs drilled with holes by water.

The top end of Ormiston Gorge is unevenly floored with occasional patches of soft sand, so the going is slow. It's hugely impressive though, and deserves unhurried appreciation. Looking up you'll see trees perched on narrow rock shelves and rocks that look as if they are barely keeping grip on the cliffs. Working your way steadily downstream you encounter pools and areas where water has lain, and you can clearly see the black high-water mark.

The main waterhole (*see* point 2) is permanent and many metres deep, and blocks the gorge. Herons sometimes perch in the trees leaning over the water and wade in the shallows. Orange arrows show the way over rocks to the right, an easy clamber up a couple of rock shelves.

On top you'll see the Ghost Gum Walk (a 2.4km loop from the parking area) heading right; this alternative route to your car climbs to vantage points over the gorge. The ghost gums along this high walk have worked roots 70m down through rock to the waterhole below!

For the full-on gorge experience remain on the lower route, through coarse sand and over pink-and-grey striped rock. Shelved rock shot through with quartz, like a Jackson Pollock painting, steps down to a bigger waterhole cupped between ascending layers of white, grey and red rock – you'll probably see a lookout-load of people overhead – and sandy beach. This is a great spot for a cooling swim, and often noisy with others who agree.

Take either set of stairs to the right-hand river bank beyond the waterhole and follow the sealed main gorge access path back to the visitor centre.

Top: *The Loop Walk brings you into the pound through almost bald hills;* **Bottom:** *Permanent water reflects red rock and blue sky in Ormiston Gorge*

8 ULURU BASE WALK

Walk:	11.6km loop
Time required:	3–4 hours
Best time:	Any time except summer, when temperatures soar
Grade:	Easy
Environment:	Sandstone monolith, red-sand desert, Aboriginal art
Best map:	This one
Toilets:	Flushing toilets at Cultural Centre and Mala carpark
Food:	Light refreshments and meals at Ininti Cafe at the national park cultural centre; supermarket, cafes, takeaways and restaurants at Ayers Rock Resort, outside the park
Tips:	There is little shade on this walk so don't take it on in summer heat; but don't be put off in rain, either – seeing the rock running with water is a rare privilege.
	While the flies can be unbearable in warmer weather they are rarely absent, so wear repellent and/or an insect hat net.
	The entire Uluru Base Walk is on a flat, compacted gravel track and you can hire bikes to cycle around.
	Visitors aged over 16 years must pay an entry fee to Uluru-Kata Tjuta National Park; details parksaustralia.gov.au/uluru/plan/passes-permits.html.

Sunset burnishes Uluru to a coppery red

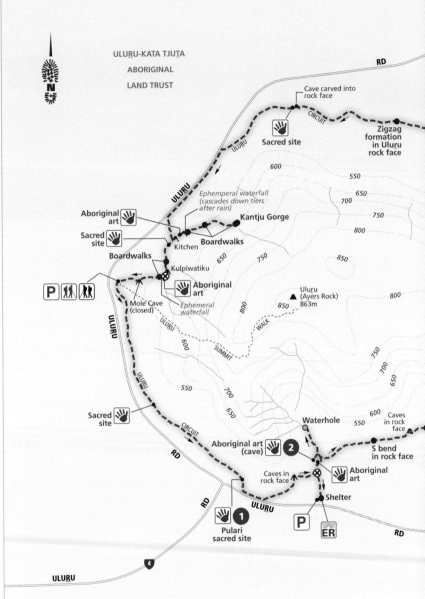

N

ULURU-KATA TJUTA
ABORIGINAL
LAND TRUST

RD

Cave carved into
rock face

CIRCUIT

Zigzag
formation
in Uluru
rock face

Sacred site

600

550

650

ULURU

700

Ephemeral waterfall
(cascades down tiers
after rain)

Kantju Gorge

750

Aboriginal
art

800

Sacred
site

Boardwalks

Kitchen

Boardwalks

650

750

850

Kulpiwatiku

P

Mole Cave
(closed)

Aboriginal
art

Ephemeral
waterfall

ULURU

600

800

Uluru
(Ayers Rock)
863m

850

800

ULURU

WALK

750

SUMMIT

700

650

ULURU

550

CIRCUIT

700

650

RD

Sacred
site

Waterhole

600

550

Caves
in rock
face

Aboriginal art
(cave)

2

S bend
in rock face

Caves in
rock face

Aboriginal
art

ULURU

Shelter

Aboriginal
art

1

Pulari
sacred site

P

ER

RD

4

ULURU

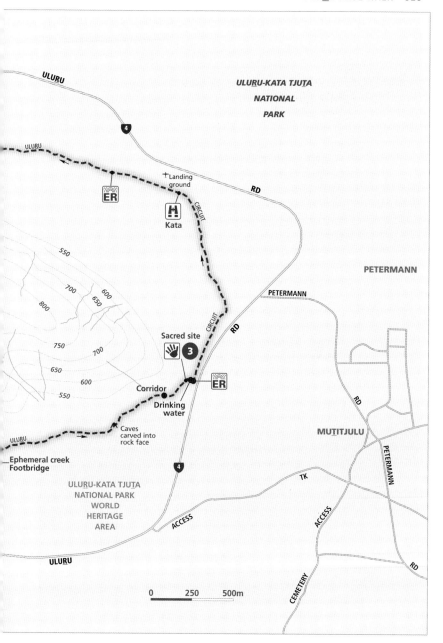

This NT landmark is fabulously textured thanks to the passage of water over time and the scars of mythological battles

Immerse yourself in geological and cultural history on this desert amble around Australia's most famous natural landmark.

The visual impact of Uluru endures and even increases with time and familiarity. Whether it's your first or umpteenth visit, the stone monolith rising from Australia's Red Centre will stop you in your tracks as you approach – and as you leave, taking more than one last look.

From afar the rock looks smooth and monochrome, but this NT landmark is fabulously textured, both by the passage of water and time and the scars of mythological battles. Its tiers, caves, stripes and scars are revealed – and best appreciated – from the 11.6km walk around Uluru.

You can start the Base Walk from several places, and departure time dictates which areas catch the sun. Uluru's arguably most visually interesting north-east flank is best seen in afternoon sunshine, so the best plan of action is to visit the Uluru-Kata Tjuta National Park cultural centre first thing. Here you can learn about Tjukurpa, the creation period and basis for the knowledge, law, religion, social structure and moral values of central desert Anangu people, before joining the free, guided 2km Mala Walk, which leaves daily at 10am from Mala carpark. Indigenous guides provide an engaging introduction to the complex cultural significance of Uluru to the Anangu people, and an overview of the rock's geological story.

The Mala Walk attracts large crowds in the milder winter months and visits several places on the Base Walk, but it's wonderful to return to those sites on your own later with newly acquired knowledge.

Start the Base Walk at Mala carpark, heading anticlockwise on a wide, compacted red gravel track, past the foot of the summit climb (for cultural and safety reasons, the Anangu request that you do not climb).

Uluru is the tip of an alluvial fan, sedimentary deposits compressed and cemented into sandstone, then folded and turned nearly 90° over hundreds of millions of years; or at least that's western science's creation story. The rock is believed to continue up to 6km underground, but no-one knows for sure.

The ongoing shaping is written all over Uluru. Early in the walk you pass a section of obviously layered rock, in places cracked and drilled with caves big and small; then a gaping 'bite' mark, the honeycomb texture within suggesting Uluru is a crusted or iced sponge! And yet just metres beyond, the rock is smooth again.

Walking among bloodwoods with scaly trunks, ahead you'll see another big hole in Uluru's flank [*see* point 1 on map], and two huge lumps of red rock that look like they have spilled onto the desert floor. This is the first of many sensitive sites on the Base Walk, places of great cultural importance to Anangu, the stories of which are handed down as family inheritance. The edge of this opening appears to have melted and dripped – it would make a remarkable photograph, but photography is prohibited (signs indicate no-photo areas).

The track loops away from this site and passes a row of information boards describing Uluru's mythological formation. Look behind you here for a pastel view of Kata Tjuta ('many domes') 50km west. [The Valley of the Winds Walk at Kata Tjuta is another fascinating foot journey.]

As you approach a footbridge over an ephemeral creek, look up and along Uluru. Depending on the light, you might see a serpent 'etched' across the steep red wall. This is woma python woman, part of a storyboard depicting ancestral activities on the rock here.

Soon after that you'll come to a track junction, with Kunija carpark to the right (an alternative, less crowded place to start the Base Walk, with a tank of drinking water and emergency radio) and Mutitjulu Waterhole to the left. Turn towards the waterhole, stopping at two cave art sites [*see* point 2]. The paintings in one are teachings of senior men to generations of Yiinka ('bush boys') preparing to become men; the other is a family cave.

Tucked well back in a deep fold, Mutitjulu Waterhole is the most reliable water source around Uluru – and the home of the mythical Wanampi ('water snake').

Emerge from the waterhole and turn left, continuing anticlockwise and coming to the very base of Uluru at probably its steepest point.

Uluṟu takes on many different moods

The rock here is like a monster wave about to crest and break over you. Walking on, look up again (a cricked neck is a real risk on this walk). See how the layers change, from running almost vertical to doubling back on themselves in a giant S-bend? Imagine the geological force needed to do this! Note, too, the thinness of the oxidised red 'crust' over Uluṟu's base blue-grey sandstone.

Through a stony corridor between Uluṟu and fallen boulders, the track swings north at another sensitive area and pulls away from the rock (*see* point 3), rounding another standalone sensitive site and running along Uluṟu's north-east face. This is the rock's most texturally interesting face, a mass of indentations, curves and caves. One series of holes looks like a giant dingo paw print.

The little shade on this walk is provided by desert oaks, and even on a sunny winter's day it can be warm. Here you also walk through bloodwoods and long-leafed corkwood trees; the latter's pale yellow grevillea-like flowers often crawl with ants collecting nectar.

The track changes tack again at Tjukatjapi, another sensitive site, where a long tail of rock has separated from the body of Uluṟu – you

can see blue sky between them – but not yet broken away at the top. Its appearance changes dramatically as you come around, and it now looks like a stingray flattened against the rock. This is an extraordinary piece of geological – perhaps mythological – artistry.

Step out onto the Uluru loop road, following it for about 500m before veering back towards the rock. At the next junction, opposite a lovely cave in which you can shelter from the sun, turn left and walk the 850m return to Kantju Gorge (which you visit on the Mala walk).

Falling water has stained the rock above this rockhole grey, but on a warm day it can be hard to imagine rain pouring down here. But even when the pool appears bone dry, this waterhole is a refuge on a hot day; more protected and leafier, so more shaded and cooler, than the scrub just metres away.

As you walk back to the track junction, divert left to a rock art site in an area of undercut stone, and into a larger 'kitchen' cave, where Anangu women, girls and small children camped. Then continue around the rock, keeping left to another rock art site as you stroll back to your car.

Clockwise from top: *One of the many caves cut into Uluru frames a walker doing the lap; remember to look up; walking around Uluru you see its tiers, caves, stripes and scars; ants gather nectar from a honey grevillea*

Hinchinbrook Island's jagged mountains watch over walkers treading the lost leg of the Thorsborne Trail

QUEENSLAND

Rainforest-clad mountains, World Heritage islands fashioned from rock and sand, too-gorgeous-to-be-true beaches, and waterfalls fed by tropical downpours – what more could you want from a walk? In Queensland you can explore the realm of ancient Antarctic beech trees dripping with moss; clamber up magnificent granite domes to stand in the shadows of balancing rocks; and appreciate Aboriginal art in a soaring outdoor gallery. Come on – take the plunge!

1	Carnarvon Gorge	338
2	Kondalilla Falls Circuit	344
3	Lake Barrine Circuit	349
4	Lake McKenzie–Central Station Loop	353
5	Mount Cordeaux	360
6	The Pyramids Loop	366
7	Ravenswood Historic Town Loop	372
8	Thorsborne Trail	379
9	Toolona Creek Circuit	392

BRISBANE

1 CARNARVON GORGE

Walk:	25km return
Time required:	9 hours, or 2 days with overnight camp
Best time:	Winter months, when it's generally dry, with mild daytime temperatures and cold nights (down to 0°C). Summer temperatures can reach above 40°C and spring and summer rains can cause flash floods and close the access road. If in doubt, check conditions with the visitor centre.
Grade:	Moderate (long)
Environment:	River gorge, creek, fern gullies, rare palms, Aboriginal art
Best map:	This one
Toilets:	Flushing toilets at visitor centre, composting toilet at Big Bend
Food:	Range of self-catering supplies, snacks and drinks, including wine, available from Takarakka Bush Resort general store, 4km back from gorge
Tips:	To explore the gorge in a more leisurely fashion you could allow two or more days and bush camp at Big Bend (10 people maximum, bookings required). This allows time to clamber up Battleship Spur for another extraordinary aerial view of the gorge.
	Other options include shorter walks in and outside the gorge and the six-day Carnarvon Great Walk, one of nine Queensland Great Walks, which loops up the creek and returns via the escarpment.

Carnarvon Gorge's sandstone walls reach 200m into the sky

The day before you do the main gorge walk, climb Boolimba Bluff, 6.4km return from the visitor centre, to get the lay of the land: a cliff-top view of Carnarvon Creek snaking through the Great Dividing Range.

Rich Aboriginal cultural connections, prehistoric plants, myriad birds and gobsmacking natural craftsmanship make this an unforgettable day walk or overnight hike suitable for anyone with kilometres in their legs.

A work-in-progress begun millions of years ago, Carnarvon Gorge is a masterpiece of natural artistry exhibited – well, not quite in the middle of nowhere (that's unfair on Queensland's central highlands), but three hours by car south and north respectively of Emerald and Roma. Access to the gorge, centrepiece of Carnarvon National Park, ends with 21km of dry-weather-only unsealed road, and exploring it can involve many more kilometres on foot.

The master craftsman of Carnarvon Gorge is Carnarvon Creek, which has sliced 200m down into pale sandstone, creating a magnificent serpentine sandstone-walled sunken garden of cabbage palms, ancient zamia cycads and maypole eucalypts reaching skyward from seas of grass. Its tributaries have widened cliff fault lines into side gorges filled with miniature waterfalls and rockpools.

The main foot trail meanders more than 9km up the creek. Visiting secondary gorges and Aboriginal art sites lengthens the return walk to about 25km but most of the going is fairly flat, so it's doable in a half-marathon day.

Our all-day itinerary begins where the unsealed access road ends, at the visitor centre in the day-use area (this is also a Queensland school holidays-only campground), where kangaroos often graze and laze. From here you walk through trees to the first of 20 easy stepping-stone creek crossings, beyond which is the track junction for Boolimba Bluff.

Turn left and walk upstream, crossing the creek six times in the 3.6km to the Moss Garden turn-off. A 1.3km up-and-back detour off

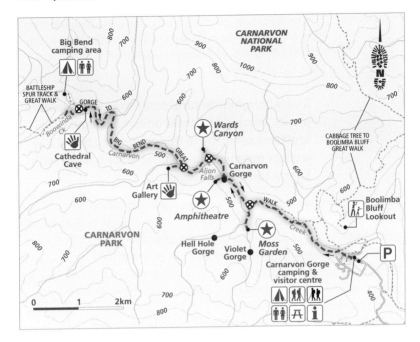

the main trail takes you to a fantasy land of vines, liverworts, lacy lichens and mosses under a canopy of tree ferns, where water dripping from sandstone ledges and tumbling down a small waterfall mark time's passing.

Back on the main trail, continue walking between soaring white sandstone cliffs that silhouette the shaggy heads of cabbage palms and open arms of grey gums. Stop on each creek crossing and watch for purply blue-and-orange flashes as azure kingfishers pluck insects from the air above the water. Look for herons and ibis in the creek and red-browed finches, superb fairy wrens and honeyeaters, drinking from grass tree flower spikes, along the track. Kookaburras and currawongs sometimes perform duets as you walk.

It is 500m from the Moss Garden junction to the Amphitheatre turn-off and another 700m to Wards Canyon, both of which we will leave for the walk back. Instead, meander another 800m to the Art Gallery, one of the best examples of stencil art in Australia and the

Walking among the king ferns and rocks of Wards Canyon

first major Aboriginal site in the main gorge system. (Baloon Cave is a smaller site and interpretive walk several kilometres downstream of the visitor centre.)

The rugged and remote country around Carnarvon Gorge deterred early explorers and sent some pastoralists packing, making it a perfect hideout for cattle rustlers and the like. But the Bidjara and Garingbal/Kara Kara people saw this region differently: as a bounteous source of food and the birthplace of five river systems, a burial place and a sacred landscape that continues to be of intense spiritual significance.

The thousands of freehand paintings and stencils of humanoid figures, weaponry, animals and animal tracks and multiple engraved vulvas on the 62m-long sandstone Art Gallery wall date back millennia. Day walkers should come at least this far before heading back.

Continue up the gorge, between sheer sandstone and through she-oaks, callistemon, soaring eucalypts and stumpy ancient zamia cycads. The cycad's hazard-orange fruits are poisonous, yet Aboriginal people knew how to prepare them and they were an important food.

Cathedral Cave, the second Aboriginal site in Carnarvon Gorge, 3.7km beyond the Art Gallery, is a magnificent wave of sandstone breaking high overhead. The massed red ochre stencils of mostly hands and boomerangs across its base make a lunch backdrop like no other in Australia.

Big Bend, below an undercut cliff where Carnarvon Creek bends left, is a further 700m and two creek crossings up the gorge, but unless you need to go to the toilet (pit) or are camping, you might like to save your energy. Having come this far, though, don't turn back without venturing a short way up Boowinda Creek, about 150m beyond Cathedral Cave.

Its sculpted curvaceous walls undercut by wet-season torrents and greened with velvety moss, the first part of Boowinda Creek feels like you are inside the intestines of some exotic beast. Explore it until it opens out (hikers continuing to Battleship Spur and the Great Walk climb up onto the escarpment further up the creek), then start back.

Retrace your steps downstream, alert for swamp wallabies grazing the native grasses as the afternoon wears on, and detour up the short, steep, signed side track through spotted gums and past a small waterfall to Wards Canyon. This pretty, shady side gorge is home to rare king fern, the world's largest fern and a dinosaur species related to the ancient flora of the Gondwana supercontinent from which Australia broke away.

A further 700m down the main gorge, detour off the trail again to the Amphitheatre. A 630m walk brings you to a steel ladder attached to the gorge wall. This climbs about 8m to a rent in the sandstone, a near-dark passage that opens into an amazing chamber within the cliff but open to the sky. Named for its shape and excellent acoustics, the Amphitheatre has been used for weddings and concerts.

Rest up here before the final 4.1km leg back, listening to other walkers' voices and the whisper of swifts and bats darting about the chamber, or, perhaps, testing the acoustics with a song.

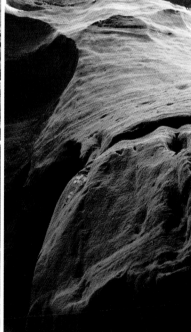

Left: *Dripping water marks time passing in the Moss Garden;* **Right:** *Moss covers the voluptuous walls of Boowinda Creek*

2 KONDALILLA FALLS CIRCUIT

Walk:	5.3km loop
Time required:	2–3 hours
Best time:	Any time, but the rainforest can be hot and steamy in summer
Grade:	Moderate (there are more than 100 steps)
Environment:	Warm tropical rainforest, plunge pools, palm-filled creek gullies, waterfalls
Best map:	This one
Toilets:	Flushing toilets in the picnic area
Food:	All manner of supplies, takeaway and sit-down food are available in Montville
Tips:	Pack your swimming gear and a towel and allow time for a dip in the pool at the top of the falls near the end of the walk. The walking track may be closed in wet weather due to flooding or rock falls, so check Park Alerts at nprsr.qld.gov.au/park-alerts/index.php and phone the Montville Tourist Information Service on (07) 5478 5544.

Plunge into the lusciously leafy world of waterfalls and tangled forest on this rollercoaster adventure walk. It's a great one for walkers of all ages – anyone with operational knees!

Cooling off in Kondalilla Falls

Kondalilla is an Aboriginal word meaning 'rushing waters', and during the wet season (usually Jan–Feb) Skene Creek wastes no time between escarpment and forested valley and roars down 90 vertical metres in a frothy spectacle. But Kondalilla Falls, one of many cascades in Queensland's volcanic Blackall Range, is beautiful at any time of year, and this popular rainforest walk concludes with a refreshing baptism with misty spray and full immersion in a plunge pool.

The walk starts from the Kondalilla Falls Rd carpark, 3.3km north-west of the Blackall Range town of Montville, where a sign for the falls and the Sunshine Coast Hinterland Great Walk directs you down steps into a grassy picnic area with tables, electric barbecues and flushing toilets.

Information boards in front of the wall of rainforest at the bottom of the lawn list the Kondalilla Falls Circuit as 4.6km (as do online sites and brochures), but that's the length of the falls loop from the swimming hole – it's about 7km return from here.

Follow the sealed walking track through thick leafy forest and down the escarpment to where pretty Picnic Creek forms a shallow waterfall over rocks. Cross the footbridge and take the unsigned track left – the steps to the right, signed Falls and Pool 1km, are the way you'll come back – and stroll through stripy piccabeen palm forest on compacted gravel and short boardwalks, with Picnic Creek gurgling through rocks below on your left for the first 300m or so.

There are eucalypts here too, some wrapped in fibrous red bark, others smooth white above dark, rough bark collars; you'll pass two huge specimens, one after the other, the second with a massive burl about 5m up.

Ignoring the track coming in on the right, walk on into more open bracken-floored eucalypt woodland, where the ground drops to Skene Creek on your left.

The track now zigzags quite steeply down the escarpment wall to a junction. Leaving the Rock Pool, to the left, for later, keep right on a narrower, rougher track that hugs the cliff. The sound of water can be loud, and you'll soon glimpse the falls through the trees.

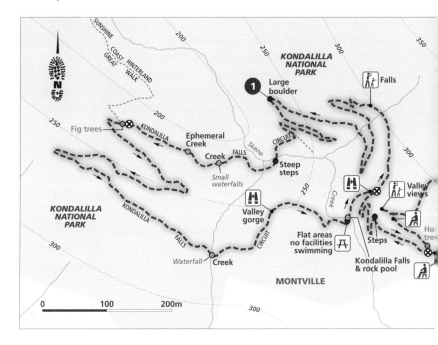

The track leads to a lookout that puts you face-to-face with the 90m drop. Looking up, you may see people who appear to be teetering on the edge. Don't panic; they are safe on the rock platform where the creek pools before launching itself over the precipice.

The track descends steeply now, becoming narrow and rough in places, though it's still not a challenging walk, before easing up slightly through piccabeen palms, mossy rocks and occasional buttressed fig trees. There are no Kondalilla Falls Circuit route markers here, so follow signs for the Sunshine Coast Hinterland Great Walk.

The track pulls away from the falls into thick rainforest before turning back on itself and slaloming down to the creek, where it forks. Our route (and the Great Walk) goes right, but first head left and clamber over rocks to the very base of the falls, where a curtain of fig roots hangs between twin cascades pouring down the base rock.

On your way back to the track junction, note the 'stone' steps; they are concrete, moulded to look like stone to minimise their visual impact.

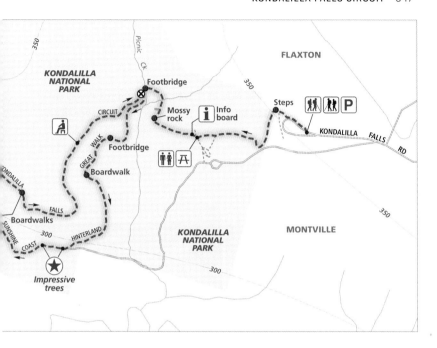

Round a massive boulder [*see* point 1 on map] and cross the creek, beyond which you immediately climb, up steps and then on track, through palms and across smaller side creeks trickling down the valley wall.

The Great Walk heads right and down at the next junction. Turn left here and zigzag uphill, passing a magnificent fig tree many metres around. Following the contours of the valley wall, with safety rails where the drop is steepest, the track emerges from palm forest into eucalypts and bristling grass trees. Having worked away from the cascade it swings back, so you are again walking to a soundtrack of falling water. The green tangle of trees and palms through which you have climbed looks a long way down.

Following the cliff-line, you'll come to the top falls, where Skene Creek fills a natural swimming pool before barrelling through a rocky chute and launching into the abyss. On a warm sunny day you'll have to share this elevated pool with others, but even when the pool is noisy with swimmers it's still refreshing. There's even a spacious flat rock on which to unwrap a picnic and lunch overlooking the creek valley and the forest-clad ranges enfolding it. (Several people have died or been permanently injured after slipping over waterfalls here and nearby, so stay behind fences and obey warning signs.)

Steep steps up the opposite side of this top station return you to the junction where you headed down into the creek valley earlier. Turn right and retrace your steps to the next junction, then turn left and follow this trail to a lookout over the creek valley (you can hear the falls, but not see them). From here you've got an easy, almost flat forest walk back to the carpark via Picnic Falls.

Clockwise from left: *Kondalilla Falls drops 90m into lush palm forest; colourful fungi grow in the moist conditions; palms weave a lattice of fronds down along the creek*

3 LAKE BARRINE CIRCUIT

Walk:	5.3km loop
Time required:	2 hours
Best time:	Any time
Grade:	Easy
Environment:	Rainforest-ringed volcanic lake
Best map:	This one
Toilets:	Flushing toilets in carpark and teahouse
Food:	Tuck into a light lunch or Devonshire tea, with locally grown tea or coffee, in the Heritage Teahouse Cafe
Tips:	Don't be put off by rain; take an umbrella and enjoy the rainforest at its dripping best. Enjoy the lake from a different perspective on one of the thrice-daily 45-minute boat cruises (lakebarrine.com.au); during February and March check Teahouse opening hours and cruise times on (07) 4095 3847.

Immerse yourself in other-worldly rainforest on this lazy circumnavigation of a volcanic lake formed long ago.

Lake Barrine, nestled on the Atherton Tablelands, 730m above sea level, is proof that beauty can be born of cataclysm. For this was not always a tranquil place where ducks paddle and vines twine towards the sun.

The track tunnels through rainforest so thick it's like walking in another world

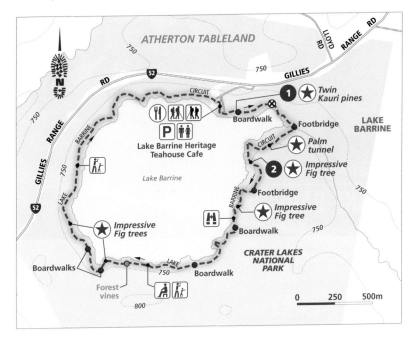

Lake Barrine is a maar (volcanic crater) formed more than 17,000 years ago, when molten rock superheated groundwater and the resulting build-up of steam, gas and pressure blasted the central core from the volcano. Back then, the forest here was open scrub – the cool rainforest now enfolding it is a youngster at just 8000 years old.

There are few prettier and more relaxing places than Lake Barrine to stretch your legs for a couple of hours, rain or shine. From the Teahouse carpark, about 10km north-east of Yungaburra and 60km south-west of Cairns via the Gillies Hwy, walk down through the Teahouse gardens to the shore and turn left, heading clockwise on the circuit track.

In cooler weather, you might see a brown-and-yellow amethystine python sunbaking along here. This is Australia's largest snake, with occasional old females, which are bigger than the males, measuring 5m long (there are unverified reports of 7m individuals). These constricting snakes are not poisonous but can still give a painful bite if disturbed, so admire any magnificent reptile you see but leave well alone.

Just 200m along you come to the famous twin kauri pines (*see* point 1 on map). Rough-barked kauri pines are the largest of Australia's native conifers and one of the first known rainforest tree species. Estimated to be more than 1000 years old, these two have grown to 2.2m in diameter and 45m high, so they pierce the canopy and overlook the surrounding forest.

The circuit track is predominantly flat with a couple of short ascents and descents. A combination of boardwalk, with chicken wire to reduce slipping when wet, footbridges and compacted gravel, it hugs the shoreline for much of the loop but veers inland and uphill to run above the water in a few places where the ground steepens.

The track tunnels through rainforest decorated with chandelier epiphytes and dangling vines, a complexity of textures and shades of green so thick it is like walking in another world. This sense is even stronger in misty conditions, when the cruise boat drifts in and out of view like the *Marie Celeste*.

Ignoring the lone side trail coming in on the left soon after the Twin Pines, continue around the lake, stopping at the occasional platforms jutting out over the blue water.

These are great places to view birds on the lake – the forest is too thick along much of the walk – and you'll almost certainly see Pacific Black ducks and white-eyed ducks. You might also spot saw-shelled turtles and long-finned eels in the water. Look out too for eastern water dragons, though it's probably not worth hanging around if one disappears under the surface, as they can hold their breath underwater for 90 min.

Back on the track, you'll assuredly encounter scrub turkeys scratching around on the forest floor. Look out for musky rat-kangaroos, about the size of a large guinea pig, and well-camouflaged olive brown Boyd's forest dragons (about 150mm long with a mustard under-jaw pouch) at head height on tree trunks.

About 1.2km around the lake you'll come to an impressive fig tree whose tendrils have strangled its host (*see* point 2); and there are other beauties 500m and 1.8km further on. But the arboreal headliner is 3.5km around the lake, a monster fig with Rastafarian strangler vines that has totally enmeshed its host and leans across the track, so you walk beneath its arch.

From here the track works north and then meanders along the lake shore to Lake Barrine Heritage Teahouse, built in the 1930s as a dance hall by surveyor George Curry, who worked with the local Council and Forestry Department to protect the lake and surrounding forest from logging and pioneered boat tours of the lake. The Curry family still run the Teahouse and the rainforest and wildlife boat tours that depart from the jetty below.

The waterfront timber teahouse served as a guesthouse, school and WW II convalescent home before it began providing visitors with oven-hot scones. To finish, tuck into a light lunch here before returning to your car.

Left: The Lake Barrine walk is beautiful on a damp, even misty day; **Right:** Tropical leaves create a wonderfully textured umbrella

4 LAKE MCKENZIE–CENTRAL STATION LOOP

Walk:	19km loop
Time required:	6–7 hours
Best time:	Mild sunny day; warmer weather for swimming
Grade:	Moderate (easy walking, but long)
Environment:	Freshwater lakes and streams, inland beach, vine forest
Best map:	This one
Toilets:	Flushing toilets at Lake McKenzie, Central Station and parking area
Food:	Reward your efforts on foot with dinner in Kingfisher Bay Resort's signature Seabelle Restaurant, eating creative combos of fresh local produce and bush tucker (kingfisherbay.com.au). Eurong, on the island's east coast, has a bakery/coffee shop, bar and restaurant.
Tips:	You don't need your own 4WD to do this walk – Fraser Island Taxis (fraserservice.com.au) offers drop-offs and pick-ups

Dip your toes in freshwater lakes and streams, hug ancient trees and get down and a bit dirty with fabulous fungi on this long loop through inland Fraser Island.

The hundreds of thousands of people who visit World Heritage-listed Fraser Island each year come to drive and fish its ocean beach, swim in

Swimming pools don't get prettier than Lake McKenzie

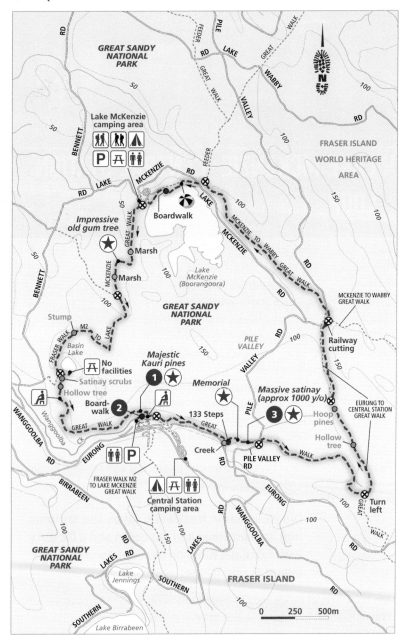

GREAT SANDY
NATIONAL
PARK

FEEDER RD

PILE

LAKE

WALK

GREAT

WABBY

VALLEY

FRASER ISLAND
WORLD HERITAGE
AREA

BENNETT

Lake McKenzie
camping area

LAKE

RD

MCKENZIE

RD

FEEDER

RD

LAKE

MCKENZIE

Boardwalk

MCKENZIE TO WABBY GREAT WALK

Impressive
old gum tree

★

GREAT WALK

Marsh

Marsh

MCKENZIE

LAKE

Lake
McKenzie
(Boorangoora)

GREAT SANDY
NATIONAL
PARK

MCKENZIE TO WABBY
GREAT WALK

RD

Railway
cutting

Stump

FRASER WALK M2 TO LAKE

Basin
Lake

M2

No
facilities

Satinay scrubs

Hollow tree

Board-
walk

Wanggoolba

WANGGOOLBA

RD

GREAT WALK

Ck

Majestic
Kauri pines

❶ ★

Memorial

★

PILE

VALLEY

Massive satinay
(approx 1000 y/o)

❸ ★

EURONG TO
CENTRAL STATION
GREAT WALK

Hoop
pines

Hollow
tree

❷

133 Steps

GREAT

Creek

RD

PILE VALLEY
RD

WALK

EURONG

Turn
left

GREAT

WALK

RD

EURONG

FRASER WALK M2
TO LAKE MCKENZIE
GREAT WALK

Central Station
camping area

RD

WANGGOOLBA

BIRRABEEN

100

GREAT SANDY
NATIONAL
PARK

LAKES

RD

RD

LAKES

RD

150

Lake
Jennings

SOUTHERN

FRASER ISLAND

RD

SOUTHERN

Lake Birrabeen

0   250   500m

pristine streams and freshwater lakes, clamber over sand blows, stare up at tall timbers and encounter wildlife. But the world's largest sand island is also a great place to hike.

A map of Fraser Island walking trails resembles a scribbly gum, with short squiggles, loops and long lines. Fraser Island Great Walk, one of Queensland's nine multi-day Great Walks, which snakes 90km through the middle of the island from Dilli Village (a research and learning centre for schools and universities) to Happy Valley Resort, facilitates shorter leg stretches too.

The all-day inland walk described here treads a section of the Great Walk as it loops through some of Fraser's famous natural treasures, none more precious than Lake McKenzie, where the walk begins and finishes, perched 100m above sea level on compacted sand and vegetable matter.

Lake McKenzie is about 12km south-east of Kingfisher Bay Resort, the nearest settlement, via sandy 4WD-only roads. Our route goes bush off the foot track to the lake from the bus parking area (adjoining the car parking area), but it's madness to set off on the hike without first finding out why McKenzie is the most popular of Fraser's 100 lakes.

So stroll down to the white sand beach and paddle in the Photoshop-blue water, but beware. McKenzie is so beautiful on a sunny day (it is a moodier creature with cloud cover) that it could rob you of your will to walk and leave you stranded lake-side for the day!

To get going, head up the track to the bus parking area and turn left at the junction about 70m short of the bitumen, toilet and fenced picnicking area (dingoes make it unsafe to eat on the beach). A sign on the side track warns that you are entering a remote area.

The fluffy, brilliant green plant flourishing here is fox tail fern. The tall trees with thick, fibrous brown bark are satinay, also called Fraser Island turpentine. And the edible mauve fruit of the midgen berry bushes are high in vitamin C and taste a little of cinnamon.

Skirt the fenced Lake McKenzie camping area – dingoes again! – and follow an easy, leaf-littered sandy track down through tall open eucalypt forest to a wetland lined with paperbarks, continuing on the flat to a joyful chorus of frogs. The scratched ground along the track is from bandicoots digging for fungi.

Ignore a trail going right to Wanggoolba Creek barge and instead head for Central Station, climbing through scribbly gums and dipping into a gully packed with cycads. The track then flattens out through lots of flowering plants and taller trees, many of which bear the scars of ringbarking.

Detour left at the next junction to Basin Lake, where those in the know enjoy more peaceful swims than are possible at Lake McKenzie. Watch blue-black dragonflies and enamel-red ones with double wings skim the water to a soundtrack of bird chatter.

Watch for honeyeaters and eastern yellow robins as you descend through forest that becomes thicker and leafier, and darker green. Piccabeen palms weave a lattice in the gully below and right.

Two arm-thick vines reaching down and across the track mark the fringes of subtropical rainforest, where you'll encounter splendid old trees. There are scaly-barked brush box, piccabeen palms crowning 15m up and vines hanging down like skipping ropes. You pass a plumb-line straight kauri pine 1m in diameter (see point 1 on map). (The biggest kauri taken off Fraser Island during 120-plus years of commercial logging was reputedly more than 3m across!)

Pass elegant white-trunked flooded gums (also called rose gums) planted in 1953, and an unusual kauri pine that has split into twin trunks, and step down into Wanggoolba Creek's tangled rainforest tunnel (see point 2).

A few metres up the boardwalk to the right along the opposite bank is an extraordinary strangler fig with vermicelli tendrils and huge epiphytes.

Continue up into Central Station to use the toilet and read about logging on Fraser from 1863 to 1991 (the year before the island was listed as a World Heritage Area), or turn around and walk upstream.

Wanggoolba Creek is so clear you can barely see the water, and the silica sand muffles any trickling and gurgling, so footsteps and voices sound loud here. Step down to the left when the boardwalk ends and follow the creek, savouring the rich, organic perfume, into massed palms reaching skyward; plants grow off plants growing off other plants here.

Ford the creek and climb 133 steps away from the water and towards Pile Valley, the domain of some true arboreal giants.

Satinay is resistant to marine borders, so satinay trunks made great wharf piles, hence the name Pile Valley. Satinay was also used to line the Suez Canal and rebuild the London Docks after WW II. But the value of living trees was also appreciated, and Pile Valley was declared a beauty spot in 1937, more than 50 years before logging ceased on Fraser Island.

There are palms here, and vines, but the superstars of Pile Valley are the satinays. The well-worn track leads to a logging survivor about 8m around and estimated to be 800–1000 years old (*see* point 3).

Follow the signs for Eurong and Lake Wabby, looping right and then behind the eastern Pile Valley parking area, and continue on a flat, broad track that cushions your footfalls through dense vine forest. Fabulous white, red, yellow and blue fungi poke their heads through the ground cover here after rain.

Keeping straight on towards Lake McKenzie (7.1km) at the next junction, beside a long-standing tree covered in burls, puts you on the old logging tramline. Dappled by filtered sunlight on clear days,

White sand slopes gently down to Lake McKenzie's too-blue water

Safe from the carloads of people who visit McKenzie, a walker takes time out at Basin Lake

the track now runs north-west through drier forest, among taller trees strung with vines where fallen logs wear shagpile moss; past trees blackened and hollowed by fire and a huge stand of hoop pine.

Turn right at a brown-and-yellow walking sign and climb out of vines and palms, going left at the next junction (Lake McKenzie 4.1km) and across a 4WD road at an M7 location indicator sign.

From here you traverse drier eucalypt forest blackened by fire and lush with regrowth. On sunny days you'll glimpse blue sky reflected in the lake through the trees about halfway along, soon after which the track works down an easy ridge into gnarly banksias.

A huge scribbly gum guards the next junction, where a track goes right to Kingfisher Bay. Turning left, you've got a short, steep climb to a road, then about 20m to the right along that road to a management track that descends, with Lake McKenzie's white sand now in view.

A narrow footpad on the left with a 'no camping, no fires' sign puts you on the beach. Leave it again, further along to the right, on the 'Main Beach Access Track', which fords a marshy area and pushes through heathy scrub to the main beach.

Any of the exits will return you to the carpark, but you need rush only if you are late for a pick-up. Otherwise, linger here, having a cooling swim or just watching pastel-soft afternoon light kiss the paperbarks rooted in the white sand.

Clockwise from top left: *Exquisite blue fungi emerge from the leaf litter; a flashy yellow pea decorates the forest; resting up beside Lake McKenzie; animal tracks score otherwise pristine sand*

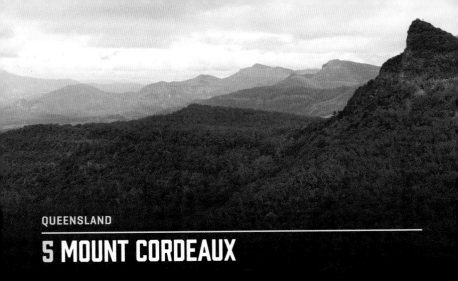

5 MOUNT CORDEAUX

Walk:	7.5km return
Time required:	2–3 hours
Best time:	Clear day for the views
Grade:	Moderate
Environment:	Cool, subtropical rainforest, unprotected volcanic cliffs, views
Best map:	This one
Toilets:	Pit toilets in The Crest parking area
Food:	None
Tips:	Take a picnic lunch and unwrap it up top

This short but breathtaking climb through verdant rainforest takes you to volcanic heights, rewarding your efforts with panoramic views.

'Wow!' sums up the view from Cunninghams Gap, south-west of Brisbane, particularly when driving east, when volcanic Fassifern Valley unfurls as you come through the break in the mountain range. The roadworks depot-like gravel parking area on the left as you crest the gap is the gateway to even better views from walks north and south of Cunningham Hwy in Main Range National Park.

One of these is the short climb to Mount Cordeaux (1135m) – Niamboyoo to the Yugarabul Aboriginal people – which starts at the eastern end of the carpark, just beyond the information board.

Volcanic Fassifern Valley reveals its full splendour to those who climb Mt Cordeaux

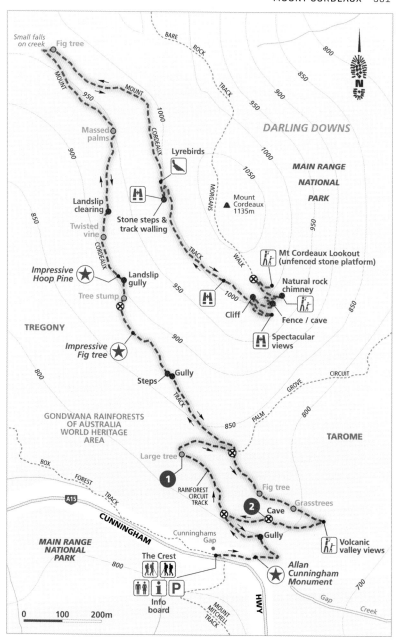

Small falls on creek

Fig tree

BARE

ROCK

TRACK

800

850

900

MOUNT

950

MOUNT

CORDEAUX

1000

Massed palms

DARLING DOWNS

Lyrebirds

900

1050

MAIN RANGE

NATIONAL

PARK

Landslip clearing

Twisted vine

850

CORDEAUX

Stone steps & track walling

MORGANS

Mount Cordeaux 1135m

950

Impressive Hoop Pine

Landslip gully

Tree stump

TRACK

WALK

Mt Cordeaux Lookout (unfenced stone platform)

Natural rock chimney

TREGONY

950

1000

850

Impressive Fig tree

900

Cliff

Fence / cave

Spectacular views

Steps

Gully

TRACK

GONDWANA RAINFORESTS OF AUSTRALIA WORLD HERITAGE AREA

850

CIRCUIT

GROVE

800

PALM

TAROME

Large tree

1

RAINFOREST CIRCUIT TRACK

Fig tree

Grasstrees

2

Cave

BOX

FOREST

TRACK

A15

CUNNINGHAM

Gully

Volcanic valley views

MAIN RANGE NATIONAL PARK

800

Cunninghams Gap

Allan Cunningham Monument

The Crest

Info board

P

HWY

Gap

Creek

700

MOUNT MITCHELL TRACK

0   100   200m

N

Initially sealed, the track climbs slightly in thick palm forest, paralleling the road and passing a strangler fig whose vines are like corset stays laced around its host.

Thirty metres up there's a stone monument to explorer and colonial botanist Allan Cunningham. In 1828 he found this 'gap' in the Main Range, which, despite its 'unforgiving' slope, facilitated the passage of Darling Downs produce to the coast, and supplies in the reverse direction. Near the cairn stand five magnificent hoop pines ringed with cracked brown bark.

The track then zigzags up and away from the road, through palms woven into a tangled green canopy of vines and epiphytes to a track junction. Ignore the stone steps going right and proceed on the Rainforest Circuit, passing a tree leaning over the track that's bedecked with epiphytes, its exposed roots reaching metres above the ground (*see* point 1 on map).

Further up, there's an old tree with buttressed trunk and encircling boardwalk protecting its shallow roots from compression. Walk around it to see huge epiphytes and look up its trunk into the canopy.

The track continues through buttressed trees, mossy roots, thick vines and palms, some close to the ground, others elevated on strappy stems.

Main Range National Park is part of the Gondwana Rainforests of Australia World Heritage Area declared in 1994. While it looks and feels like somewhere a dinosaur might graze, the background drone of trucks grumbling up to Cunningham's Gap keeps you in the present. But the forest also rings with the long cracks of male whipbirds and the females' double-barrelled pistol-shot replies.

Turn left at a four-way junction towards Mt Cordeaux, ascending stone steps, rounding the hill and crossing a bracken-crammed gully probably carved by a landslide. Steady climbing brings you to a pseudo junction where what looks like a footpad branches left. Our stone-lined track steps up to the right and fords another landslip; from the next one you can see mountain ranges beyond the trees.

Under the cover of piccabeen palms, the track shortly doubles back on itself where a creek runs 6m down a rockslide. Lyrebirds make the scratches you see on the forest floor, so listen for these expert mimics and watch for a curl of lyre/harp-like tail feather among the foliage.

Where the track doubles back again, further up the landslides crossed earlier, you get a wide-angle view down the Main Range into the valley – and can now see the semitrailers you heard earlier. Higher still, the conical peak on the south side of Cunningham's Gap shows itself.

You then emerge from moss- and lichen-trimmed forest to stand among grass trees covering a steep exposed mountain slope. This is a breathtaking viewing area, looking across the valley's ruffled floor to Lake Moogerah and distinctive pointed peaks.

Having ducked back into rainforest, the track crisscrosses uphill and pushes across the base of a mossy cliff. Then it steps out into grass trees again for another view of Cunningham Hwy and the Gap, both far below you now.

Shorter and steeper zigs and zags through grass trees and tea-tree put you on a fenced lookout commanding a spectacular scene reaching east to the coast and south down the Main Range ramparts. Even when it's windy here, you can still hear bellbirds chiming in the forest below.

Stunning views glimpsed between trees on the climb

Grass trees add bristles to the view south down the Main Range from Mt Cordeaux

There's an interesting natural chimney drilled vertically down into the rock at the end of this lookout – a volcanic vent, perhaps.

Proceed past a sign warning of sheer cliffs to another track junction. Mt Cordeaux Lookout is 65m up to the right, but you could also venture on to Bare Rock (2.8km ahead) for gobsmacking views of the northern reaches of Main Range National Park. This would extend the return hike to 12.4km.

The lookout track climbs stone steps and runs along rock covered in lichen and moss and studded with paper daisies. More stone steps put you on Mt Cordeaux Lookout.

Forming the western part of the Scenic Rim, a splendid arc of mountains reaching from Mt Mistake to Springbrook in south-east Queensland, the Main Range is a remnant of a massive shield volcano active more than 20 million years ago. You are standing on its western rim.

The eastern rim has long-since eroded away, but the peaks rising from the farmed valley below are plugs, dykes and sills, created when magma filled vertical pipe-like fissures, forced its way across older rock strata and penetrated between beds of rock strata.

To your left rears the top of Mt Cordeaux, its face a vertical garden planted with giant spear lilies, whose elongated sword-shaped leaves can reach 3m long. In late winter and spring the lilies produce flower spears tipped with blood-red blooms that grow 5m high, which makes for an unforgettable show.

From the lookout, retrace your steps to the Rainforest Circuit track and walk straight ahead (you came up on the right before), treading a good, wide track down through strangler figs, walking stick palms, and flame trees whose red flowers litter the trail from late spring into summer; through eucalypts and grass trees, to fenced cliff-edge Fassifern Valley Lookout for your last view on foot.

Three tracks meet here; you'll continue on the one going up steps to your right as you step down to the lookout. The third track snakes to Gap Creek Falls (9.8km there and back). The falls plunge 100m, but are only really worth visiting after heavy rain – the return walk is uphill, and tiring in hot weather.

From the fire-tolerant fringing eucalypt forest at the lookout, step back into rainforest and make your way downhill, past a (labelled) black booyong tree heavy with epiphytes; a fallen tree's exposed root ball (*see* point 2), a natural cave in which people have obviously sat; and a thick vine wrapped around another tree like a python.

Turn left at the next junction, onto the track you walked up earlier, and follow it back to the memorial and carpark.

6 THE PYRAMIDS LOOP

Walk:	5.7km loop
Time required:	3 hours (plus summit and creek time)
Best time:	Cool sunny day
Grade:	Moderate
Environment:	Bald granite domes, rocky creek, riparian eucalypt woodland
Best map:	This one
Toilets:	Flushing toilets in Bald Rock Creek picnic/day use area and Bald Rock Creek camping area
Food:	None
Tips:	This walk involves scaling a broad-but-steep exposed granite slope that can be slippery after rain; wear proper shoes or boots with non-slip tread. Walking poles help with balance and take the pressure off your knees on the descent.

Expect close encounters with balancing rocks and uninterrupted views over one-of-a-kind Queensland geology on this vertigo-testing hill climb.

Crafted by sedimentation, volcanic activity, fracturing and weathering over millions of years, the rocky country characteristic of Girraween National Park exists nowhere else in Queensland. Girraween and neighbouring Bald Rock National Park, just over the NSW border,

Sunlight gilds a magnificent twisted eucalypt

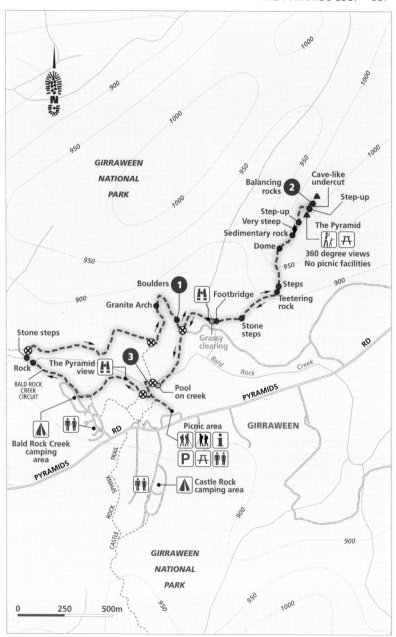

N

GIRRAWEEN
NATIONAL
PARK

Balancing
rocks ②

Cave-like
undercut

Step-up

Step-up
Very steep
Sedimentary rock
Dome

The Pyramid

360 degree views
No picnic facilities

Boulders ①

Granite Arch

Footbridge

Steps

Teetering
rock

Grassy
clearing

Stone
steps

Stone steps

Rock

The Pyramid
view ③

BALD ROCK
CREEK
CIRCUIT

Bald Rock
Creek
camping
area

Pool
on creek

PYRAMIDS

GIRRAWEEN

RD

Bald Rock Creek

RD

Picnic area

P

PYRAMIDS

ROCK SPHINX TRAIL

CASTLE ROCK

Castle Rock
camping area

GIRRAWEEN
NATIONAL
PARK

0   250   500m

Left: *A balancing rock stands tall on the Pyramid;* **Right:** *Countless wet seasons have cut patterns in the stone along Bald Rock Creek*

together protect about 17,000 hectares of granite hills, boulder clusters and magnificent tors.

A walking track snakes over exposed ridges and through shady woodlands almost to the top of Mt Norman (1267m), the park's high point – rock-climbing skills are needed to bag the summit. However, the pick of the walks is the shorter and more dramatic Pyramid Track, up a granite dome rising just 200m above Bald Rock Creek. The route described here, via the Bald Rock Creek Circuit, is a short lasso-shaped celebration of nature's work with stone.

The walk starts in the Bald Creek day use area (parking, flushing toilets, picnic tables, free electric barbecues), 8.4km (all sealed) off the New England Hwy and 26km south of the agricultural town of Stanthorpe. Before heading off on the walk, pop into the park visitor information centre in the day use area, if only to see the 1984 photograph of snow in Girraween!

From the carpark, cross the lawn (toilets on your right) to a gravel track leading to a junction. The sign points straight ahead to the Pyramid, but turn left onto the Bald Rock Creek Circuit, then keep right at the next junction, treading a broad track through eucalypts and banksias and away from the Pyramid, visible through the trees. You may spook wallabies and kangaroos lazing in the grass here.

The track ends on an unsealed road in Bald Rock Creek campground (hot showers) and resumes about 100m along the road to the right, just beyond a low-fenced group camping area. Step back into fire-blackened woodland splashed with bright green regrowth. Just beyond a sign warning that granite rocks are slippery when wet, the track drops down onto a broad, natural granite pavement beside a tempting waterhole. Cross the creek on stepping stones, turning right at the next junction (towards the Pyramid).

Walk on, crossing granite pavements laid in woodland. Looking up, you'll see boulders and what look like standing stones on the hills to the left. Mt Norman and the park's southern reaches then come into view on your right.

Turn left at the next junction, to the Pyramid and Granite Arch, and amble through woodland scattered with granite boulders and tors, some rounded and fat-bottomed, some so undercut they look like they will soon topple over. Climbing gently, you'll approach and duck under Granite Arch, a tor balanced on two others.

Seven hundred floral species have been identified across regional open forests, woodlands, heaths, shrublands and sedgelands in this region. Twenty-five eucalypt species grow in the park, and here you are among stringybarks, twisted, striped trees and others peeling to smooth honeycomb-yellow trunks.

Soon after passing a huge rock, more than 20m long (see point 1 on map), the track forks. Turning left you'll see rocks perched on the Pyramid's sloping face; to the right, you get another eyeful of Mt Norman.

Relatively flat and easy to this point, the track now fords a small creek then steps steeply up through scattered boulders and rounds a rocky outcrop, depositing you at the base of a broad granite slope reaching skyward. Start up the slope, following the route marked by stripes of white paint, steeper and steeper. Take your time, and stop often to admire the unfolding view and study the textured dykes traversing the slope.

Keep climbing between two great granite blocks that have cracked away from the main hill, then clamber over a jam of smaller rocks, beyond which Mt Norman, and the park's other landmarks, The Sphinx and Castle Rock, are clearly visible to the south.

Cross the slope now, towards a huge boulder that appears about to roll down the hill. This traverse is less steep, but the granite is striped with lichen dampened by running water, so take care and avoid obviously wet areas. [Algae and lichen produce weak acids that break down minerals into clay, and plant roots widen cracks in the rock, so the age-old shaping of Girraween is ongoing.]

From that 'teetering' rock you've got a few more metres up to a plateau of sorts, then another clamber up onto the Pyramid's flat-topped 'point'. The 360° view from here takes in the park's signature peaks and unexpected cleared land below, a relic of the area's settlement and farming.

Kambu-wal Aboriginal people hunted, traded and gathered in this country for millennia before the first squatters arrived in the 1840s. The selectors who followed brought sheep, cattle, vegetables and fruit trees. It is hard country, and many selectors abandoned their blocks, although more orchards were planted in the 1920s and 1930s, and small-scale timber felling continued until 1958.

Although it can be windy, this flat top is a great spot for a snack-with-a-view, but the Pyramid's main attractions are the fantastic formations one level back down: massive balancing rocks (*see* point 2), undercut stone, and nooks and crannies where you can sit and look out over the park. The dome beside you, which looks like it's wearing a suede-like skin, is Second Pyramid (also called Bald Pyramid, for obvious reasons). Accessible only by rock climbers, this is the largest single granite slab in the park.

When you are done up top, retrace your steps, taking care on the descent. Some people find it easier to zigzag down the steepest sections rather than head straight down.

Don't be surprised if you notice more weird and wonderfully shaped stones in the forest as you descend than you did climbing the steps; more flowers, too. Girraween means 'place of flowers', and the park puts on a wildflower show from late July, which peaks in September and October. But there is always something in bloom. Look out for pretty bluebells, snowy heaths, native cherry, whispering rock she-oak and nodding greenhood orchids. The white hemispherical flower with a faint pink blush is a herb, commonly called candytuft, among other names.

Back at the Granite Arch junction saunter ahead on an easy, compacted sand track, passing great chunks of rock on your right. Skirting a lagoon on Bald Rock Creek, you reach another junction. Walk straight on again here, towards Bald Rock Creek day use area.

This brings you to a beautiful length of creek (*see* point 3) where water, which pours gin-clear over miniature waterfalls, has sculpted ripples and drilled holes in the granite. Cross two footbridges and veer left, up stone steps, and follow the signs back to your wheels in the day use area.

Blue sky pools along Bald Rock Creek

7 RAVENSWOOD HISTORIC TOWN LOOP

Walk:	5km loop
Time required:	2 hours
Best time:	Sunny day; summer can be unpleasantly hot and wet
Grade:	Easy
Environment:	Mining relics, heritage buildings, undulating outback
Best map:	This one
Toilets:	Flushing toilets in the park near the bridge
Food:	The Railway and Imperial hotels both serve counter meals. Snacks are available from the general store.
Tips:	Soak up the atmosphere of this historic town by staying overnight, camping, or sleeping in a cast-iron bed under a tin ceiling in a gold-era hotel

Step back to a noisier, busier time as you follow the faded footsteps of gold miners around north Queensland's oldest inland town.

Founded in the first flush of north Queensland gold fever, Ravenswood is a historic gem, albeit a tiny, time-worn one in an often dusty and unrefined setting. In fact, you'd be excused for thinking you'd stumbled on an abandoned film set, for who, other than a director, would erect lace-trimmed hotels in the middle of nowhere? Or strew poppet heads, chimneys and stampers through the surrounding scrub?

A rusty curlicue gate guards the cemetery on a hill above Ravenswood

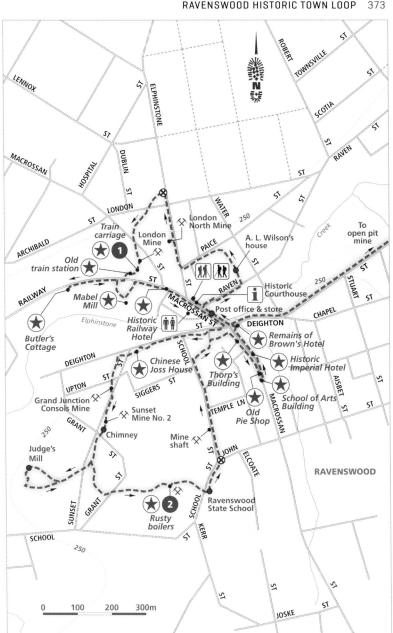

LENNOX

ST

ELPHINSTONE

ROBERT ST

TOWNSVILLE ST

MACROSSAN

HOSPITAL ST

DUBLIN ST

LONDON ST

SCOTIA ST

RAVEN

ARCHIBALD

ST

Train carriage

London Mine

London North Mine

WATER ST

250

A. L. Wilson's house

Creek

To open pit mine

1

Old train station

PAICE ST

RAILWAY

Mabel Mill

Elphinstone

Historic Railway Hotel

MACROSSAN ST

RAVEN ST

250

STUART ST

ST

Butler's Cottage

SCHOOL ST

ST

Historic Courthouse

Post office & store

DEIGHTON

CHAPEL

Chinese Joss House

Thorp's Building

Remains of Brown's Hotel

DEIGHTON ST

UPTON ST

SIGGERS ST

Historic Imperial Hotel

AISBET ST

Grand Junction Consols Mine

Sunset Mine No. 2

TEMPLE LN

Old Pie Shop

School of Arts Building

MACROSSAN

GRANT

Chimney

Mine shaft

ST

ST

ELCOATE

Judge's Mill

ST

JOHN ST

RAVENSWOOD

SUNSET

GRANT ST

ST

2

Rusty boilers

SCHOOL ST

Ravenswood State School

KERR ST

SCHOOL

250

0   100   200   300m

JOSKE ST

ST   ST

But Ravenswood is neither a movie set nor a ghost town, and its 200-odd residents – down from the 5000 in its heyday – include workers employed at Mt Wright underground gold mine, 11km from town.

This stroll around North Queensland's oldest inland town starts at Ravenswood courthouse, cnr Raven and Barton/Macrossan sts, 90km east of Charters Towers and 130km south of Townsville by sealed road.

The weatherboard courthouse (c. 1884), which overlooks the town from under a verandah, along with neighbouring police buildings, was removed in the 1950s and used as stockmen's quarters until its

Top: *The lace-trimmed Railway Hotel is one of two gold-era drinking establishments in town;*
Bottom: *Bougainvillea softens a view of gold era relics*

restoration to Commissioner's Hill in 1987. The courthouse is now a museum, open a few hours daily, which sells *Ravenswood Five Heritage Trails* by Diane Menghetti, a book telling the town's history through text and photographs and detailing the many sights visited on the combined-trail walk described here.

From the courthouse, walk up Raven St and follow the yellow arrow left up concrete steps to the site of A.L. Wilson's house.

After the first flush of the gold rush, gold-mining success at Ravenswood relied on continually improving and adapting extraction methods. The British investment that made this possible was secured by local mine manager and entrepreneur A. Laurence Wilson, and saved the industry and town.

Ravenswood boomed from 1900 to 1912, but the 'uncrowned King of Ravenswood' couldn't stem the cost increases and yield drops that saw Ravenswood become a virtual ghost town by 1917. (More efficient modern techniques led to mining resumptions over the years, though not all were successful.)

All that remains of Wilson's ostentatious house are the red-brick chimney and few square metres of herringbone paving, which you pass before turning left down Paice St.

Head towards Ravenswood's landmark two-storey Railway Hotel, built in 1902, but turn right before it, into Elphinstone St. Pass mango trees and the fenced London North Mine, then swing left through the St Paul's Church of England site. You may spook wallabies on this grassy stretch.

A mown trail leads to the London Mine and mullock heap. The London lode produced about 11,500 ounces of gold between 1903 and 1913, and you can see down the meshed shaft up which much of that yield surfaced.

A train carriage (*see* point 1 on map), about 30m beyond the London Mine, identifies the railway precinct (a branch line off the Townsville–Charters Towers railway reached Ravenswood in 1884). Check out the historic photographs lining the walls of the station building, to the right, facing Railway St, then continue another 200m along the road to Butler's Cottage.

A family home until the 1980s, this corrugated iron-clad, earth-floored cottage was severely damaged by Cyclone Aivu in 1989 and painstakingly restored by local identify Steve Hancock. Wander around the site, checking out the interior under lift-and-prop hinged iron shutters and noting the miner's cradle on the porch, made with cross-cut-saw-blade legs.

Amble back to the Mabel Mill site, opposite the station, whose successive entrepreneurial owners experimented with all manner of ore treatment systems from the 1870s. The site extends across the creek, but here you have a photogenic red brick chimney and five-stamper battery.

Now walk east into town, passing the red-brick Railway Hotel, built by a part-owner of the London Mine; then the courthouse and post office–general store (c. 1878) on the left.

Cross treed Elphinstone Creek and turn right up Deighton St, the centre of Ravenwood's Chinese population and site of nearly 30 market gardens in the 1880s. Pass the brick ambulance building, from which horse-drawn ambulances once departed, and the Joss House (temple) site on your way to the continuation of Mabel Mill. The gravel walking track at Partridge's Mill, within this area, loops around some of the most interesting rusty mining relics in Ravenswood.

Red-tailed black cockatoos hang out in the eucalypts in this heavily worked area. They'll flash red tail feathers ahead of you, flying tree to tree as you walk south from Mabel Mill (don't follow the track along the powerlines).

The way now marked by a few red arrows, take the right of two unsealed vehicle tracks to the square red-brick boiler stack of Grand Junction Consols Mine, which produced only a few ounces of gold. Then proceed past the octagonal stack of Sunset Mine No. 2 (the field's largest gold producer) to Judge's Mill. This treatment plant operated for just four years, from 1938, but a short loop trail accesses some more interesting equipment.

Now walk east along a pit mine fence to a couple of rusty boilers (see point 2) left over from the Duke of Edinburgh Mine. Then, ignoring a track left to a mullock heap and another chimney, continue east towards

Left: *Corrugated iron-clad Butler's Cottage was carefully restored after being smashed by a cyclone;* **Right:** *The weatherboard courthouse (c. 1884) is now the museum*

sealed School St and swing right to look over the Buck Reef West Pit. Looking for blue arrows now, descend the road and turn left opposite the State School, which has operated continuously since 1873.

Where the bitumen turns right, giving a leafy tunnel view of the candy-striped Imperial Hotel, continue straight, on a gravel track leading to a ramp with an okay view over the town (best in morning light). Then walk downhill between house and road to a small park, and turn right into the main street.

The lovely two-storey building on your right is Thorp's Building. Note the exposed steel girder out front as you step inside to peruse gifts, handmade craft, woodwork and pottery for sale and collections of pick heads, old magazines, bottles, biscuit tins, and rock samples that help you differentiate Burdekin River sediment from petrified wood and pyrite.

Further along the road are the School of Arts hall and library and the Old Pie Shop. From here, double back to the Imperial Hotel, the only

One of many relics of the mining era scattered around Ravenswood glows in the early sun

other of Ravenswood's 30-odd hotels to survive. Through its gunslinger saloon doors is a circular bar and magnificent carved divider, inset with original stained-glass panels that have miraculously survived more than a century of celebrations and commiserations. The Imperial is reputedly haunted, which only adds to its appeal.

Having taken refreshment here, walk west towards the creek. The steps to nowhere on the corner are all that remain of Browne's Hotel, once Ravenswood's grandest establishment.

If you're up for an additional 2.5km on foot, turn right into Deighton St and follow the signs to the lookout over the town's vast open-cut pit, via the lovely weatherboard Catholic church on the hill. Otherwise, you could do this side trip by car, and add on the short drive to the cemetery in the hills just east of town.

To finish, saunter west from the steps to nowhere back to your car.

8 THORSBORNE TRAIL

Walk:	32.7km one-way
Time required:	4 days
Best time:	April to September; the island is warm year round but is hot and very humid in summer. Heavy rain can fall at any time.
Grade:	Moderate
Environment:	Beaches, headlands, paperbark wetlands, eucalypt forest, tropical rainforest, waterfalls, crocodile-inhabited lagoons
Best map:	*Thorsborne Trail–Hinchinbrook Island 25k Topographic 2 Sheet Map Pack* available from World Wide Maps at worldwidemaps.com.au
Toilets:	Hybrid pit toilets at all campsites (no toilet paper provided)
Food:	Cardwell cafes, restaurants, pubs and supermarkets cover most bases; Lucinda Jetty Store's crisp fish and chips make a great celebratory feast at the end of the walk
Tips:	Heed all crocodile warning signs. Hinchinbrook's sandflies and mosquitoes can be voracious, so take repellent and cover up in camp around dusk and dawn. Rubbish bins are not provided; carry out all refuse. Tides on Hinchinbrook range up to 4m; refer to a Lucinda tide table before departure and be aware of tides when crossing creeks. There is mobile reception in several places, so pack your phone in case of emergencies.

Hinchinbrook Island is on show from the top of Zoe Falls

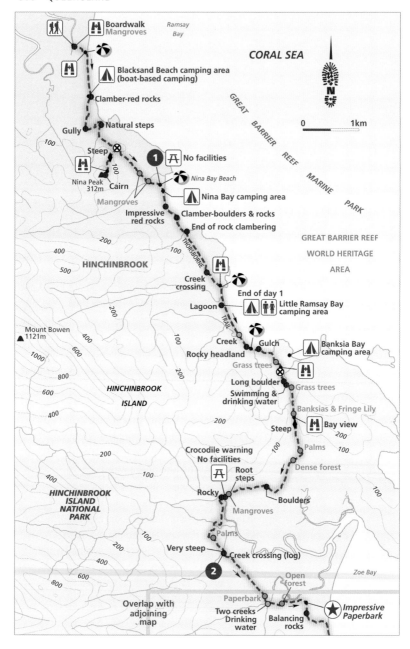

Boardwalk
Mangroves

Ramsay Bay

CORAL SEA

N

0   1km

Blacksand Beach camping area
(boat-based camping)

Clamber-red rocks

Gully   Natural steps

Steep

Nina Peak
312m   Cairn

Mangroves

GREAT BARRIER REEF MARINE PARK

1   No facilities

Nina Bay Beach

Nina Bay camping area

Impressive
red rocks   Clamber-boulders & rocks

End of rock clambering

GREAT BARRIER REEF

WORLD HERITAGE

AREA

THORSBORNE

HINCHINBROOK

Creek
crossing

End of day 1

Lagoon   Little Ramsay Bay
camping area

TRAIL

Mount Bowen
1121m

Creek   Banksia Bay
camping area

Rocky headland   Gulch

Grass trees

HINCHINBROOK
ISLAND   Long boulder

Swimming &
drinking water   Grass trees

Banksias & Fringe Lily

Steep   Bay view

Palms

Crocodile warning
No facilities   Dense forest

Root
steps

HINCHINBROOK
ISLAND
NATIONAL
PARK   Rocky   Boulders

Mangroves

Palms

Very steep   Creek crossing (log)

2

Zoe Bay

Open
forest

Paperbark

Two creeks   Balancing
Drinking   rocks
water

*Impressive
Paperbark*

Overlap with
adjoining
map

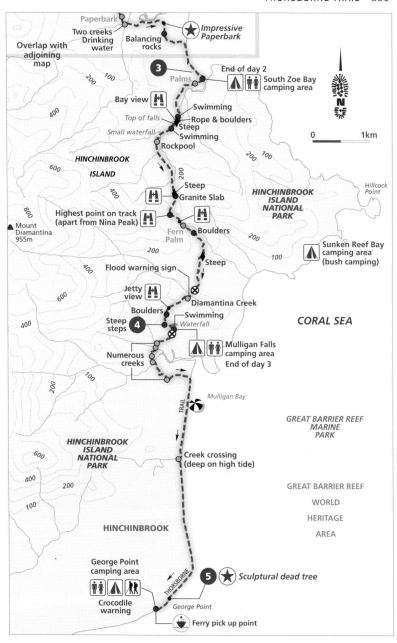

Paperbark
Two creeks
Drinking water
Balancing rocks

★ *Impressive Paperbark*

Overlap with adjoining map

3 Palms

End of day 2
🏕 🚻 South Zoe Bay camping area

Bay view 🔭

Swimming
Rope & boulders
Steep
Swimming
Rockpool

Top of falls
Small waterfall

HINCHINBROOK

ISLAND

Steep
Granite Slab 🔭

Highest point on track
(apart from Nina Peak) 🔭

Fern Palm

Boulders

HINCHINBROOK
ISLAND
NATIONAL
PARK

Hillcock Point

Sunken Reef Bay
camping area 🏕
(bush camping)

Steep

Flood warning sign ⊗

Jetty view 🔭

Boulders
Steep steps 4

Diamantina Creek

Swimming
Waterfall ⊗

CORAL SEA

Numerous creeks

🏕 🚻 Mulligan Falls
camping area
End of day 3

Mulligan Bay ⊛

GREAT BARRIER REEF
MARINE
PARK

HINCHINBROOK
ISLAND
NATIONAL
PARK

Creek crossing
(deep on high tide)

GREAT BARRIER REEF

WORLD

HERITAGE

AREA

Mount
Diamantina
955m

▲ HINCHINBROOK

George Point
camping area

🚻 🏕 🚶

Crocodile
warning

5 ★ *Sculptural dead tree*

George Point

⚓ Ferry pick up point

THORSBORNE

TRAIL

N

0 — 1km

Explore an island jewel over four fabulous days, hiking from broad white-sand beach to hilltop vantage point, paperbark swamp to rainforest, and crocodile hangout to pristine waterfall.

Separated from North Queensland's coast by a narrow channel inhabited by dugongs and navigated by migrating whales, Hinchinbrook Island is a magnificent sea creature whose forested flanks rise to a spine of mountain peaks. The Thorsborne Trail, on the island's east coast, is a four-day close encounter.

Named after the late Arthur Thorsborne, who shared a lifelong passion for nature conservation with his wife Margaret, the Thorsborne Trail introduces walkers to Hinchinbrook's diverse habitats, taking walkers through eucalypt forest, rainforest, melaleuca swamps, heaths, rocky mountain slopes and mangrove forests. About 700 plant species have been identified across 30 plant communities in the region.

Protected since 1932, Hinchinbrook Island National Park sits within the Great Barrier Reef World Heritage Area. A maximum of 40 people per day are allowed on the trail, and camping permits must be pre-booked (qld.gov.au/camping). Access is by private vessel (pick up the brochure *Marine Wonders of Hinchinbrook: a guide to using the Hinchinbrook transit lanes*) or commercial water taxi; contact Absolute North Charters (absolutenorthcharters.com.au), which operates out of Lucinda and cruises up beautiful Hinchinbrook Channel to deposit walkers up north; or Hinchinbrook Wilderness Safaris (hinchinbrookwildernesssafaris.com.au). Taxi schedules vary with season and tide, and transfers must be secured prior to booking camping permits.

Most people walk the trail from north to south (orange arrows), as described here, but you can walk it in reverse (yellow arrows). Side trails are marked with blue arrows. The colour scheme is designed to prevent you heading in the wrong direction if you lose your bearings.

The Thorsborne Trail is neither a graded nor hardened walking track, and it can be rough. It is cleared once a year, at the end of the wet season, although rangers do spot work if alerted to major problems.

Rock-strewn Little Ramsay Bay is where you camp on the first night

The view of Hinchinbrook Island from the mainland

It is fairly well signed and walkers have piled cairns in the places where it isn't immediately obvious where to go, but this walk is not recommended for first-time overnight hikers.

DAY 1: 8.6KM – Ramsay Bay to Little Ramsay Bay (via Nina Peak)

The walk begins with a spectacular boat journey from either Cardwell or Lucinda, across or up Hinchinbrook Channel and around the island's north coast into Missionary Bay. These follow transit lanes established to protect the dugongs that graze sea grasses in the channel – but fortunately no-one told the dugongs to keep clear! Dugongs and manatees are members of the Sirenia (sea cow) family, solitary, herbivorous mammals commonly claimed to have inspired the mermaid myth. If you are lucky enough to spot a dugong during the boat trip, you may wonder at the mental state of any sailor who saw them as sexy!

Sheltered by a north-jutting peninsula comprised of four rocky outcrops, Missionary Bay is lined with mangroves. These, along with those in the channel, form one of the largest mangrove areas on continental Australia, made up of 31 species. Estuarine crocodiles inhabit the mangroves, and you might spot one – if the magnificent mountain ridge releases your gaze – as the boat snakes through this sea of green.

The boat lands you on a floating jetty (crocodile warning sign) with steps up to a boardwalk. This cuts through the mangroves to a line of black fence posts leading to Ramsay Bay, the first of many popular photo stops on this trail.

Walk south on the beach to its end and follow the orange arrows around a red granite headland. This involves clambering over and around boulders, smaller rocks, and slabs; a short, sharp climb up a rock face and a hard right hand turn at a gulch. The trail then follows a ridge before descending onto Blacksand Beach at a creek; here you loop out onto the beach and then back into forest, between two majestic melaleucas (paperbarks).

About 3km into the walk you reach a saddle, with an unsigned, unmaintained footpad leading up to the right. Leave your pack here and head up Nina Peak. Five hundred metres climbing, with steep step-ups where walking poles are a hindrance, puts you on a natural lookout. Push on another 100m to the top (312m elevation) for a jaw-dropping view south to Little Ramsay Bay, east to Nina Bay, north to Missionary Bay, where serpentine waterways snake through the green mangroves, and west to that gaze-raising mountain ridge.

Back on the saddle, follow a rocky track studded with exposed roots that runs to Nina Bay, from she-oaks and grass trees down into leafy tropical forest where you cross seasonal creeks lined with paperbarks. A shady area just short of Nina Bay makes a good lunch spot (see point 1 on map).

Refuelled, walk south on the beach. At low tide it is often decorated with the artwork of bubbler crabs, which sift organic matter from sand and discard the remaining pellets in lines radiating from their holes. From the water's edge you get another great view of the ridges.

At the end of the beach, cross another rocky section and climb a small cliff. Look for green turtles off the shore as you follow the headland to Boulder Bay and rock-hop around to the next headland. Orange markers show the way over a low ridge to Little Ramsay Bay.

White-bellied sea eagles may watch from aloft as you walk along the bay's rock-strewn beach and cross a creek running down the sand (you may get wet feet, depending on the tide). The camping area is in the trees up on the right, overlooking a lagoon that mirrors the sun-blushed mountain ridge behind.

For drinking water, wade back across the creek and follow it inland until you find water flowing over rocks.

If you need quiet to sleep, you have come to the wrong place. Hinchinbrook's forests are noisy with wildlife. Store all your food – empty wrappers, too – in the metal food bins provided to protect your supplies and your pack from overnight invasion by fawn-footed melomys and giant white-tailed rats, cute natives with a penchant for hikers' food.

Day 2: 10.5KM – Little Ramsay Bay to Zoe Bay

Continue south on Little Ramsay Bay, crossing a creek before rock-hopping around a red granite headland to a smaller unnamed beach cut by another creek lined with paperbarks. The trail continues along a rocky ledge above a larger beach, then climbs a grass treed ridge offering colourful sea views.

Past a side trail (600m return) to Banksia Bay, where there is a small camping area, the trail descends to a small waterfall where Banksia Creek runs down compressed rock layers into a deep plunge pool frequented by yabbies and red dragonflies. This is a good spot to top up your drinking water – even when there is nothing falling into the plunge pool there is often a narrow flow to the left of the pool – and have a refreshing swim. It doesn't compare with the waterhole at day's end, but why ration yourself? Change into your swimmers, strip off, or just immerse yourself clothes and all – you'll soon dry.

After climbing up and over Banksia Creek to a saddle, you've got a steep, fairly rough descent down a rocky creek through banksias and she-oaks. The trail then flattens out in palm forest and crosses creeks where magnificent old paperbarks grip the rocky bed with gnarled roots. You'll then step from beneath a lattice-like canopy of palm fronds into a light-filled stand of immature paperbarks. Ahead, through the palisade of precision-straight white trunks, is a lower, more dense and darker green mangrove swamp.

Turn right (there's a faded arrow) and walk through paperbarks and between mangroves and thicker palm forest. The trail then ducks back into the tangle on the right and winds through more open forest to a crocodile warning sign on the approach to North Zoe Creek.

Having crossed North Zoe Creek's wide, rocky bed diagonally, between two tempting waterholes frequented by salties, the trail meanders through palm swamps to narrower Fan Palm Creek.

You've got several more creek crossings between here and Zoe Bay so prepare to get your feet wet, and take care when rock-hopping. A fallen tree bridges one creek, in a steep, narrow gully (see point 2).

In places lumpy with exposed roots – some so big you have to step up and over them – the trail winds through paperbark wetlands and palm forest, passing huge trees and assorted stacked and stand-alone boulders; one forms an archway, another projects over the trail. The beautiful trees with coppery, papery bark are red beech. Beware wait-a-while tendrils (also called lawyer vine), which can hook clothing and pull hanging items off packs.

Suddenly, you'll hear the sea! Soon after, you'll see it, and feel the breeze.

The trail deposits you on the beach at Zoe Bay (which is often strewn with sand dollars), about 400m north of the mouth of South Zoe Creek. Camping areas are dotted among the fringing forest towards the end of the beach.

Pitch your tent, or at least dump your pack, then continue along the trail, which leaves the beach via the last camping area beside the creek. Follow it 1km through buttressed blue quandong (their vivid blue fruit often litters the trail) and blush touriga, also called alligatorbark trees because of their scaly trunks, to Zoe Falls (no camping permitted) to rinse off the sweat. After a slippery entry over rocks you are in deep water and can swim across to the falls, which zigzag down a granite cliff.

Look up at the cliff-top where the water comes from and you'll probably see swifts darting about, one of the many species of bird found on the island. Arthur and Margaret Thorsborne's work included monitoring migratory pied imperial-pigeons, big white birds with black wing-tips. Back on the beach, look out for kingfishers and white-bellied sea eagles.

The trail crosses multiple dry and wet creeks along the way

South Creek backs up behind the beach and forms a tranquil lagoon (*see* point 3) perfect for crocodiles, and a sign warns against nearing the edge. Crocodile sightings are rare, but lace monitors strut about the leaf litter along the edge of the beach, and cute native rats (melomys) frequent the camp so, again, store all food in the provided bins.

Zipped into your tent, looking up through mosquito netting (a fly is unnecessary at many times of year) and a loose forest canopy at brilliant stars, it can feel as if there's infinitely more between you and the mainland than one ridge of mountains.

DAY 3: 6.8KM – Zoe Bay to Mulligans Falls

Day three begins with a repeat walk to Zoe Falls, prettiest in a wash of morning sun – a post-breakfast dip, anyone? – from which you climb steeply, out of rainforest and up onto the granite slabs capping the falls. A thick white rope helps you scale a boulder short of the top, where sweeping views of Zoe Bay and swimming holes fashioned by water delay many walkers.

When you're ready, cross South Zoe Creek on stepping stones just above the falls, then narrower tributaries as you walk through grass trees and she-oaks. A spur leads to the highest point on the main trail, a saddle 260m above sea level that gifts a great view back to the sea and the mountains and, on the clearest day, the Palm Islands and Magnetic Island to the south.

The long, straight line visible on the sea ahead as you walk on is Lucinda Jetty, the longest service jetty in the southern hemisphere. It reaches 5.76km out into Georges Bay, and the curvature of the Earth was taken into account in its design.

The trail now traverses a landscape drawn in black (burnt trees and grass-tree trunks), green (flourishing new foliage) and red (the beautiful granite underfoot). This is the result of a planned burn to control acacias competing with the rare blue banksia, which has blue-grey cylindrical flowers, knobbly cones and red new foliage and is found only on Hinchinbrook and the immediately adjacent mainland. The stalky red flowers that bloom along here are the wonderfully named herb *Haemodorum coccineum*, commonly called Bloodroot (First Australians use the plant's roots and fruits to make red, brown and purple dyes for colouring fibres).

Dipping in and out of creek gullies lush with coral fern and insectivorous sundews, one very steep and the footing loose, the trail works downhill towards a spread of sea and island. Ignoring the side trail to Sunken Reef Bay, you'll come to a sign warning of flash flooding.

Diamantina Creek is subject to flash flooding but drops quickly; take particular care crossing the creek if it is swollen by rain, and if you are not confident, wait for it to drop. This is the widest creek on the trail, but it is filled with rocks that make sure-footed stepping stones. Cross almost to the far bank and rock-hop upstream to where the track resumes (arrow).

As you start the last kilometre of trail, a fabulous beach view taking in the mouth of Diamantina Creek opens up on the left, only to disappear as you descend stone steps (*see* point 4) around stacked boulders and zigzag into a rainforest gully. The trail flattens out amid palms and assorted trees, and brings you to a junction, with George Point ahead and Mulligan Falls to the left.

Turn left into the Mulligan Falls camping area, where tent sites are strung along a rooty track. The camping area and walking track end just short of where water tumbles down a rocky slope into a chute, which empties into a large waterhole furnished with semi-submerged boulders – perfect for stretching out on after a swim.

Experience suggests this campsite is the most visited by melomys, and these cute placental mammals have no hesitation in climbing into a coffee mug or an empty freeze-dried meal pouch. Buff, chestnut, black, blue and red noisy pittas hop about camp too, unperturbed by two-legged animals armed with zoom lenses.

DAY 4: 6.5KM – Mulligan Falls to Georges Bay

This is the shortest and easiest day on the Thorsborne Trail, unless the tide forces you up into the soft sand on the beach and fills Mulligan Creek, threatening a chest-high wade. But there is no reliable drinking water along the way, so fill up at the falls before leaving camp.

From here the trail heads through rainforest to the coast, crossing four creeks before popping you out onto Mulligan Bay for a 5km beach stroll.

For the first time since day one you can stride out, but you probably won't, because you'll stop to take just a few more photos of the island's mountainous spine, from the water's edge or Mulligan Creek, which cuts through the sand to the sea about 2km down. The last creek on the Thorsborne Trail is best crossed at low to mid tide, when you'll probably get just your feet wet.

With Lucinda Jetty lengthening across the horizon, continue down the beach and past a magnificent dead tree, bleached by salt and sun (*see* point 5), to George Point, the signed pick-up point (picnic table and pit toilet) for transfers across Georges Bay to the mainland, where celebratory fish and chips at Lucinda Jetty Store await!

Clockwise from top: *A hiker trails footprints down the beach on the last day; water backed up behind Little Ramsay Bay beach reflects the mountain range rearing up behind; a hiker splashes through a creek flowing into Little Ramsay Bay; cooling off in Mulligans Falls, on the last night*

9 TOOLONA CREEK CIRCUIT

Walk:	18.5km loop
Time required:	6 hours
Best time:	Overcast day for the most intense rainforest experience; sunshine for the best views from the ridge. January to March are generally the wettest months; winters can be cold.
Grade:	Hard (rough uphill track with creek crossings)
Environment:	Warm and cool subtropical rainforest, mountain creek, Antarctic beech forest, ridge-top vantage points overlooking New South Wales
Best map:	This one
Toilets:	Flushing toilets in the National Park parking area, just before O'Reilly's Rainforest Retreat
Food:	Sit-down lunches and morning and afternoon teas available at the licensed Mountain Cafe & Gift Shop; drinks, snacks and some lunch provisions in the Mini Mart; both opposite the national park information centre
Tips:	Toolona Creek can rise quickly after heavy rain so check at the information centre before setting off. Rainforest can be very dark in cloudy and wet weather, so carry a torch. Take a raincoat and a warm jacket just in case; the forest can be cold and wet. Summer rains bring leeches, so wear repellent.

Walkers encounter prehistoric Antarctic beech trees high on the ridge

A Lamington National Park classic and one of Australia's most beautiful day walks, this lasso-shaped hike crisscrosses a tumbling mountain creek as it climbs to a ridge populated by ancient Antarctic beech trees cloaked in moss.

The perilously rugged rainforest-clad McPherson Range and neighbouring Nightcap (*see* p. 55) and Tweed ranges, just over the NSW border, form the battlement-like walls of one of the world's largest erosion calderas, fashioned when the Tweed Shield Volcano erupted 20–23 million years ago. The ranges' deep folds, ancient flora and pouring waterfalls are protected within the Gondwana Rainforests of Australia World Heritage Area, a collective of eight sites in NSW and Queensland.

Some of Queensland's best forest walks are the McPherson Range trails in Lamington National Park, and the all-day Toolona Creek Circuit, in the Green Mountain (western) section of the park, is a stunner.

It begins opposite the main entrance into family-owned O'Reilly's Rainforest Retreat, which nestles in the national park, 76km from the Gold Coast. The last 36km are winding and often narrow, and unsuitable for vehicles towing caravans and recreational vehicles longer than 4m.

The O'Reilly family's love affair with the McPherson Range began in 1911, when eight cousins took up dairying selections in the rainforest; and it continues unabated. Bernard O'Reilly became a reluctant hero, and his beloved mountain home a household name, in 1937, after making a solo trek through the mountains in search of a plane lost in a storm nine days earlier, discovering the wreckage, and dashing for help after finding survivors.

O'Reilly's Rainforest Retreat (oreillys.com.au) conducts epic 35km guided day walks to the Stinson crash site on a regular basis.

The half-length Toolona Creek Circuit plunges you immediately into thick, tangled forest, passing an information board and ducking under a historic Lamington National Park archway, to a fig tree whose roots clasp a boulder, its corset-like trunk having strangled its host tree. This is one of countless magnificent trees on the walk. Another stands

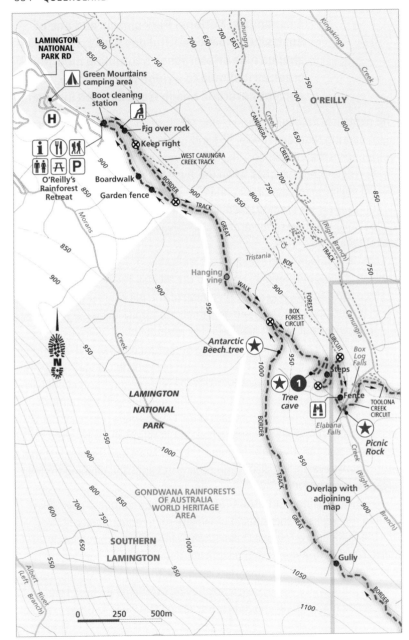

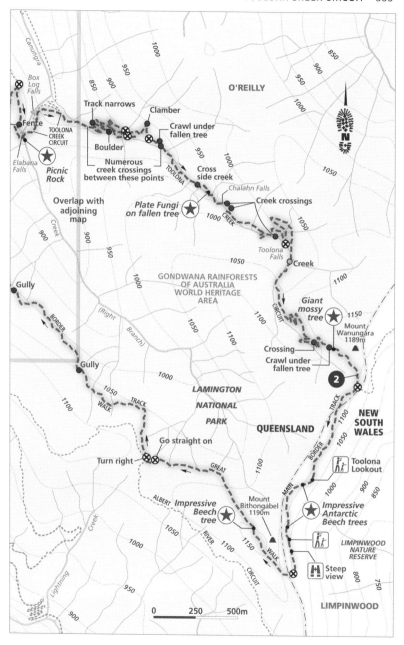

Toolona Creek forms dozens of pretty waterfalls as it tumbles through the forest

at the first track junction, where the unsealed West Canungra Creek track loops left.

Ignoring another track on the right, leading back to O'Reilly's, remain on the Border Track, which runs up to the mountain ridge, along the Queensland–New South Wales border and down into the Binna Burra section of the park, a fabulous 20km walk.

A broad and compacted track with occasional exposed roots, the Border Track climbs steadily through a leafy tangle of buttressed black booyong trees, staghorns, vines hanging like skipping ropes from the trees and umbrella-like tree ferns. Little sun penetrates the thickest forest and in wet weather it can be quite dark, with only occasional bright patches where falling trees have ripped open the canopy.

Where the track divides, a couple of kilometres up the range, veer left for the Toolona Creek circuit. Descending immediately, the track doglegs around a massive rough-barked eucalypt, past which there's a tree whose roots have formed a small cave (*see* point 1 on map). Further on, stone and concrete steps detour to a splendid Arol or bush box tree with a hollowed base several metres around.

The exposed roots can be slippery, particularly after rain, so take care as you continue down the main track. Watch too for where the track turns hard left down some stone steps (there is an orange arrow on a tree) just before a rocky creek gully; the creek bed ahead looks confusingly like a walking track.

At the next junction turn right towards Picnic Rock (a map shows where you are). Coming down a very steep slope crowded with buttressed trees and ferns, you'll hear Toolona Creek below, and see the equally steep opposite gorge wall.

Picnic Rock is a flattish area above a tumbling waterfall, perfect for a snack or dipping your toes on warm days. Taking extra care if the rocks are wet, cross the creek and follow the track uphill and to the left (there's a white arrow on a green board).

This is the first of multiple creek crossings over the next 4km, so if you feel uncomfortable or unsafe here or on any subsequent crossing, turn back. You'll probably get wet feet at more than one place, and walking poles can be helpful.

Take in a beautiful view of the ranges from the vehicle lookout just short of the ranger station and O'Reilly's Rainforest Retreat

Very narrow, and in places zigzagging steeply up walls to which the rainforest clings, the track works its way upstream through a fairyland of moss and lichen where trees entwine branches above, creating gothic tunnels. The track is fairly easy to follow and there are few markers, other than orange arrows at most creek crossings, however in a couple of spots it is not immediately clear which way to go.

Approaching a small waterfall, you'll see what looks like a duplicate track on the left. This is our route, but don't step up yet. Wait until you reach the spot where it doubles back (people taking shortcuts adds to the track confusion). If the only way on appears to be to clamber down the step-like roots of a huge tree onto the rocky creek bed below the falls, turn around and look back the way you came; you'll see the track better from this perspective.

Trees fall onto the track too, so be prepared to do some clambering.

Shortly after passing Toolona Falls, the tallest cascade on the walk, where the creek tips over the edge of a horseshoe of granite, light penetrating the canopy signals you are nearing the ridge.

Still climbing, but less steeply, with the creek on your right, squeeze between two trees with splayed mossy bases (*see* point 2).

Shortly after this you run into the wider Border Track with Binna Burra signed left (13.8km) and Green Mountains and O'Reilly's right (7.6km). Turn right and follow the Border Track along the ridge. Toolona Lookout – really just a break in the trees – rewards you on a clear day with a great view of the mountain-ringed erosion caldera and Mt Warning, its jagged central plug.

The Border Track can be boggy, but walk through the mud rather than widen any damage. It's because of that dampness that every tree up here, standing and fallen, is covered in moss; so too are the vines that reach down to the ground like hairy tentacles.

And then there are the Antarctic beech trees! Multiple trunks shaggy with greenery, exposed roots entwining, these ancients look like creatures from Tolkien's Middle Earth. The track meanders past one particularly extraordinary individual – you'll know the one – which has stood here for thousands of years.

When you can tear yourself away from their august presence, continue along the Border Track.

Ignoring a side track to Bithongabel, head towards Green Mountains, initially along the ridge and then steadily and gently downhill through smaller Antarctic beech trees in mossy vestments. Stepping out easily on a wide track, you'll start to leave these beauties behind and re-enter the lush and leafy world of strangler figs, staghorns and tree ferns.

Seven hundred metres beyond the Toolona Circuit junction where you left the Border Track earlier, turn left towards O'Reilly's Guesthouse via the Booyong Boardwalk. This takes you slightly uphill and then along the fenced Botanical Gardens. Lyrebirds are often spotted here.

If you have the energy, loop left onto O'Reilly's Tree Top Walk. Otherwise keep to the boardwalk, which passes massive strangler figs and an excellent example of how wonga vine twists as it grows, producing a thick, multi-ply woody 'rope'.

The boardwalk ends about 20m from where you stepped into the forest six hours before. Watch for handsome black-and-yellow regent bowerbirds, king parrots, crimson rosellas and other birds in the resort gardens and fringing rainforest as you make your way back to your car.

Stepping out on the famous Overland Track in Tasmania's World Heritage Wilderness

TASMANIA

The island state has an unrivalled reputation for challenging treks in World Heritage wilderness, and country doesn't get any wilder than this. But Tasmania's walking menu is as varied as the food it produces, and you don't have to flog yourself to get a taste of its pedestrian treats. Stroll the streets of one of Tassie's oldest towns; poke your nose over some of Australia's highest sea cliffs and walk its most famous long-distance track. And that's just the entrée!

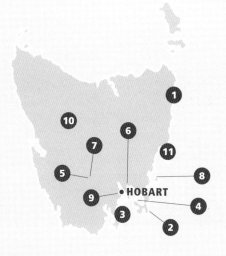

1	Bay of Fires	402
2	Cape Hauy	407
3	Cape Queen Elizabeth	412
4	Coal Mines Historic Site Loop	418
5	Growling Swallet & Junee Cave	424
6	Historic Richmond Town Loop	430
7	Lake Dobson & Tarn Shelf Loop	436
8	Maria Island Loop	441
9	kunanyi/Mount Wellington Summit Loop	449
10	Overland Track	456
11	Wineglass Bay & Hazards Beach Loop	471

BAY OF FIRES

Walk:	8.5–22km return
Time required:	Between 3 hours and all day (plus swimming, paddling and picnicking time)
Best time:	Sunny day (or stormy, for a shorter, dramatic walk)
Grade:	Easy
Environment:	White sand ocean beach, lichen-covered granite outcrops, coastal heath and lagoons
Best map:	This one
Toilets:	Flushing toilets on Binalong Bay foreshore and pit toilets in Swimcart Lagoon day-use area
Food:	Slim but good pickings in Binalong Bay, with eat-in and takeaway seafood at Moresco Restaurant; cafes, coffee, restaurants, fast food and a supermarket in St Helen, 11km south-west
Tips:	Take your bathers and a picnic lunch and spend the day soaking up the natural beauty, or pack a tent and camp out overlooking the waves

You can walk for kilometres along this string of beaches and bluffs

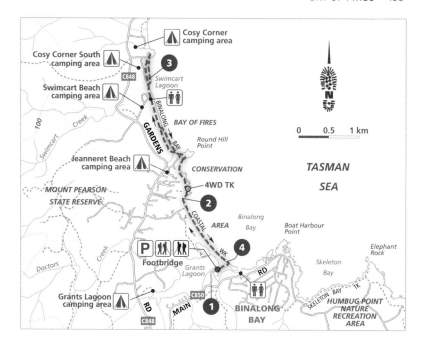

White beaches, blue water and orange granite give this easy beach walk a visual punch, making it a walk unlike any other in Tasmania.

The Bay of Fires, on Tasmania's north-east coast, was named by English navigator Tobias Furneaux, who saw numerous fires, lit by coastal Aboriginal people, burning along this shore when he captained HMS *Adventure* up the coast in March 1773. But this stunningly gorgeous region might just as well be named for its signature granite boulders, which are covered in orange lichen and glow like hot coals in early and late sunlight.

The beauty extends for many kilometres, protected within conservation areas, state reserves and Mt William National Park. One of the simplest walking pleasures in the island state is leaving footprints in the white sand and clambering about the low-slung granite outcrops that separate the beaches. Walk for an hour, all day, or even take a

Lichen turns the granite boulders a fiery orange

tent and camp overnight before heading back. Or spoil yourself with a luxurious four-day guided Bay of Fires Lodge Walk (bayoffires.com.au) further up the coast.

The area is of continuing cultural significance to Tasmania's Aboriginal community, and Aboriginal sites should be respected and left untouched (there are middens in the dunes).

The walk described here is on the most accessible stretch of coast, immediately north of the village of Binalong Bay, 11km north-east of St Helens. It starts in the Grants Lagoon day area, a sandy parking spot beside a footbridge in Humbug Point State Reserve. As you come into Binalong Bay look for an unsigned dirt road on the left (*see* point 1 on map), just after Main Rd swings right, and drive down it about 300m into the reserve. If you reach a grassy picnic area with toilets and parking on the left you have missed the turn.

Cross the footbridge over the serpentine lagoon outlet and follow the sandy track to a junction, taking the right-hand track, with Humbug Hill to the east, its slopes colonised by Binalong Bay houses. Step down onto a beautiful white beach and head left along the sand towards its rocky end, accompanied by a rhythmic wash of waves, passing holiday homes nestled in the dunes.

A footpad on the land side of the first rocky point (see point 2) leads to a spectacular gulch among the granite. Follow the narrow track going bush from here, which gives rocky and rooty passage through tea-tree and she-oaks and around the point to another couple of hundred metres of white beach.

The colour of the sand is a product of the granite's high quartz content. Lichen, a symbiosis between a fungus and an alga, gives the crazed, cracked granite points separating the beaches their distinctive and vibrant orange hue.

You'll probably see camps set up in the scrub to your left as you amble along this beach. Behind you is a great view of Binalong Bay township.

Tread the sandy track that clambers over Hill Point to gorgeous Swimcart Beach, a longer sweep of sand, with campsites strung along its edge and a day-use area with toilets tucked back in the scrub.

Along here you'll come to Swimcart Lagoon, on Swimcart Creek, its tannin-stained water contrasting the pale sand through which the creek sometimes breaks to meet the blue ocean. Salmon, flounder, eastern king prawns and black bream inhabit the lagoon, and if you're really lucky a magnificent white-bellied sea eagle, Australia's second largest bird of prey, with a wingspan reaching 2m, will pluck a meal from its waters in front of you.

Continue along the track and explore the next beach (see point 3), over another rocky point, before turning back.

If prepared for a long day out, with water, food and sunscreen, you can tread another 7km or so along beach, headland and unsealed road to The Gardens, a place of stunning beauty, with a white-sand bay nestled against a mass of sculpted granite covered in orange lichen.

Also accessible by car, The Gardens was named by Lady Jane Franklin, wife of Sir John Franklin, Lieutenant Governor of Van Diemen's Land (now Tasmania) from 1837 to 1843. Lady Franklin rode her horse here from Georges Bay and found it abloom with wildflowers. If you're tempted to walk to The Gardens from Binalong Bay just remember that you'll have to walk back again or arrange a lift.

Packing a tent opens up even more options. Walking another 16km north from The Gardens up the coast puts you on Policeman's Point at the outlet of Ansons Bay. You can't cross the outlet and it's a long walk around this bay, so travel north on foot ends here.

However far you go along this glorious shoreline, look for wooden steps up off the beach [*see* point 4] as you return to Binalong Bay, near the walk's end. Leave the beach here and follow a sandy track along a fence line, which is part of a Landcare project, turning left at the next track back to your car.

Clockwise from top: *A rounded boulder juts from the sand beside Swimcart Lagoon; boulders and white sand are strung along the shore; getting a feel for the rock*

2 CAPE HAUY

Walk:	10.3km return
Time required:	3–4 hours
Best time:	Sunny day (much of the walk is exposed, and it can be unsafe in bad weather)
Grade:	Moderate (with quite a few steps and some steep sections)
Environment:	Tranquil bay, coastal forest, exposed saddles, sheer sea cliffs and precipitous drops
Best map:	*TASMAP's Tasman National Park 1:75,000 Map & Notes*
Toilets:	Pump-out pit toilets at Fortescue Bay
Food:	Scallop pies, a Tasmanian tasting plate and lavender panna cotta are among the treats on the menu (and in the display fridge) at Port Arthur Lavender (portarthurlavender.com.au), on Arthur Hwy just south of the Fortescue Bay turnoff
Tips:	While most children of all ages will love the thrill of this walk, there are dangerous unfenced drop-offs, so don't let youngsters walk ahead unsupervised.
	Book a tour with Tasman Island Cruises (tasmancruises.com.au) for a gobsmacking sea-level perspective of Cape Hauy.
	Entry fees apply for all Tasmanian National Parks and a range of passes are available; details at parks.tas.gov.au.

Dolerite cliffs rear out of the inky ocean off Cape Hauy

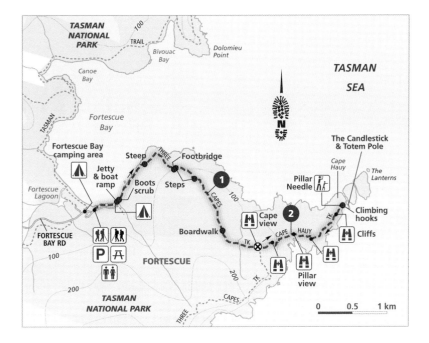

The opportunity to poke your nose over a cliff plunging more than a hundred metres into inky ocean makes this much more than just a spectacular coastal walk.

Tasmania boasts thousands of kilometres of shoreline, from wild and rugged to ridiculously pretty. Trying to nominate any one section as the most spectacular would be asking for trouble. But it would take award-winning debating skills to argue against the title going to the Tasman Peninsula, where the ocean slams into the highest sea cliffs in the southern hemisphere.

The multi-day Three Capes Track (threecapestrack.com.au), between White Beach and Fortescue Bay, which partially opened to the public in November 2015, caters for independent hikers sleeping in tents and public huts and commercially guided groups overnighting in private lodges, but you can also enjoy the drama of capes Pillar, Raoul and Hauy on shorter overnight and day hikes.

Half-day walks don't have more wow factor than the return tramp to Cape Hauy, which points seaward from Fortescue Bay like an ancient, gnarled finger. The walk starts in Fortescue Bay's day-use carpark, 12 unsealed kilometres off the Arthur Hwy, a drive that takes you through eucalypt forest regrown since it was razed by loggers in 1971. The signed walking track starts at the eastern end of the day use area. Fortescue Bay laps the rocks to your left as you follow the track east through a camping area and into the bush beyond a jetty and boat ramp.

Stage one of the Three Capes Track project was a multi-million dollar upgrade of the Cape Hauy track. Some walkers think it has been over engineered – to the point of being almost a footpath – but the country through which it passes is no less astounding for this new work.

First up, you tread a flat, metre-wide compacted track through eucalypts, banksias and tea-tree. Then the steps start, and there are plenty. Stonework that would set a stonemason's heart aflutter climbs steadily along the coast before turning inland, there gaining about 150m in height over a kilometre, among stringybarks and blue gums that dwarf banksias and native cherry trees. Look for pink or white Parson's Bands (orchids) growing beneath.

The steps end on a plateau of sorts (*see* point 1 on map) populated by tea-tree, banksias and grand old eucalypts, and the trail rises and falls gently as it continues south and east. The pretty purple flowers growing beside a long boardwalk are fairies' aprons.

The forest now is dominated by Oyster Bay pines and she-oaks. If the she-oaks are in bloom it's worth taking a closer look – the females erupt in tufts of red flowers while the males produce flower spikes. The forest's diverse colours and textures make up for the lack of a view.

About 3.5km into the walk you reach a junction with signs pointing right to Cape Pillar via Mount Fortescue and left to Cape Hauy (two hours return). Turn left for your first glimpse of the sea and a faceful of wind (the remainder of the walk is very exposed to the elements). Descending steeply on stone steps and packed earth you can clearly see the walking track snaking out along the cape below, a yellow line through wind-cropped green heath bookended by dolerite columns and cliffs.

Stick your nose over the edge, if you dare, to see blue water pounding the cliff more than 100m below

The track skirts the edge of a steep, rocky cove before climbing again (*see* point 2). As you start uphill you'll see Cape Pillar around to your right. (An overnight walk to Cape Pillar puts you atop Australia's tallest sea cliffs, with 300m drops into the ocean.) A stand-alone dolerite column sticks out from the sentinel-like cliff just south of the cove, and Fortescue Bay is now visible behind. From further along the narrowing cape you can see the battlement-like cliffs that run north from Fortescue Bay to Tasman Arch, one of the peninsula's most visited tourist spots. The walking track continues through a waist-deep sea of coastal heath often festooned with stalks of candy-floss pink common heath bells.

Gaps in the natural rock wall along the cape's southern edge give vertiginous views of the Tasman Sea and a 20m long rock shard that has split from the cliff but not yet let go.

After dipping down to the left and doing an S-bend, the track ends suddenly on a small, unsigned rock shelf with a view sweeping clockwise from the sea cliffs north of Fortescue Bay to Cape Pillar and the neighbouring, upthrust Tasman Island, beyond which the next landfall is Antarctica.

It appears as if the cape extends further, but the dolerite formations beyond this rocky aerie are separated from it by a sheer drop. If you dare, crawl to the edge and poke your nose over the cliff, where you'll see inky water thumping into rock more than a hundred metres below. To your left you'll just see the top of the Totem Pole, a dolerite column that looks like it was pushed through from below by a subterranean stitcher.

The subject of many photographs promoting Tasmania, this remarkable geological exclamation mark is popular with freestyle sports climbers (no bolting), and voices and the tinkle of climbing equipment sometimes carry across the gap. The two metal D-rings bolted to the cliff beneath your nose are rock climbing anchor points!

When you've had your fill of this jaw-dropping view, raise yourself from horizontal and retrace your steps to Fortescue Bay.

Left: *The cliff drops away just metres from the walking track;* **Right:** *Walking through forest between Fortescue Bay and the cape*

3 CAPE QUEEN ELIZABETH

Walk:	13km return
Time required:	4 hours (longer if you loll on the beach)
Best time:	Sunny day
Grade:	Easy to moderate
Environment:	White beaches, rocky cape, rock stacks, coastal heathland
Best map:	This one
Toilets:	None
Food:	Bruny Island Cheese (brunyislandcheese.com.au), which sells artisan cheeses, coffee and cake and seasonal homemade ice-cream, and the Oyster Bar at Get Shucked (getshucked.com.au) are just up Bruny Island Main Rd from the walk carpark
Tips:	Time your walk so you can include the low-tide route around Mars Bluff. Check times at surf-forecast.com/breaks/Neck-Bay/tides/latest.

White sand, turquoise water, geological artistry, massed wildflowers and only moderate hills make this one of Australia's great short coastal walks.

Adventure Bay, on South Bruny Island, is the most important bay in Australia's pre-white settlement history. The who's who of European visitors to this sheltered harbour include Captain James Cook, and

Looking south from Moorina Bay Beach

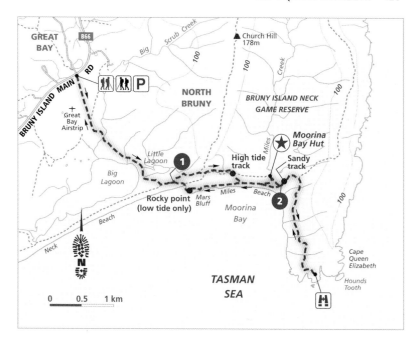

Rear Admiral Bruni D'Entrecasteaux, after whom the island and the channel separating it from mainland Tasmania are named. Among the exhibits in the museum at Adventure Bay is the stump of the tree to which, tradition says, Cook tethered his ship, the *Resolution*, in 1777 to clean its hull. Bruny Island was also the only Australian port-of-call for the mutiny-bound HMS *Bounty* in 1788, and Captain Bligh's crew became the first sawyers in Tasmania, starting a timbering industry in the island state (and on Bruny) that, controversially, continues.

That period of relatively intense visitation in the late 18th and early 19th centuries is only a fraction of Bruny's human timeline, however. Nuenonne Aboriginal people, who call the island Lunnawannalonna, hunted its hills and fished its waters for millennia before tall ships sailed into Adventure Bay, and for many years Bruny was Hobart's secret backyard playground.

Treading any of Bruny Island's walking tracks gives you an appreciation of why it has been so popular for so long.

The walk ends on a rocky cape where cliffs plunge into the sea

The Cape Queen Elizabeth walk starts in a small parking area beside Bruny Island Main Rd, 4km north-east of the ribbon-like isthmus – The Neck – linking North Bruny Island and hillier, more forested South Bruny. Head east from here on a flat, gated and unused 4WD track, through a corridor of eucalypts and banksias separating farmland and Bruny's airstrip, where scenic flights take to the air (islandscenicflights. com). The trees are often a-chatter with birds, and on warm days hum with bees (and flies).

About 700m along, the track sweeps left through bracken, she-oaks and tea-tree, and from the next bend you can look across Big Lagoon to the distinctive dolerite columns that give South Bruny's Fluted Cape its name. Tasmania's 12 endemic bird species can all be seen on Bruny Island – including the rare forty-spotted pardalote, if you are very lucky – and more than a hundred other species live on or visit the island. Look for waterbirds on Big Lagoon and majestic white-bellied sea eagles overhead.

Cape Queen Elizabeth comes into full view as you pass smaller, ephemeral Little Lagoon on the left.

Narrower and sandier but still easy going, the track wanders through twisted rough-barked eucalypts and into dunes greened with sand-hugging heath. You'll hear waves and taste salty breeze before the ocean shows itself.

About 300m beyond the lagoons the track divides (see point 1 on map). The tide determines which way you go: right, on the low-tide route to Moorina Bay via the beach (fantastic and fun geology) or, if the tide is high, left, up and over Mars Bluff (sweeping views of lagoons and The Neck). Don't attempt the low-tide beach route more than an hour or so either side of low water – and even then you'll probably get wet feet! If conditions give you the choice, take the 'high road' first and come back from the cape on the lower route, as described here, which gifts you the rugged geology at the foot of the Bluff as a grand finale.

Assuming conditions allow this, turn left at the junction and work your way up and over Mars Bluff on a footpad, remembering to look back at the broadening view over the lagoons and isthmus and South Bruny's dolerite sea cliffs. From the top you descend gently to wooden steps that deposit you in soft sand behind a dune. (The lone post with sun-bleached marker arrow atop this dune helps people walking in the reverse direction find this track after visiting the cape.) Stroll along Miles Beach, with Moorina Bay to your right.

Moorina Bay is named after a sister of Truganini, the famous Indigenous woman born on Bruny Island around 1812. A spokesperson and leader of Tasmanian Aboriginal people, and briefly a guerrilla fighter with Victoria's first Australians, Truganini was for many years described, erroneously, as the last Tasmanian Aboriginal person.

About 600m along the beach, detour left, up Miles Creek, to Moorina Bay Hut in the dunes. Two walkers built this rustic shelter in the 1950s, from planks of sawn timber they found in the wreck of the *Swift*, a ketch abandoned after grounding and washing ashore in a heavy storm in 1935.

Back on the beach, continue along the bay. Just before the sand ends in a pile of rocks (*see* point 2) turn off the beach onto a narrow, sandy track that climbs into the dunes. Above the beach, turn right onto a track running along the cape's southern flank. This undulates through eucalypts with thick, coarse trunks and others peeling in streamers of bark; through stands of tea-tree; through bristling banksias and drooping she-oaks; with views to the south.

As you near the cape's point, trees give way to shrubs and then stunted coastal heath, and you pass through an area drilled with shearwater (mutton-bird) burrows. The smell of these birds infuses the rest of the walk.

Cape Queen Elizabeth's crown is a web of tracks, but finding your way is only an issue coming down, and even then, the plants are low enough to keep your bearings: look for rock cairns and occasional ribbons.

The wonderful view from the top sweeps from The Neck, Adventure Bay and Fluted Cape (another great walk) to the south, around to the Tasman Peninsula and north into the nooks and crannies of Hobart's waterways. And immediately below, over the precipitous edge, is a fist of dolerite columns.

Now retrace your steps to Miles Beach and amble to its southern end (tide permitting) for the walk's geological finale.

In the lee of the cliff just short of a rock stack is an extraordinary arch fashioned from layered, crazed dolerite. Walk around and through this architectural natural sculpture, before rounding the rock stack that blocks passage into the tiny next bay at high tide. Continue through a taller, narrower archway and a rock corridor to elongated Neck Beach, passing undercut and eroded stone.

It's a short walk from here to the high-tide junction and the track back to the car.

Top: *A remarkable rock formation arches over Moorina Bay Beach;* **Bottom:** *Stepping out on Moorina Bay Beach*

4 COAL MINES HISTORIC SITE LOOP

Walk:	4.7km loop
Time required:	2 hours
Best time:	Any time
Grade:	Easy
Environment:	Coastal eucalypt scrub, convict-era ruins
Best map:	This one
Toilets:	Pit toilet in carpark
Food:	No food on site; bakery, cafe and pub fare in Nubeena, 11km south of Premaydena
Tips:	Don't be put off by grey skies; they only add to the atmosphere of this historic site

Walk in the footsteps of convict labourers and their minders on this disarmingly pretty stretch of Tasmanian coast.

Convicts who reoffended after transportation to Van Diemen's Land, as Tasmania was known in the early 19th century, found themselves at Port Arthur, the infamous penal settlement on the Tasman Peninsula. Port Arthur targeted reform through hard physical labour and severe punishment, and conditions were harsh. An even more dreaded destination, however, were the coal mines on the peninsula's north-west coast.

Norfolk Bay's blue water laps the shores of this World Heritage convict site

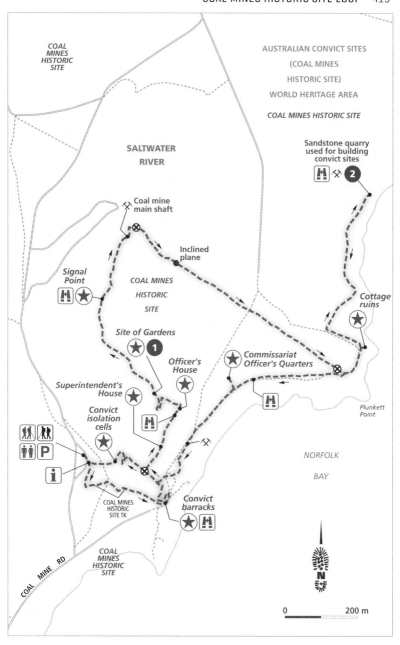

COAL
MINES
HISTORIC
SITE

AUSTRALIAN CONVICT SITES
(COAL MINES
HISTORIC SITE)
WORLD HERITAGE AREA

COAL MINES HISTORIC SITE

SALTWATER
RIVER

Sandstone quarry
used for building
convict sites
2

Coal mine
main shaft

Inclined
plane

Signal
Point

COAL MINES
HISTORIC
SITE

Cottage
ruins

Site of Gardens **1**

Officer's
House

Commissariat
Officer's Quarters

Superintendent's
House

Convict
isolation
cells

Plunkett
Point

NORFOLK

BAY

COAL MINES
HISTORIC
SITE TK

Convict
barracks

COAL MINE RD

COAL
MINES
HISTORIC
SITE

N

0   200 m

The rocky shore comes into view from the side trail to the quarry

But this reputation may have been unjust. While the 'worst class' of convicts laboured underground in unstable mine shafts, often harnessed to others and always under threat of solitary confinement in subterranean punishment cells, most men at the coal mines worked above ground, quarrying rock, building prisoner barracks and civilian quarters, splitting timber and tending vegetables.

The Coal Mines Historic Site is one of 11 sites in Tasmania (*see* Maria Island Loop, page 441), Norfolk Island, Western Australia and New South Wales (*see* Finch's Line & Devine's Hill, page 20) that form the Australian Convict Sites World Heritage property. This walk revisits a dramatic chapter in Australia's short but action-packed European history.

To get there you turn west off the Arthur Hwy at Taranna, south of Eaglehawk Neck, the infamous isthmus that links the Tasman and Forestier peninsulas, which in Port Arthur's day was guarded by a chain gang of vicious dogs. Drive along the B37 to Premaydena then turn north up the C341, following this road 13km (mostly unsealed) north.

Your journey back in time begins when you step through an obvious break in the tea-tree fringing the parking area, and continues on a flat walking track that snakes through woodland to a chicane of timber and rammed earth. Information plaques on the wall above a rusty chain outline the site's timeline. Watch for superb fairy-wrens flitting about the leaf litter as you continue through woodland into the site.

The track emerges from the trees beside the main settlement or 'Square', founded in 1838, and swings around in front of the ruined convict barracks, their every sandstone block pitted with tool marks. Climb the rise and wander around the settlement. A second-floor fenced area within the first building gives a view down into the solitary confinement cells (and out over the blue water of Norfolk Bay).

Now head towards the rear of the 'square' and take the right-hand track to the Military Precinct. Ascending gradually through banksias and tall eucalypts, with a broadening view of water and peninsula, you pass the remains of the Superintendent's House (built in 1837), home to tyrannical Superintendent Cook and more moderate managers.

The track turns left at the remains of the brick six-room Senior Military Officer's House, which from 1837 to 1842 housed the garrison commander, who also acted as magistrate. Under the sadistic Lieutenant Barclay, the miners became known as Barclay's Tigers because of the flogging scars on their backs.

After a short detour left to the beautiful remains of the sandstone officers' outbuilding, you reach the garden site (see point 1 on map), a grassy clearing where convicts once grew hectares of potatoes, carrots, turnips, cabbages and leeks.

From here the track, now lined with delineating logs, climbs through cypress pines, thick, velvety moss growing in their shade, and tops out at Signal Point. The convict-manned signal station operated here was a branch line of the semaphore system that enabled Port Arthur to communicate with Hobart in just 15 minutes. There must have been far fewer trees back then, to facilitate signal-flag sightings, but now eucalypts frame scraps of farmland and water views.

Descend slightly from here to the deepest coal mining shaft, down which convicts were lowered by windlass to work a coal face, or run out the coal-laden boxes, or pull and push them to the shaft. This shaft reached 92m into the hill but is now a fairly shallow fenced hole. The rusty boiler behind powered the steam engine, which superseded convict labour to pump water from the constantly flooding mine.

Turn right at the track junction immediately beyond the shaft and descend the inclined plane. A gravity-powered cable transfer system operated on this slope, with empty wagons being hauled back up to the mine by the weight of those laden with coal running down to the jetty.

There are other unfenced shafts either side of the inclined plane, so don't leave the wagon route. Just continue downhill (ignoring a cross road) to Plunkett Point, where aqua water laps white sand.

You could turn right here and make your way back to the settlement area, but we're making the 1.4km return detour to the quarry first. So turn left and follow a sandy track with occasional exposed roots north along the bay's rocky shore to the quarry via photogenic stone cottage ruins. The track tunnels through tea-tree, which blocks the breeze, but you still get refreshing views of Norfolk Bay.

Unfinished stone blocks (see point 2) that were abandoned on the track the day the mine closed signal you've reached the quarry. Ignore the rougher track going left and continue ahead and down. Walk into the quarry area and compare the clean stone faces cut by convicts with the voluptuous curves nature has fashioned in the rock face.

Back at Plunkett Point, walk south-west along the shore on a sandy track often lined with stalks of pink and white common heath. Ignore the intersecting wide track on the left but do step up to the right to the ruins of the Commissariat Officers' Quarters (1842). There are some particularly colourful stone blocks here.

On your return to the Coal Mines settlement square, which soon comes into view through the trees, walk up through the buildings again, passing the track to the Officers' Quarters you took earlier and continuing to the punishment cells at the rear of the site. Tread the mesh walkway through the building and past the restored and original isolation cells, in which convicts were locked for days at a time, deprived of light, sound and human company. Then escape along the track heading west to the carpark.

Clockwise from top: *One of the convict-built ruins of the main Coal Mines Site settlement; exploring the ruins; multiple shades of blue make up the bay and sky on a sunny day; other ruins are tucked away in the forest along the walk*

5 GROWLING SWALLET & JUNEE CAVE

Walk:	3.6km (in two parts)
Time required:	2 hours (plus 15-minute drive)
Best time:	Misty day for the best atmosphere
Grade:	Easy (but can be muddy)
Environment:	Rainforest, river, karst cave system
Best map:	This one
Toilets:	None
Food:	Waterfalls Cafe, within Mount Field National Park visitor centre, sells a range of drinks, takeaway food and table meals
Tips:	The forestry road into Growling Swallet is gated and locked. You must pre-book the key with the national park rangers (03 6288 1149) and pay a $300 security deposit when you collect it at the visitor centre at the Mount Field National Park entrance.
	The forestry road can be rough in winter, so check the road condition with the park rangers.
	Entry fees apply for all Tasmanian National Parks and a range of passes are available; details at parks.tas.gov.au.

Water has piled rocks and logs in the mouth of Growling Swallet

Pairing one of Tasmania's best rainforest walks with a leafy riverside ramble, this easy two-part walk initiates you in the mystery and magic of limestone caves and underground rivers.

Nature performs a now-you-see-it-now-you-don't conjuring trick with the Junee River, whose peat-stained mountain tributaries disappear into an extensive karst (limestone) cave system only to reappear on the far side of the range as a gin-clear river. These two short walks visit one of the most spectacular entrances into the system and the cave through which the Junee River resurfaces.

The delightfully named Growling Swallet (sinkhole) is tucked inside Mt Field National Park's southern boundary, but access is through plantation forest. From the turn-off to the national park proper, and the visitor centre, 67km north-west of Hobart, via North Norfolk, drive about 15km further along Gordon River Rd (B61) and through Maydena until you see large tourist signs for the Styx Valley and Big Tree pointing up Florentine Rd. Follow this wide, well-maintained forestry road about 16km north to gated F8 East, on the right. Beyond the gate (see point 1 on map) (the lock is tucked under a small metal canopy on the left upright) drive 2km east on a rougher, narrower, occasionally sandy road best travelled in a 4WD or AWD vehicle (some conventional vehicles get through).

If you can't be bothered arranging to pick up the key from the visitor centre and are up for 4km extra leg work you could walk in from the gate; however, there are commercial beehives along here and the mosquitoes can be fierce, so reconsider this option if you are allergic to either.

F8 East ends at a wall of forest, where there's space for a handful of cars, and the walking track disappears into the foliage at around one o'clock (with the road directly behind you). A sign about 5m in warns that there are numerous deep hidden shafts in this area and that flash flooding can occur in the creek and cave system; there's a Mt Field National Park sign shortly after.

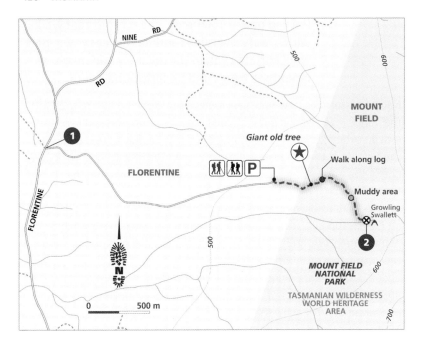

This track doesn't appear on park maps and isn't permanently marked, but you'll often spot pink and orange ribbons guiding the way. The route is easy to follow, with the only possible confusion at the end.

Beyond the national park sign, the trail rambles through thick myrtle and sassafras forest, whose leafy canopy looks like green confetti tossed into the air, passing centuries-old eucalypts and the stumps of others felled for timber. About 300m in there's a magnificent tree, its coarse, red-barked trunk about 20m around, and lumpy with burls. A hundred metres further on there's another old-timer whose trunk is limbless for about 30m before bursting into a Rastafarian top knot of leafy branches.

Immediately beyond this second notable forest character, a tree branch has grown down towards the track and then looped skyward again, creating a throat-high booby trap for the distracted.

Rooty in parts and boggy after rain – boots and gaiters are recommended and walking poles handy – the track snakes between,

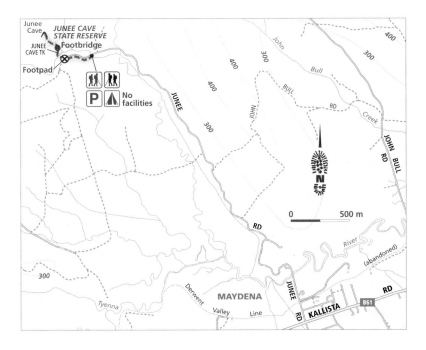

over and around fallen trees colonised by lichens and velvety mosses. It also runs 20m along a toppled trunk.

About 1.3km into the walk, with the sound of rushing water now quite loud, you'll see a tree festooned with coloured ribbons (*see* point 2). Turn right and walk down into the creek gully. (If you come to a small cavers' camping clearing with old fireplaces, you have gone a few metres too far.)

Descending right and then scrambling steeply left lands you beside a stream that washes around and over mossy rocks before disappearing into a cave mouth at the base of a limestone formation, like an ancient temple being reclaimed by the jungle. Tree ferns umbrella overhead and every branch and trunk is shaggy with old man's beard.

Work your way across to the boulders in the creek for a better look down into Growling Swallet, so named because it growls after heavy rain when water pours into the cave. Getting your feet damp is usually the only risk here, though extra care is needed to navigate a fallen tree and rocks to get closer to the mouth.

Growling Swallet is part of the Junee Florentine cave system, consisting of 30km of passages and more than 295 cave entrances. Decorated with limestone formations and home to creatures such as Tasmania's cave spider – the females have a leg span up to 180mm – this cave system is hard, wet, technical and includes the deepest cave in Australia. Only experienced, fully-equipped cavers should venture beyond the logs stacked at Growling Swallet's mouth.

From the growling – or perhaps just grumbling, or even gurgling – sinkhole, retrace your steps to the car and drive south back to the bitumen and then left, back towards the visitor centre. Turn left again onto Junee Rd (signed for Junee Cave) just as you come into Maydena, and follow this narrowing, dirt road to its end, at a turning area beside pretty Junee River.

Continue in the same direction on foot (there's an orange arrow and sign), treading a forestry road between the river and plantation timber, with Mount Field National Park mountains on your left. The Junee Cave walking track heads right off the road about 300m up.

Starting downhill, this easy track curves through thick forest noisy with birds and fords a footbridge over the fast-flowing clear river. Walk upstream and through a tree-fern tunnel to a boarded platform in the shadow-filled mouth of Junee Cave, through which the river re-emerges into the light.

The tannin-browned river that disappeared underground through Growling Swallet is filtered by the limestone before it surfaces again and runs clear past this platform. Imagine the twists and turns along that journey, the cracks and caverns through which the river works, as you watch the river and listen to it burble. Then return to your car when you're done.

The Junee River flows through lush fern forest before disappearing underground through Growling Swallet

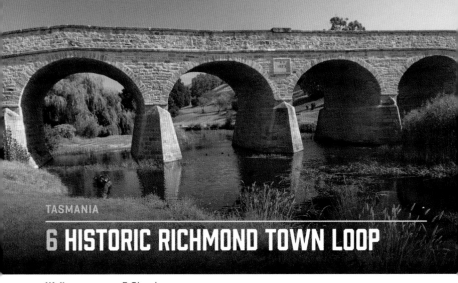

6 HISTORIC RICHMOND TOWN LOOP

Walk:	5.2km loop
Time required:	2 hours
Best time:	Sunny day
Grade:	Easy
Environment:	Village streets, convict-era gaol, colonial buildings, riverbank
Best map:	This one
Toilets:	Flushing toilets in the Forth St parking area near Richmond Gaol
Food:	Everything from oven-fresh scones to pub fare is available along Richmond's main street
Tips:	Richmond is on the Convict Trail (tasmanian-convict-trail.com), a fascinating 205km self-drive tour from Hobart to Port Arthur and back, highlighting the region's history and scenery

Follow in the footsteps of convicts, military officers, innkeepers and a Dickens character as you explore the streets of one of Tasmania's most historic towns.

Settled in the early 19th century after the discovery of coal, the fertile Coal River region north-east of Hobart became known, with neighbouring Pitt Water, as 'the granary of Australia' – and is now a renowned wine region. This walk dips into the fascinating history of

Richmond Bridge is said to be haunted by several ghosts

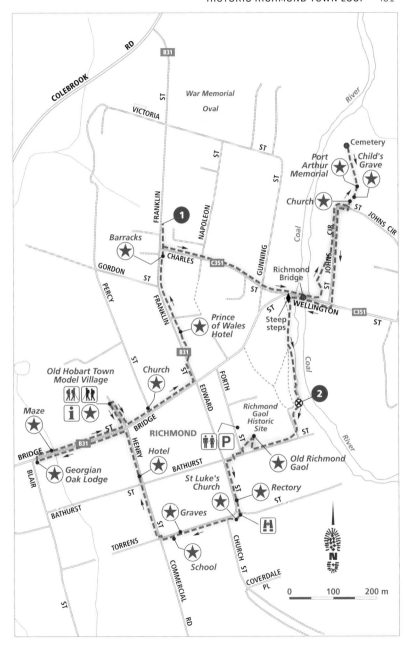

Richmond, the town established at the point where a sandstone bridge was built across the Coal River to facilitate travel to the east coast and Tasman Peninsula.

The walk starts at Richmond's visitor information centre (up a laneway off Bridge St), which is also the entrance to Old Hobart Town. Wander around this faithful, outdoor, scale model of 1820s Hobart before heading off around Richmond.

From there, turn left into Bridge St and pass Fry Cottage (1835), now the Woodcraft Shop, which sells an array of Tasmanian timber products. Note the stone front step, worn by the passage of feet over nearly 200 years. Imagine what stories it could tell!

The congregational church on the next corner was built in 1873, making it a youngster, but the supermarket, just before the next corner, dates from 1836.

Turn left at the supermarket carpark and walk along the east side of Franklin St. Now a private residence, the two-storey red brick building was once the Prince of Wales Hotel, one of numerous hotels that accommodated early travellers quenching their thirsts.

Have a sticky beak over the picket fence at the old hotel's elegant Georgian lines before strolling on to the cluster of white-painted cottages on the corner of Charles St. Now holiday accommodation, these buildings were the Richmond Barracks, built of convict-made bricks in 1830, when Richmond became one of Governor Arthur's police districts.

You are going to turn right here, but first walk a bit further along Franklin St and look across the road at the early workers' cottages (see point 1 on map). On this side you'll see some new houses, built in sympathy with the original, simple historic design.

Retrace your steps, then turn down Charles St and walk east and downhill to a junction with more lovely old brick cottages on your right. Directly ahead is Richmond Bridge, the oldest bridge in Australia still in use.

The construction of a bridge over the Coal River enabled settlers to push further east, to the coast and Tasman Peninsula in search of good land. Commenced in 1823 and built by convicts from sandstone

A convict-built Georgian steam mill, now a private home, sits beside the river

quarried by convicts and hauled in hand carts to the river by convicts, Richmond Bridge is said to be haunted by several ghosts, including George Grover. Himself a convict, transported for stealing, Grover was by all accounts a nasty piece of work who whipped prisoners like horses during the rebuilding of the bridge piers in 1829. Three years later, the 27-year old 'wicked Flagellator' was thrown over the bridge to his death while drunk, probably by some of the men he brutalised; he is buried in the grounds of St Luke's Church, which you'll pass later on the walk.

Turn left immediately across the bridge and walk down the grassy bank to view its beautiful arches. Then head up St John's Cirque to the oldest Catholic Church in Australia still in use, which sits prettily on a rise behind some beautiful gum trees. The church interior is fairly plain but, inside and out, you can see convict tool marks in every stone.

A historic burial ground overlooks the Coal River from a rise behind the church. Some of the oldest and most interesting headstones, at the back, have developed severe lists.

Return to the bridge and cross back over the river, turning hard left at the end of the stonework and heading down the steep, worn original steps – if you can cope with the pitch (otherwise just amble down the wheel-friendly path beyond). The three-storey Georgian building sitting proudly on the opposite bank was convict-built as a steam mill in 1853. It later became a butter factory.

Walk downstream through linear parkland, keeping to the lower walking track, which passes lovely old wooden boats for hire and awful plastic swans you can paddle on the river.

Continue along the river to a track (see point 2) up to a carpark, and from there walk up Bathurst St, between almond trees, with the clocktower/spire of St Luke's Church to your left. Just before the crossroad, turn right to Richmond Gaol (1825), the oldest gaol in Australia.

Allow at least an hour to wander around this remarkable piece of history and read about the people who lived and worked here. One notorious prisoner was Ikey Solomon, London fence and pawnbroker and repeat escapee, who was transported to Van Diemen's Land in 1831 (having sailed to Australia voluntarily after his wife was

Left: *St John's is the oldest Catholic church in Australia still in use;* **Right:** *Looking into the whipping yard in Richmond Gaol*

transported from Britain). Solomon is widely believed to have been the inspiration for Fagin in Charles Dickens' novel *Oliver Twist*.

On exiting the gaol, head back across the lawns and towards the church seen earlier. Wander up Edward St (the little sandstone cottage on the corner was Richmond Dispensary, c. 1830) to St Luke's Church, passing the stone-block rectory on the left.

As you approach the church gate you are treated to a watercolour view of river and farmland to the left.

St Luke's Anglican Church is the oldest church in Richmond, its foundation stone having been laid in 1834 by Governor Phillip himself. Convict James Thompson was granted his freedom as a reward for the interior timberwork.

Now walk up Torrens St, passing the burial ground (1845) on the site of the original congregational church. Directly opposite is the oldest still-operating primary school in Australia (1834). Turn right into Commercial Rd and walk to Bridge St, passing the old Richmond Hotel – note the faded 'wine and spirits' paintwork.

Turn left into Bridge St and walk to Georgian Oak Lodge (1830), perhaps via the homewares shops along the way, all in stone cottages. Built as a gentleman's town residence and subsequently used as a rectory, school, doctor's surgery and family home, Oak Lodge is run by volunteers as a local museum and is open most days 11.30am–3.30pm (or by appointment).

Cross the street and head back up to the visitor information centre, perhaps getting lost in Richmond Maze on the way.

7 LAKE DOBSON & TARN SHELF LOOP

Walk:	5.2km loop
Time required:	2 hours
Best time:	Sunny day, autumn to spring (the walk is snowbound in winter, although snow can fall at any time of year)
Grade:	Moderate
Environment:	Alpine lake, unsealed road (snowbound in winter), ski field, exposed mountain slopes, ancient pencil pine forest
Best map:	*TASMAP's Mount Field National Park 1:50,000 Map & Notes*
Toilets:	Flushing toilets at Mount Field National Park visitor centre
Food:	Waterfalls Cafe, within Mount Field National Park visitor centre, sells a range of drinks, takeaway food and table meals
Tips:	Allow time at the visitor centre before or after the Lake Dobson walk to wander through fern forest and truly tall timbers to three-tiered Russel Falls, one of Tasmania's prettiest cascades. Entry fees apply for all Tasmanian National Parks and a range of passes are available; details at parks.tas.gov.au.

Climb from the weird and wonderful world of giant heath to an exposed alpine plateau on this short alpine taster in Tasmania's 'backyard' national park.

The main range rises above the Tarn Shelf lookout

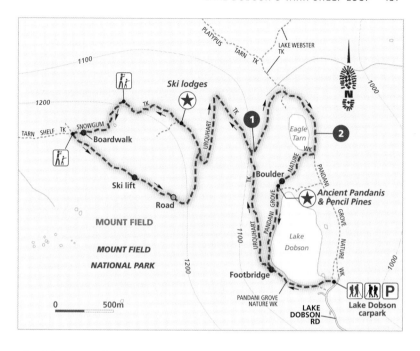

The island state's most diverse national park, with attractions ranging from stunning waterfalls amid some of the world's tallest timbers to tarns on alpine moors, Mount Field is an easy 80km drive north-west of Hobart via the beautiful Derwent Valley. Declared in 1916 (which makes it Tasmania's joint first national park, along with Freycinet Peninsula) and part of the Tasmanian Wilderness World Heritage Area, Mt Field is the city's popular 'backyard' playground, with kilometres of walking tracks for summer visitors, and downhill skiing and tobogganing for lovers of the white stuff (which can also fall in summer).

This walk starts in the Lake Dobson carpark, 15km beyond the ranger station and picnic area at the park entrance on an unsealed road that initially winds through towering trees whose upper branches almost touch overhead. The carpark marks the end of road access for the public; ski-club members with a gate key can drive further in summer on a jeep track.

The walking trail drops obliquely from the carpark to the lake's shoreline, and you'll almost immediately have boardwalk underfoot. Tread the boardwalk around the lake, through needle-sharp scoparia and beautiful old pencil pines. Look out for platypus in the lake; your best chance of seeing them is in the early morning and at dusk, but these extraordinary animals can show themselves any time.

Ignore a side track on the left (Wellington Ski Club), but veer left at the next junction onto Erquhart Track, which climbs gently away from the water. The shaggy, Dr Seuss-ish plants here are pandani, the world's tallest heath; Mt Field is the most accessible place in Tasmania to see these Gondwanaland relics. (For an easier, lower-altitude walk, stay on the lower track and circumnavigate the lake.)

A short, uneven climb puts you in gorgeous forest given height by alpine gums and fagus (deciduous beech) and texture by pandani and scoparia. Meander through this forest and emerge from its cover at a U-bend on the jeep track (see point 1 on map), where a sign warns you to beware of vehicles and skiers.

Turn left and climb the jeep track, turning off it again on the third U-bend, where Snowgum Track is marked to the right.

Resuming just beyond the second of two ski lodges on this ridge, Snowgum Track undulates through pandani and magnificent old snow gums with impressive girths, offering views down to alpine lakes.

The track turns hard left at a jumble of rocks decorated with cream and orange lichen that presents a spectacular view over Lake Seal and the park's rugged interior. There are so many lookouts up here that this rocky vantage point doesn't have an official name, let alone a sign, but it deserves one. There is no better place on this walk to stop and ponder the nature of things.

Turn your back on the view, and watch for occasional route marker arrows as you follow a rocky and boarded track away from the lookout. This lands you at a four-way boardwalk junction almost atop Mawson Plateau, with ski runs to your left and Lake Seal Lookout signed to the right.

This lookout is an area rather than a specific spot or formed structure. Hikers' feet have cut a web of tracks to a jumble of rocks, so just approach the cliff edge and take in the splendid vista down to Lake Seal and across to the Tarn Shelf, a famous walking destination.

If you have plenty of time you could proceed to the Tarn Shelf before heading back. Or, with pre-planning, do the fabulous all-day loop walk that traverses the shelf and returns to the carpark via Lake Webster. Otherwise, enjoy the panorama, then return to the boardwalk junction and head south-east across the plateau towards the ski runs, through prickly alpine heath and low-growing tea-tree. Cross the ski tow and descend to the tow huts and the winter-season emergency and first-aid shelter. From here, follow the jeep track downhill through snow gums, enjoying an aerial view of Lake Dobson and miniature parked cars down to your right.

Stay on the jeep track all the way to the bottom, passing the ski clubs and Snowgum Track on the left and the footpad (on the right) you came up earlier from Lake Dobson, and entering taller eucalypt forest.

Soon after Platypus Tarn Track, going left on a bend, you'll reach pretty Eagle Tarn (see point 2), which often plonks with frogs. Immediately beyond this tarn, turn right onto the Pandani Grove track;

An ancient pencil pine stands beside crystal clear Lake Dobson

An unnamed natural lookout presents a grandstand view of Lake Seal and its enfolding mountains

this skirts the smaller lake before plunging into a fantastical, shady grove of ancient pencil pines and pandani, with the odd gum tree giving some height.

Pencil pines are one of several conifer species endemic to Tasmania. All are slow growing and long lived, in favourable conditions, with the Huon pine, famed for its beautiful golden timber, reaching ages in excess of 2000 years. The conical pencil pine, predominantly found around sub-alpine lakes, lives beyond 1200 years and some of the old-timers you see here may be of that vintage.

All endemic pines (rainforest and alpine communities) are highly susceptible to fire, and the Tasmanian Wilderness World Heritage Area has been declared a 'fuel stove only area' in the hope that this will limit further losses.

Continue through slightly more open forest of pandani, which rattle percussively as you brush past, and deciduous beech, whose pretty, corrugated leaves turn red-gold in autumn before falling like confetti on the ground. Then follow the lake shore back to the carpark.

8 MARIA ISLAND LOOP

Walk:	18km loop
Time required:	2 days (or 5–6 hours if not spending the night)
Best time:	Clear, dry day
Grade:	Moderate to hard (easy without the mountain climb)
Environment:	Precipitous sea cliffs, primordial forest, mountains, beach, convict settlement
Best map:	*TASMAP's Maria Island National Park Map & Notes*
Toilets:	Flushing toilets beside Commissariat Store and in Darlington
Food:	None on the island; Triabunna (where the ferry departs) has a pub, fish-and-chip caravan, and a supermarket for supplies
Tips:	There are two ferry departures a day to Maria Island (mariaislandferry.com.au); dolphins often ride the boat's bow wave.
	Entry fees apply for all Tasmanian National Parks and a range of passes are available; details at parks.tas.gov.au.
	For a less rushed Maria Island experience divide this walk into two day walks either side of a night spent in a penitentiary cell; book at mariaislandferry.com.au/maria/accommodation-on-maria).

Maria Island's oldest building, the Commissariat Store (c. 1825), is now the National Park ranger station

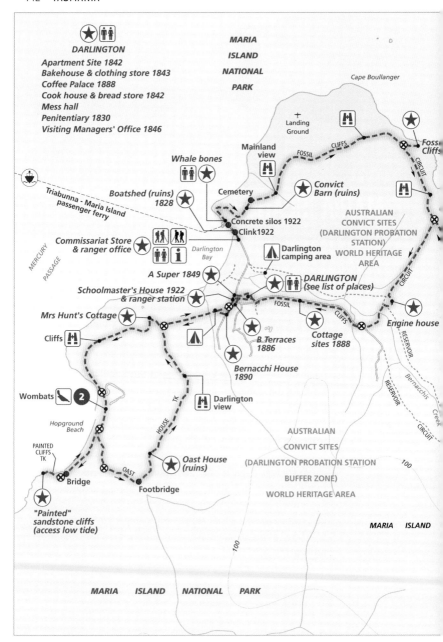

DARLINGTON

Apartment Site 1842
Bakehouse & clothing store 1843
Coffee Palace 1888
Cook house & bread store 1842
Mess hall
Penitentiary 1830
Visiting Managers' Office 1846

MARIA ISLAND NATIONAL PARK

Cape Boullanger

Landing Ground

Mainland view

Fossil Cliffs

FOSSIL CLIFFS

CIRCUIT

Whale bones

Cemetery

Convict Barn (ruins)

AUSTRALIAN CONVICT SITES (DARLINGTON PROBATION STATION) WORLD HERITAGE AREA

Boatshed (ruins) 1828

Triabunna - Maria Island passenger ferry

Concrete silos 1922
Clink 1922

Commissariat Store & ranger office

Darlington Bay

Darlington camping area

DARLINGTON (see list of places)

MERCURY PASSAGE

A Super 1849

Schoolmaster's House 1922 & ranger station

FOSSIL CLIFFS

CIRCUIT

Mrs Hunt's Cottage

Cliffs

B Terraces 1886

Cottage sites 1888

Engine house

RESERVOIR

Bernacchi House 1890

Darlington view

HOUSE TK

RESERVOIR

Bernacchis Creek

CIRCUIT

Wombats 2

Hopground Beach

AUSTRALIAN CONVICT SITES (DARLINGTON PROBATION STATION BUFFER ZONE) WORLD HERITAGE AREA

100

PAINTED CLIFFS TK

Bridge

OAST

Oast House (ruins)

Footbridge

"Painted" sandstone cliffs (access low tide)

MARIA ISLAND

100

MARIA ISLAND NATIONAL PARK

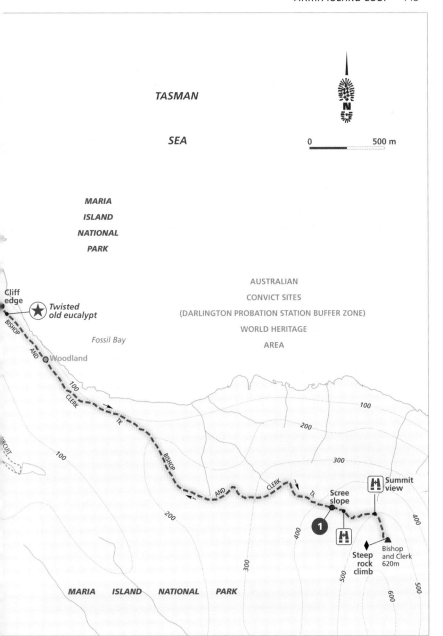

TASMAN

SEA

0   500 m

N

MARIA
ISLAND
NATIONAL
PARK

AUSTRALIAN
CONVICT SITES
(DARLINGTON PROBATION STATION BUFFER ZONE)
WORLD HERITAGE
AREA

Cliff
edge

★ Twisted
old eucalypt

Fossil Bay

Woodland

BISHOP

AND

CLERK

TK

100

CIRCUIT

100

BISHOP

AND

CLERK

TK

100

200

300

200

300

400

500

Scree
slope

1

Summit
view

Steep
rock
climb

Bishop
and Clerk
620m

400

500

600

MARIA   ISLAND   NATIONAL   PARK

Mountains, tangled forest and windswept cliffs provide a stunning backdrop for this walk through another fascinating chapter in Tasmania's history.

'... to find a gaol in one of the loveliest spots formed by the hand of Nature in one of her loveliest solitudes creates a revulsion of feeling I cannot describe ...' So wrote Irish political prisoner William Smith O'Brien, transported to Van Diemen's Land in 1849, of first seeing Maria Island.

Settled in 1825 as a convict station, and subsequently home to Italian business entrepreneur Diego Bernacchi (silk, wine and concrete) in the late 19th century, and a concrete factory in the 1920s, Maria Island remains one of the loveliest spots formed by nature's hand – and now people visit voluntarily.

This walk, coincidentally shaped like convict leg irons and chain, showcases north Maria's geological and human history. Boot-camp pace would have you completing this walk between the first incoming

Left: *Red brick frames the view out of an engine house;* **Right:** *Up close, the Painted Cliffs look like caramel*

ferry from Triabunna and the last departing one, but it's more rewarding to take it slower and stay overnight. You can camp or unroll a sleeping bag in the penitentiary (booking required; see 'Tips'), in a six-bed dorm with wood-burning stove that once slept 66 convicts. More indulgent again would be to splurge on a private guided four-day walking holiday with Maria Island Walk (mariaislandwalk.com.au).

This walk begins and ends at the Commissariat Store, Maria's oldest building, which overlooks the jetty where the ferry docks. Built in 1825, the two-storey dolerite-and-limestone store, designed to house months of supplies, is now the national park visitor centre, where you collect maps and find out which 'cell' you've been assigned. Trolleys are provided to wheel your gear 400m up to the cluster of buildings of Darlington settlement.

From the store, walk back towards the jetty and past the National Portland Cement Company concrete silos (1920s). The bleached whale bones on the shore are evidence of a bloody earlier industry.

You'll already have seen Cape Barren geese – and probably stepped in their poo – because the small population of these elegant grey birds, introduced in 1968 as part of a program to save several endangered species, has thrived. A similar philosophy saw the controversial release of captive-bred Tasmanian Devils on Maria in November 2012 in the hope of saving the carnivorous marsupial from the contagious tumour disease threatening its survival, so look out for white-spotted black devils bowling along the harbour.

Gravel road becomes grassy track as you loop right and up to a red-brick Convict Barn (1844) on Cape Boullanger that houses rusty machines and wooden wagons. Hugging the cape's contour, the easy trail then passes the picket-fenced cemetery (half a dozen marked graves with unimpeded views of Tasmania's east coast) and the airstrip.

Step down into the Fossil Cliffs quarry site to fossick, or just look along Maria's sea cliffs to Bishop and Clerk, your destination (weather permitting). Named for its perceived likeness to a clergyman following a bishop wearing a mitre – can you see it? – Bishop and Clerk (620m) is the second highest point on the island after Mount Maria (711m).

The Fossil Cliffs are a formidable slope on a cloudy day

About 500m beyond the cliffs is a junction: climb Bishop and Clerk (8km return from here) or loop right back to Darlington? Leaving out the mountain climb shortens the walk to an easy 10km day trip. The way to the top is almost unremittingly uphill and increasingly rocky, the stone is slippery when wet, and there is no view in rain and mist. But on a sunny day, you're rewarded with a gobsmacking panorama, and you can straddle a deep crevice for a photo that will curl the toes of your less-adventurous friends and family, making the ascent very worthwhile.

If climbing, keep along the cliff-line and uphill, past a eucalypt that looks like it was hand-wrapped in its twisted bark. She-oak needles soften your footfalls as you continue through flatter woodland.

Now for the push to the top, on a narrowing, rocky track through thicker, damper forest dripping with bark streamers and old man's beard and patched with lichen and moss. It feels so like the land that time forgot, you might almost expect a dinosaur to poke its head through the canopy.

A tree tunnel pops you out at the bottom of a scree slope (*see* point 1 on map). Follow orange arrow markers up the switchback track, catching your breath at old eucalypts with roots buried beneath the stones. From the top of the scree slope, the trail winds through forest and around boulders.

An expanding view encourages you up a short but steep boulder face (with a couple of okay footholds) to the jaw-dropping summit sweep of island, sea and mainland.

Back down at the Darlington junction, turn left and follow the signs to the settlement, turning left again onto a gravel road at the red-brick engine house (1888). Ignoring tracks coming in from the sides (the ends of Reservoir Circuit), walk through scruffy eucalypt forest and step into the heart of the village between the mess hall (on your right) and the penitentiary (long building on your left).

The penitentiary verandah is a great late lunch spot, with seats and posts to lean against as you watch Cape Barren geese grazing. Common wombats also trundle around the settlement in the late afternoon and evening. This is the place to end day one of the walk if you are staying overnight.

Darlington comprises a dozen or so red-brick and whitewashed stone buildings dating from the convict era and Diego Bernacchi's reign. Read about transported young Irelander William Smith O'Brien in the single-storey terrace cottage where he lived. Listen to taped anecdotes of more comfortable island life in the elegant, weatherboard Coffee Palace (1888). Then continue south-west to the red-brick and weatherboard Bernacchi houses.

From here, walk down to the colonnade of Cypress pines and turn left onto Maria's only road, following it uphill past the camping area (right) and a simple 1920s cottage overlooking the town and harbour. Heading downhill now you'll see a ribbon of white beach ending in shallow cliffs, whose stripes are just visible, even from this distance.

A sign immediately before a bridge directs you right onto Counsel Beach for a sandy stroll to the cliffs. You can also stay on the road, passing wetlands (*see* point 2) where you are almost guaranteed to see a wombat (ignore the Oast House track going left and continue to the Painted Cliffs sign).

Counsel Beach ends in a delicious toffee-like swirl of smooth and pitted sandstone striped yellow, white and red. Low tide gives you the best access to these Painted Cliffs, which continue well around the point.

Head back to Darlington by walking north along the road and turning right onto the Oast House Track, which forks a few hundred metres into a sea of bracken. Follow the Oast House track left (Mount Maria, the highest point on Maria island, is straight ahead), through eucalypts peeling rough bark to yellow trunks. Beyond a wetland thrumming with insects and frogs, you come to the Oast House (1884) ruins. Hops were dried here for making beer during the Bernacchi era, and one of the two circular kilns still stands, several metres tall, but minus its conical roof and cowl.

From the clearing's eastern corner the track curls through woodland littered with bark streamers to the road. Follow it back to Darlington – and down to the jetty for the ferry, when you can bring yourself to leave.

Left: *A whitewashed convict cottage opens to a rusty wheel;* Right: *Bees buzz about a flowering gum in the settlement*

9 KUNANYI/MOUNT WELLINGTON SUMMIT LOOP

Walk:	13.8km loop
Time required:	5–7 hours
Best time:	Clear day
Grade:	Hard
Environment:	Tree-fern gullies, eucalypt forest, exposed alpine plateau
Best map:	*TASMAP's Wellington Park Recreation 1:20,000 Map & Notes*
Toilets:	Flushing toilets at The Springs picnic area and on the summit
Food:	Pub lunches and dinners, takeaway pizzas and homemade cakes are all on offer at Fern Tree Tavern
Tips:	There is no drinking water on this walk, so take enough for the whole day

Loop through fern-filled gullies and eucalypt forest and traverse exposed slopes as you summit Hobart's landmark mountain for a hard-to-beat view of southern Tasmania.

Tasmania's capital spreads over the Derwent River estuary like a colony of colourful molluscs, and from nowhere is this description more apt than the top of kunanyi/Mt Wellington, the natural sentinel that protects Hobart from the worst of westerly storms. Often covered in snow, which can fall here even in summer, the mountain is both the

Spectacular views abound on the walk to Hobart's high point

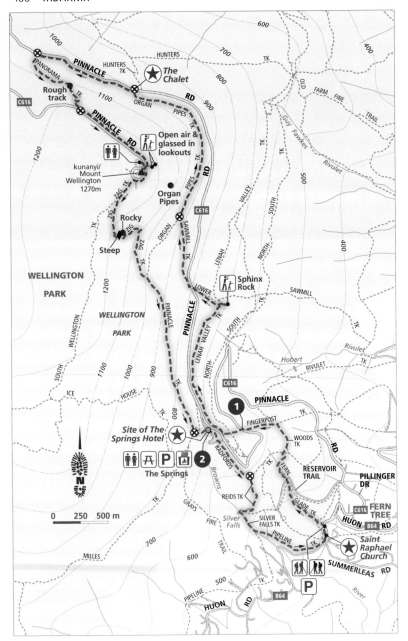

city's spectacular backdrop and the barometer by which residents check the weather.

Officially named Mt Wellington in the 1820s, in honour of the duke who beat Napoleon at Waterloo, Hobart's mountain was renamed kunanyi/Mt Wellington to acknowledge that places had Aboriginal names first. Kunanyi means 'mountain' in palawa kani, a constructed composite of original Tasmanian Aboriginal languages.

Walking tracks in Wellington Park reveal the 'noble forest', 'most extensive views', 'elegant parasols' of tree ferns, and the 'huge angular masses of naked greenstone [dolerite]' that Charles Darwin described in his book, *The Voyage of The Beagle*, after climbing kunanyi/Mt Wellington in 1836. This walk links several tracks into a grand day tour.

The walk starts in a small parking and picnic area on the mountain side of Summerleas Rd, just short of Fern Tree village, 13km from Hobart's CBD. The parking area can accommodate half a dozen sensibly parked cars. There is roadside space for a couple more, but the road is narrow and winding, so it's safer to park in Fern Tree and walk back.

The track disappears into thick forest from the picnic area, up stone steps beside a small seasonal waterfall. Follow the creek feeding the fall up a ferny gully, ignoring other tracks and footbridges left and right. Cross a restricted-use vehicular track and scale the stone steps opposite, up which you'll see a fabulous old gum tree.

Climbing from tree ferns into smooth-barked eucalypts, you'll intersect multi-use Radfords Track [mountain bikes permitted]. Here stands a memorial to George H. Radford, who died coming down Mt Wellington on 19 Sept 1903 during the first recorded footrace from Hobart to the pinnacle. The modern-day equivalent is the annual Point to Pinnacle, promoted as the world's toughest half-marathon.

Cross Radfords Track, and continue north on an easy, vehicle-wide track through tall eucalypt forest for about 300m, then turn left up Fingerpost Track, a steeper, narrower, rocky track. Cross sealed Pinnacle Rd, which snakes to the summit, and ascend the stone steps opposite [*see* point 1 on map], shortly after which you reach another track junction with the road immediately ahead. Watching for mountain bikes, cross North–South Track [there are toilets in The Springs parking area, down to your left) and turn right onto Lenah Valley Track, parallel with the road.

Lined with prickly mountain berry bushes – the females produce plump pink-to-red fruit – this flattish track ambles through eucalypts and traverses a boulder slope. Gaps between tree trunks provide a preview of the view to come.

About 1.3km from The Springs, on a sharp left bend, a side trail tunnels through tea-tree to Sphinx Rock (a childproof gate prevents overeager youngsters from rushing out onto this unfenced lookout).

While you obviously need to view this sandstone outcrop from afar to see any similarity to the famous Egyptian monolithic creature, the impressive view from Sphinx Rock takes in Hobart, the Derwent estuary and the Tasman Peninsula. Up to your left is the spectacular dolerite Organ Pipes formation.

Immediately beyond the Sphinx Rock side trail, turn left onto Lower Sawmill Track, and climb through a swathe of spiky heath plants from which soar alpine gums. The track becomes rougher here, and crosses another boulder slope, the rocks underfoot decorated with rosettes of white lichen.

Lower Sawmill Track ends at Pinnacle Rd. Continue on Sawmill Track, which starts about 20m north up the road and climbs through sedgy grass, tea-tree, elegantly striped eucalypts and alpine mintbush to the Organ Pipes.

A mountain-side wall of dolerite columns visible from afar, the Organ Pipes is one of Tasmania's most popular rock-climbing venues. As you walk north, with stone columns reaching skyward above and Hobart and surrounds spread below, you may hear voices and the tinkle of rock-climbing gear.

After descending to The Chalet, a stone shelter beside Pinnacle Rd, walk about a kilometre up the road to Panorama Track (on the left). A bit of a stretch up stone steps puts you on a rocky track that scrambles up through alpine gums and scratchy alpine heath, and rounds boulders.

Steep steps put you on Pinnacle Rd, with kunanyi/Mt Wellington's signal tower ahead. Follow the road to the top, where you'll find toilets, boardwalk-linked viewing platforms and a stone-and-glass lookout that shelters you from the bitter winds that often blow here.

When you're done ooh-ing and aah-ing at Hobart and southern Tasmania spread at your feet, and have ticked off the summit proper (a trig point on a rock pile), keep on along the road (a one-way loop) to the television and radio signal broadcasting tower.

Clockwise from top: *Hobart colonises the flats below kunanyi/Mt Wellington; it's a rocky climb to the Organ Pipes; an alpine gum sports colourful stripes*

Turn left immediately beyond the tower onto ZigZag Track, and traverse kunanyi/Mt Wellington's wind-scoured rocky plateau, treading a slightly uneven but beautifully stone-paved pathway through metre-high heath towards another fabulous dolerite wall.

South Hobart and Bruny Island [*see* p. 412] come into view beyond this tubular wall, and the view reaches east to take in Hobart as you descend further.

Now it's down the ZigZag Track, steep and rocky, with chains run between posts in places where nothing would prevent a rapid descent

More spectacular views from the mountain

if you went over the edge. Go steadily and enjoy the 180° panorama of estuary and islands bookended by fabulous vertical geology.

The view vanishes as you drop into trees, there coming to another junction, with Organ Pipes Track running uphill. Turn right down Pinnacle Track and cross the path of a landslide, looking up at the swathe of damage and down at the boulder that caused it, resting just off the trail.

Wider and less rocky now, so you can step out at last, the track crosses a grassy fire trail running along power lines and proceeds down into tea-tree forest, towards The Springs. Stone track and stone steps descend through leafy forest to a one-way bitumen road. Turn right towards the 'No Entry' sign and pick up the walking track again opposite the grassy site of The Springs Hotel (1907), following this downhill. Cross the one-way loop road again (The Springs picnic area is to the left), then step down onto an unmarked walking track (see point 2).

Signs a short way along announce this is a multi-use track, so watch for mountain bikes as you navigate chicanes fashioned from fallen trees and rocks, designed to slow cyclists.

Turn right down Reids Track (no bikes permitted), a steep track lined with mossy rocks and tall gum trees. Turn right again at the bottom, towards the swish of running water, and amble to Silver Falls, where Brown's River cascades prettily from a low ledge into a walled pool that empties into a stone-lined creek. (The stonework is part of the Waterworks scheme (1861), which took water from Mt Wellington to South Hobart.)

Cross the footbridge and follow the wide, formed Pipeline Track down the burbling river beneath a canopy of fern fronds. The track then recrosses the creek and diverges from the water. Benches along here might tempt you to stop and listen to the forest, but soon the loudest sound will be cars.

You come out on Pinnacle Rd opposite Fern Tree Tavern. Stay on this side of the road and walk left to the carpark, passing the pretty, Swiss-style Anglican Church of St Raphael, one of the few Fern Tree buildings to survive the devastating 1967 bushfires.

10 OVERLAND TRACK

Walk:	65km one-way
Time required:	6 days (more with side trips)
Best time:	October to May (the track is snowbound in winter)
Grade:	Moderate (hard side trip)
Environment:	Alpine moors, temperate rainforest, Tasmania's highest mountain
Best map:	*TASMAP's Cradle Mountain-Lake St Clair National Park 1:100,000 Map & Notes*
Toilets:	Composting toilets at Kitchen Hut and all overnight stops
Food:	Snacks are available from the cafe in the Cradle Mountain visitor centre, and more substantial breakfasts and dinners at Cradle Mountain Lodge. All manner of refreshments, including celebratory alcoholic beverages, can be purchased at the walk's end in the Lake St Clair visitor centre restaurant.
Tips:	Bookings are required, and the Overland Track Fee paid, for the official walking season (1 Oct–31 May) at bookings. overlandtrack.com.au. A National Park Pass is also required. Children aged 17 and under must be accompanied by an adult. Personal Locator Beacons (PLBs) for emergency assistance in life-threatening situations can be hired from Parks and Wildlife Service Tasmania and at the Cradle Mountain and Lake St Clair visitor centres; there is a helicopter pad at each hut. Unless you plan to walk the final 17km down Lake St Clair

Tarns reflect blue sky above the Overland Track

(not described here), you'll need to book passage on the Ida Clair ferry to finish the walk (phone 0362 891 137 or email sceniccruises@lakestclairlodge.com.au). You must check in at the Overland Track counter in the Cradle Mountain visitor centre to collect your Overland Track Pass; remember to also log out at Lake St Clair on completion.

With jaw-dropping ice-carved mountains, windswept moors, pristine alpine lakes and ancient forests, it's no wonder this Tasmanian classic is Australia's most popular long-distance walk.

When Austrian-born amateur botanist Gustav Weindorfer scaled Cradle Mountain with his Tasmanian wife Kate in 1910, he declared, 'This must be a national park for the people for all time.' The awesome glaciated landscape that won his heart, and which he championed until his death in 1932, was declared a scenic reserve in the 1920s and the much-expanded Cradle Mountain–Lake St Clair National Park was included in the Tasmanian Wilderness World Heritage Area in 1982.

Many of the national park's wonders can be experienced on day walks and overnight hikes, but those hiking the Overland Track get the full impact. Thousands walk this much-loved – some say overloved – track annually, and from 1 October to 31 May numbers are restricted, and you must walk north–south.

There are seven public huts (and two emergency-only refuges), each with bunk beds or bed shelves, a communal eating area, rainwater tank and heater, but no cooking equipment, lighting or toilet paper; pods of toilet waste are helicoptered out.

But extreme weather helped fashion this spectacular landscape and rain, ice and even snow can occur even at the height of summer, so you must carry a tent for emergency shelter. In any case, you might prefer camping on the timber tent decks at each hut to 'sleeping' indoors with snorers.

Guided Overland Track hikes with Wilderness Expeditions Tasmania (wildernessexpeditions.net.au) and Tasmanian Wilderness Experiences

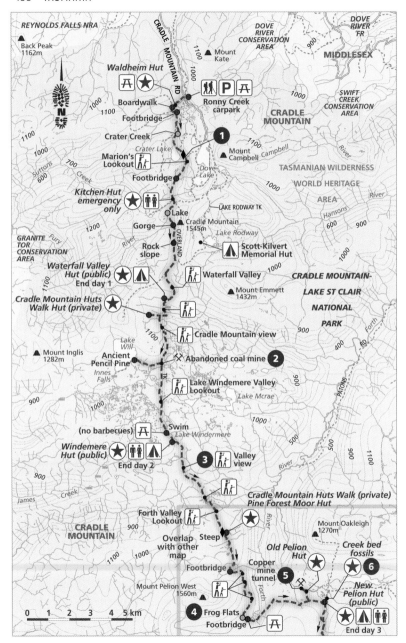

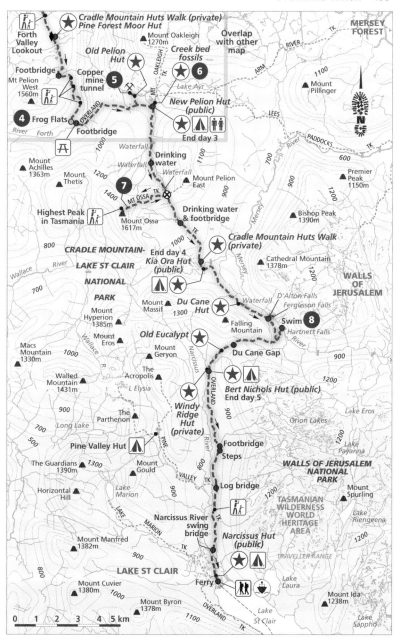

(twe.travel) are a safer option than walking alone. And if a 10kg pack, private huts with drying rooms and hot showers, and nightly three-course dinners with Tasmanian wine sound more like you, then there's the Cradle Mountain Huts Walk (cradlehuts.com.au).

However you go, you'll soon understand why this walk is so popular. You'll soon have wet and muddy feet, too. Accept this – embrace it even – and the journey will be even more enjoyable. Many kilometres of the Overland Track are boarded, but boggy areas remain. Cutting new tracks to keep boots dry only widens the damage, so unless your depth-finder walking pole disappears into the mire, walk through it. Muddying your feet helps protect this fragile country – and it's fun!

Several side trails branch off the Overland Track. This walk takes several short detours and climbs Mt Ossa, Tasmania's tallest peak. It finishes with a ferry ride down Lake St Clair.

DAY 1: 12.7KM – Ronny Creek to Waterfall Valley Hut
The Overland Track begins at Ronny Creek carpark in Cradle Mountain–Lake St Clair National Park's north. A good alternative to car shuffling, which involves a 200km drive back to Cradle Mountain after the hike, is bussing into Cradle Mountain visitor centre and out of Lake St Clair (tassielink.com.au) and riding the shuttle bus to Ronny Creek to start.

Rain highlights the glorious colours of snow gums

After signing the walkers' registry at Ronny Creek, follow the boardwalk south through buttongrass moorland, where wombats trundle at dusk. Carpeted with tight-knit coralfern and central lemon boronia, this moorland bristles with spiky palm-like plants whose serrated leaves dry to papery ringlets. Found only in Tasmania, these are pandani, the world's tallest heath plant, which grow to 10m.

Cross Ronny Creek by footbridge and climb through tea-tree and elegant eucalypts into gorgeous green rainforest, where Crater Creek foams around boulders and beneath moss-wrapped fallen trees. Crater Falls, upstream, is a good spot to fill your water bottle.

King Billy pine, an endemic Tasmanian conifer, grows only millimetres a year, so the three broad-girthed trees guarding this watering spot could be more than a thousand years old. Exit the creek gully but continue upstream, looking for red and yellow Christmas bells on the creek's steep bank.

The track lands you beside a weathered boat shed on the rocky shore of Crater Lake, which isn't actually a crater but rather a deep, bowl-shaped depression carved by a glacier. The ancient wall of rock wrapped around it, which runs with ribbon waterfalls after rain, dates from the breakup of the Gondwana supercontinent.

Now for the steepest leg of the Overland Track, up to Marion's Lookout. Crater Lake drops behind and Dove Lake spreads out below as you haul yourself up bolted chains to an exposed ridge (*see* point 1 on map) leading to the lookout. Even in rain, the view from Marion's will leave you slack-jawed. An almost palpable presence to your right, Cradle Mountain rears above Dove Lake like a giant chipped axe head (its name apparently comes from a perceived likeness to a miner's cradle). Opposite sits Lake Hanson, on a loop walk, and below, the easier and shorter but no less spectacular Dove Lake circuit track.

Beyond Marion's Lookout, rocky track, stone-paving and boardwalk traverse Cradle Plateau, cutting through small-leafed alpine plants hunkered down against the often fierce winds en route to Kitchen Hut, an emergency refuge whose timber shingles are greyed with age. This is the perfect spot to take a break, and for meeting other dripping hikers in wet weather.

Clockwise from top: *Boardwalk emerges from forest onto Pine Forest Moor; descending from Mt Ossa, Tasmania's tallest peak; the river bed below Hartnett Falls is the perfect spot to cool off in warm weather*

Just past Kitchen Hut, the Cradle Mountain summit track (3 hrs return, clear weather only) breaks left. The Overland Track climbs through pandani and deciduous beech, Australia's only native winter-deciduous tree, whose tiny crinkle-cut leaves turn yellow in autumn and then festoon the ground. Here too are massed mountain rocket shrubs that produce long-stemmed white and pink flowers in summer and high-vis orange-red fruits in autumn. The now rocky and often muddy track skirts Cradle Mountain, its dolerite fingers thrusting skyward to your left, and rough-hewn Barn Bluff soon comes into view.

Wooden steps climb to a panorama of Waterfall Valley, prettiest when water streams down its cliffs. The track emerges from pandani and oh-so-fashionable black, white and grey beech trunks into a sea of prickly scoparia. When covered in white, yellow, orange, red and pink summer flower spikes, this spread looks like a feature garden in a flower show.

The Waterfall Valley public huts (1950s and 1994), your home for the night, are 150m off the track, on flats below Barn Bluff. A family of spotted-tailed quolls lives under the old hut.

DAY 2: 9.2KM – Waterfall Valley to Windermere Hut via Lake Will
Back on track, head briefly downhill to the Waterfall Valley cliff-line and tread its edge, past pink and grey snow peppermints, twisted and gnarled like wizards frozen mid-spell.

In all but the bleakest weather, when you can't see anything except your feet on the boardwalk, Barn Bluff (1559m) dominates this section of track, its lower slopes culminating in a wall of dolerite columns. On reaching the next rise, however, the track, snaking towards the horizon across water-pooled buttongrass, might lower your gaze, albeit briefly.

Just before Lake Holmes on your left, a side trail heads right (see point 2). Leave your pack here and stroll 1.5km to Lake Will, crossing a seam of coal unprofitably prospected in the 19th century by Joseph Will, after whom the lake is named. If the weather gods are kind, you can see the remote Eldon Range, to the south, from this detour.

Lake Will's quartzite beach is a lovely spot for morning tea. The pencil pine leaning out over the tannin-stained water is estimated to be about 1500 years old.

From the lake junction, the Overland Track climbs through heathland striped hot pink in summer with grass trigger plants. Look closely: each flower is armed with a trigger that daubs pollen on unsuspecting insects.

A rocky pile topping the next hill offers a feet-stilling, breathtaking view over Lake Windermere and smaller tarns, with Mt Pelion West straight ahead and Mount Oakleigh's signature dolerite crown to the south-west. And there's no drop-off in wow factor as you descend to Windermere.

Rounding boulders and passing old pencil pines, the track follows the shoreline to picnic-perfect fallen trees and a paved path into the lake. Drop your pack here and take a refreshing dip or push on to the Windermere Hut (500m) to stash your things, then come back for a couple of lazy lakeside hours.

DAY 3: 16KM – Windermere Hut to New Pelion Hut

The longest hut-to-hut section on the Overland Track begins by venturing from snow peppermint woodland to myrtle beech forest. A rocky trail then crosses moorland bristling with antennae-like buttongrass; this is the beginning of Pine Forest Moor.

An unmarked but obvious side trail on the left (*see* point 3) about 1.5km along leads to a lookout that hands you Pelion West, Mt Ossa's torn-paper profile, and Mt Oakleigh on a plate. Clearly visible from here too are the flat paths of two glaciers and the moraine deposited between them, which, once back on the main trail, you cross on boardwalk and rocky track. Carved words on the boardwalk coming out of a patch of forest confirm this is Pine Forest Moor. The only things brave enough to stand tall here are lichen-bearded track marker posts.

Shortly after skirting a mossy tarn reflecting Mt Pelion West, there's another track junction. Turn left to the River Forth Gorge lookout and take a breather, watching the colour play as shadows drift across the treed mountain slopes reaching up from the river.

An ankle-threatening crazy paving of rocks, tangled roots and mud plunges you into wet eucalypt forest, fording several creeks before climbing through woolly tea-tree, myrtle beech and pandani. An equally rough track heads down the other side.

You are now on part of the 120km long Innes Track (officially the Mole Creek Track), surveyed in 1896 by Edward George Innes's party and cut by Public Works Department gangs for a rail line to Tasmania's west coast mining areas. The rail line was never built, but the track found favour with miners, drovers and hikers.

The prospective supply line lands you on Frog Flats (*see* point 4), a grassy spread ringed by mountains and inhabited by leeches. Rest here, because after crossing the River Forth by footbridge you climb again: through damp forest and tree ferns. Fallen trees reveal how shallow roots are in this forest. Beech orange fungi grow like grape bunches on the myrtle trees.

The track tops out in open forest. Then it's down onto Pelion Plains, an Impressionist working of yellow, red, brown and green shrubs and grasses and elegant yellow gums below Mt Oakleigh. Leave your pack at the junction for Old Pelion Hut (you can see New Pelion Hut ahead) and walk unencumbered to the oldest building in the national park.

Old Pelion is the sole survivor of several huts that were built by the Mt Pelion Prospecting Company in the 1890s but soon abandoned because the copper content of the plains was too low. The log-and-plank bunk beds date from the 1930s, but some of the King Billy pine roof and wall timbers are thought to be original. An unsigned track behind the hut leads 300m north-west along Douglas Creek to a mullock heap and copper mining tunnel (*see* point 5) that burrows about 20m – take a head torch – into the hill.

With your pack back on, you've got another 800m to New Pelion Hut for the night.

Antennae-like button grass heads bristle on the moors

The 8km return walk to Mt Oakleigh's summit ridge via some of the park's worst bogs (or best, if waist-deep mud rocks your boat) begins behind New Pelion Hut. It branches off Arm River Track, a popular shorter route from the east into New Pelion Hut to climb Mt Ossa (a three-day option) or Ossa and Oakleigh (four days). Much less taxing is an afternoon stroll about 200m along Arm River Track, to a footpad branching right (*see* point 6) to a river beach awash with fossils.

DAY 4: 13.5KM – New Pelion Hut to Kia Ora Hut via Mt Ossa

Day four begins with an easy walk through moors and forest and a short detour down an unsigned boarded track, about 1.5km in, to a pretty cascade at the confluence of two creeks. A smaller tiered waterfall about a kilometre further on is the last place to get drinking water for the climb to Pelion Gap (and Mt Ossa).

An unremitting 1.7km ascent through beech trees draped with lichens, liverworts and mosses ends beneath a spread of sky resting on the encircling mountains. If you can tear your gaze from Mt Ossa, turn around for a view north to Cradle Mountain.

At 1617m, Mt Ossa is Tasmania's tallest peak. Summiting it is a climb, not a walk, with exposed slopes, rock hopping, steep drops and places where you'll wish your legs were longer. The view from the top on a clear day takes in much of Tasmania, but life-threatening weather can come in fast; don't climb in foul conditions or if cloud hides the summit.

Leave your pack with the others on the roomy boarded area at the Mt Ossa junction (you need to take water, a snack and a wind- and water-proof jacket), but remember to remove foodstuffs from zipped pockets. Overland Track currawongs, one of more than 80 bird species recorded in Cradle Mountain–Lake St Clair National Park, have learned to unzip packs in search of goodies.

The 6km return Ossa climb snakes through living and skeletal dead pencil pines as it works up and around Mt Doris, another impressive dolerite mountain construction. Doris's flanks are carpeted with bright green cushion plants, colonies of plants that grow low and tight to protect their stems from the harsh conditions and produce tiny white flowers.

Coming around Doris, the view back across the gap disappears and another valley spectacle opens up to the north. And rearing up to your left are the Gates of Mordor, twin towers of fluted dolerite between which the Ossa trail is clearly visible, scaling a steep, rocky slope. About 1.5 hrs of climbing puts you through the 'gates' on a false summit [*see* point 7], with a final push to the plateau and its crowning red boulders.

When George Frankland in 1835 gave several Lake St Clair landmarks names from Greek mythology he started a trend continued by other cartographers and the hikers who followed. The Titans stacked Mt Pelion atop Mt Ossa to ease ascent to heaven during their war against the gods, and there are certainly places on Ossa where you might pray for divine intervention.

The plateau is carpeted with cushion plants, snow gentians and tarns that pool blue sky on sunny days. And from the edge, the country plunges into valleys and rears again as columnar massifs. Distinctive Frenchman's Cap, another famous Tasmanian walking destination, is visible on clear days.

Back down the mountain you've got roughly 4km, mostly downhill. Heathland makes way for grassland and red-striped gums that frame Ossa on the right and august Cathedral Mountain ahead. The descent and today's walk ends at Kia Ora Hut, among tea-tree.

DAY 5: 14KM – Kia Ora Hut to Bert Nicholls Hut (Windy Ridge)

Today is a celebration of waterfalls, beginning with an easy walk through eucalypts and button grass and lichen-covered beech to historic Du Cane Hut. Pioneer bushwalker, trapper, prospector and bowler hat-wearer Patrick (Paddy) Hartnett built this hut, from King Billy pine, in 1910 as a base for winter snaring of quolls, brushtail possums and wallabies for their pelts. Lucy Hartnett spent three winters here with her husband, cooking, caring for their son Billy, and treating the plush skins for sale in Europe.

The hut was extended in the 1930s to accommodate the increasing number of hikers (it is now an emergency-only refuge) and changed several more times, but it retains the huge, timber chimney in which the skins were dried. A Hartnett grandson helped repair the hut in 1992.

Beyond Du Cane is some of the oldest rainforest in the national park. The track is very rough and interlaced with roots, and slows your pace through shadow-filled forest of myrtle beech and ancient, fissured King Billy pines. Deep in the forest is a track junction with lichen-patched wooden signs directing you deeper into the rainforest to D'Alton Falls, which pours down a rocky slope in a great curtain of white foam after good rains, and Fergusson Falls. A plaque on one of the trees at the junction remembers Albert 'Fergy' Fergusson, a long-time Lake St Clair ranger and 'bushwalker's friend'.

Another side trail, a kilometre on, visits Hartnett Falls (named after Paddy Hartnett). This detour breaks out of the shadows into eucalypt forest, flattening out among button grass and pandani, and brings you to a footworn area where the Mersey River falls to a rocky river bed. There is a spider's web of foot pads here; one follows the cliff-line downstream before descending steeply to a side stream (*see* point 8); note where this lands you, because it is easy to overshoot when heading back. Across the stream and upriver is a pebbly river beach facing up the gorge to the falls.

This is a popular spot for an invigorating – that's Tasmanian for 'cold' – swim, but the rocks underfoot are slippery, so take water sandals. With care you can walk up the flow towards the cascade.

From the Hartnett Falls junction the Overland Track climbs to Du Cane Gap, sometimes steeply, sometimes on boardwalk, through rainforest, woodland, pine pockets and snow gums, with mountain ridges showing themselves above the treetops. At the gap (1070m) – small and treed, not open like Pelion Gap – look up to your right. The fantastic rise of dolerite columns is appropriately called Falling Mountain; this is the end of the rugged Du Cane Range. To your right stands the Traveller Range.

From Du Cane Gap you descend through arguably the most beautiful forest on the Overland Track, with magnificent, multi-coloured alpine yellow gums merging into almost luxuriantly mossy myrtle rainforest. Tree stumps with indentations from timber cutters' standing boards tell of a time when this forest was viewed very differently.

Clockwise from top left: *Old man's beard (also called Spanish moss) grows shaggy on a track marker; paper daisies bloom on the moor; a button grass seed head stands proud; a wooden sign marks the top of Du Cane Gap; rain beads pretty wildflowers*

The track leads to the newest public hut on the Overland Track, a large, hard-to-heat structure built to replace one destroyed by fire and named in honour of trapper, ranger and pioneer guide Bert Nicholls, who blazed the track in 1930.

DAY 6: 10.5KM – Bert Nicholls Hut to Lake St Clair Jetty

While your last day is not all descent, it would be petty to call the few short, slight ascents 'hills'. Following a moraine left by a retreating glacier, and heading down the Narcissus Valley, it's the easiest section too, albeit with an occasional mud hole for old time's sake.

The track meanders through silver banksias and woolly tea-tree beneath towering stringybarks and cabbage gums and passes a flat, grassy frost hollow on the right. Ridgelines peek through the trees, but after the attention-grabbing geology of previous days it is restful to focus on the forest, particularly when summer wildflowers are on show. Purple fairies' aprons, silver banksia and slender riceflowers are some you might see. And you could well hear more birds today than on the past five days combined; look out for yellow-tailed black cockatoos.

Boardwalks skirt rainforest and snake through heathland planted with gums towards the might of Mt Olympus and tiny Narcissus Hut, and a one-person-at-a-time swing suspension bridge takes you over Narcissus River.

The mosquitoes at the recently renovated 1963 Narcissus Hut are voracious, but the composting loo behind has the best view of any on the track.

You're all but done now, with just 350 flat metres to the jetty near the mouth of the Narcissus River. Confirm your arrival for the ferry pickup on the hut radio and then head down to the jetty. If game, take a ceremonial plunge in the cold river before the 20-minute ride down Lake St Clair, Australia's deepest natural lake, to your journey's end.

11 WINEGLASS BAY & HAZARDS BEACH LOOP

Walk:	12km loop
Time required:	4 hours
Best time:	Sunny day for the bay at its beautiful best
Grade:	Moderate
Environment:	Granite peaks, beach, forested isthmus, rocky shore
Best map:	*TASMAP's Freycinet National Park 1:50,000 Map & Notes*
Toilets:	Flushing toilets in Wineglass Bay carpark
Food:	Two options at Freycinet Lodge, within the national park: snacks and tasty, casual lunches in Richardson's Bistro; and dinners of scrumptious, seasonal Tasmanian produce in The Bay Restaurant (bookings essential). Pub, takeaway and other food is available in Coles Bay, outside the park; fresh local seafood at Freycinet Marine Farm, on Coles Bay Rd.
Tips:	Don't be put off by a crowd on the track; on a sunny day the elevated view of Wineglass Bay makes it worth joining the throng. Entry fees apply for all Tasmanian National Parks and a range of passes are available; details at parks.tas.gov.au

The Hazards in all their majesty

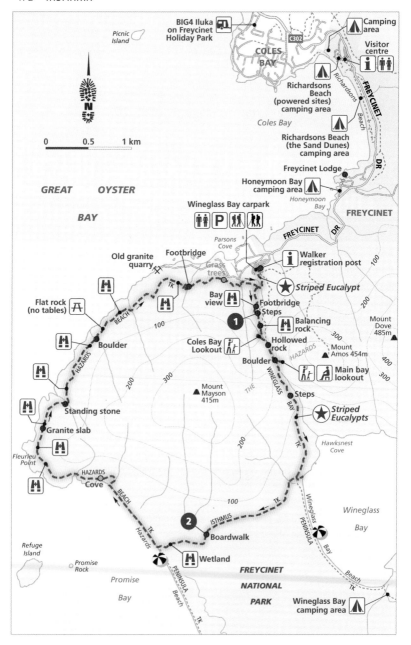

One of the most beautiful beaches in Australia? Undoubtedly. THE most beautiful? You decide on this loop walk up to Wineglass Bay and back via beach and rugged shore.

Most visitors to Freycinet National Park, halfway up Tasmania's east coast, come for one thing: to walk to Wineglass Bay lookout and add to the already countless pixels that have captured this picture-postcard view. Fewer continue down to the beach itself; fewer still walk on from there across the isthmus to Hazards Beach to complete a scenic loop. But that doesn't mean you'll have this walk to yourself: it is very much about sharing!

Starting in Wineglass Bay carpark, about 4km from Coles Bay and the national park boundary, just go with the flow, treading a fairly easy gravel track up through white-flowering tea-tree, grey-and-yellow striped peppermint eucalypts, and the pretty pink granite featured in all Freycinet promotions, usually blushing at dawn or sunset. (A combination of pink feldspar and orange lichen produces this distinctive hue.) Look for a particularly beautiful twisted and striped eucalypt soon after the track ducks under a balancing rock and squeezes between lumps of rock.

Wineglass Bay lookout sits in the saddle between mounts Mayson and Amos, two of the landmark five-in-a-row granite knuckles collectively called The Hazards. These rocky rises, as well as Coles Bay, come into view as you climb.

Part way up there's a junction, where a one-way descent track disappears downhill on the left – yes, it gets that busy! The climb continues up stone steps (*see* point 1 on map).

A voluminous bowl of water contained by a crescent of sand and forested mountains, Wineglass Bay is impressive even on a cloudy day. But when sunshine blues the sea and greens the hills, and the white sand gleams, you'd be hard pressed to argue that this isn't Australia's prettiest beach.

When you tire of the view or the crowd (whichever comes first) keep on the south-east heading, down Wineglass Bay Track. A sign warns that this is steep and can be slippery, and it is certainly very different from the formed track you came up. With stone steps, exposed roots and granite underfoot, descend through tea-tree, smooth and rough eucalypts, drooping she-oaks and banksias to Wineglass Bay beach.

This is a beautiful spot to picnic on a granite boulder, have a cooling swim or leave footprints in the sand; it's 1.7km to the end of the beach, where you'll find a camping area used mostly by hikers treading the multi-day Freycinet loop down the main peninsula. But remember that it's another 8km and about 3 hours to the carpark.

When you're ready to push on, leave the beach where you stepped onto it and head south-west on a flat track that crosses the isthmus tethering The Hazards to the main peninsula. Visible through the trunks of eucalypt woodland trees is broad Hazards Lagoon, often noisy with frogs.

Six frog species have been recorded in the park, including the nationally threatened green and gold frog, which lives in Hazards Lagoon. Some two-thirds of Tasmania's endemic bird species frequent the Freycinet Peninsula region too, and you'll probably hear many different calls on this leg of the walk.

Having forded an area of sedgy grass and coral fern on boardwalk (*see* point 2), climb up and over white dunes and down onto yellow Hazards Beach, then walk right (north-west) along sand littered with oyster shells.

For millennia before European settlement, Oyster Bay Aboriginals harvested oysters and marine vegetables in these waters during autumn and winter. Native oysters still grow here, but Pacific oysters, mussels, scallops, abalone and sea urchins are farmed in Great Oyster Bay and Mercury Passage. You can savour the harvest at Freycinet Marine Farm, on the Coles Bay road.

At the end of Hazards Beach, the track heads inland and works its way around Mt Mayson's rocky base, snaking in and out of forest. Bennett's (red-necked) wallabies are often seen among the tea-tree and she-oaks. Rock slabs, slippery in places, present fantastic views into pretty rocky coves whose lapping green water contrasts the pink-orange granite. As you dip down steps and emerge from gullies, look up at the fantastic boulders decorating the Hazards' jagged ridgeline. Slow down when the track emerges from trees and enjoy the extended views across Coles Bay and up the bald granite mountain slopes.

With only a kilometre to go you'll start to see grass trees. The track then doubles back on itself and heads down a leafier, greener creek gully, flattening and widening as it continues through an area of young and mature tea-trees sandwiched between bay water and sky-reaching rock.

At the junction with the Wineglass Bay Lookout track, turn left and wind your way back to the carpark.

Clockwise from top left: *Pretty common heath decorates the walk; lichen burnishes the rocks; Oyster Bay waters lap Hazards Beach under a stormy sky*

INDEX

ABC Range SA 167, 168, 180, 182
Aboriginal carvings/engravings/
rock art
NSW 17, 18, 72
NT 288–9, 290, 296, 298–9,
327, 335
Qld 338, 339, 340, 342
Aboriginal Dreaming stories
NT 309, 311–12, 320, 322,
330, 332
SA 178
WA 213
Aboriginal middens/sites
NSW 14, 71
NT 299, 305, 309, 310–11,
331, 332, 333, 335
Qld 342
Tas. 404
Adelaide Summit to Sea SA
148–59
Admiral's Arch SA 184
Adventure Bay Tas. 412, 413, 416
Aire River to Johanna Beach Vic.
78–83
Albany WA 199, 220, 240, 243
Alice Springs NT 278, 280, 282,
305, 317, 322
Alice Springs Telegraph Station NT
278–83, 312
Alligator Creek SA 163, 165
Alligator Gorge SA 160–5
Alpine NP Vic. 108–15, 116–21
Amphitheatre (Carnarvon Gorge)
Qld 340, 343
Amphitheatre (Jatbula Trail)
NT 298
Ansons Bay Tas. 406
Anzac Hill NT 281, 282
Arabanoo Lookout NSW 72
Arankaia Walk NT 319, 320
Arm River Track Tas. 466
Army Jetty WA 247
Art Gallery (Carnarvon Gorge) Qld
340, 342
Atherton Tablelands Qld 349–52
Australian Alps Walking Track
(AAWT) 109, 112, 113, 114,
127, 128
Australian Convict Sites World
Heritage property 420
Ayers Rock Resort NT 327

Bald Pyramid Qld 370
Bald Rock Creek Qld 366,
368, 371
Bald Rock Creek camping area Qld
366, 369
Bald Rock Creek Circuit Qld
368, 369
Bald Rock Creek day use area Qld
366, 368, 371
Bald Rock NP NSW 366
Baloon Cave Qld 342
Balor Hut NSW 26, 29, 30
Banksia Bay Qld 386

Banksia Creek Qld 386
Bare Rock Qld 364
Barn Bluff Tas. 463
Basin Lake Qld 356
Bathurst Lighthouse WA 250
Battleship Spur Qld 338, 342
Bay of Fires Tas. 402–6
Belair NP SA 153
Bellbird Picnic Area Vic. 139, 144
Belougery Spire NSW 29
Berlang camping area NSW 3
Bert Nicholls Hut to Lake St Clair
jetty Tas. 470
Bibbulmun Track WA 217–25,
240–5, 274
Bickley Battery WA 247, 250
Bickley Bay WA 247
Biddlecombe Cascades camping
area NT 295
Big Bend Qld 338, 342
Big Cathedral Vic. 89
Big Hole NSW 2–7
Big Lagoon Tas. 415
Binalong Bay Tas. 402, 404,
405, 406
Binna Burra section, Lamington NP
Qld 397, 399
birdwatching
ACT 46
NSW 4, 23, 52, 64, 75
NT 281, 282, 286, 294, 298,
309, 310, 325
Qld 340, 343, 351, 356, 362–3,
376, 385, 387, 390, 399
SA 175, 178, 180, 185,
188, 194
Tas. 405, 415, 421, 445, 447,
466, 470, 474
Vic. 88, 90, 97–101, 106,
119–20, 133, 143–4
WA 207, 214, 216, 231,
237–8, 243, 247, 255, 260–1,
266, 272
Bishop and Clerk Tas. 445, 446
Black Spur Vic. 87
Black Swamp SA 185
Blackboy Hollow WA 211
Blacksand Beach Qld 385
Blue Gum Flat SA 160, 162, 164
Blue Lake NSW 37
Blue Mountains NP NSW 47–54
Bluff Knoll WA 198–203
Bluff Mountain NSW 30, 32
Boodjidup Bridge WA 211
Boolimba Bluff Qld 339
Boowinda Creek Qld 341, 342
Booyong Boardwalk Qld 399
Border Track Qld 397, 399
Boulder Bay Qld 385
Brachina Gorge SA 168
Brainy Cut Off WA 224
Breadknife, The NSW 29, 30
Brown's River Tas. 455
Bruny Island Tas. 412–17, 454
Budawang Wilderness NSW 62,
65, 66
Bullen Range Nature Reserve
ACT 45

Bundeena NSW 8, 18
Bungle Bungle Range WA 212,
213, 286
Bunyeroo Creek NSW 166, 168, 170
Bunyeroo Gorge SA 166–70
Burning Palms NSW 14
Buxton Roadhouse Vic. 84
Byangee Mountain NSW 66

Cairns Qld 350
Canal Rim Walk Vic. 104, 107
Canberra ACT 41
Canyon Track Vic. 89
canyoning, NSW 7
Cape Arid NP WA 227
Cape Boullanger Tas. 445
Cape Freycinet WA 207, 211
Cape Hauy Tas. 407–11
Cape Jervis WA 149, 174, 183
Cape Le Grand Coastal Trail
WA 227
Cape Le Grand NP WA 226–33
Cape Leeuwin WA 206
Cape Naturaliste WA 206
Cape Pillar Tas. 408, 409,
410, 411
Cape Queen Elizabeth Tas.
412–17
Cape Raoul Tas. 408
Cape to Cape Track WA 204–11
Cardwell Qld 379, 384
Carnarvon Creek Qld 339, 342
Carnarvon Gorge Qld 338–43
Carnarvon Great Walk Qld 338,
342
Carnarvon NP Qld 338–43
Carro Track SA 152
Carruther's Peak NSW 37, 38
Castle, The NSW 66
Castle Cove Beach Vic. 81
Castle Rock Qld 370
Cathedral Cave Qld 342
Cathedral Gorge WA 212–16
Cathedral Gorge Trail WA 214–16
Cathedral Mountain Tas. 467
Cathedral Range South Loop
Vic. 84–90
Cathedral Range State Park Vic. 87
Cemetery Walk NT 282
Central Station Qld 353, 356
Chalet, The Tas. 452
Chalka Creek Vic. 97
Channels Waterhole NT 301
Charles Darwin Walk NSW 47
Charlotte Pass NSW 33, 36, 39, 40
Charters Towers Qld 374
Cleland Conservation Park SA 149,
152, 153
Clontarf Reserve NSW 71
Club Lake Creek NSW 36
Coal Mines Historic Site Tas.
418–23
Coal River Tas. 430, 432
Coalmine Beach to Treetops WA
217–25
Coast Track, The NSW 8–19
Coastal Cliffs Walking Trail SA 193
Cobungra Gap Vic. 109, 113
Coles Bay Tas. 471, 473, 475

Collier Creek Wetlands WA 217
Conservation Hut NSW 47, 50, 52
Conto Campground WA 204, 207
convict sites
NSW 20, 25
Tas. 418–23, 430, 432–5,
444, 445
Convict Trail Tas. 430
Cooks Mill Vic. 84, 88, 90
Coonabarabran NSW 26, 28
Coromandel Railway Station to
Kingston Park Beach SA 155–9
Cotterill's Lookout NT 308
Counsel Beach Tas. 447–8
Cradle Mountain Tas. 457, 461,
463, 466
Cradle Mountain–Lake St Clair
NP 456–70
Cradle Mountain Lodge Tas. 456
Cradle Mountain summit track
Tas. 462
Cradle Mountain visitor centre Tas.
456, 460
Cradle Plateau Tas. 461
Crater Bluff NSW 30
Crater Cove NSW 72
Crater Creek Tas. 461
Crater Falls Tas. 461
Crater Lake Tas. 461
Crater Rim Walk Vic. 105
Crest parking area, The Qld 360
Cronulla NSW 8, 9, 12, 18
Crystal Creek NT 294, 297
Crystal Falls NT 298
Cultural Centre NT 327
Cunninghams Gap Qld 360,
362, 363
Curracurrong Creek NSW 16
Curracurrong Falls NSW 15

Dagda Gap NSW 30
D'Alton Falls Tas. 468
Darling Range WA 242, 244
Darlington Tas. 441, 445, 446,
447, 448
Dave Evans Bicentennial Tree WA
259, 261
Deep Rock Picnic Area Vic. 141
Delaney Lookout WA 220
Den Fenella Lookout NSW 51
Deua NP NSW 2–7
Devil's Peak Walk SA 175
Devine's Hill NSW 20, 22, 24–5
Dharug NP NSW 22, 24
Diamantina Creek Qld 389
Dibbins Hut Vic. 109, 113
Didthul NSW 62–6
Dight's Falls Vic. 143
Dilli Village Qld 355
Dobroyd Head NSW 72
Domes Walk WA 214, 215
Douglas Creek Tas. 465
Dove Lake Tas. 461
Dow's Camp NSW 32
Drought Busters Walk SA 178,
180, 182
Du Cane Gap Tas. 468, 469
Du Cane Hut Tas. 467, 468
Du Cane Range Tas. 468

Dutchmans Stern SA 171–6
Dutchmans Stern Conservation
 Park SA 173

Eagle Rock NSW 16
Eagle Tarn Tas. 439
Eaglehawk Neck Tas. 420
East MacDonnell NP NT 322
Echo Track SA 154
Edith Falls NT 290, 291, 295,
 298, 303
Edith River NT 300, 301
8 Mile Flat Vic. 116, 117–19, 120
Eldon Range Tas. 463
Emerald Qld 339
Encounter Bay SA 182
Era NSW 14
Erquhart Track Tas. 438
Esperance WA 227
Eurong Qld 357

Fairfax Lookout NSW 75
Fairfield Park Boathouse Vic.
 139, 143
Falling Mountain Tas. 468
Falls Creek Vic. 108, 109
Fan Palm Creek Qld 387
Farmyard Vic. 87, 90
Fassifern Valley Lookout Qld 365
Fergusson Falls Tas. 468
Fern Tree Tas. 449, 451, 455
Finch's Line NSW 20–4
Finke Gorge NP NT 316–20
Finke River NT 315, 316–18
Fletchers Lookout NSW 54
Fleurieu Peninsula SA 152,
 174, 189
Flinders Chase NP SA 183–8
Flinders Ranges SA 162–4,
 167–8, 171–6, 180, 182
Flinders Ranges NP SA 166–70,
 177–82
Fluted Cape Tas. 416
Flying Fox Wetland Walk Vic. 144
Fortescue Bay Tas. 407, 408, 409,
 410, 411
Forty Baskets Beach NSW 74
Fossil Cliffs Tas. 445, 446
14 Mile Creek Vic. 119
Frankland River WA 217, 221,
 223–4
Fraser Island Qld 353–9
Fraser Island Great Walk Qld 355
Frenchman's Cap Tas. 467
Freycinet Lodge Tas. 471
Freycinet NP Tas. 471–5
Friends Nature Trail Vic. 87
Frog Flats Tas. 465

Gap Creek Falls Qld 365
Garden Lake WA 255
Garden of Eden waterhole NT 309
Gardens, The Tas. 405, 406
Garie Beach NSW 8, 15
Gates of Mordor Tas. 467
George Driscoll Sea to Summit
 Walk SA 149
George Gill Range NT 304,
 305, 310

Georges Bay Qld 389, 390
Georges Bay Tas. 405
Georges Point Qld 389, 390
Ghost Gum Walk NT 325
Giant Tingle WA 222–3
Giles Track NT 310
Girraween NP Qld 366–71
Glen Helen Gorge NT 315
Glen Helen Resort NT 311
Gold Coast Qld 393
Golden Pipeline Heritage Trail
 WA 271
Goldfields Water Supply Scheme WA
 271, 272, 273, 274
Gondwana Rainforests of Australia
 World Heritage Areas 56–7, 58,
 362, 392
Gosse Bluff NT 315
Gould's Circuit NSW 29
Grampians NP Vic. 91–5
Grand High Tops NSW 26–32
Grand Stairway NSW 53
Granite Arch Qld 369, 371
Grants Lagoon Tas. 404
Great Barrier Reef World Heritage
 Area Qld 382
Great Ocean Walk Vic. 78–83
Great Otway NP Vic. 78–83
Great Oyster Bay Tas. 464
Greater Blue Mountains World
 Heritage Area NSW 21, 48–9
Green Mountain section, Lamington
 NP Qld 393, 399
Grotto Point NSW 72
Growler Creek Vic. 133, 137
Growling Swallet Tas. 424–9

Halfway Hut Vic. 136
Halls Gap Vic. 91, 92
Hamersley Range WA 265
Hancock Gorge WA 262–3, 265,
 267–8
Hangman's Cave NSW 25
Happy Valley Resort Qld 355
Harrietville Vic. 109
Hartnett Falls Tas. 468
Hattah–Kulkyne NP Vic. 96–101
Hawkesbury River NSW 20–5
Hazards, The Tas. 473, 474–5
Hazards Beach Tas. 471,
 473, 474
Hazards Lagoon Tas. 474
Healesville Vic. 87
Heartbreak Crossing WA 259
Hedley Tarn NSW 37
Hellfire Bay to Lucky Bay Walk
 226–33
Henrietta Rocks Lookout WA
 251
Hermannsburg NT 316
Heysen Range SA 167, 168
Heysen Trail SA 149, 152, 170,
 174, 176, 189, 192–4
Hill Point Tas. 405
Hilltop Lookout WA 222
Hinchinbrook Channel Qld
 382, 384
Hinchinbrook Island Qld 379–91
Hinchinbrook Island NP Qld 382

Hobart Tas. 421, 425, 430, 437,
 449, 451, 453
Hollow Butte Tree WA 223
Hollow Mountain Vic. 91–5
horseriding, Vic. 120
Hotham Heights Vic. 108, 109
Howqua River Vic. 116–21
Howqua Track Vic. 118
Humbug Hill Tas. 404
Humbug Point State Reserve
 Tas. 404

Indian Ocean 206, 207
Innes Track Tas. 464

Jamison Creek NSW 47
Jamison Lookout NSW 50
Jarnem campground NT 284, 285
Jarnem Loop NT 284–9
Jatbula Trail NT 290–303
Jawbone Creek Vic. 90
Jawbone Peak Vic. 89
Jawbone Track Vic. 90
Jibbon Head NSW 18
Jindabyne NSW 33, 36
Joffre Gorge WA 265
Johanna Beach Vic. 78, 80, 81, 83
Johanna River crossing Vic. 78, 81
Junction Pool Lookout WA 265
Junee Cave Tas. 424, 428
Junee River Tas. 425, 429

Kalbarri WA 234, 235
Kalbarri NP WA 234 9
Kambah Pool ACT 41, 46
Kanes Bridge Vic. 141
Kangaroo Island SA 183–8
Kangaroo Island Wilderness Trail
 SA 184
Kantju Gorge NT 335
Karijini NP WA 262–8
Kata Tjuta NT 332
Katherine Gorge NT 290, 291, 294
Katherine River NT 291
Kathleen Springs NT 310
Katoomba NSW 50
Keep River NP NT 284–9
Kep Track WA 271
Kermit's Pool WA 268
Kestrel Falls NT 310
Kia Ora Hut to Bert Nicholls Hut
 (Windy Ridge) Tas. 467–70
Kimberley, The WA 212–16
King Beach SA 189, 192, 194
Kingfisher Bay Qld 358
Kingfisher Bay Resort Qld 353, 355
Kings Canyon NT 304–10
Kings Canyon Resort NT 304
Kings Canyon Rim Walk NT
 305, 309
Kings Creek Walk NT 305, 310
Kings Tableland NSW 50
Kingscote SA 183, 185
Kingston Park Beach SA 148, 159
Kingstown WA 247
Kitchen Hut Tas. 456, 461, 462
Kondalilla Falls Circuit Qld 344–8
Kondalilla NP Qld 344–8
Kosciuszko NP NSW 33–40

kunanyi/Mt Wellington Summit Loop
 Tas. 449–55
Kunija carpark NT 332
Kununurra WA 214

Lake Albina NSW 38
Lake Baghdad WA 255
Lake Barrine Qld 349–52
Lake Barrine Heritage Teahouse
 Qld 349, 350, 352
Lake Cave WA 208
Lake Dobson Tas. 436–40
Lake Eildon Vic. 117
Lake Hanson Tas. 461
Lake Herschel WA 255
Lake Holmes Tas. 463
Lake Konardin Vic. 99
Lake McKenzie Qld 353, 355, 356,
 357, 358
Lake McKenzie–Central Station
 Loop Qld 353–9
Lake Moogerah Qld 363
Lake Mournall Vic. 96–101
Lake St Clair Tas. 457, 460, 470
Lake St Clair visitor centre Tas. 456
Lake Seal Tas. 439
Lake Seal Lookout Tas. 438
Lake Surprise Vic. 104, 107
Lake Torrens SA 170, 175
Lake Vincent WA 255
Lake Wabby Qld 357
Lake Webster Tas. 439
Lake Will Tas. 463
Lake Windermere Tas. 463, 464
Lake Yerang Vic. 107
Lamington NP Qld 58, 392–9
Larapinta Trail NT 282, 311, 312,
 313–15, 322–3
Lava Canal Walk Vic. 104, 105, 107
Leeuwin–Naturaliste NP WA
 204–11
Leliyn/Edith Falls NT 290, 291,
 295, 298, 302, 303
Leliyn Loop Trail NT 303
Lenah Valley Track Tas. 452
Little Cathedral Vic. 89
Little Garie NSW 14
Little Hellfire Bay WA 227
Little Lagoon Tas. 415
Little Marley Beach NSW 17
Little Oberon Bay Vic. 137
Little Ramsay Bay to Zoe Bay Qld
 385, 386–8, 390
Little River Vic. 87, 88
London Mine Qld 375
Long Hill Camp SA 164
Long Pool NT 303
Long Tunnel Extended Gold Mine
 Vic. 126–7
Lookout Track WA 216
Loop, The WA 234–9
Lorikeet Loop Walk SA 154
Lower Sawmill Track Tas. 452
Lower Waterfall SA 153
Lucinda Qld 379, 382, 384, 390
Lucinda Jetty Qld 389, 390
Lucky Bay WA 226, 231–3
Lughs Throne NSW 30
Lyrebird Lookout NSW 52

Mabel Mill Qld 376
MacDonnell Ranges NT 281, 282, 314, 322
Machinery Spur Track Vic. 109, 112
McPherson Range Qld 393
Magnetic Island Qld 389
Magpie Creek Gully SA 156
Maiden Bush WA 258, 259
Main Range NP Qld 360–5
Main Range Track NSW 33–40
Main Yarra Trail Vic. 143
Mala carpark NT 327, 331
Mala Walk NT 331, 335
Manly NSW 67, 70, 72, 75
Manly Scenic Walkway NSW 67, 70, 75
Mansfield Vic. 116, 118
Marble Arch NSW 2, 3, 5, 7
Margaret River WA 204, 206, 207, 211
Maria Island Loop Tas. 441–8
Marion's Lookout Tas. 461
Marley Beach NSW 17
Marley Creek NSW 17
Mars Bluff Tas. 412, 415
Martins Hill Vic. 136
Marysville Vic. 84, 87, 89
Mawson Plateau Tas. 438
Maydena Tas. 425, 428
Mereenie Loop NT 305
Merri Creek Vic. 141, 143
Merritt's Creek NSW 40
Mersey River Tas. 468
Messmate Track Vic. 88
Miles Beach Tas. 416
Miles Creek Tas. 416
Milligan Creek Qld 390
Missionary Bay Qld 384, 385
Mole Creek Track Tas. 464
Monadnocks campsite WA 240, 244
Monadnocks Conservation Reserve WA 242
Montville Qld 344, 345
Moorina Bay Tas. 415, 416
Moorina Bay Beach Tas. 417
Moorina Bay Hut Tas. 416
Mormon Town Track Vic. 128
Morton NP NSW 62–6
Morwell Vic. 123
Moss Garden Qld 339, 340, 343
Mount Amos Tas. 473
Mount Beauty Vic. 109
Mount Brown Summit Walk SA 175
Mount Buller Vic. 118
Mount Cordeaux Qld 360–5
Mount Cordeaux Lookout Qld 364
Mount Cuthbert WA 243, 244
Mount Difficult Range Vic. 95
Mount Doris Tas. 466–7
Mount Eccles NP Vic. 102–7
Mount Feathertop Vic. 109
Mount Field NP Tas. 424–9, 436–40
Mount Fortescue Tas. 409
Mount Gillen NT 282
Mount Hotham to Falls Creek Vic. 108–15

Mount Howitt Vic. 117
Mount Kosciuszko via Main Ridge NSW 33–40
Mount Loch Vic. 109, 112
Mount Lofty SA 148, 149, 159
Mount Lofty to Coromandel Railway Station SA 149–55
Mount Manning NSW 24
Mount Maria Tas. 445, 448
Mount Matheson NSW 58, 59–60
Mount Mayson Tas. 473, 474
Mount Mistake Qld 365
Mount Nardi NSW 58
Mount Norman Qld 368, 369, 370
Mount Oakleigh Tas. 464, 465, 466
Mount Oberon Vic. 133, 134
Mount Oberon Saddle Vic. 130
Mount Ohlssen–Bagge SA 177–82
Mount Olympus Tas. 470
Mount Ossa Tas. 460, 464, 466, 467
Mount Pelion West Tas. 463, 464
Mount Remarkable NP SA 160–5
Mount Solitary NSW 50
Mount Sonder NT 282, 311–15, 323
Mount Sugarloaf Vic. 84, 87, 89
Mount Tennant ACT 45
Mount Toolbrunup WA 201
Mount Vincent WA 242, 243, 244, 245
Mount Warning/Wollumbin NSW 55, 59, 61
Mount Wellington Tas. 449–55
Mount William NP Tas. 403
Mount Wright gold mine Qld 374
Mount Zeil NT 312, 314
Mount Zero Vic. 94
mountain-bike riding
    NSW 39
    Tas. 451
    Vic. 143
    WA 220, 222, 223, 271, 272
Mournpall Lake Walk Vic. 98
Mournpall Track Vic. 97, 98, 99
Mpulungkinya Walk NT 316–20
Mulligan Bay Qld 390
Mulligan Falls to Georges Bay Qld 389, 390
Munda Biddi cycling trail WA 220, 222, 223, 271, 272
Mundaring WA 269
Mundaring Park WA 269
Mundaring Weir WA 220, 269–74
Murchison River gorge WA 235–9
Murrumbidgee Discovery Track ACT 43
Murrumbidgee River Corridor ACT 41–6
Mutitjulu Waterhole NT 332

Namadgi NP ACT 109
Nangare Track SA 152
Narcissus Hut Tas. 470
Narcissus River Tas. 470
Narcissus Valley Tas. 470
Narrow Neck Peninsula NSW 50

Narrows, The SA 160, 162, 163, 165
National Pass Loop NSW 47–54
Natural Bridge Vic. 106
Nature's Window WA 236, 238
Neck, The Tas. 415, 416
Neck Beach Tas. 417
New Pelion Hut to Kia Ora Hut via Mt Ossa Tas. 464–5, 466
Newland Head Conservation Park SA 193, 194
Nightcap Bluff NSW 55–61
Nightcap NP NSW 55–61, 393
Nightcap Track NSW 58–61
Nigli Gap NT 285, 286, 289
Nimbin NSW 55, 58
Nina Peak Qld 385
Nitmiluk NP NT 290–303
Norfolk Bay Tas. 421, 422
Norman Bay Vic. 137, 138
Norman Point Vic. 137
Nornalup Inlet WA 222, 225
North Bruny Island Tas. 415
North Era NSW 8, 9, 14
North Harbour Reserve NSW 74
North–South Track Tas. 451
North Zoe Creek Qld 387
Northam WA 271
Northern Rockhole NT 295
Nubeena Tas. 418

Oast House Track Tas. 447, 448
Oberon Bay Vic. 130, 133, 136, 137
O'Connor, C.Y. 269, 271, 272
Ogma Gap NSW 32
O'Halloran Hill Recreation Reserve SA 158
Old Pelion Hut Tas. 465
Oliver Hill WA 246, 252
O'Reilly's Rainforest Retreat Qld 392, 393, 399
O'Reilly's Tree Top Walk Qld 399
Organ Pipes Tas. 452, 455
Ormiston Creek NT 321, 323, 324
Ormiston Gorge NT 323–5
Ormiston Pound NT 322, 324
Ormiston Pound Loop NT 315, 321–6
Otford NSW 8, 9, 12
Otway Ranges Vic. 78, 80
Overland Track Tas. 456–70
Oxer Lookout WA 265

Painted Cliffs Tas. 444, 448
Palm Islands Qld 389
Palm Valley NT 316–20
Pandani Grove Track Tas. 439
Panorama Track Tas. 452
Parachilna SA 152, 174
Parsons Beach SA 189
Pelion Gap Tas. 466
Pelion Plains Tas. 465
Pemberton WA 258
Penneshaw SA 183
Perisher NSW 33
Perth WA 220, 240, 242, 246, 247, 269, 271
Piccaninny Creek WA 216

Piccaninny Creek carpark WA 212, 214
Piccaninny Creek Lookout WA 216
Piccaninny Gorge WA 216
Picnic Creek Qld 345
Picnic Falls Qld 345
Picnic Rock Qld 397
Pigeon House Mountain NSW 62–6
Pilbara WA 262–8
Pile Valley Qld 357
Pincham carpark NSW 26, 28
Pine Forest Moor Tas. 464
Pine Island Reserve ACT 41, 43
Pink Lake WA 255
Pinnacle Track Tas. 455
Pipe Bridge Vic. 143, 144
Pipeline Track Tas. 455
Platypus Tarn Track Tas. 439
Platypus Waterhole Walk SA 185
Plunkett Point Tas. 422
Point Hut Crossing ACT 41, 43
Policeman's Point Tas. 406
Porongorups WA 201
Porpoise Bay WA 251
Port Arthur Tas. 418, 421, 430
Port Hacking NSW 9
Port Hedland WA 265
Poverty Point Bridge Vic. 128
Premaydena Tas. 418, 420
Pretty Valley Pondage Vic. 109, 114
Prevelly WA 204, 211
Princes Rock Lookout NSW 50, 54
Purnululu NP WA 212–16, 286
Pyramid Track Qld 268
Pyramids, The Qld 366–71

Queen Victoria Lookout NSW 52
Queens Cascades NSW 53
Quorn SA 171, 173, 176

Radfords Track Tas. 451
Rainforest Circuit Qld 362, 365
Ramsay Bay to Little Ramsay Bay (via Nina Peak) Qld 384–6
Ravenswood Historic Town Loop Qld 372–8
Rawson's Pass NSW 33, 39
Razorback Vic. 87, 89, 109
Recherche Archipelago WA 227
Red Gorge WA 265
Red Range SA 182
Red Robin Gap Vic. 112
Red Robin Mine Vic. 113
Red Rocks Gorge ACT 46
Redbank Gorge NT 311, 312, 313
Redgate Beach WA 204, 208, 209–11
Reef Beach NSW 72, 73, 74
Reids Track Tas. 455
Remarkable Rocks SA 184
Richmond Tas. 430–5
Richmond Bridge Tas. 432–3
Richmond Gaol Tas. 434–5
Ridgeway Hill Walking Trail SA 193
Ritchie's Hut 116–21
River Forth Tas. 465
River Forth Gorge Lookout Tas. 464

Riverside Walk NT 22
Roaring Meg junction Vic. 130, 136
rock climbing
Tas. 411, 452
Vic. 94–5
WA 265
Rock Pool Qld 345
Rocky River Bridge SA 187
Rocky River to Sea SA 183–8
Roma Qld 339
Ronny Creek to Waterfall Valley Hut Tas. 460–3
Rosetta Head SA 189, 195
Rottnest Island WA 246–56
Royal NP NSW 8–19
Russel Falls Tas. 436

Saint Bernard's Walking Track Vic. 90
St Helens Tas. 402, 404
St Mary Peak SA 178, 182
Sandy Bay NSW 71
Sandy Camp Pool NT 299, 301, 302
Sappers Bridge WA 224
Sawmill Track Tas. 452
Sealers Cove Vic. 133
Seaman's Hut NSW 39
Second Pyramid Qld 370
Serpentine Lake WA 252
17 Mile Creek NT 294, 296, 299
17 Mile Falls NT 299
Shoalhaven River NSW 2, 3, 4
Siding Spring Observatory NSW 29–3
Signal Point Tas. 421
Silver Falls Tas. 455
Simpson Desert 317
Skene Creek Qld 345, 347
Snake Lagoon Hike SA 183, 184, 187
Snowgum Track Tas. 438, 439
Snowy River NSW 36, 39, 40
South Bruny Island Tas. 412–13, 415
South Era NSW 14
South Hobart Tas. 454
South Wall Return Walk NT 309
South Zoe Creek Qld 387, 388, 389
Southern Ocean 184, 188, 189, 202, 206, 220
Spencer Gulf SA 171, 173, 175
Spencer Hill Walk NT 282
Sphinx, The Qld 370
Sphinx Rock Tas. 452
Spirey Creek NSW 28, 29
Spit Bridge to Manly NSW 67–75
Springbrook Qld 365
Springs, The Tas. 449, 451, 452, 455
Stanthorpe Qld 368
Stirling Range NP WA 198–203
Stony Creek gorge SA 175
Stringer's Creek Vic. 123, 126
Studley Park Boathouse Vic. 139, 141, 144

Sturt Gorge Recreation Park SA 156, 157
Sturt River SA 156, 157
Sugarloaf Peak Vic. 84, 87, 89
Sugarloaf Saddle Vic. 84
Sullivan Rocks to Monadnocks Campsite WA 240–5
Summit Lookout NT 314
Sunshine Coast Hinterland Great Walk Qld 345, 346–7
Sweetwater Pool NT 291, 302, 303
Swimcart Beach Tas. 405
Swimcart Creek Tas. 405
Swimcart Lagoon Tas. 402, 405, 406
Swindlers Spur Vic. 109
Sydney NSW 9, 18, 22, 67
Sydney Harbour NP 68–9, 72

Takaraka Bush Resort Qld 338
Taranna Tas. 420
Tarn Shelf Tas. 436, 439
Tasman Arch Tas. 410
Tasman Island Tas. 411
Tasman Peninsula Tas. 408, 416, 432
Tasmanian Wilderness World Heritage Area Tas. 437, 440, 456
Tawonga Huts Vic. 114
Telegraph Saddle Vic. 123, 136
Telegraph Station (Alice Springs) NT 278–83, 312
Telegraph Track Vic. 132, 133, 136
The Breadknife NSW 29, 30
The Castle NSW 66
The Chalet Tas. 452
The Coast Track NSW 8–19
The Crest parking area Qld 360
The Gardens Tas. 405, 406
The Greater Blue Mountains World Heritage Area NSW 21, 48–9
The Hazards Tas. 473, 474–5
The Kimberley WA 212–16
The Loop WA 234–9
The Narrows SA 160, 162, 163, 165
The Neck Tas. 415, 416
The Pyramids Qld 366–71
The Sphinx Qld 370
The Springs Tas. 449, 451, 452, 455
Thelma Head NSW 14, 15
Thistle Cove WA 230, 231, 232
Thomson Bay WA 247, 250
Thomson River Vic. 128
Thomson River Station Vic. 123, 128, 129
Thorsborne Trail Qld 379–91
Thredbo NSW 36
Three Capes Track Tas. 408–11
Three Sisters NSW 50
Tidal River Vic. 130, 132, 133, 138
Tjukatjapi NT 333
Tnorala (Gosse Bluff) NT 315
Todd River NT 280–1, 282

Tom Roberts Horse Trail SA 153
Toolona Creek Circuit Qld 392–9
Toolona Falls Qld 398
Totem Pole Tas. 411
Townsville Qld 374
Traveller Range Tas. 468
Tree Tops Walk carpark WA 217, 225
Triabunna Tas. 441, 443
Trig Hill NT 281, 282
Tuggeranong Creek ACT 45
Tyers Vic. 123

Ulladulla Vic. 64
Uluru Base Walk NT 327–35
Uluru–Kata Tjuta NP NT 327–35
Underclift Track NSW 50
Upper Pool NT 303
Upper Waterfall SA 153

Valley of the Giants WA 217
Valley of the Waters NSW 50, 52
Valley of the Winds Walk NT 332
Victor Harbor SA 192
volcanic craters/calderas
NSW 54, 59, 61, 393
Qld 350–2
Vic. 102–7

Wadjemup Hill WA 253
Wadjemup Lighthouse WA 250, 252, 253
Wadjemup Walk Trail WA 246–56
Waitpinga Beach SA 189, 192, 194
Waitpinga campground SA 189, 192
Waitpinga Cliffs SA 189–95
Walardi Campground WA 24
Walhalla Vic. 109, 122–9
Walhalla Goldfields Railway Vic. 123
Walpole WA 217, 220
Walpole Inlet WA 217
Walpole–Nornalup NP WA 217–25
Wanggoolba Creek Qld 356
Wards Canyon Qld 340, 343
Warren NP WA 257–61
Warren River Lookout WA 260, 261
Warren River Loop WA 257–61
Warrumbungle NP NSW 26–32
Watarrka NP NT 304–10
Waterfall Hike SA 153, 154
Waterfall Valley to Windermere Hut via Lake Will Tas. 463–4
Waterloo Bay Vic. 133, 134, 136
Wattamolla NSW 17
Wattamolla Creek NSW 17
Weano Gorge WA 262–7, 268
Wedding Cake Rock NSW 17
Wells Cave Track Vic. 84, 89
Wentworth Falls NSW 47, 50, 53, 54
Wentworth Pass NSW 52, 53
West Canungra Creek circuit Qld 397
West Island Conservation Park SA 194
West MacDonnell NP NT 305, 311–15, 316

West MacDonnell Ranges NT 282, 311, 312
West Spirey Creek NSW 32
whale-watching
NSW 12–13
Vic. 138
WA 204, 207
White Beach Tas. 408
wildflowers
NSW 18, 20, 26, 33, 41, 67
SA 153, 162, 171, 180, 183
Tas. 405, 412, 469, 470
Vic. 81, 90, 108, 113, 122, 130, 134
WA 199, 207, 217, 226, 234, 240, 265, 267, 269–75
wildlife-watching
ACT 45
NSW 5, 14, 15, 23, 32, 64, 71
NT 309
Qld 339, 342, 343, 350–1, 384, 386, 388, 390
SA 156, 164, 174, 176, 185
Tas. 438, 445, 447, 461, 474
Vic. 89, 104, 106, 144
WA 227, 231, 233, 251, 256
Wilmington SA 160, 162
Wilpena Creek SA 178
Wilpena Pound SA 166, 175, 177, 178, 182
Wilpena Pound Resort SA 166, 167, 177, 178, 180
Wilsons Promontory Lighthouse Vic. 130–8
Wilsons Promontory NP Vic. 130–8
Wimmera Plains Vic. 94
Windermere Hut to New Pelion Hut Tas. 464–6
Wineglass Bay Tas. 471–5
Wineglass Bay beach Tas. 473, 474
Wineglass Bay carpark Tas. 471, 473
Wineglass Bay Lookout track Tas. 475
Wineglass Bay Track Tas. 473–4
Wisemans Ferry NSW 20, 22, 23, 24
Wollumbin NSW 59, 61
Wonoka Formation SA 168

Yarra Bend Vic. 139–45
Yarra River Vic. 141
Yeagarup Dunes WA 261
Yengo NP NSW 24
Yungaburra Qld 350
Yurrebilla Trail SA 154

ZigZag Track Tas. 454–5
Zoe Bay to Mulligans Falls Qld 386, 388–90
Zoe Falls Qld 387, 388

Acknowledgements
The publisher would like to acknowledge the following individuals and organisations:

Commissioning editor
Melissa Kayser

Managing editor
Marg Bowman

Project manager
Lauren Whybrow, Kate Armstrong

Editor
Vanessa Lanaway

Cartography
Bruce McGurty, Emily Maffei

Design
Philip Campbell

Layout
Megan Ellis

Index
Max McMaster

Pre-press
Splitting Image, Megan Ellis

Photography credits
Cover: Spectacular views on the Mount Hotham to Falls Creek walk in Victoria's high country (Melanie Ball)
Back cover: On the track from Mount Hotham to Falls Creek (Melanie Ball)
Other images: All images used in the internal pages are © Melanie Ball

Maps in this book
The maps in this publication have been produced by combining digital topographic data with field-collected GPS data. They have been specifically designed and drawn to complement the author's narrative description of each walk and to enhance the walker's experience. These maps can be used as a supplement to navigating and identifying the location of features described, but are in no way intended to replace authoritative topographic maps that, at better scales, will show much more of the natural and man-made features.

Feature walks on the maps are highlighted and are easily identified among other useful topographic elements. General relief of the landscape is shown with contour lines and heights at 50-metre intervals. The maps also include roads, tracks, rivers and creeks giving the walker an appreciation of the geography of the area. A wide variety of points of interest have also been incorporated focusing on helping the walker identify attractions such as lookouts, natural features, picnic areas and important facilities.

Explore Australia Publishing Pty Ltd
Ground Floor, Building 1, 658 Church Street,
Richmond, VIC 3121

Explore Australia Publishing Pty Ltd is a division of Hardie Grant Publishing Pty Ltd

hardie grant publishing

Published by Explore Australia Publishing Pty Ltd, 2016

Concept, maps, form and design © Explore Australia Publishing Pty Ltd, 2016
Text © Melanie Ball, 2016

A Cataloguing-in-Publication entry is available from the catalogue of the National Library of Australia at www.nla.gov.au

The maps in this publication incorporate data © Commonwealth of Australia (Geoscience Australia), 2006. Geoscience Australia has not evaluated the data as altered and incorporated within this publication, and therefore gives no warranty regarding accuracy, completeness, currency or suitability for any particular purpose.

Copyright imprint and currency – VAR Product and PSMA Data
"Copyright. Based on data provided under licence from PSMA Australia Limited (www.psma.com.au)".

Hydrography Data (May 2006)
Transport Data (February 2016)

Department of Sustainability and Environment, Victoria

ISBN-13 9781741174830

10 9 8 7 6 5 4 3 2

Printed and bound in China by 1010 Printing International Ltd

Publisher's note: Every effort has been made to ensure that the information in this book is accurate at the time of going to press. The publisher welcomes information and suggestions for correction or improvement. Email: info@exploreaustralia.net.au

Publisher's disclaimer: The publisher cannot accept responsibility for any errors or omissions. The representation on the maps of any road or track is not necessarily evidence of public right of way. The publisher cannot be held responsible for any injury, loss or damage incurred during travel. It is vital to research any proposed trip thoroughly and seek the advice of relevant state and travel organisations before you leave.

www.exploreaustralia.net.au